KINGDOM PROLOGUE

KINGDOM PROLOGUE

GENESIS FOUNDATIONS
FOR A COVENANTAL WORLDVIEW

Meredith G. Kline

Wipf & Stock
PUBLISHERS
Eugene, Oregon

Wipf and Stock Publishers
199 W 8th Ave, Suite 3
Eugene, OR 97401

Kingdom Prologue
Genesis Foundations for a Covenantal Worldview
By Kline, Meredith G.
Copyright©2006 by Kline, Meredith G.
ISBN: 1-59752-564-2
Publication date 2/1/2006

PREFACE

For several decades, at some half a dozen theological schools, I have taught a course whose mixed curricular genre is reflected in the diverse names it has borne, like Old Testament Hermeneutics, Old Testament Redemptive History, Old Testament Biblical Theology. A lecture-syllabus emerged volume by volume until there were three, which then were combined into one, entitled *Kingdom Prologue* (see the Introduction below for an explanation of this name). Slight revisions accompanied repeated reprintings of the privately produced version and more extensive but still minor revisions were involved in the present published edition.

As intimated by the subtitle, *Genesis Foundations for a Covenantal Worldview*, the immediate literary focus of this study is the book of Genesis and its account of the formative ages in the eschatological movement of the kingdom of God from creation to consummation. As also indicated by the subtitle, our biblical-theological commentary on Genesis is designed to uncover the foundations of God's covenantally administered kingdom with its major historical developments and its institutional structures and functions. In this way *Kingdom Prologue* seeks to provide an introductory sketch of the over-all shape of the biblical worldview and the character of biblical religion.

The lecture-syllabus origin of this work accounts for its no-footnote, no-bibliography format. One controlling factor in the selection of themes and issues for special attention has of course been a concern for relevance to the state of theological discussion and controversy in the schools where the lectures represented by *Kingdom Prologue* were given, these being in one case eclectically evangelical but for the most part confessionally Reformed.

I would express my appreciation to John Anderson of the Gordon College Printing Services for his repeated kindnesses in the course of the private production and reprinting of this work. The appearing of the present publication is due to a truly remarkable labor of love on the part of multi-talented, great-hearted friends at the Park Woods Orthodox Presbyterian Church, Overland Park, Kansas, creators of Two Age Press. And to Jonathan B. Kline, my grandfatherly gratitude for lending the aid of his computer expertise and literary sensibility and for his all-around brightening of the hours of editing.

Kingdom Prologue, born in the classroom, is dedicated to the hundreds and hundreds of students who have taken that course of many names, the joy of my professorial life, and so played a midwifery role in the book's protracted parturition.

Meredith G. Kline

CONTENTS

INTRODUCTION

Kingdom Prologue engages in a biblico-theological analysis of the foundational revelation contained in the book of Genesis. Taking the kingdom of God as our central, organizing theme, we inevitably find ourselves fully involved with the subject of the divine covenants of Scripture; for to follow the course of the kingdom is to trace the series of covenants by which the Lord administers his kingdom.

The early chapters of Genesis report two occasions in the history of "the world that then was" when God's people were organized as an earthly kingdom, one in Eden and another in the Noahic era. But the title of the present work assumes a later stance at the Abrahamic Covenant, and the kingdom as promised in that covenant was not established even in its preliminary, prototypal form until the mediatorial mission of Moses inaugurating the old covenant, as narrated in Exodus. From that perspective – and in view of the fact that the book of Genesis as a whole performs the function of historical preamble in the canonical documentation of the old covenant – Kingdom Prologue is an appropriate designation for the Genesis history.

Because the subject of biblical covenants and ancient treaties has been under intensive investigation and lively dispute, some introductory observations are in order here about the nature of those biblical arrangements we call "covenants." Our chief interest in these comments is in those covenantal arrangements in which God was one party.

Of the biblical words usually rendered "covenant" the primary one in the Old Testament is the Hebrew *berith*, for which the Greek *diatheke* was the translation choice of the New Testament writers. What is it that constitutes the peculiar *berith*-character of that which is so denominated?

Repeatedly we read of a *berith* being "made." The *berith*-making is accomplished through a solemn process of ratification. Characteristically this transaction centers in the swearing of an oath, with its sanctioning curse. Clearly a *berith* is a legal kind of arrangement, a formal disposition of a binding nature. At the heart of a *berith* is an act of commitment and the customary oath-form of this commitment reveals the religious nature of the transaction. The *berith* arrangement is no mere secular contract but rather belongs to the sacred sphere of divine witness and enforcement.

The kind of legal disposition called *berith* consists then in a divinely sanctioned commitment. In the case of divine-human covenants the divine sanctioning is entailed in God's participation either as the one who himself makes the commitment or as the divine witness of the human commitment made in his name and presence.

A good indication that the act of commitment with the obligations thus undertaken is basic to the meaning of *berith* is provided by the numerous statements about keeping and remembering the *berith* or being false to it and transgressing it. In fact, the two possible ways of treating a *berith*, by observing or violating it, are the most conspicuous and pervasive ideas found in immediate association with that term in the Bible. Also, a common synonym for *berith* is *chesed* with its connotation, if not primary force, of loyalty and fidelity, underscored at times by its combination with the term, *'emeth*, "truth."

Further, pointing to the centrality of commitment and specifically oath-commitment in the *berith* arrangement is the common use of words for oath (or curse) as synonyms for *berith*. For example, Moses instructs Israel assembled in the plains of Moab: "(You stand here) to enter into the covenant of Yahweh your God and into his oath-curse which Yahweh your God is making with you this day" (Deut 29:12[11]). In the marriage allegory of the Sinaitic Covenant in Ezekiel 16 the Lord says: "I sware unto you and entered into a covenant with you" (v. 8). *Berith* may also be the direct object of the verb of swearing (cf. Deut 4:31; 7:12; 8:18). See also Genesis 26:28.

So much was oath-commitment definitive of the *berith* that the act of making a *berith* was denoted by the imagery of the oath ritual performed when ratifying a *berith*. Thus, since the characteristic ratification rite was one of slaying and cutting up animals to symbolize the curse that would befall the breaker of the oath, "cut a *berith*" became the idiom for this transaction.

Etymology possibly affords another indication of the oath-commitment significance of *berith*, for its original meaning may well be "bond". Use of this term for the Old Testament covenants would then have in view the binding obligation undertaken in the ratificatory oath. For the idea of the oath as a bond see, for example, Numbers 30:2ff. (3ff.), especially the expression "binding oath" (v. 13[14]). And for the association of bond and *berith* note the phrase "bond of the covenant" (Ezek 20:37; cf. Jer 27:2; Dan 6:8). But whatever the etymology of *berith* (and this is still under debate), the proper meaning of the word used to translate it in the New Testament is clear. *Diatheke* means a disposition, especially (in extra-biblical usage) a testament, and its use as a rendering for *berith* points to an understanding of the latter as a solemnly transacted commitment.

This understanding of the meaning of *berith* is confirmed by the extra-biblical evidence of analogous phenomena in the ancient world, particularly certain political arrangements whose formal equivalence to the divine covenants in the Bible is established by striking and extensive parallels in their ratificatory rituals and documents and in their administrative procedures. For these similar covenantal arrangements are regularly called "bonds (i.e., obligations) and oaths." Moreover, the making of these covenants too is referred to as a cutting of the covenant, or it is denoted by some expression descriptive of a particular oath-curse ritual consisting in the dismemberment of some specific animal.

The evidence for *berith* as an obligation solemnly undertaken or imposed has increasingly impressed investigators of the matter and a vigorous case has been made opposing as unwarranted the translating of *berith* by "covenant," with its connotation of relationship. It is even suggested that "command" would be a suitable rendering, and in support of that is the fact that "law" and various terms for commandment are employed as synonyms for *berith* (cf. Jer 33:25). Those who defend the continued use of the translation "covenant" have to acknowledge that *berith* is in the first instance a matter of commitment (given or exacted). They contend, however, that *berith*-arrangements are bilateral in that they involve negotiations (even if one party sovereignly proclaims or imposes the terms) and that the *berith*-making occurs in the context of an existing relationship or mutual understanding, often a cordial relationship, which the *berith* then further defines. It should be observed, too, that *berith* is not always used in its simple primary and proper sense and that some justification for rendering it by "covenant" can be found in the secondary extensions of its meaning. For the idea of the act of oath-commitment, which may be obvious enough in passages that deal with *berith*-making or ratification, shades off in other passages into the idea of the contents of the commitment. And we can think of those contents *per se*, or as written down as the text of a *berith*-document (we find references in the Bible to the "words of the covenant," "the tables of the covenant," "the book of the covenant") or as embodied in the order of life or the relationship that they promise or stipulate. These nuances are so interrelated that it is difficult to say which one is dominant in some passages. For possible examples of *berith* referring to the contents, whether promissory or obligatory, see Exodus 31:16; Numbers 25:13 (cf. Neh 13:29; Mal 2:8); 2 Samuel 23:5 (cf. Ps 89:39); 1 Kings 20:34; and Psalm 50:16. For possible examples of *berith* used for the resultant alliance or relationship or order, see Genesis 17:4; Exodus 23:32; Job 5:23; Psalm 83:5(6); Isaiah 28:15, 18; Ezekiel 30:5 and Hosea 12:1. In view of these secondary uses of *berith* and because of the long and firmly established place of the word "covenant" in English versions of the Bible and in theological formulations it would seem expedient to continue to make use of "covenant" in translating *berith* and *diatheke*.

It was stated earlier that there is a close connection between divine covenant and divine kingdom. Viewed as commitment transactions with their rituals, documents, and stipulated terms and procedures, covenants function as administrative instruments of God's kingly rule. Indeed, the connection is sometimes closer than this. As we have observed, *berith* in some passages denotes the actual historical realization of the arrangement defined in the covenantal stipulations and sanctions. Covenant thus becomes a particular administration of God's kingship, whether in the bestowal of his holy kingdom as a royal grant on a special covenant people as their peculiar inheritance or in the sovereign government of a temporal world order whose benefits are common to all alike (as in the postdiluvian common grace covenant of Gen 9). It is in this sense that covenant is used to designate the major divisions of covenant theology.

Converging lines of evidence have indicated that what is designated *berith* is primarily a legal disposition, characteristically established by oath and defined by the terms specified in oath-bound, divinely sanctioned commitments. We have also found that there is a functional aspect common to the divine *berith* transactions which provides warrant for those engaged in theological analysis to employ the term covenant in the sense of kingdom administration.

In adopting these conclusions we are rejecting certain counterproposals in which the covenant concept gets unduly restricted. These would make essential to the definition of covenant as a biblical theological category features that are not present in all *berith* arrangements, features pertaining to the substance of the covenantal commitment or to the resultant covenantal order.

Thus, with respect to the substance of the covenant commitment it has been held that nothing is properly called covenant except sovereign administration of grace and promise. However, as will be argued below, there are *berith* arrangements in the Bible that are informed by the principle of works, the opposite of grace. One of these is the original order in Eden. In postlapsarian history, where we encounter covenants both of works and grace, the identity of the party who takes the ratification oath is an indicator of which kind of covenant it is in a particular case. It must be noted here that not all oaths of covenantal commitment function as ratification oaths. For example, the role played by the oath ritual of circumcision (Gen 17) is that of a supplementary seal added to the Abrahamic Covenant, which had been ratified by God's oath on an earlier occasion (Gen 15). More precisely, in the situation after the Fall it is the presence or absence of a human oath of ratification that provides the clue as to the governing principle, for divine oath is at least implicit in the ratification of all divine-human covenants, whether of works or grace. If the covenant is ratified by divine oath alone, it is a covenant of grace, either saving or common. But when the covenant-making includes a human oath of ratification, as in the case of Israel's oath in the Sinaitic Covenant (Exod 24), the arrangement is informed by the works principle. (On the complex relation of works and grace in the old covenant, see further below.) Man's ratificatory oath is a commitment to perform the obligations imposed by his Lord, while the divine oath in such a works covenant is a commitment to enforce the sanctions appropriately, rewarding obedience with the promised blessing and recompensing disobedience with the threatened curse. But our immediate concern is simply to observe that in view of the data indicating that some biblical covenants are of the works variety, the fundamental feature of divinely sanctioned commitment in our definition of covenant may not be restricted to commitment of sovereign grace and promise.

Improper restriction of the biblical theological definition of the *berith* concept has also occurred by inclusion of what is effected by the covenantal transaction. Some suggest that the main component in this definition should be the effecting of a religious relationship, more specifically, a holy fellowship in love between God and a chosen people. If we were limiting our analysis to those covenants in which God bestows his holy kingdom on a sanctified community, we might properly include in an expanded definition of covenant this feature of the union and communion of God and man in recognition that this is the acme of blessedness secured in these covenants and the chief end in view, under the glory of God. However, if our definition is intended to cover all the divine covenants in Scripture, this feature of special relationship must be omitted, for there is also the common grace covenant (cf. Gen 9) in which God commits himself to maintain a certain order of life but does not therein bestow his holy kingdom and communion on an elect people.

Once we are satisfied that we have arrived at a proper concept of covenant and have in mind employing the succession of divine covenants as a general scheme for a biblical theology, the question arises whether we should classify as covenants various arrangements that are not specifically labelled *berith* or *diatheke* in the Bible. This problem takes a couple of different forms. One involves the traditional procedure of covenant theology whereby the individual *berith-diatheke* transactions of redemptive history are combined into ever more comprehensive "covenant" entities, culminating in what is usually called the Covenant of Grace, which encompasses all the redemptive administrations from the Fall to the Consummation. If it is recognized that there is a fundamental unity among all the individual covenants brought under the overarching Covenant of Grace, the process of identifying higher levels of covenantal unity is surely proper, for the biblical authors themselves already did that kind of systematizing of the covenants. For example, in Psalm 105:9,10 (cf. 2 Kgs 13:23; 1 Chr 16:16,17) there is a virtual identifying of God's separate covenantal transactions with Abraham, Isaac, and Jacob. And the separate covenants enacted by Moses at Sinai and in Moab and the later renewals of this arrangement in Joshua 24 and elsewhere in the Old Testament are repeatedly spoken of by later Old Testament authors and by New Testament authors as one covenant of the Lord with Israel, which the Book of Hebrews refers to as the "first" over against the "new" or "second" covenant (Heb 8:6-8). In principle then there is biblical precedent for the systematic organizer of the covenants to identify the over-all unity of the redemptive covenants by some such term as the Covenant of Grace.

Another form of the problem is involved in the original order produced at creation. In this case, covenant theology applies the term covenant to the situation even though the Bible (at least in the immediate record of Gen 1-3) does not use the term *berith* to describe it. We shall take up this matter in the introductory comments of Part I, Section A.

In the foregoing, *Kingdom Prologue* has been referred to as a biblico-theological study. Biblical theology is an exegetical discipline that processes biblical revelation in a way that contributes directly to the church's task of theological formulation, a task undertaken in the interests of covenantal instruction and discipline and world witness. More specifically, biblical theology in the classic tradition of Geerhardus Vos has as its distinctive feature a concern with the historical progress of special revelation as disclosed in the Bible. That history is divided into its significant periods, determined from the biblical account, and the contents of revelation are described epoch by epoch, being so set forth as to reflect the peculiar revelatory emphases of each period. The result is a diachronic display of a series of synchronic summaries of special revelation in its successive stages.

As it turns out, the significant eras of special revelation are coordinated with the sequence of the Lord's covenant enactments and his epochal acts of creation and redemption associated with them. The best example of this is the Bible itself with its major divisions into Old and New Testaments, the covenantal constitutions for the old and new covenants respectively. For Vos, then, delineating the progress of special revelation is broadly the same as expounding the contents of the several divine covenants.

The present work, in that it traces the course of the successive covenantal administrations (within the Genesis limits), is doing something similar. It differs, however, in that it makes the kingdom of God rather than special revelation the central theme. Our main focus is on the historical drama of the covenantal kingdom with its epochal events of covenant transaction and kingdom establishment. What is in Vos's *Biblical Theology* the infrastructure, the particular historical pattern in which the periodicity principle gets applied, becomes here the surface structure. By unfolding and developing that infrastructure, *Kingdom Prologue* performs, in part, a prolegomenon function for the program of biblical theology, while also serving the enterprise of systematic theology by contributing very directly to the formulations of covenant theology.

PART I

THE KINGDOM IN THE WORLD THAT THEN WAS

Beyond the prologue (Gen 1:1-2:3), Genesis is divided by its superscription formula, "these are the generations of...," into ten sections beginning successively at the following verses: 2:4; 5:1; 6:9; 10:1; 11:10; 11:27; 25:12; 25:19; 36:1 (cf. v. 9); and 37:2. What follows the formula is always an account of the descendants of the person named. This is a genealogical record or, more broadly, an historical narrative of the developments associated with the family in view. In the introductions to such accounts there may be allusions to the origins of the person named in the formula (see Gen 2:4; 5:1; cf. 25:12,19), but it is not to those origins that the term "generations" in the superscription refers. Not ancestry, not the past, but posterity and the future is in view in that term.

An attempt has been made to construe the formula in question not as a superscription for what follows it, but as belonging to the material which precedes it. That preceding material is then regarded as an originally independent document for which the formula is thought to serve as a colophon. For several quite decisive reasons, however, that interpretation of the data must be rejected. It is unable to understand the formula in any consistent, uniform way. Sometimes it must take the person named as the principal subject of the preceding narrative or as the one whose origins are presented there, but at other times as the one who wrote or possessed the preceding "document." Actually, there are cases where neither sense suggested by the colophon view is at all suitable (see, e.g., 25:12,13; 25:19; 36:1; 37:2). For example, on this view it would have been Esau who preserved the record about Isaac and Jacob (36:1); and Jacob, the record of Esau's descendants, Edomite king list and all (37:2). Also, removing the formula from the section following it in some cases leaves the following section (or supposed tablet) beginning in a most abrupt manner (see, e.g., 2:5; 5:3) and it has the further effect, of course, of leaving the last section of Genesis (37:2b-50:26) without either heading or concluding colophon. Moreover, the more generally accepted view of the generations-formula as a superscription is the interpretation obviously required when that formula is used in contexts outside the Book of Genesis: see Numbers 3:1; Ruth 4:18; and Matthew 1:1 (which reflects the variation on the formula found in Gen 5:1).

The first occurrence of the generations-formula in Genesis 2:4 requires further examination. This superscription to the first of the ten sections of "generations" consists not just of Genesis 2:4a but of the fourth verse in its entirety: "These are the generations of the heavens and the earth when they were created, in the day that the Lord God made earth and heaven." The chiastic form of this verse taken as a whole argues against a major break after verse 4a. The generations-formula of verse 4a is expanded in verse 4b just as it is in Numbers 3:1, where the expansion (v. 1b) once again begins "in the day that..."

In keeping with the consistent meaning of the generations-formula throughout the book of Genesis, Genesis 2:4 must be understood as the superscription not for an account of the origins of the heaven and the earth, but rather for an account of their subsequent "family" history. Genesis 2:4 is not the heading for a second creation story *per se*, but for the sequel to the story of the origins of the heaven and earth and all their hosts – a sequel which continues up to the Flood (2:4-4:26).

But if the Genesis 2:4 heading refers to the whole prediluvian period, what are we to make of verse 4b: "in the day that the Lord God made earth and heaven"? How can the world-age extending from Adam to the Noahic flood be identified as belonging to the day of creation? The use of this same idiom in Leviticus 6:20(13) is illuminating. There the Lord directs that "in the day" that Aaron is anointed he shall present a certain offering, which in fact was offered not during the seven-day period of the anointing-consecration but subsequently and indeed as a perpetual offering thereafter. What the priest did afterwards is said to be done "in the day of" his anointing in the sense that the anointing event marked a turning point and gave a distinctive character to his subsequent life and ministry. In the usage of an equivalent idiom (consisting of the preposition "in" plus the infinitive) we similarly find that an introductory event is used to identify an era, so that what happens later is said to happen "when" the founding event occurred. For example, in Deuteronomy 4:46 Israel's victories in the Transjordan area some forty years after the exodus are described as happening "in their going forth from Egypt." (Compare too Gen 33:18; 35:9; Deut 23:4[5]; 27:4,12; Josh 5:4.) In this same way, Genesis 2:4, the heading for a survey of the entire prediluvian history, views that whole age under the horizon of its great founding event, the original creation, and thus classifies that whole time as belonging to "the day that the Lord God made the earth and the heavens."

The scope of the family history of heaven and earth as related in the first section of Genesis (2:4-4:26) is panoramic. It develops the theme of the entrance of sin and its escalation in the apostate line of Cain through the entire prediluvian age. Then we find that the second section of Genesis (5:1-6:8) matches the vast sweep of the first section, its narrative once again covering the whole era extending from creation to the great deluge, now from the viewpoint of the covenant line, whose history it traces through Adam's son Seth down to Noah.

It would indeed appear that by far the largest part of the many millennia of all human history is covered in the brief record contained in roughly chapters 2 through 6 of the book of Genesis (or through chapter 8, if we include the Deluge episode). And, measuring again simply in terms of the passage of time, considerably more than half of the history from the Flood to the present is dealt with in Genesis 9 through 11.

The reader of Genesis may fail to appreciate the vastness of this historical span from Adam to Abraham because it is presented in such an extremely condensed form, while all the rest of the Bible from Genesis 12 on to the end is devoted to the relatively short span of about two thousand years from Abraham to Christ and the apostolic age. But both the brevity of the biblical account of the long pre-Abrahamic ages and the extended treatment given to the subsequent era introduced by the patriarchs are explained by the particular purpose and nature of the Scriptures. The Old and New Testaments are designed to serve as constitutions respectively for the kingdom of Israel and for the church of the new covenant. And, of course, the Bible's concentration on the climactic advent of Christ and the Israelite epoch of revelation immediately preparatory to it also reflects the supreme significance of this focal period of history with its decisive redemptive events.

It is not only because of the brevity of the Genesis treatment that there is not a more general awareness of how large a proportion of man's time on earth falls within the pre-Abrahamic or even prediluvian history. Some readers of the Bible find themselves unable to attribute so great a duration to that history because they misconstrue the Adam-to-Noah genealogy in Genesis 5 and the Noah-to-Abraham genealogy in Genesis 11. If these genealogies are (mistakenly) taken as an unbroken line of descent, the result is a division of all history from Adam to the present into three fairly equal and all relatively short parts: the first, from Adam to the Flood (or to

Abraham, who, on this exegesis, would come only some three centuries after the Flood); the second, from the Flood (or Abraham) to Christ; and the third, from Christ to the present.

Actually, however, the genealogies of Genesis 5 and 11 must be understood as a selective listing of only the more significant (presumably) names, which allows for indefinitely lengthy gaps here and there between the individuals who are selected for inclusion in the list. The selective interpretation is not only completely compatible with the idiom of the genealogical genre, but it is clearly signalized by the symmetrical composition of the two genealogies with their pattern of conventional numbers – ten names each, following the LXX in Genesis 11:12,13 (cf. Luke 3:36), with three sons for the last individual in each case. The validity of this interpretation is made completely certain by historical considerations, some inner-biblical and some arising from the integration of biblical and other evidence, both archaeological and literary. As an example of the latter we may mention the epic tradition that in the days of Gilgamesh, several centuries before Abraham, the Flood was already viewed as an event of remote antiquity. One is, therefore, left free by the biblical representations in Genesis 5 and 11 to date the Flood no more recently than the close of the most recent ice age, at the latest, and to allow to the prediluvian history of Genesis 2 through 6 all the millennia that may be shown by further investigation to have elapsed.

An intimation of the true dimensions of the times so briefly surveyed in Genesis 4 through 6 is given in 2 Peter 3:5-7. There, all of man's history on earth is divided in two at the Flood, and the prediluvian times are viewed not merely as an early stage in the present course of events but virtually as a separate world history by themselves, the history of another world that preceded the present world. The apostle speaks of "the world that then was," the original heavens and earth created by the word of God, a world that perished in the judgment of the Flood, and he sets that prediluvian world over against the present heaven and earth, the world produced at the Flood, which is also moving towards a destiny of divine judgment.

This cosmic interpretation of the prediluvian age was derived by Peter from the book of Genesis itself. He was adopting the perspective that informs each of the first two generations-sections of Genesis when he viewed the whole course of events from the beginning to the Deluge as comprising a single coherent age, the first major era in man's history. If we consider how this way of organizing the history submerges the distinction made by the Fall into prelapsarian and postlapsarian history, the distinction that is of such tremendous theological import, we will appreciate more fully the peculiarity of this cosmic perspective and the directness of Peter's dependence on the Genesis historiography as his source for it. And all the more so, when we further notice how the apostle follows the lead of Genesis 2:4 in its identification of the prediluvian world as a world characterized by the founding event of creation. Obviously reflecting the portrayal of the origin of the earth and heavens in the Genesis creation-prologue, Peter characterizes "the world that then was" as a world formed by the word of God out of the water (v. 5).

This perspective on the prediluvian world-age is then reinforced and sharpened as Peter goes on to set "the heavens and the earth which are now" (v. 7a) over against the world that then was. He thereby makes the Flood episode in which the old world perished (v. 6) to be at the same time an act of re-creation. We are thus instructed to see in the Deluge not only a kind of return to the not-yet-habitable state of Genesis 1:2, but a virtual re-enactment of Genesis 1:3-2:3 as well, a restructuring by which the present habitable world was brought forth out of the chaotic waters. The effect of this radical cosmic reading of the Flood as a creation event and of the postdiluvian stage of the world as a virtual new heavens and earth is that the prediluvian world stands out sharply as a separate world that has come and gone, a world that began in the waters of the original creation and ended in the waters of deluge-judgment. The picture conveyed by Peter is that of a world that had a total history, that had its beginning, developed its culture and witnessed the course of the great conflict of heaven and hell to a final climax, had its eschaton, and made way for a new world.

What makes all this of special importance to Peter's Christian readers is that he also presents that overall, complete world-history from the creation to the Flood as a paradigm that is being followed again in the history of the present world. Peter appeals to this ancient pattern as instructive for our understanding of the eschatological course of our present world, in particular, as affording warning of cosmic divine judgment to come (v. 7). This insight into the nature of the prediluvian world was acquired by Peter from his Lord (cf. Matt 24:37-39; Luke 17:26,27). "As the days of Noah were," Jesus had said, "so shall also the coming of the Son of Man be" (Matt 24:37).

For our analysis of Genesis, Peter's overall division of human history into two cosmic eras provides a principle of organization by which our study is divided into two major Parts. But as was noted earlier, another two-part division of human history, which is of fundamental importance in biblical theology, is hidden under Peter's cosmic perspective. For his broad category of the world that then was spans the two eras that are separated by the Fall of man. This division marked by the Fall has even more radical significance for humanity than that produced by the Noahic deluge. For as basic a distinction as that between the order of creation and the order of redemption is what differentiates between these two eras separated by the Fall. This great divide in history is brought out in the organization of our material here by subdividing Part I (The Kingdom in the World That Then Was) into two Sections. Section A will deal with the pre-Fall age and the creational covenant and Section B will begin the analysis of the post-Fall age and the administrations of redemptive covenant, in the period up to the Flood.

CREATIONAL COVENANT

Covenant theologians have generally taken the position that the covenant concept can accommodate the entire history of the kingdom of God. Thus, the original creational stage of the kingdom and the entire subsequent redemptive phase have been comprehended under the headings of Covenant of Works and Covenant of Grace. Since here in Section A of our study we will be dealing with the data of Genesis 1-3 under a covenantal heading, this is the place to discuss the biblical warrant that exists for regarding the pre-Fall kingdom as a covenantal affair.

It is to be observed in the first place that even though the term *berith* does not appear in the immediate biblical record of the creational kingdom, the substance of covenant is the stuff that forms the contents of Genesis 1-3. It is, therefore, altogether appropriate to give the covenantal phenomena that are found here the label that identifies them elsewhere. That, by the way, is what covenant theology does elsewhere when, for example, it extends the category of Covenant of Grace to the redemptive situation before the days of Noah (although the term *berith* does not appear until Gen 6:18) or when it subsumes the Abrahamic history in Genesis 12-14 under the category of the Abrahamic Covenant (although the term *berith* does not appear in that history until the Gen 15 transaction).

Actually, it is possible that the Bible itself, in later references back to Genesis 1-3, applies the term *berith* to the situation there, just as 2 Samuel 23:5 and Psalm 89:3 refer to God's covenantal revelation to David as a *berith*, though that term is not employed in the account of it in 2 Samuel 7. Isaiah 24:5 and Hosea 6:7 have been suggested as instances of this. Although the meaning of both passages is disputed, the everlasting covenant of Isaiah 24:5 definitely appears to refer to the creational arrangements and Hosea 6:7 probably refers to Adam as the breaker of a covenant. Also, comparison of Jeremiah 33:20,25 and Jeremiah 31:35-37 suggests that the former applies the term *berith* to God's ordering of the world of nature as described in Genesis 1, though the use of the term *berith* here possibly reflects the use of *berith* in Genesis 9 for the postdiluvian reestablishing of the order of nature according to the measure of common grace. Even though the Jeremianic reference would not be to the Genesis

1-3 arrangement precisely, it would nevertheless show that covenants may be found in historical narratives from which the term *berith* is absent.

Certainly the substance of *berith* was present in the kingdom order described in Genesis 1-3. It was characterized by precisely those elements that constitute a covenant, for it was produced through divine words and acts of commitment and it was subject to the sanctions of ultimate divine blessing and curse.

The words and acts that expressed God's creational commitments had the character of oaths and bonds. Of God it can truly be said that his word is his bond. The author of Hebrews says that when God added his oath to his promise to Abraham there were then two immutable things on which Abraham's faith could rest – "two" because God's previous simple word of promise was itself the equivalent of an immutable oath (Heb 6:13-18). Similarly, God's making of promises to David in 2 Samuel 7 is referred to in Psalm 89:3 as the swearing of an oath. Since, when God is the speaker, the truth character of a simple word of commitment is guaranteed as by oath, to identify the speaker as God is to identify the word as an oath. Hence, the divine self-identification, "I am Yahweh," may be understood as an introductory oath-formula. Thus, in Ezekiel 20:5, God's swearing (literally, lifting up his hand) to Israel is explained as an act of making himself known to them, saying "I am the Lord your God." God's spoken self-identification is here regarded as an equivalent of the physical oath-gesture of raising the hand to heaven, a verbal counterpart to a theophanic appearance in the oath-stance. In the Exodus 6 passage, which is apparently the one chiefly in view in Ezekiel 20:5, God's words of commitment are bracketed within the introductory and concluding oath-formula: "I am Yahweh" (vv. 2 and 8). This means that the ancient treaty-form as adopted by the Lord God when making covenant with his people was tantamount to a divine oath document, for the customary self-identification of the suzerain in the preamble was now a divine self-identification and so a virtual oath-formula (see Exod 20:2a; cf. Gen 17:1ff.; 26:24; 28:13; 35:11). Accordingly, the Sinaitic Covenant could be interpreted as a divine pledging of troth (see Ezek. 16).

In the beginning God's covenanting bond-words took the form of creative fiats. By these fiats God dictated into existence a covenantal kingdom order and implicit in the structuring-defining words spoken by the beneficent Creator was his oath commitment to maintain by faithful providential oversight the good world he had made and given its meaning. As noted above, Jeremiah interprets the establishment of the order of heavenly luminaries with their control of the day-night cycle as a divine covenantal commitment (Jer 31:35-37 and 33:20,21), with the implicitly covenantal character of the original creation process becoming explicit in the postdiluvian reestablishment of that order. The divine creation fiats were then covenant fiats too.

Before the first creative fiat is heard in Genesis 1:3, the divine speaker is portrayed in Genesis 1:2 as God the Spirit overshadowing the deep-and-darkness. As we shall be observing further below, this form of divine presence is to be identified with the Glory-cloud epiphany. At the ratification of the old covenant at Sinai, this cloud-pillar form of theophany represented God standing as witness to his covenant with Israel. Once again at the ratification of the new covenant at Pentecost, it was God the Spirit, appearing in phenomena that are to be seen as a New Testament version of the Glory-fire, who provided the confirmatory divine testimony. And the book of Revelation pictures the consummation of creation's history as involving a reappearance of the Glory-Spirit of Genesis 1:2, now enveloping the incarnate Son, his hand lifted in oath to heaven as he swears by himself, the Creator, that the mystery of God was to be completed (Rev 10:1,5-7; cf. Rev 1:15; 2:18).

As I have written elsewhere: "In the interpretive light of such redemptive reproductions of the Genesis 1:2 scene, we see that the Spirit at the beginning overarched creation as a divine witness to the Covenant of Creation, as a sign that creation existed under the aegis of his covenant lordship. Here is the background for the later use of the rainbow as a sign of God's covenant with the earth (Gen 9:12ff.). And this appointment of the rainbow as covenant sign in turn corroborates the interpretation of the corresponding supernatural light-and-clouds phenomenon of the Glory (the rainbow character of which is explicit in some instances) as a sign of the Covenant of Creation." (*Images of the Spirit*, pp. 19f.) The effect of the Genesis 1:2 portrayal of the Creator in oath-stance is to reinforce powerfully the commitment character of his ensuing words of creative fiat recorded in Genesis 1:3ff.

Another act of the Glory-Spirit with special covenantal significance appears at the sixth day climax of the creation narrative, namely, the forming of man in the image of God. Elsewhere in the Bible this creative act is interpreted as a marriage, as a covenantal pledging of troth by the Creator. (Here only a brief summary is presented of my review of the biblical data in *Images of the Spirit*, chapter 2).

One of the biblical figures for the bestowing of the divine image on man is that of covering him with a robe emblematic of God's Glory. The outstanding instance of this symbolism in the Old Testament is found in the placing of the sacred vestments on the high priest of Israel. Now in the allegory of Ezekiel 16 such an act of investiture with the image of God is used as a symbol for an act of covenant ratification. Presenting the Sinaitic covenant-making in nuptial imagery, Ezekiel depicts the divine pledging of the marriage troth as God's act of adorning the bride-Israel with the sacred vestments of his Glory-likeness. The prophet thus interpreted the Sinai covenant-making as a redemptive re-creation event culminating (as did the original creation) in the production of a covenant people fashioned in God's image, and he interpreted that climactic episode of investiture with the divine image as an act of divine commitment, sealing the marriage covenant. The specific historical reality behind Ezekiel's portrayal of the covering of the bride with her divine husband's robe of glory was the bringing of Israel at Sinai under the overshadowing canopy of the Glory-cloud. And that was, of course, the counterpart in the exodus re-creation to the Glory-Spirit's overarching of the deep-and-darkness in the original creation, preparatory to his creating of mankind in his Glory-likeness on the sixth day. Thus, for the Creator to adorn mankind with his image in the beginning, was, from the biblical perspective, to create mankind in a covenant of marriage, as bride of the Maker-Lord, with all the commitment of promise and obligation inherent in such an alliance.

In a special sense then the particular divine fiat to create man as one invested with the Glory-image of God was a covenantal fiat. Right here it is, of course, patent that the covenantal relationship of God and man had its origin in the very act of creating man. It is not the case, as some theological reconstructions would have it, that the covenant was superimposed on a temporally or logically prior noncovenantal human state. The covenantal character of the original kingdom order as a whole and of man's status in particular was given along with existence itself. For the Creator of Genesis 1 gave name and existence simultaneously in his creative fiat – and his creative fiat-names were covenantal fiat-names of divine commitment, especially so the fiat-name that called man into being in the divine image.

By investing man with the divine image, God appointed him to privileged status over the rest of creation (Gen 1:26-30). This sovereign determination of the relationship between man and the world can be viewed as an instance of God acting as third party or mediator in the arranging of a covenant between two parties. (Such mediation of covenants by a third party is attested in ancient international diplomacy.) In the account in Jeremiah 27:2-8, God's giving of dominion over the nations to Nebuchadnezzar is portrayed in symbolic act and word as the imposing of the yoke of a vassal treaty upon those nations, obliging them to serve the Babylonian suzerain. Nebuchadnezzar's position is described in terms evocative of the narrative of man's original dignity in Eden. (Reflection of the primal situation of man is still clearer in the picture of Nebuchadnezzar's suzerainty in Dan 2:38.) Accordingly, the Creator's giving of the earth and its creatures into man's hands in Eden may be viewed as the placing of the covenantal yoke of man's lordship upon the earth.

Such authoritative mediating of a covenantal order by the Creator clearly involved commitment on his part to supervise and enforce that covenant. In fact, divine arranging of a kingdom order wherein nature serves man's well-being is at times in the Bible expounded as a covenant that God makes between himself and man, God committing himself therein to secure man in a state of peace (see Ezek 34:25; Hos 2:18[20]). Viewed in these terms, the Lord's assignment of dominion to man over the world under conditions of Edenic beatitude (Gen 1:28) can be seen as signalizing a covenantal relationship between God and man. Indeed, it is likely that the later identification of episodes of subordination of nature to the service of man in terms of a covenant of God with man reflect an understanding of the original order with its similar relationship of man and nature as such a covenant.

Conspicuous among the stipulated terms of the original divine-human relationship were the paired divine sanctions of life and death, the curse of death threatened against any breach of fealty and the blessing of life promised for loyal obedience. Now divine sanctioning is an essential element in covenants. Moreover, in a divine covenant the divine sanctions coalesce with the commitments made by God as one party to the covenant, for here, uniquely, the covenant suzerain is himself the divine witness and enforcer of the sanctions of the covenant. Thus, in pointing to the notable role of the dual sanctions in Eden, we are also adducing further evidence of the presence there of the feature of commitment, which is the hallmark of covenants.

In part, the blessing sanction of the Edenic arrangement was expressed in the sign of the Sabbath, and this may be singled out as of particular interest for the covenantal identity of the original kingdom order. (We assume here conclusions that will be reached in our discussion of God's Sabbath below.)

For one thing, the setting of man's kingdom labors in a sabbatical framework imitative of the pattern of God's work of creation was an expression of man's identity as image of God and as such the sabbatical ordinance also served to identify man as a creature in covenant with God. By the Sabbath ordinance God made covenantal commitment that man with his God-like endowment would move on in the way of obedience to a consummation of rest, indeed, to the glory of God's own Sabbath.

Also, the Sabbath ordinance appointed for man's observance celebrated the reality of the archetypal Sabbath of the Creator's seventh day, and in doing so highlighted aspects of the creation order that were distinctly covenantal. God's entrance upon his Sabbath rest was an enthronement of the Creator, an assumption by him of his rightful position as Lord of the world, of all lands and peoples. The Sabbath ordinance thus called upon all earthly kingship to acknowledge itself to be a vassal kingship under the heavenly Suzerain. Now such a relationship is the kind of covenantal relationship that was defined by the ancient suzerain-vassal treaties. Agreeably, when God later made covenant with Israel, adopting for this purpose the form of these ancient political covenants, he appointed the Sabbath ordinance as a seal of this covenant (Exod 20:8-11; 31:16,17), signifying thereby that the people and the land belonged to him (cf., e.g., Lev 25:2-4). The Sabbath declared that Yahweh was covenant Lord of the kingdom of Israel. And if the Sabbath ordinance serves as a symbolic sign of God's covenantal lordship in the holy kingdom of Israel, it is surely because the original divine Sabbath represented the Creator's covenantal lordship over the world. Indeed, this connection is conspicuous in the appointing of the Sabbath to Israel. For this later Sabbath observance is explained as a remembering of God's creation acts, a celebrating of the glory of his covenantal kingship first established by his work of creation and now being reestablished through the redemptive sanctifying of a covenantal people renewed in God's image under God's lordship (Exod 20:8-11). In short then, the Sabbath ordinance in Eden was a sign of the covenant of God with man already in effect there. The very fact that the Genesis creation prologue is cast in sabbatical form tells us that the creation of the world was a covenant-making process.

Further, there is the familiar fact that the biblical accounts of redemptive covenants, the old and the new covenants, depict these covenant histories as divine works of re-creation. The point here is much the same as we were making about the appointing of the Sabbath ordinance as a sign of the covenant to Israel, but with our view extended now to include all the creation motifs that are used in the Scriptures to set forth the nature of God's covenantal action through Moses and Jesus Christ, the mediators of the old and new covenants. In interpreting these later covenants as creational, the biblical authors reflect their understanding of the creation as covenantal.

It is especially significant for our present thesis that in the Mosaic economy there was a reproduction of the creational order as a whole (within the limitations of the fallen situation and with the adjustments resulting from the redemptive process), including specifically the nature of the original Edenic order as a holy paradise-kingdom and as a probationary-works arrangement. The covenant identity of the reproduction points compellingly to the covenantal nature of the original.

Another such parallel is found in the Bible's use of the two-Adams scheme in its comprehensive analysis of God's government through history. If the role of Christ as the second Adam is recognized as covenantal, this scheme provides further clear warrant for classifying the arrangement made with the first Adam as covenantal.

Our conclusion is, therefore, that Genesis 1-3 teems with evidences of the covenantal character of the kingdom in Eden. We have in fact seen that the covenantal identity of this creation order was given to it with its very existence, particularly in the creation of man, its head, in the image of God. The creational covenant will here be called "The Creator's Covenant of Works with Adam." By continuing the use of the term "works" we preserve an important advantage that the traditional name, "Covenant of Works," has when combined with use of "Covenant of Grace" for redemptive covenant – the advantage of underscoring the fundamental law-gospel contrast. And our additional terms, "Creator's" and "with Adam," will serve to bring out the parallelism between this covenant of works and what we shall be calling "The Father's Covenant of Works with the Son" (i.e., the eternal intratrinitarian covenant), namely, the parallelism of the two Adams scheme, each of these covenants involving, as it does, an Adam figure, a federal representative under probation in a covenant of works.

As the analysis of this covenantal administration of God's kingdom lordship with its dual sanctions unfolds in the following chapters, we will see that it involves not only the bestowal of the kingdom on a holy people of God but an offer to make the kingdom given in creation a permanent possession on a glorified level of existence. Described in terms of varieties of international covenants familiar at the time of the writing of the book of Genesis, the original covenant with Adam was thus a suzerain-vassal covenant plus the proposal of a special grant to the vassal for loyal service.

Within the Scriptures are treaty texts (like the Decalogue) produced for particular covenant ratification transactions and displaying the literary-legal form attested in the contemporary ancient international treaties. The several standard sections of this treaty-form provide serviceable categories for analysis of the creational covenant. The first two chapters of the following analysis include data that would be found in the preamble and historical prologue, the opening sections of the treaty form. Chapter Three corresponds to the section of treaty stipulations or law; Chapter Four, to the sanctions section. Finally, Chapter Five will trace the history of the creational covenant, with the tragic failure of the first man to obtain the proposed grant of the eternal kingdom. Our use of the standard sections of the ancient treaty-form in this way should not be misunderstood as suggesting that the earliest chapters of Genesis have the literary form of a treaty. However, the fact that these treaty sections serve as satisfactorily as they do as an analytical framework for describing the sum and substance of these chapters does support illuminatingly the identification of the creation order as a covenantal arrangement.

Chapter One

LORD OF THE COVENANT-KINGDOM

Ancient vassal treaties opened with two sections setting forth the claims of the great king upon the vassal's allegiance and service. They stated who he was and what he had done. The first section identified him by his name and titles; the second, by a historical survey of his previous dealings with the vassal. Our concern in this chapter is to draw out of the biblical account of God's covenant with Adam a revelation of the names of God contained there and to indicate the lordly claims of those names upon the life and devotion of man. In the second chapter we shall be considering the further claims of God on man that were made by the gift of kingship and the bountiful blessings of the garden-kingdom of God.

A preoccupation with the question of God's name-identity is evident in the Pentateuch, the Mosaic documentary witness to the old covenant. This interest in the name(s) of God emerges from the very outset in the book of Genesis, where the self-disclosure of Israel's covenant Lord is traced back through the centuries of patriarchal promise to the distant Deluge and prediluvian ages, and yet farther back to man's beginnings and the dawn of history.

In connection with the record of those beginnings an especially effective answer to the question of Yahweh's identity is given by arranging the divine names in a striking pattern. In the creation account proper (Gen 1:1-2:3) only the generic term for God, Elohim, is used for the Creator. In the narrative of man's history in the garden (2:4-3:24) the compound designation, Yahweh-Elohim, predominates. In fact, this compound divine name is used as often within this brief compass as it is in all the rest of the Old Testament. Then, beginning with chapter 4, Yahweh and Elohim are both used singly, with the choice of one or the other determined in each instance by various theological and literary considerations. Clearly, the remarkable combination of the name Yahweh with Elohim in the account of the pre-Fall history in Genesis 2 and 3 is designed as a pointed declaration that Yahweh, the Lord of redemptive history, is Elohim, the Creator-God of Genesis 1.

Yahweh, Israel's Lord, is thus identified in Genesis 2 and 3 as Elohim, and Elohim in turn is identified in the creation account of Genesis 1:1ff.

Elohim appears there as the subject of the series of mighty verbs of creative action, as the dominant central figure of the vast creative drama exalted absolutely above everything else in the cosmic scene. While the account is indeed a revelation concerning the actual origins of the world, it is primarily a self-disclosure of the Creator himself, an apocalypse of Elohim. Unveiling the cosmic beginnings, it reveals there the glory of the eternal Elohim, the almighty Maker of the heavens and the earth.

As was intimated above, this hymnic celebration of the Creator placed at the opening of the canonical revelation of the old covenant thus serves the same purpose for which the preamble was designed in the international treaties current at the time the book of Genesis was written. The overlord, dictating the treaty to his vassals, named himself in this opening section, and along with his name he identified himself by an assortment of grandiose titles. The reading of the preamble was intended to instill in the vassal a dread of the great king of the treaty. Similarly, Yahweh, Lord of Israel, begins his covenant Word by identifying himself, and he does so not for the purpose of satisfying the noncommittal curiosity of philosophical speculators but to inspire in his servant people the fear of their Lord, and so impart to them the secret of covenant life.

I. GOD, THE ALPHA-AUTHOR

A. Creator of All

"For of him and through him and to him are all things" (Rom 11:36a). That all things are of God is affirmed in grand simplicity in the Genesis prologue (Gen 1:1-2:3). Summarizing the creative work of Elohim, the record states: "Thus the heavens and the earth were finished and all the host of them" (Gen 2:1). All the visible creation is meant and the invisible realm of angelic beings besides. Such seems to be the understanding of the statement reflected in the confessional prayer of Nehemiah 9:5ff. For Genesis 2:1 is evidently in view in the acknowledgment made there of the Lord as Creator of "heaven, the heaven of heavens, with all their host, the earth, and all things that are therein, the seas, and all that is therein," and this "host of heaven," described as worshipping God (v. 6), would be the invisible spiritual hosts of heaven (cf. 2 Chr 18:18; Pss 103:20,21; 148:2).

There is an echo of this reading of the Genesis revelation of creation in the Pauline confession of the Son: "For by him were all things created, that are in heaven, and that are in earth, visible and invisible, whether they be thrones, or dominions, or principalities, or powers" (Col 1:16; cf. John 1:1-3). And in Revelation 10 the same perspective informs the oath of Christ, portrayed in this vision as the Glory-Angel, who swears "by him who lives forever and ever, who created heaven and the things that are therein, and the earth and the things that are therein, and the sea and the things that are therein" (10:6). On the lips of the One who has just been described as coming down from heaven (10:1) and as lifting up his hand in oath to God in heaven (10:5), the words "heaven and the things therein" would surely seem to refer to the invisible realm of God's presence among his angels.

Given this understanding of Genesis 2:1, a referent must then be found in the preceding account for the mention of the creation of angels in the Genesis 2:1 summary statement and the only possible such referent is Genesis 1:1. According to its idiomatic force, the phrase "the heaven and the earth" in that verse denotes a totality and in the light of the kind of biblical data mentioned above it is not just the totality of the visible creation but of creation visible and invisible that is meant. The terms "heaven" and "earth" have the meanings here that they have, for example, in the prayer petition: "Thy will be done on earth as it is in heaven."

Another line of evidence confirms the interpretation of the "heaven" of Genesis 1:1 as the invisible heaven. From the treatment of the creation theme in Proverbs 8 it appears that Genesis 1:1 is the record of an event at a "beginning" time that preceded the episodes delineated in verses 2ff. (rather than a summary of the total creation history). For as picked up in Proverbs 8:22,23, that "beginning" is explicitly equated with a time before the waters of the earth's vast deep (cf. Gen 1:2) were divided vertically or bounded horizontally and before any of the other achievements of the creation "week" (Prov 8:22-30). Therefore, according to Genesis 1:1, a "heaven" existed in distinction from an "earth" at a time prior to developments described in the following verses. Then as the "earth" from which the "heaven" is distinguished in verse 1 is singled out in verse 2 and becomes the exclusive subject of the subsequent narrative, a decisive fact emerges for the identification of the "heaven" of verse 1. For from this "earth" of verses 1 and 2 eventually is derived not only the land and seas but the *visible* heavens. Thus, on day two (Gen 1:6-8) the separation of the waters above from those below involves the appearance of the firmament of heaven, the vault of the sky, while the waters above are themselves the heavenly sea of the clouds (perhaps paralleled in Ps 148:4 by "the heaven of heavens," though that phrase seems to denote the invisible celestial realm in Deut 10:14; 1 Kgs 8:27; Neh 9:6; and Ps 115:16). All the visible heavens are thereby accounted for as byproducts of the structuring of the "earth." Sun, moon, and stars do not come into consideration here for in terms of Genesis 1 they are not the heavens but the luminaries that are placed in the heavenly vault; they are the host of (the visible) heaven. (They too owe their existence to God's creative fiat [Gen 1:14-18]. In actual fact, they existed at the time the earth was in its deep-and-darkness stage [Gen 1:2] – the Genesis 1 narrative being arranged thematically rather than by chronological sequence – but there is no specific mention of them in the first two verses.) We conclude then that the "earth" referred to in Genesis 1:2 included within it, though not yet separate from it, all that constitutes the visible heavens (in the biblical vocabulary). This means that the "heaven" that is distinguished from that "earth" at the prior point in view in Genesis 1:1 can only be the invisible heaven, the realm of angels.

Recognition that the "heaven" of Genesis 1:1 is the invisible heavens corroborates the conclusion that this verse is not a heading that summarizes the creation process narrated in verses 2 ff., for that process does not include the production of the invisible heavens. Also, the Proverbs 8 interpretation of the "beginning" in Genesis 1:1 as a time prior to and not overlapping developments described in verses 2ff. rules out the exegesis that would relativize the "beginning" by treating verse 1 as a dependent statement, coordinate with verse 2 and subordinate to verse 3. On either this approach or the view of verse 1 as a summary heading, Genesis 1 would no longer contain a direct declaration of the original absolute creation. Over against such conclusions we maintain that Genesis 1:1 is an independent statement, not however one that summarizes what follows but rather one that refers to the "beginning" time which preceded the history recorded in verses 2 ff. So understood, Genesis 1:1 affirms that this beginning time witnessed the origins of the cosmos as a whole, visible and invisible, and in particular the absolute act of origination, creation *ex nihilo* and *in nihilum*, that is, without a context of prior created reality (cf. Heb 11:3).

Genesis 1:1 sets the Creator at the beginning in holy majesty above and apart from all creation visible and invisible as the One eternally before all things. According to Proverbs 8, the divine Wisdom was present at the earliest creation of God, and God, the One to whom Wisdom relates before the primeval beginning, is simply there, unquestioned, presupposed, the Eternal, the Lord and there is none else (cf. Isa 40:21,28; 43:10). Similarly, in Paul's Christological exposition of the Genesis 1 event, conjoined to the declaration that all things in heaven and earth were created by the Son is the statement: "and he is before all things" (Col 1:17; cf. John 1:1f.).

In sum, Elohim is revealed in the Genesis prologue as God alone, the Eternal, the Creator of all things visible and invisible.

B. Sovereign Architect-Builder

Creation as described in the Genesis prologue is strictly a constructive process, without any undercurrent of conflict. Elohim, the Creator, is portrayed not as a mighty warrior but as an omnipotent artisan, not as a cunning conqueror but as an omniscient architect. There is no sense of the tumult of war in the account; everything proceeds in orderly and stately fashion according to architectonic plan.

A major building motif is the dividing of the world structure into compartments suitable for habitation by various types of creatures. For God "created it not to be empty but formed it as a place to live" (Isa 45:18). Overhead, as a sheltering cover for the earthlings, was spread the sky, called "the firmament" with reference to its canopy-like appearance. In it were installed heavenly lamps to illumine the darkness of the dwelling-place by day and night. What is thus barely suggested of architectural imagery in Genesis 1 is carried out in more picturesque detail in other biblical reflections on the creation account. The Lord himself in his challenging disclosure to his servant Job pictures himself in the process of creation with measuring line in hand, defining the spaces, determining the dimensions according to specifications, setting the building on foundations and laying the cornerstone, enclosing the living areas by boundary-walls with their doors and bars (Job 38:4ff.). In the version of the creation days from the wisdom perspective given in Proverbs 8:22ff., the divine wisdom that directs and delights in the founding and bounding of the world-habitation is personified as a master-builder. (Or, as otherwise interpreted, it is the Lord himself, rather than his wisdom, who is designated the master-builder.) Elsewhere too in the Old Testament in poetic cosmological allusions the world is imaged as an architectural structure with the earth as one four-cornered floor and the heavens an upper story, its chambers supported by beams and having windows, with the mountains as the columns on which this heavenly story is raised, while the earth is founded on pillars with bases in the depths. All this needs no demythologizing by us, for in its biblical form it is not mythopoeic in the first place. What is required for a proper assessment of this kind of cosmology is simply an appreciation of the figurative quality of the poetic treatment.

Another architectural dimension of creation comes to view in the course of biblical revelation. Creation was designed to serve a far more exalted function than the housing of a variety of creature-beings in the several distinctive areas of the earth. The cosmic structure was built as a habitation for the Creator himself. Heaven and earth were erected as a house of God, a palace of the Great King, the seat of sovereignty of the Lord of the covenant.

"Thus says Yahweh: heaven is my throne and the earth is my footstool" (Isa 66:1a; cf. Matt 5:34,35). Creation was royal construction. The establishing of the world order was the establishing of the throne room of the King of kings. From the heights of his holy cosmic house God rules, robed in heaven's majesty (Ps 93). The lyric exposition of Genesis 1 in Psalm 104 similarly views the creation as God's residence-garment (vv. 1-3). From the creation of the world, God sits as king above the circle of the world within the heavenly curtains (Isa 40:21-23). "Yahweh is in his holy temple, his throne is in the heavens" (Ps 11:4; cf. 103:19; Mic 1:2,3).

In ancient mythological cosmogony the theme of a house for the god occupies a climactic place. Thus, in the Canaanite version, when Baal emerges from the conflict as the conqueror of the dragon-power of chaos and thereby as the stablilizer of world-order, he has a house built for his enthronement. The mythological "creation" process thus culminates in the celebration of the hero-god's exaltation as king in a palace which is an archetype of the actual temples where the god was worshipped, the latter also being representational of the cosmic world of the god.

As observed above, the creation as described in the Genesis prologue is a work of construction without trace of struggle. The Genesis account itself does not make even a poetic use of the conflict theme current in extra-biblical cosmogony, the theme of the slaying of the chaos monster by the hero-god as the means of founding the world order.

Elsewhere in the Bible that theme and imagery are used, usually to portray God's redemptive triumph over the powers of Hell. Sometimes it is used to describe the Creator's government of the world of nature, particularly his control of the more tempestuous phenomena and especially the raging waters of the sea (Job 9:13, cf. 8[RSV]; 26:12,13; cf. 3:8; Pss 65:7; 89:10). The latter instances might well include the divine providential rule and ordering of forces of nature operative during as well as after the creation era (notice the clear allusions to creation in Job 9:8,9 and 26:10) and in this qualified sense it might then be said that the Bible does on occasion make a literary use of the conflict motif with reference to God's activity during creation. In such passages (cf. too Pss 74 and 89) the distinction between the unique, closed era of the "six days," marked by the series of supernatural acts of origination, and the postcreation era is allowed to fade while the broader theme of God's providential control and direction of nature, which overlaps both eras, is brought into focus. However, even in this limited sense that God's providential activity during the creation "week" is at times described in terms of a conflict with chaotic forces it is purely a matter of poetic literary idiom, not a theological adoption of the cosmogonic myth, either whole or piecemeal.

The pagan cosmogonic myth, a garbled, apostate version, a perversion, of pristine traditions of primordial historical realities, could not pass through the conceptual grid that forms the consistent framework of the teachings of Scripture except as already demythologized poetic idiom. Even among the ancient myth-makers themselves the practice is attested of redacting earlier cosmogonic myth with polemic intent. In order to propagandize for some new development in the cult, they would so adapt the myth that the old god who was to be eclipsed would be replaced by his rival, the current favorite, in the role of heroic conqueror of the chaos monster in the mythopoeic drama of cosmic origins. The adoption of the earlier myth was thus for the purpose of rejecting its message, if not at the conceptual level of its mythological cosmogony as such, at least at the political level of rival cultic claimants. The Bible's use of the cosmogonic conflict myth is with similar, but incomparably more radical, polemical intent. When the biblical revelation identifies Yahweh, the living and true God, as the Creator who slays the dragon, it is not a mere matter of substituting one deity for another while maintaining the essence of the myth. In its adaptation of the myth the Bible demythologizes the myth as such. It demythologizes the hero-god, it demythologizes the dragon (whether identifying him as Satan or as tempestuous nature), it rejects the mythical cosmogony and cosmology root and branch.

There is no serious suggestion in Scripture of the existence of divine adversaries with whom the creating God had to contend. Indeed, while the conflict motif is used in the Bible as a literary figure for the kind of general ordering of nature whose beginnings reach back into the creation era, such as God's bounding of the seas, that motif is apparently not used in any way whatsoever with reference to God's acts of absolute creation. Theomachy is not used in the Bible even in poetic idiom as providing the pre-material for the creation of the world. Not even in figurative imagery is there a suggestion of the use of the vast carcass of a vanquished deity as the material for man's world, as in the case of Marduk's cosmogonic conquest of Tiamat in the Mesopotamian tradition. Even where the Sea-monster might appear in a creation context, it is not there as a pre-existing thing but as (the symbol of) a creature made by God. The biblical revelation of world origins by divine creation in the strict sense thus remains unobscured.

Certainly in the Genesis prologue itself, the creation fiats are not battle cries but architectural directives. According to Genesis 1, creation is a purely production process. The goal in view is not to struggle through to a precarious victory but to complete a building. The biblical account thus stands apart from the Canaanite cosmogony of the Baal epic, and other ancient cosmogonies of that type. The right of the latter to be called creation accounts has been challenged because they do not include the concept of world creation in the strict sense but only the idea of an ordering of chaos. Even the other major ancient type of cosmogony, which began with the theme of theogony, did not understand creation as absolute origination *ex nihilo* or *in nihilum*, but as a birth process issuing from original binary deity. If we judge from the biblical concept of creation, neither of these major types of ancient pagan cosmogonies falls properly in the category of creation. Both rather represent mythologically distorted reinterpretations of aspects of the primeval revelation of creation which lies behind and is faithfully represented in the Genesis creation account.

God has no adversary in his original creating. He does not build with trowel in one hand and sword in the other. There is no need for the sword. More than that, there is no need for the trowel. This builder does not use tools. He does not really work with his hands. The word of his will is his all-effective instrument. Further still, he does not need even materials.

There is no theogony in Genesis 1, and no theomachy as a means to provide the raw material of creation. The world order is not explained there in terms of a tension between interacting forces of staticism and flux as represented in the theogonic and cultic deities of the Near Eastern cosmogonic myths or as propounded in more abstractly dialectical principles in Greek philosophy. God's almighty fiat not only shapes the world-material to his purpose; that simple sovereign word actually brings the material itself into being.

"Thus says Yahweh ... I, Yahweh, am the Maker of all things, who stretched out the heavens, I alone, and spread out the earth – who was with me?" (Isa 44:24; cf. 45:18). There was no strange god with him, no other as hindrance or helper. Elohim, alone in the beginning, created heaven and earth.

C. Glory-Spirit Archetype

God's name-nature was revealed not only in the process and the products of his sovereign creative action but through an epiphanic Presence. Genesis 1:2b refers to this divine reality: "The Spirit of God was hovering over the face of the waters." [I have treated this subject in some detail in *Images of the Spirit*, chapter 1, and present a summary of that discussion here.]

An interpretation of this "Spirit" hovering as on wings above the dark watery waste (cf. Gen 1:2a) is provided in the Song of Moses in Deuteronomy 32. The use in Deuteronomy 32:10,11 of two rare words found nowhere else in the five books of Moses except in Genesis 1:2 (where one describes the Spirit's bird-like action and the other denotes the inchoate state of deep-and-darkness) points to the parallel circumstances in the situations depicted in the two passages. Deuteronomy 32 refers to God's work of redemptive re-creation in the exodus event. The song recalls how God was present with Israel in the desolate wilderness wasteland, hovering like an eagle over his people as he fashioned for himself anew a holy sanctuary. And the form of his overshadowing presence there was, of course, that of the Shekinah cloud of glory. Elsewhere in the Bible this Glory-cloud is at times called simply "the Spirit" (Neh 9:19f.; Isa 63:11-14; Hag 2:5). The usage in Genesis 1:2 is similar, though the Spirit here is probably best understood as the heavenly reality, the invisible cosmos-filling glory of the divine Presence, of which the Glory-cloud was a localized manifestation.

The Glory-Spirit was a visible divine signature. It is frequently referred to as God's "name" and at times it is even viewed as a divine name-banner lifted on high over the land and people. In the introduction to Section A, we noted that the Glory-cloud was sometimes viewed as a divine witness pillar, as the Lord standing in oath-stance on occasions of covenant ratification. This witness pillar function and the identity of the Glory-Spirit as a divine name-signature are obviously closely related.

All that the Glory-cloud represented would constitute the meaning of this "name." It represented God's personal presence and it was therefore called the face or presence. In it God was present in power to act and therefore it was also called his arm or hand. Bright luminosity characterized the visible appearance of the Shekinah; hence, it was designated by the word glory and other terms suggesting its radiant beauty. This glory was a royal splendor for the epiphanic cloud formation as a whole was the throne-room of God, his heavenly court or palace-temple within which he sat in majesty amid the angelic hosts as King of Glory. This cloud was indeed the invisible Glory-temple of heaven appearing in a veiled visibility in the midst of earthly creatures. And since it represented a presence of God in power for action (often for judgment) the cloud, though a royal sanctuary-structure, was also a vehicle; it was the chariot God rode in stormy terror through the skies. Multiple aspects of God's nature were thus revealed in the Glory-Spirit-Name. In sum, this Name-theophany declared God to be heavenly Lord and Judge of all the earth, "glorious in holiness, fearful in praises, doing wonders" (Exod 15:11).

Hovering over the face of the waters in the beginning, the Glory-Spirit was the Creator-King present in almighty power, poised to fashion deep-and-darkness into a heaven on earth and promising to transform the death realm into a realm of abundant life.

More than that, the Glory-Spirit provided a preview of the finished creation-structure, for this theophanic Spirit-formation was a divine paradigm as well as a divine power for the work of creation. Cosmos and man alike were to be formed after this archetypal temple pattern. The Creator-Word who was in the beginning and made all things (John 1:1-3) would articulate this heavenly temple pattern in creative fiats and the world that came into being at his behest would be a cosmic replica of the royal sanctuary of the Glory-Spirit. So God identified it by way of comparative contrast with another temple replica constructed by Israel: "Heaven is my throne and earth is my footstool. What manner of house will you build for me?" (Isa 66:1). At the climax of creation history the Creator-Word replicated the Spirit-paradigm in man. Thus man too is a temple of God, a living temple fashioned in the image of the archetypal Glory-Spirit.

The Spirit-Glory manifests the divine presence at creation's origins and signifies that God's name is Alpha and the First and the Beginning. As the overshadowing Glory was present at the beginning of the first creation, so it was again present at epochal beginnings in the history of re-creation in both old and new covenants – at Sinai, at the incarnation, baptism, and transfiguration of the Son of God, and at Pentecost. And because the Spirit's presence in redemptive re-creation is once more both as power and as paradigm, the consummation of redemptive history witnesses the appearing of the eternal cosmic-human temple of God. Accordingly, in the Glory-Spirit of Genesis 1:2 we see an earnest not only of the finished creation as described at the close of the Genesis prologue but of creation at the end of all history as revealed in the prophetic visions of the Revelation. We behold in the Spirit-Presence hovering over the world at its beginning the shape of the world to come.

Inherent in God's name-identity as Creator of all things visible and invisible, the Alpha-Author, is the lordly claim of ownership and absolute authority. Such is the reasoning of the Psalms when they confess: "The earth and its fullness belong to Yahweh, the world with all who live on it; for it is he who founded it on the seas, who established it above the oceans" (Ps 24:1,2) ... "to him belongs the sea, for he made it; and the dry land, which his hands formed" (Ps 95:5) ... "Acknowledge that Yahweh is our God, for he has made us – made us who were not his people to be the sheep of his pasture" (Ps 100:3). As the signature of the Creator-Author, the Glory-Spirit of Genesis 1:2 was the sign of God's sovereign claim to ownership of all the world. At the beginning the creation existed under the insignia of God's covenant lordship. The Glory-Spirit of Genesis 1:2 is thus another evidence that the creation record of the Genesis prologue is at the same time the record of the making of a divine covenant with man.

Each of the opening two verses of Genesis 1 speaks of both the visible and invisible realms. The latter is referred to in verse 1 as "the heavens." And the "Spirit" of verse 2 evokes that same invisible heavenly court of the Lord with its celestial hosts. The name of God thereby revealed was therefore not only covenant Lord of the visible world of men, but Lord of hosts –

King of the heavenly temple, Lord of the angelic hosts. Together the opening two verses, along with the entire creation account, affirm that all things are "of him," that he is Lord of all.

II. GOD, THE OMEGA-CONSUMMATOR

Elohim is the First – he is also the Last. Witness is given in the Genesis prologue to the truth that all things are *unto* him. The force of this truth as a compelling witness to his covenantal lordship and as a constraining claim upon man's service is equal to that of the affirmation that all things are of him. It is particularly through the overall form of the creation narrative that this aspect of his sovereignty is expressed. God sets forth his creative acts within the pictorial framework of a Sabbath-crowned week and by this sabbatical pattern he identifies himself as Omega, the One for whom all things are and were created, the Lord worthy to receive glory and honor and praise (cf. Rev 4:11).

It is the seventh day of the creation week, the climactic Sabbath to which the course of creative events moves, that gives to the pattern of the week of days as a whole its distinctive sabbatical character, and it is then in the unfolding of the significance of the Sabbath day that the disclosure of the Omega name of God will be found.

A. Sabbath and Consummation

First and most obvious, the Sabbath marks the completion of God's work of creation. As a celebration of the finishing of the world-temple, the Sabbath proclaims the name of the Creator to be Consummator. To be the builder who arrives at the seventh day of completion, to be the Sabbath attaining Creator, is to bear the name "the Last" along with the name "the First."

From the outset it was evident by the very mode of his working that the divine worker would complete his cosmic enterprise. He who can speak an effective "Let there be" must inevitably arrive at his Sabbath and say, "It is finished." None could resist or deny or silence his fiat. Such effortless authoring by omnipotent words was an infallible presage that this worker would prove to be a Sabbatarian Creator.

With each successive fiat the cosmic house took shape in progressive fulfillment of the divine architect's unfathomably vast conception. Hence the work process of the six days is marked by the judicial refrain of divine approbation: "God saw that it was good." This succession of judgments expressing the builder's pleasure in the work of each day led to the final verdict of delighted satisfaction: "God saw everything that he had made and behold it was very good" (Gen 1:31a; cf. Exod 39:43). The work of Elohim eventuated in the completion of the cosmic masterpiece and in the Sabbath that proclaimed the name of this Lord of the covenant to be not only Author but Finisher.

At the beginning stood the Glory-theophany, the divine Alpha. By virtue of its nature as an archetypal pattern it was a prophetic sign of creation's goal. And the Sabbath at the completion of creation answers to that paradigm-promise of the Glory-Spirit (Gen 2:2; cf. 1Kgs 6:38). The Glory is the Sabbath reality present beforehand; it is the earnest and archetype that guarantees the Sabbath's coming. The Sabbath is the Glory come to expression as the consummation of history. Pneumatology is the realm of eschatology. Together, the Spirit and the Sabbath revealed that Elohim is Alpha and Omega.

B. Sabbath and Enthronement

A corollary of the completion of work is the resting of the worker – that is another meaning of God's Sabbath. The effortless fiat character of the work of the six days forestalls any misconception of the Creator as a wearied workman who must recoup his spent strength on the seventh day. (The highly anthropomorphic "was refreshed" of Exod 31:17 certainly does not intend to suggest otherwise, nor does "he rested" in Exod 20:11.) The Creator's Sabbath rest is much more a matter of taking satisfaction and delight in his consummated building. So it is with the Wisdom-figure in the architectural delineation of creation in Proverbs 8 (see vv. 30f.).

But this rest of God may be more specifically understood as a royal kind of resting. The royal nature of the rest follows from the royal nature of the work. God created the heaven and the earth to be his cosmic palace and accordingly his resting is an occupying of his palace, a royal session. The dawning of the Sabbath witnesses a new enthronement of Elohim.

The Scriptures in effect interpret God's Sabbath rest at the completion of his cosmic house as an enthronement when they present the converse of this idea by portraying God's enthronement above the ark in earthly replicas of his cosmic house as a Sabbath rest. Thus, after identifying heaven and earth as his throne-house (Isa 66:1a) the Lord asks Israel: "What manner of house will ye build unto me and what shall be the place of my rest?" (Isa 66:1b; cf. 2 Chr 6:18,41f.; Acts 7:49). And David spoke of his intention "to build a house of rest for the ark of the covenant of the Lord and for the footstool of our God" (1 Chr 28:2), while Psalm 132 exhorts: "Let us go to his dwelling place; let us worship at his footstool. Rise up, Yahweh, from your resting place; arise from the ark of your strength" (vv.7,8; cf. Num 10:35,36) ... "for Yahweh has chosen Zion; he has desired it for his dwelling [or seat]. This is my resting place forever; here I will dwell [or sit enthroned]" (vv.13,14). When God's seventh day resting is referred to in the Sabbath commandment in the Decalogue (Exod 20:11), the verbal root of *menuchah*, "rest," the term used for God's temple enthronement in these passages, is employed in the place of the verb *shabath* used in Genesis 2:2.

Another indication of the royal nature of God's Sabbath rest is afforded when the Bible interprets the entrance of God's covenant people Israel upon their royal inheritance as the securing of a Sabbath rest. Thus, Israel's occupation of the promised land is described as God's gift of "rest" (*menuchah*) to them (Deut 3:20; 12:9; 1 Kgs 8:56). In fact, in Hebrews 4, Israel's dominion-rest in Canaan (viewed as forfeited by the generation in the wilderness but typologically achieved through Joshua's conquest of Canaan) is expressly interpreted in terms of the Creator's seventh day rest (vv. 3f.), while the corresponding antitypical experience of God's people in the new covenant is called a *sabbatismos*, "a Sabbath rest" (v. 9), a participation in the divine rest of the ongoing seventh day of creation (v. 10; cf. vv. 3-5). The identification of Israel's kingdom inheritance as a Sabbath experience is also evident in the fact that the sabbatical years and especially the Jubilee Sabbath were occasions for the restoration of the people of God to the possession of their allotted land. This means then that God's own Sabbath, the archetype of Israel's sabbatical occupation of the kingdom in Canaan, must also be seen as a royal resting in kingdom sovereignty.

Inasmuch as the final attainment of Sabbath rest by the people of God will be a participation in God's seventh day of creation, his everlasting Sabbath, what is revealed of the eternal state of rest following upon the re-creation of heaven and earth will also illuminate the divine Sabbath rest of Genesis

2:2. And surely the quintessence of the eternal City in which God's people find their rest is the enthronement of the Lord God Almighty and the Lamb (Rev 21:5,22f.; 22:1-3). The figure of the Lamb reminds us that this is the consummation of a history of redemption and all the features of this picture cannot be projected back into Genesis 2:2. But beyond doubt, the enthronement of the divine Glory belongs to and is indeed the heart of the continuity between the original stage of the creation's seventh day and that later stage in which the redeemed participate.

A feature of redemptive Sabbath that underscores its royal character is that it is rest from battle, a victory celebration. During the wilderness march the ark was said to rest when it resumed a stationary position in the midst of Israel after leading an advance heralded by Moses' call: "Rise up, O Yahweh, and let thine enemies be scattered" (Num 10:35,36). Also, the establishing of God's house of rest in the days of David and Solomon was the sequel to attainment of rest (through royal conquest) from all foes of the theocracy (2 Sam 7:1,10,11; cf. Deut 12:10; 1 Chr 22:9f.). So too, the eternal Sabbath of the New Jerusalem follows upon God's victory in the final judgment over the Satanic hordes (Rev 19 and 20). It is in the treatment of this theme of redemptive re-creation that the Scriptures make their most striking use of imagery drawn from the pagan cosmogonic myth – the slaying of the dragon by the hero-god, followed by celebration of his glory in a royal residence built as a sequel to his victory. Thus, in the New Testament Apocalypse it is by vanquishing dragon and beast that the Lord prepares for the final scene of the appearance of his temple-throne (Rev 20:2,10). By gaining rest from all his enemies round about, Christ secures the throne of the consummated temple in the realm of the eternal Sabbath. This figurative utilization by the Bible of a cosmogonic pattern that has as its climax the building of a throne-house for the victorious god-king gives dramatic emphasis to the message that the production of a house for God's enthronement as cosmic King is the ultimate objective of the work of re-creation.

Even in these redemptive re-creation accounts that portray God's victory as an overcoming of monstrous powers, the idea conveyed is not at all that God was obliged to wrest world dominion as the spoils of battle from the clutches of eternal rivals. The absolute lordship of God is the presupposition and explanation of his triumph, not its sequel. The battle, therefore, is not the means by which God acquires the throne, but is rather a sovereign exercise of that imperium which belongs to him as the Creator who sits enthroned from the Flood, yea from everlasting (Ps 29:10). The battle and the conquest are in fact acts of divine judgment against transgressing subjects.

Since, in the case of the original creation, Sabbath enthronement was not preceded by conflict with rebel adversaries but came at the completion of a purely constructive process, there could be no question of an initiation of God's world dominion by defeat of another god who previously possessed sovereignty. Neither is there any suggestion of the Creator's attaining at some point to a sovereignty he had formerly lacked. To predicate an enthronement of God on the seventh day of creation history is not to deny that the creative activity of God is from the beginning an exercise of an ultimate and absolute sovereignty which he enjoys as an original and everlasting prerogative of his very godhood. It is simply saying that creation produced a new theater for the manifestation of God's eternal majesty, and when the heavenly throne and earthly footstool had been prepared, God assumed his rightful royal place in that new sphere.

Nor was the Sabbath enthronement of the seventh day the first expression of the reality of divine enthronement within creation history. For according to Genesis 1:2, as we have seen, the Glory of the Lord stood over the creation while yet the earth was without form and void, and that Glory is the manifestation of God enthroned in the midst of the heavenly hosts. Here again we encounter the paradigmatic nature of the Spirit-Glory. As a revelation of the God of the throne it was archetypal of God's Sabbath enthronement. [See further my *Images of the Spirit*, chapter 4, for a discussion of the relationship of the Glory-Spirit and the Sabbath in redemptive eschatology, particularly in the prophecy of Isaiah. The immediately following comments echo the treatment of the theme of the Sabbath and the day of the Lord in that same context.]

Another aspect of the Sabbath closely related to its character as a royal resting or enthronement is its identity as the day of the Lord. The divine Sabbath, that seventh day of the enthroned Creator-King, whose dawning marked the completion of creation history, is the heavenly reality that breaks into history in subsequent judicial episodes known as the day of the Lord, and ultimately in the *parousia*-day of the Lord Christ which inaugurates the eternal participation of the entire new mankind in the divine Sabbath. Like the later occurrences of the day of the Lord and especially the last one, the divine Sabbath of the creation history was a time of God's pronouncing judicial verdict (his self-glorifying approbation of his creative handiwork), a day of his consummating of a creation of heaven and earth, and a celebration of the perfecting of a temple of God, the Omega manifestation of the Alpha archetype of the Glory-Spirit. As the inception of the day of the Lord, the divine Sabbath of the Genesis creation prologue is a revelation of the Creator reigning from his heavenly throne as the Judge of all the world.

In summary then, the Sabbath, or day of the Lord, and the Spirit-Glory, which is the archetypal earnest of the divine Sabbath, are exponential of divine enthronement. By portraying Elohim as the cosmic builder who attained to the royal rest of the Sabbath day, the Genesis prologue identifies him as Great King of the world, the one enthroned as eternal Judge over the cosmic temple and as sovereign Lord over the covenant community.

C. Sabbath and Consecration

A hierarchical pattern of dominion can be traced through the creational record, a pattern of ascending consecration with the Sabbath as its capstone. In the topically arranged narrative, the several elements of creation's history are distributed within the figurative chronological schema of days so as to bring out this hierarchical order in strong relief. Within the first three day-frames is described the origin of three vast spheres over which rule is to be exercised. Then in day-frames four through six the rulers of each of these spheres is presented in proper turn, each arising at the divine behest and ruling by divine appointment. But the rising chain of command does not stop with the six days; it ascends to the seventh day, to the supreme dominion of him who is Lord of the Sabbath.

The fourth day-frame depicts the creation of the sun and moon and their royal appointment "to rule over" the day and night, the realms described in the parallel first day-frame. Their rule is expressed in their defining of the boundaries of their realm, as they "separate" the light and darkness (Gen 1:16-18). Then the fish and the birds of day five, the lords of the waters below and the sky above, the realms of the parallel second day-frame, are given the blessing-commission to enter into possession of their domains to their utmost limits. The terms that describe their commission – to be fruitful, to multiply and fill (Gen 1:22) – anticipate the royal mandate that was to be given to man. The sixth day-frame introduces those who are to rule over the dry land of the parallel third day: land animals and man. The lordly beasts are authorized to serve themselves of the natural tributary produce of their land-realm (Gen 1:30), a prerogative they share with man (Gen 1:29). The investiture of man with kingship (Gen 1:26-29) brings the lines of authority to their apex within the six days. The scheme of the parallel days proves too restrictive here. For the scope of man's lordship is not confined to the dry-land realm of day three but extends over all the earth. Moreover, man's dominion extends not only over all the subject-realms of earth defined in days one to three but over all those rulers whose dominions are described in days four through six. The series of terms that describes man's royal functions and prerogatives also points to the supremacy of his kingship. Those concepts that were used singly to indicate the dominion of the other rulers are all included in the account of man's royal appointment. He rules, indeed subdues; he multiplies and fills; he appropriates the tributary produce.

But all this pomp and majesty of the six days simply subserves the revelation of the ultimate and absolute dominion celebrated in the seventh day. Even during the pageant of the creature-kings in the narrative of days four through six, their royal splendor is paled by the surpassing glory of the Creator-King who commands them into existence, identifies them in his fiat-naming of them, and invests them with their subordinate dominions. And then when the creation apocalypse has reached the vicegerency of the God-like creature-king of the sixth day, and moves beyond it, we observe the glory of all the creature-kingdoms of all six days being carried along as a tributary offering within the gates of the Sabbath day to be laid at the feet of the Creator-King, now beheld in the brilliance of his epiphany as Sabbath Lord.

The meaning of the original Sabbath (Gen 2:2) is mirrored in the Sabbath ordinance (Gen 2:3), the record of which emphasizes that the Sabbath is set apart as sacred to the Creator. It belongs to the Lord of the covenant and it witnesses to God's ultimate proprietorship of the land and to his lordship over the total life of man. Observance of the Sabbath by man is thus a confession that Yahweh is his Lord and Lord of all lords. Sabbath-keeping expresses man's commitment to the service of his Lord.

All the creation of the six days is consecrated to man as the one set over all the works of God's hand, as the hierarchical structure of Genesis 1 shows, but man himself in turn is consecrated to the One who set all things under his feet. Man is king over creation, but he is a vassal-king, he reigns as one under the Creator's authority, obligated to devote his kingdom to the Great King. And through that consecration of man to the Creator which is required in the Sabbath stipulation, all that belongs to the six days is consecrated to the Sabbath-Lord. In the Sabbath sanctified unto God all the works of the six workdays leading to and issuing in the Sabbath are hallowed unto God.

The pattern of ascending dominion in the creation record is thus designed to teach the ultimate truth that all created reality is under the Creator's lordship, that God's kingdom embraces all creation.

The several aspects of the revelation of Elohim conveyed through the sabbatical form of the Genesis prologue interlock. The consummation of the cosmic palace issues in the Creator's cosmic enthronement, and to the King enthroned in the Sabbath-Glory all creation owes allegiance. Read in this perspective, the Genesis prologue is seen to be so constructed that at the same time it is declaring that all things are of God, it is declaring that all things are unto God, "to whom be glory forever" (Rom 11:36). Genesis 1:1-2:3 is therefore at once history and law, both covenantal, and these two witnesses together attest to the exalted name of God as Lord over all.

Conclusion
As part of the Old Testament Scripture given to Israel as its covenant canon, the Genesis prologue performed for them the essential function of a treaty preamble. It answered the question "Who is Yahweh?", identifying Israel's Redeemer-God with Elohim the Creator. And manifestly the God who in the beginning bounded the vast seas by lordly fiat and the God who made the dry path through the sea in the exodus salvation-act were one and the same. Indeed, it was only because Yahweh was Elohim, the Lord of nature, that he had been in a position to save his people, making the darkness light before fleeing Israel and bringing the waters thundering over the chariots of Egypt. So too in the future, Yahweh, Lord of the covenant, King of creation, would be able to use nature to execute the sanctions of his covenant. He would be able to unleash chaos as an agent of his judgments and he would be able also to accomplish a re-creation of nature that complemented the personal renewal of his people and perfected the beatitude promised in his covenant.

It may be assumed that the general substance of the revelation of the Genesis prologue identifying God as the Sabbatarian Consummator of creation formed part of God's special preredemptive revelation to man in the garden. At least, that assumption seems justifiable if one regards the Sabbath ordinance as a creation ordinance (on this see further below). And in that case the original of the sabbatical creation tradition represented by the prologue to Genesis will have performed for the creational covenant at the beginning the function for which treaty preambles were later designed. It will have made known to the man-vassal at once that his covenant Lord was to be reverenced with godly fear and served with all the heart – for his name was Author-and-Finisher, King of heaven and earth.

Indeed, quite apart from such a disclosure to man of the sabbatically structured history of creation, all natural and supernatural revelation in Eden joined in chorus clearly proclaiming to Adam the meaning of his world as a covenantal order under the sceptre and protection of its Creator. Beholding the revelation of God as Creator, the man-vassal was confronted with God's claims, calling for confession, commitment, doxology. The personified divine Wisdom in Proverbs 8:22-9:6 appeals to her participation in the work of creation as the basis of her summons to men to heed her voice, come to the covenant banquet in the cosmic house she has built, and follow the covenant way of wisdom and life. That, refracted through the medium of wisdom literature, is the point of the claims of God's names revealed to man in the Creator's covenant with Adam.

Chapter Two

HOLY THEOCRATIC KINGDOM

In the second principal part of the international treaties of the Mosaic age, the historical prologue, the covenant overlord narrated the history of his previous relationship with the vassal leading up to the present treaty negotiations. One common feature of this survey was an account of the benefits that had accrued to the vassal. There might even be mention of authority over a specified territory that was being conveyed to the vassal by this very treaty. The recollection of these benefits should dispose the vassal to a ready acceptance of the new treaty confirming and perpetuating the advantageous relationship existing under the old treaty. If the preamble was designed to inspire fear as a motive for the vassal's allegiance, the historical prologue was calculated to inculcate a sense of obligation if not gratitude, or at least to enlist the vassal's enlightened self-interest in view of the suzerain's alleged favors.

On the analogy of the historical prologue of the treaties our purpose in this chapter is to show how man's covenantal devotion was constrained by the claims of the Creator's goodness. Creating mankind in the divine image, God honored them with the gift of kingship and bestowed on them the blessings of his holy theocratic kingdom, a sanctuary-paradise.

I. ROYAL INVESTMENT AS IMAGE-SON

God's gift of kingship to man was inherent in the fact of man's creation as the image of God and may therefore be dealt with through the study of the latter. In this way, too, additional aspects of God's creational goodness to man will emerge since the *imago Dei* is broader than kingship, comprehending such further benefits as sonship. (The treatment of the *imago Dei* theme here is a shortened recasting of what may be found more fully elaborated in my *Images of the Spirit*, especially chapter 1.)

A. Spirit-Paradigm of the Image

In the passages in Genesis 1 and 2 describing the creation of man there are indications that the Glory-Spirit of Genesis 1:2 is the particular divine original in view when man is said to be made in the image of God. The very form of the creative fiat of Genesis 1:26 calling for the making of man in God's image tells us that we have to do here with the Glory-theophany, and thus with the heavenly assembly or council. For the Creator speaks in the deliberative plural idiomatic of the council: "Let us make man in our image, after our likeness." And in Genesis 2:7 it is by the quickening breath of the Spirit that man is said to have been made a living soul. This vitalizing function characteristic of the Spirit is attested elsewhere in Scriptures, at times in passages that allude to Genesis 2:7 (see especially John 20:22).

In the whole process of creation the Glory-Spirit was present not only as a powerful Architect-Builder but as a paradigmatic Archetype. As the divine heavenly temple, the Glory-epiphany (invisible or visible theophanic cloud) was the Alpha-model for the creation of other temples. The visible cosmos of heaven and earth was one such royal habitation of God. Man was another. Man was a replica of the Glory-Spirit in that, for one thing, he was made to be the temple of the Creator-Spirit.

In order to see something more of the multifaceted truth of man's image-likeness to the Glory-Spirit, we shall now review further the nature of that divine Paradigm, noting some of the glory-features of the Spirit that enter into the glory-image bestowed on man. Central and quintessential was the glory of lordship, embodied in the Lord of Glory enthroned as King of kings in the midst of the angelic hosts of the divine council. This royal office of the Creator had ethical and physical (or visual) dimensions of glory. There was the glory of holiness, righteousness, justice, goodness and truth that characterized the rule exercised in the heavenly court. And there was the glory of epiphanic light that manifested this majestic Presence of the Judge of all the earth. These official, ethical, and visual facets of the Glory-Spirit-Paradigm were to find their creaturely counterparts in man, made in the image of his royal Creator.

B. The Glory of the *Imago Dei*

Because the Glory-Spirit is the particular divine model in view for the *imago Dei*, the latter consists, on the level of creaturely analogue, of those glory-features that are paramount in the archetypal Spirit. Man is made with the glory of an official dominion, a dominion that is holy, righteous and true in its ethical character, a dominion that has promise ultimately of a perfected manifestation in the luminosity of human glorification. This conclusion as to the meaning of the *imago Dei* drawn from the fact that the Glory-Spirit stands as the specific divine Archetype behind the image ectype is borne out by those biblical passages that refer to man as image of God.

Coupled with the image-of-God concept in both the fiat and fulfillment sections of the record of the creation of man in Genesis 1:26-28 is the idea of man's dominion over the world, the dominion that images the dominion of the God-King enthroned in the divine council of the Glory temple. Commenting on this Genesis 1 passage, Psalm 8 expresses the *imago Dei* idea as a likeness of man to the members of that divine council – "Thou hast made him a little lower than the angels" (v. 5a[6]) – and then expounds this status as a royal crowning with glory and a dominion over all the earth (vv. 5b-8[6-9]).

The next mention of man's image-likeness to God comes in Genesis 3:22, where it is defined in terms of a knowing of good and evil. Since the latter refers to the exercise of judicial discernment (elsewhere noted as a God-like characteristic – see 1 Kgs 3:9, 28), this passage is a further index of the prominent place of the official-judicial aspect of glory in the biblical concept of the image of God.

In both the other passages in the book of Genesis where man is described as the image of God, the concept has royal-judicial associations. This is less obvious in the first of these, Genesis 5:1f., a passage we shall return to when dealing with the relation of the image and sonship concepts. But the second, Genesis 9:6, clearly identifies image-bearing and judicial authority by citing man's nature as the image of God as the explanation for his being authorized to inflict capital punishment upon murderers.

For our present purposes the evidence of the book of Genesis will suffice to illustrate the point, but a survey of all the Scriptural data would disclose that consistently the image of God is identified in terms of a glory like that of the Glory-Spirit. While the judicial glory continues to be conspicuous wherever the Bible touches upon the history of man's re-creation in the image of God in Christ Jesus, the ethical and visual glory elements in the image idea also become prominent.

By virtue of his creation in the image of God, man under the original covenant had the status of ruler of the earth under God, a glory that reflected the dominion exercised in the heavenly court by God and the angelic hosts. As image of God, man also possessed the ethical glory of a state of simple righteousness, with the prospect of moving on to the greater glory of confirmed righteousness. And a further promise of man's image status was that of transformation into the likeness of the epiphanic light. Man was given the hope of an eschatological glorification that would change him into a transfigured glory-image of the radiant Glory-Spirit.

C. Image of God and Son of God

Man's identity as a child of the Creator is suggested by the special intimacy of the mode of God's creating him. Setting the Bible's description of the origin of man apart from its account of the origin of the subhuman creatures of land and sea and sky are the special consultation involved in the former (Gen 1:26) and the immediacy of God's personal touch and breath in bringing forth Adam and Eve (Gen 2:7, 21f.). Though with a careful restraint, biblical revelation thus intimates that this creating of man is a kind of divine authoring analogous to human procreation. What is thus simply suggested of father-son imagery in the record of creational origins becomes virtually explicit in the record of the birth of Seth in Genesis 5:1-3. In this passage a statement of Adam's creation in the likeness of God is directly juxtaposed to a statement that Adam begat a son in his own likeness and image. Clearly we are being advised that there is a similarity between these two processes, both of which result in products like their authors. Adam's fathering of a son provides a proper analogy to God's creating of man and the relationship of Seth to Adam is analogous to man's relationship to his Maker. Such is the understanding of the Genesis 5 genealogy reflected in the Lucan use of it when, tracing back the lineage of Jesus, the evangelist concludes: "...Seth, which was (the son) of Adam, which was (the son) of God" (Luke 3:38). The Lucan birth narrative throws an interesting light on the overarching creative presence of the Glory-Spirit in Genesis 1. Luke records Gabriel's words to Mary in which the origin of the second Adam is attributed to the overshadowing presence and power of the Glory-Spirit (as was the case with the first Adam) and the explanation for calling the holy one thus produced the Son of God is found in this special creative involvement of the Glory-Spirit (Luke 1:35). Here then is another indication of the father-like nature of God's act of creating man in the beginning.

Since the Spirit's act of creating man is thus presented as the fathering of a son and that man-son is identified as the image-likeness of God, it is evident that image of God and son of God are mutually explanatory concepts. Clearly man's likeness to the Creator-Spirit is to be understood as the likeness which a son bears to his father. And that understanding of the image concept, according to which the fundamental idea is one of representational similarity, not representative agency, is further and unmistakably corroborated by Genesis 5:1-3 as it brings together God's creation of Adam and Adam's begetting of Seth, expressing the relation of the human father and son in terms of the image-likeness that defines man's relation to the Creator. To be the image of God is to be the son of God.

II. KINGDOM ENDOWMENT

Human kingdoms provide useful analogies for describing the kingdom of God in Eden, but none of these by itself is altogether adequate. Indeed, we find that a certain amount of adaptation is involved whenever the Bible depicts the kingdom of God at any stage of its history in terms of political forms taken over from the nations of the world, for these models do not provide a perfect fit for the religious realities entailed in God's kingdom relationship to his people.

We have discussed the suzerain-like identity of the Lord of the covenant-kingdom in the preceding chapter and, in so doing, have employed the analogy of those great kings of the nations in biblical times who extended their dominion over neighboring vassal kings through treaty-diplomacy. If, instead of this more complex empire model, we were to use a simple kingdom model (at least if we used only the latter), we might seem to be suggesting that God was king over the human community and nothing beyond that. But, of course, man and the visible world of man's experience were not the totality of the realm ruled by God. In the beginning God created the invisible heavens and their hosts as well as the earth with mankind and the various other kinds of earthlings. And the original and proper seat of the divine sovereignty was in this invisible heavenly sphere. So even without speculating about the possibility of yet other creations, what is revealed to us about the creation to which we belong indicates the appropriateness, in describing God's kingdom, of our employing at times at least the model of the great king who dwells in his own proper domain but unites other nations in covenant under his suzerainty. This model of the great king and his vassal kingdoms can also accommodate, as the simple idea of a king and his subjects could not, the fact that man is given the status of a vassal king over the earth.

Yet, there are features of God's covenant-kingdom, in part present from the beginning and in part contemplated as an eschatological goal, for which the model of a simple kingdom with the closer relations that obtain between the king and his subjects in their shared homeland provides a better analogy than the suzerain-vassal form of political structure. For instance, in this chapter we shall be taking account of the way in which God made his dwelling with man right there in Eden. Moreover, the hope was held out to man to become participant in that realm of the heavenly council which was the primal domain of the Lord God within his creation. With reference to such features the simple kingdom model would be more suitable even for the original preredemptive situation. And the simple king-subjects analogy appears still more appropriate when we come to the kingdom of God in redemptive history, where divine and human kingship meet in the person of the Lord Christ, the king of righteousness exalted in the midst of his brethren. In fact, so intimate is the religious relationship at all times that any political analogy must seem inadequate by itself to describe it and we must turn to the sphere of the family for supplementation of the picture.

A. The Kingdom as Sanctuary

1. Site of God's Throne-Presence

Stationed in Eden was the localized, visible Presence of the Creator-King. After introducing the Glory-Spirit at the critical point in creational beginnings marked by Genesis 1:2, the biblical record affords several indications of the continuing presence of this theophanic Glory and in particular of its settling in the garden area where man was located. Thus, as noted above, there is an allusion to the members of the divine council found within the Glory-cloud when God is about to create man in the divine image (Gen 1:26), and to the Spirit in the narrative of the quickening of the man-creature (Gen 2:7). [On this, see *Images of the Spirit*, chapter 1.] And in the account of man's Fall, the garden location of the Glory is evidenced by the fact that God is present there in this theophanic form, called "the Spirit of the (judgment) day," to pronounce judgment on the violation of his covenant (Gen 3:8). [On this, see *Images of the Spirit*, chapter 4.] In this same connection, there is another reference to the heavenly hosts who belong to the Glory-cloud phenomenon in the mention of the cherubim who figure in the judgment scene as guardians of God's holy presence (Gen 3:24). Similarly, the prophet Ezekiel pictured the cherub-attended Glory as present there "on the holy mountain of God" (Ezek 28:13ff.). Agreeably, when the prophets depict the redemptive restoration of the pristine kingdom order, they portray along with the river and tree of life the return of the Glory-cloud, the spring-source of the life-giving river and the crowning beauty of the glorious Edenic scene (cf., e.g., Isa 4:2-6; 40:5; 59:19; 66:18f.; Ezek 43:2ff; Hab 2:14; Rev 21 and 22). [See also *Images of the Spirit*, chapter 2.] By positioning his Glory upon the holy mount of Eden's garden, God placed there the claim of his Name. Later, when God, in the form of the Shekinah, enters the sanctuary in the midst of Israel, that is described as a putting of his name there (Deut 12:5,21; 14:24) or a causing his Name to dwell there (Deut 12:11; 14:23; 16:2,6,11; 26:2). The Glory-Spirit was, therefore, a divine name-banner hovering on high over the domain of Eden, which, being thus identified, claimed, and consecrated by God's Name, was holy land.

Man's homesite was hallowed ground. The garden of Eden was not only the original land flowing with milk and honey, it was the original holy land. Paradise was a sanctuary, a temple-garden. Agreeably, Ezekiel calls it "the garden of God" (28:13;31:8f.) and Isaiah, "the garden of the Lord" (51:3).

A clear indication that the garden had been set apart as a holy place, a cultic site of God's special Presence, is found in the measures taken to guard its sanctity after man's Fall. To prevent access to the tree of life, the Lord stationed at the east of the garden the cherubim, those holy beings who attend the divine Presence (Gen 3:24). Also marking the garden of Eden as a sacred place was the divinely appointed symbol of the covenant religion, the tree of life that was in the midst of the garden, intended to be a sign and seal of man's perfected life with and in his holy God. Consonant with the fact that the garden was the place of divine theophany, it was the site of special oracular revelation. It was the holy place where man heard the voice of God speaking to him, telling him what he must know of God's covenant beyond the covenantal revelation available through creation, the revelation which he found within him and in the world outside, instructing him so that he would know how to glorify and enjoy his Creator forever (cf. Gen 1:28-30; 2:16ff.; 3:8). Another indication of the sanctuary character of the garden is the re-emergence in redemptive history of paradise motifs in decorative architectural detailing of the sanctuary of God in Israel (1 Kgs

6:18,29,32,35; 7:18ff; cf. Ezek 41:18ff.) and in prophetic portrayal of the eternal royal dwelling-place of the Lord (Ezek 47; Rev 21 and 22).

At the center of this creation kingdom, on the mountain of Eden (archetype of Zion, its redemptive restoration), God was revealed in his royal Glory. This holy mountain of God (as Ezekiel called it) was the vertical cosmic axis of the kingdom, extending from earth to heaven. In it the kingdom had a central cultic focus that proclaimed its nature as a holy realm, a sanctuary-kingdom.

Chosen as the focal throne-site of the Glory-Spirit, the garden of Eden was a microcosmic, earthly version of the cosmic temple and the site of a visible, local projection of the heavenly temple. At the first, then, man's native dwelling-place coincided with God's earthly dwelling. This focal sanctuary in Eden was designed to be a medium whereby man might experience the joy of the presence of God in a way and on a scale most suited to his nature and condition as an earthly creature during the first stage of his historical journey, walking with God.

2. Theocracy

The peculiar kind of kingdom established in Eden at the beginning (and later redemptively renewed) differs radically from other kinds of world kingdoms that arose after the Fall. This distinctive form of kingdom we call theocracy. Whatever analogies exist between the theocracy and the other kingdoms, however many falsely proclaimed theocracies there may be, there is only one genuine theocratic kingdom under the special rule of the living God. And in the beginning it was the only kingdom on earth.

Theocracy implies an external realm. It does not refer to a spiritual reign of God in the hearts of his people by itself, but includes the geopolitical dimension. On the other hand, theocracy involves something more than a general providential rule of God over men and nations. It denotes a particular kingdom realm that God claims in a special way as his own.

This special claim is registered by God's setting up his royal residence in the midst of the theocratic land and declaring this site or structure his palace-sanctuary by the special revelation of his Presence, there enthroned. As we have already observed, the Lord assumed the seat of his sovereignty on the mountain of God in Eden, manifesting himself there in his Glory-Name, and by so doing he laid the claim of his name upon the creation kingdom.

By making the Edenic kingdom his dwelling-place God sanctified it to himself; he imparted to it that holiness which is peculiar to theocracy.

In a theocracy the people of the realm as well as the land itself are specially consecrated to God. This special religious relationship is defined through covenants, divinely determined and instituted, in which God identifies with this kingdom-people, bestowing on them his name to be borne and confessed by them. Because the name of God is identified with the theocratic people and is at stake in their history, the covenants that govern this relationship contain guarantees of dominion and power and glory for the loyal theocratic community.

God's name was borne by the kingdom-people in Eden. To be created in God's image was to be God's covenant children, and to have God as Father-Lord was to bear his name as surname. (Isa 44:5. cf. *Images of the Spirit*, chapter 2). By the bestowal of God's name they were acknowledged as belonging to him, set apart as his holy theocratic family. Their theocratic identification with God's name appears in the covenant service they performed. In their exercise of dominion over the earth they came as vicegerents in the name of the Great King. And in their priestly office they made doxological confession of God's name in worship and witness.

As seen in the original form of the kingdom of God in Eden, a theocracy is a cultic kingdom through and through. God is King of the entire realm; all of it has the character of a holy house of God. A theocratic kingdom is a holy nation, a kingdom of priests. Membership in the kingdom involves participation in the sanctuary of God, for the kingdom is God's sanctuary. To break covenant by unfaithfullness to the God of the sanctuary is to be cut off from the kingdom, for God is the King of the kingdom. It is this sanctuary identity of the theocratic kingdom that sets it apart in holy uniqueness from all the other kingdoms found in the postlapsarian world.

In the world as first created there was no community except the holy covenant community and all the world was consigned to its dominion under God. (Our purview here is confined to the visible world of man. If we were considering theocracy as inclusive of the heavenly hosts, the question would arise as to how to relate the sphere of Satan and his demonic company to our concept of cosmic theocracy, a question which, at the consummation of human history, assumes the form of how we are conceptually to relate the realm of hell to the new heavens and earth.)

Since the original earthly theocracy was a universal kingdom there was of course no place outside of it where a nontheocratic kingdom might emerge. Nor could there have arisen within this worldwide theocratic realm the institution of the state as that was appointed in the fallen world within the framework of common grace. For since such a state would not be God's sanctuary and its requirements for citizenship would not be identical with those for priesthood in the cult of the Lord, its existence would have been a contradiction within the theocratic order, violating the holiness of the covenant-kingdom instituted in Eden.

This is not to say that a structured form of government at the human level was incompatible with God's supreme authority in the theocracy. However, such a governmental structure would have to be confessionally subservient to the lordship of the Great King enthroned in the theocratic sanctuary and subordinately oriented to the theocratic cultus. It would have to be a priestly servant of the God-King, charged with the function of guardianship of the sanctity of the kingdom. (For the specific, i.e., family, form of human government, see the next chapter.)

In the kingdom in Eden there was an institutional coalescence of the cultic and the political in the identity of the head of the covenant-kingdom as God-King. This is entailed in the theocratic principle. At the level of the God-King the political and the cultic are not distinguishable. His palace is holy; his temple is royal. His temple and palace are one. At the human level of the theocracy the cultic and the political are distinquishable, but only as two theocratic functions. There is the directly cultic priestly function and there is the royal function of culture, which is cult-oriented. However, these distinguishable human functions, no matter how formally organized, would not become separated into discrete institutions (like the church and state) but would remain institutionally integrated as two functional components of the one holy institution of the theocracy. Accordingly, not only could the state as we know it not exist in the original theocratic world order, but neither could a church institution arise of the kind found in the course of redemptive history in this world. Theocracy is not a combination of church and state institutions. It is a simple unique institution, a structure *sui generis*. It is the kingdom realm whose great king is the Lord, where all activity is performed in the name of the God-King enthroned, confessed, and worshipped in the cultic epicenter, whence theocratic holiness radiates outward, permeating all, so that the whole realm, land and people, is a sanctuary of the Creator-Lord.

B. The Kingdom as Divine Protectorate

1. Consecration-Sacrifice-Death in Paradise

Certain obligations might be assumed by the suzerain in the relationship governed by an ancient treaty even though the emphasis in such a relationship fell heavily on the obligations imposed on the vassal. The treaty document itself might contain guarantees of the continuance of the vassal's dynasty or of his possession of certain cities. Such guarantees might take the form of a promise to extend into the future benefits bestowed in the past. Also, if only to protect his own interests, the suzerain would undertake to assist his vassal against enemy attack. The vassal kingdom was accordingly a protectorate under the guardianship of the treaty overlord.

Such was the nature of the kingdom established by the Creator at the beginning; the covenant servant in Eden found himself in a divine protectorate under God's guardian care. Everything he encountered in this realm spoke to him of his Lord's sovereign goodness. Manifested in God's creative acts, that goodness continued to be displayed in perfect constancy in his providential government of his creatures. The Lord of the covenant who created man's world order also preserved it.

Man's homeland in Eden is proverbial in the Bible as the paradise ideal, well-watered and fertile (cf. Gen 13:10; Isa 51:3; Ezek 36:35; Joel 2:3). There grew all manner of trees, the glory of the vegetation kingdom; there roamed all manner of representatives of the animal kingdom. Accessible nearby too were the resources and treasures of the mineral world (Gen 2:11f.). All these kingdom-spheres of creation were richly stocked with provisions to satisfy man's physical needs and delight his aesthetic sensitivities. Nor had the Creator left man socially unfulfilled; he had blessed the man with the woman, the woman with the man. He made mankind male and female, king and queen over the garden of Eden.

The original covenant order was thus everywhere one of beatitude, for there in the garden the Creator raised his hands over man in protective, prospering benediction. When fully disclosed, the terms of the covenant did include the threat that blessing might turn to curse. But if and when that curse befell the world, the blame would belong entirely to man, the vassal, and not at all to the Suzerain. The original condition of man traceable to creative fiat alone could reflect only the pure goodness of the

Creator. The covenantal kingdom-protectorate was at the first a realm of unmixed blessing.

Traditional ideas of the nature of man's original Edenic state have tended on the one hand to go beyond the biblical representations in the idealizing of the natural element and on the other hand to underestimate the biblical evidence for the supernatural element in the composition of the kingdom of God in Eden. Involved here is the question of the meaning of the biblical concepts of blessing and curse. We may get at this by asking whether it necessarily follows from the pure blessedness of man's original state that the earth at that time was without anything violent or dangerous, that the ground was without thorns and thistles, that there was no death in the world.

This question may be approached by examining the pattern of consecration we have previously noticed in the description of creation in Genesis 1:1-2:3. Consecration is one of the chief structural principles of the covenantal order of life. At its highest level, consecration has been identified as the essence of religion, but at an elementary level it may be defined as simply the subordination of the interests of one person or thing to those of another. Such subordination of interests assumes various forms and among the specific forms of subordination-consecration met with in the phenomena described in the creation record sacrifice and death are especially important. In the interrelationship of the lower orders of creation to one another there were forms of subordination that did not amount to sacrifice. For example, the realms of light and darkness, the order of day and night, are pictured in Genesis 1 as subordinate to the dominion of the sun and moon, but this was simply a matter of regulation, a royal defining of boundaries. When we move along, however, to the use made of the soil by the plants or to the way the air is utilized by the birds and beasts or the waters by the fish of the seas, something more is involved. There is here a royal exacting of tribute, an assimilation of lower elements into higher orders and in this process these elements undergo conversion and loss. We may regard this as an elementary form of sacrifice. When something belonging to the organic, living level of creation is sacrificially consecrated to the interests of a higher creature, as when plants are assigned as food for animals and men (Gen 1:29,30), death is an appropriate term for this form of sacrifice (cf. John 12:24; 1 Cor 15:36). In this elementary sense at least, death was thus part of the pattern of consecration that informed the world-structure from its beginning.

In these various examples of consecration that were present in creation the Creator provided instructive nature-parables of the kingdom. They illustrated the consecration principle which was a significant element in the meaning of both the obligations and the sanctions of the covenant. For example, in these nature-parables man saw exemplified the kind of subordination and devotion that was required of him as the covenant-vassal by his Lord and he saw something of the meaning of the death with which he was threatened in the curse sanction of the covenant.

2. Death, Blessing, and Curse

A question that calls for consideration in this connection is whether the idea of man, before the Fall, sacrificing animal life for his own higher interests is compatible with the Bible's representations concerning the original state of blessedness. Since all creatures were subordinated to man's dominion and, as we have seen, sacrifice and death enter the original order as particular expressions of the consecration principle, there would appear to be no obvious principial objection to man's having had the right to kill animals to provide himself with animal flesh for food or animal skins for clothing or for other purposes. Moreover, it is generally conceded, even by some who resist the idea of man's being authorized from the beginning to take animal life, that study of natural history shows that all manner of animals had lived and perished even before man appeared on earth. Indeed, Psalm 104:21 seems to indicate clearly that the Creator had from the outset granted to predatory beasts to feed on other animals. And if that is so, it would have been anomalous if animal flesh had not similarly been consecrated to the higher interests of man, who was set in authority over all the works of God's hands. This conclusion is supported by the apostle Paul's comments in 1 Timothy 4:3-5, which reflect the terminology of Genesis 1:31, itself immediately connected to God's statement concerning his provision of food for his creatures (vv. 29,30). Paul asserts that the foods some were proscribing (and probably meat is chiefly in view) were good and had in fact been created by God to be received with thanksgiving (cf. 2 Pet 2:12).

The counterarguments often drawn from statements concerning man's diet in Genesis 1:29 and 9:3 are not cogent. In Genesis 1:29 the explicit assignment of the plant world to man for food is not restrictive, as though that were the only kind of food permitted to him. The theme of this passage is man's kingship over the animal and vegetable realms. Since animals were designed to serve man in a great variety of ways – not only as food but as helpers in agriculture, as means of transportation, as beasts of burden, etc. – the general fact of man's dominion over them is all that is stated. When it comes to the vegetable kingdom, however, its usefullness as food for man, whether by direct consumption or indirectly through the fattening of animals, is clearly the distinctive contribution it makes to man and hence man's dominion over vegetation is described in those specific terms. Moreover, there is a special literary purpose in the reference to the permission for the use of plants for food in Genesis 1:29, namely to prepare for the exceptional stipulation in Genesis 2:16,17 prohibiting the use of the fruit of the tree of knowledge. These considerations show how unwarranted is the assumption that the silence of this passage concerning man's use of animal flesh as food must be intended as a prohibition of such.

We will deal only briefly here with Genesis 9:3. For a more detailed treatment see the discussion below of the postdiluvian common grace covenant. If Genesis 9:3 were interpreted as simply permitting the eating of meat as well as vegetables, it would, in any case, not be the first such authorization even in the postlapsarian period, judging from Genesis 4:4 (cf. 3:21). However, what Genesis 9:3 actually authorized was the eating of all kinds of meats, thus removing the prohibition against the eating of unclean animals that had been instituted for Noah's family within the special symbolic situation in the ark-kingdom. Instead of posing a problem for our thesis, Genesis 9:3 is another argument for it. For by its allusion to an earlier special situation where the eating of meat had been temporarily restricted to the flesh of clean animals, this passage discloses the fact that the eating of meat had been permitted all along and was not a privilege first granted after the Deluge.

Against our thesis, appeal has also been made to the idyllic prophetic descriptions of an eschaton in which carnivores are turned herbivorous; but this objection too is not compelling. For one thing, it must be remembered that the future world is not a simple return to conditions at the beginning. It is necessary to see if a given feature of the prophesied future may be a new feature introduced in the act of consummating the kingdom order. Moreover, such prophecies can hardly be pressed in the literal sense since we find that in other prophetic portrayals of the world to come, at least at the literal level, the redeemed are depicted as feasting, with no suggestion of vegetarian scruples. More significantly, something of the nature of the eschatological condition is evidenced in the resurrection manifestations of

Christ; and in particular the episode of the risen Lord's eating of the fish suggests that the sacrifice of such a living creature to the use of higher beings ought not to be considered as an imperfection in the order of things.

How then can we say that man's original state was one of unmixed blessing if the likes of death were present in his world? The validity of that assertion resides in the fact that blessing for man does not consist in the absence of things like death, but rather in man's dominion over them, or putting it the other way, in their subordination to man and in their serving man's interests. Similarly, the curse on man consists in the reverse of this relationship; not in the mere presence of things like death but in man's falling victim to them. Blessing and its opposite, curse, as they relate to man are simply the consecration principle working in two different directions. When the subhuman realm is consecrated to man, a state of beatitude exists; when man is made subservient to or victim of the subhuman, a state of curse exists.

Thus, the presence of subhuman death in the natural order at the beginning was not a glaring exception to the blessedness of man's first estate, because death was then working for the maintenance and renewal of man's life. Man standing in his righteousness as king upon the earth, sustaining his life through the death of plants and animals, their life in turn nourished by the sacrifice of the soil – that is the state of beatitude. Man, the sinner, felled and laid low in the earth, dust unto dust, reduced to a part of the soil to nourish vegetation growing above him – that is the state of cursedness. It is only when death thus victimizes man himself as the wages of his sin that it assumes the character of the great last enemy to be destroyed by Christ. In Romans 8:19ff. (reflecting Isa 24:4ff.) the personified earth mournfully groans over the postlapsarian role it must play as Sheol. It especially laments that it must serve as the cover, concealing the blood of the martyr-saints.

The Bible does not require us, therefore, to think of the character and working of man's natural environment before the Fall as radically different than is presently the case. To be sure, the garden God prepared as man's immediate dwelling was a place eminently expressive of divine goodness and favor. Nevertheless, the elements that could be turned against man were already there in nature. Man's state of blessedness is thus seen to be primarily a matter of God's providential authority over creation, controlling and directing every circumstance so that everything works together for man's good and nothing transpires for his hurt or the frustration of his efforts. God gives his angels charge over the one who stands in his favor lest he should dash his foot against a stone (Ps 91:12). Blessing consists not in the absence of the potentially harmful stone, but in the presence of God's providential care over the foot. Adam's world before the Fall was not a world without stones, thorns, dark watery depths, or death. But it was a world where the angels of God were given a charge over man to protect his every step and to prosper all the labor of his hand.

It appears then that the secret of human beatitude is in the spiritual dimension of man's relationship to his covenant Lord. To stand in God's favor is the beginning of blessing and that is why the fear of the Lord is the beginning of wisdom.

3. Divine Shield

Divine protection was present in Eden in the supernatural form of the Glory-cloud, a sheltering canopy over the mountain of God. By reason of this theophanic Presence, Eden was a sanctuary in the sense of place of security and preservation as well as in the sense of holy place. Both the sanctifying and protective functions of the Glory are conspicuous in the Isaiah 4 picture of the garden of God in its eschatological restoration as the new Jerusalem. The overarching presence of the Glory-Spirit constitutes the place a holy assembly of the Lord, but that covering of glory is also a shade from the heat and a sheltering refuge from the storm (Isa 4:5,6; cf. Ps 105:39). The divine Presence imparts blessedness as well as holiness. The theophanic Glory that made Eden a temple also made it a paradise where the occupants of the garden were protected by the divine sheltering canopy from anything that could mar their blessedness.

The Glory-cloud as described in Isaiah 4 is a covering (*sukkah*). Psalm 105:39 similarly says that at the exodus God spread that Glory-cloud for a covering (*masak*). Note also the use of the verb *sakak* in Psalm 140:7, which says that God covers the psalmist's head in battle, and in Psalm 91:4, which says with reference to the Glory-cloud with its winged cherubim, "He will cover you with his feathers and under his wings you will find refuge." The description of God in the Psalm 91 context is replete with terms and images also found in Isaiah's Glory-cloud description: the secret hiding place, the shade (v. 1), the refuge (vv. 2,9). From the analogy that emerges between God's protective overshadowing of Eden and of Israel at the exodus we may determine more fully the nature of man's original beatitude. Psalm 91:11 was cited previously for its description of the sovereign providential care which secured the blessedness of man in Eden. The providential working was through angelic agency (Ps 91:11), and in the Psalm 91 context that would be a further reference to the winged protection of the Glory-cloud. Viewing the sovereign providence operative in Eden in the light of this divine guidance and provisioning of Israel in the wilderness, we may better understand the combination of natural and supernatural agencies at work in the Edenic protectorate. The divine communication of knowledge to man in his original estate was by both natural and special revelation, and there was a similar blend of natural and supernatural providential working in God's general care of man.

Another image of God's protective presence arising from the nature of the cloud-theophany is that of the shield (see Deut 33:29; Pss 3:3, with its parallels between "my shield" and "my glory"; 91:4; 144:2, cf. vv. 5 ff.). Psalm 84:11 declares Yahweh God to be "a sun and shield" (possibly a reflection of the dual function of the Glory-cloud as both light and shade). On the other hand, both "sun" and *magen* may be titles identifying God as covenant suzerain. "Sun" is found as a title for Egyptian and Hittite suzerains and *magen* is perhaps here and in some other biblical texts to be equated with the (disputed) Punic *magon*, "suzerain" (and related to a root *mgn*, "bestow"). If the references to God as *magen* are to be understood in the traditional way, "shield", it might then be significant that the site in Eden protected by the theophanic shield is called a *gan*, "garden, enclosure," from the same root as *magen*, "shield" namely, *gnn*, "cover, surround."

Isaiah's interpretation of the Glory-cloud as a canopy and pavilion (*sukkah*) recalls David's graphic depiction of the storm theophany in Psalm 18. Comparing the dangers that threatened him to the chaotic watery depths, David describes the divine intervention by means of the cherub-vehicle as a veritable reenactment of the divine mastering of the waters when the foundations of the earth were established at creation (cf. Ps 46). And he too designates the Glory-cloud as God's secret place and *sukkah*, "pavilion" (v. 11; cf. also Job 36:29). As seen in the Isaiah 4 vision of Eden renewed, the cloud-pavilion, God's heavenly tabernacle, forms a canopied dwelling-place for God's people. The original Eden too was a sanctuary for God dwelt there, a sanctuary which the gracious Creator opened to man as his dwelling. Man's true home was the house of the Lord. More than that, since it was God who in his theophanic cloud-pavilion formed the tabernacle in Eden, it was God himself who was man's temple-home.

There, under the shadow of the Almighty's wings, man would find the language of Psalm 91 manifestly applicable and confess that Yahweh was his refuge, the Most High was his habitation (Ps 91:9, cf. 2).

Conclusion

In the original relationship between the Lord of creation and Adam, the beneficence of the Creator-Lord was evidenced in the provision that had been made on every hand for man's well-being. The whole world, man's total situation, natural and supernatural revelation complementing each other in a twofold witness, pressed on man the claims of the goodness and wisdom of the Lord of the cosmic realm and called on him for a response of grateful covenantal devotion and service.

In the Decalogue-treaty of the Lord's covenant with Israel at Sinai, after the preamble, "I am Yahweh your God," came the brief historical prologue, "who brought you out of the land of Egypt, out of the house of bondage" (Exod 20:2). To the man and the woman with whom God made the covenant in Eden he could say, "I am Yahweh, Lord of creation's Sabbath, enthroned in heavenly glory above the cherubim hosts, who brought you out of the mud-clay of the ground and breathed into you life." Israel's covenantal election and calling is represented in the Bible as a "creation", so radical is the renewal God accomplishes in the process of man's redemption. But it was by an act of literal creation that God brought Adam and Eve into covenant relationship to himself. The original covenantal administration of the kingdom was in this respect unique. God not only formulated a covenant order by the word of his authority, but he dictated that order into existence by the word of his power. As previously observed, the divine fiats were covenant fiats as well as creation fiats, hence, the Lord of the covenant did not simply address the covenant servant, calling him to the fulfillment of his covenant service, but he creatively called man into being in the status of covenant servant.

Nothing could more plainly show that this covenant was a sovereign administration of God's lordship. The vassal had had nothing to say about the terms of the covenant; he did not previously exist. Whatever he was or had, everything was a gift of creation. And how lavishly the Creator's goodness had been expressed. For he had made man in his own Glory-image, raising him from the dust of the earth to crown him with glory and honor, giving him royal status among the angels of heaven (Ps 8:5-8). Stated from the side of the covenant lord, the claim of this Lord upon his vassal's covenantal allegiance was one of absolute right, the claim of the love of a Creator from whom all blessings flowed, who had brought man out of nothing into the paradise-sanctuary of God.

The original homeland of man might well have been named Immanuel. God was with man, man's dwelling-place was God's dwelling-place. That was the greatest glory of paradise and the supreme and ultimate blessedness of human life. The covenant servant had been created for friendship and fellowship with his Lord. He was qualified for this holy communion by the nature with which God's creating hand endowed him. And he found to his delight that his transcendent Maker was not a god far off, but the immanent Immanuel. Man did not have to make a long pilgrimage to come to God's dwelling. There was no great wilderness to pass through, no perilous ascent on high or journey down into the depths was necessary to find God. For man was by creation's arrangement a house-guest at home in the house of God.

Still other features of the covenant that will be surveyed in subsequent chapters on covenant law and covenant sanctions made distinctive contributions to man's beatitude, enhancing the claims of the Creator-Lord on his earthly servants' love and devotion. The psalmist's attitude toward the statutes of his Lord whereby he saw them not as a burden but as a delight was first experienced by man in the garden. As Adam received God's directives for living so as to continue in the favor and blessing of his Maker, his heart already sang, "O how love I thy law." And the covenant sanctions proferred to man an increase in blessing far beyond all he enjoyed at the first as the original gifts of creation. The Creator had so made man that he could undergo a consummating transformation. Along with present honors and joys man was thus given the hope of advancing to new dimensions in his experience of God's presence and of his own dominion over creation.

At the contemplation of the claims of the Creator's goodness, gift upon gift, the covenant servant must wonder: "What shall I render unto the Lord for all his benefits toward me?" (Ps 116:12) – and resolve in grateful praise: "Bless the Lord, O my soul, and forget not all his benefits" (Ps 103:2). Truly, all things were of and through the Lord God and from that followed the claim that he was also the One to whom are all things.

As we consider what we have seen of God's relation to man through creation and providence, we see the shape of another social model emerging besides that of lord and servant. God creatively produced man as a son in his own image, provided for him and protected him. In these elements we have the original of fatherhood. From God's fatherhood man might learn what his own father role should be and from his own fatherly love he would in turn derive new understanding and appreciation of the divine affection and care.

The Lord of the covenant, the Lord of the Edenic sanctuary in its double role of home-protectorate and temple, was thus man's Father and his God. So from the very beginning man was taught to pray trustingly: "Our Father which art in heaven," and to add worshipfully: "Hallowed be thy name." From the revelation of the covenant law and sanctions man would learn to continue his Lord's prayer: "thy kingdom come, thy will be done on earth as it is in heaven."

Chapter Three

LAW OF THE CREATION THEOCRACY

After the preamble and historical prologue, ancient suzerainty treaties continued with a section of stipulations defining the services to be rendered by the vassal to the overlord. Along with the specific obligations concerning tribute, military assistance and the like there might be a general statement of the essential lord-servant character of the relationship envisaged in the treaty, with its fundamental demand for the dutiful submission and loyalty of the subordinate party. Similarly, in our treatment of the law of the Creator's Covenant of Works with Adam we may distinguish between the basic demand, entailed in the nature of the covenant relationship between God and man, and the specific duties assigned to man, having to do particularly with the historical development of God's kingdom.

I. LAW OF THE IMAGE-SON OF GOD

Inherent in man's nature as the image-son of God were the primary ethico-religious principles of his life.

A. The Imitation of God

Likeness to God is signified by both image of God and son of God. Man's likeness to God is a demand to be like God; the indicative here has the force of an imperative. Formed in the image of God, man is informed by a sense of deity by which he knows what God is like, not merely that God is (Rom 1:19ff.). And knowledge of what one's Father-God is, is knowledge of what, in creaturely semblance, one must be himself. With the sense of deity comes conscience, the sense of deity in the imperative mode. The basic and general covenantal norm of the imitation of God was thus written on the tables of man's heart (Rom 1:32; 2:14f.). And naturally then we find that this ultimate standard continues as the constant canon of human conduct, being reiterated in a variety of ways in subsequent revelation, preredemptive and redemptive. See, for example, Leviticus 11:44f.; Matthew 5:44-48, noting especially the relation between the ideas of children of God and imitation of God in verse 45; and Ephesians 4:24,32; 5:1,2, noting again here that the call to imitate God is addressed to

Christians "as beloved children (of God)." The law of the imitation of God is the law of the image-bearing child of God. It is the comprehensive norm, the unifying principle for the complex of specific covenant stipulations.

Presently we shall observe the application of the imitation of God norm in the commissioning of man to perform various functions in the kingdom program. Here we simply observe in briefest, most general outline how the divine Examplar was man's standard in his several major areas of relationship: God loves himself supremely and glorifies himself; therefore, man must love God supremely and make it his primary objective to glorify God – here, the imitation of God and the love of God coincide. And the glorifying of God also coalesces with the imitation of God, for it is by reflecting the holy Glory-light of the divine Original that the human image glorifies God. God loves his covenant children; therefore, they must love one another. God reigns over the cosmos, creating it a holy temple of his Glory; therefore, his human image-bearer must exercise dominion (under God) over the world, sanctifying it for the presence of the Creator-Lord. God hates Satan and his evil company; therefore, man must hate the Devil – and since this is the converse of loving God, here again the imitation of God and the love of God strikingly coincide.

B. Service of Love

Both image of God and son of God bring out man's secondary or subordinate position in relation to God, even while both call attention to the dignity of man's likeness to God. Though the image is like the Spirit-Archetype, the image is not the original but secondary. Though the son is like the Creator-Father, the son is derived and therefore under the authority of his Author, obliged to render obedience to his divine parent. To be image-son is, in covenantal terms, to be the covenant servant. (In fact, in the language of ancient treaty diplomacy father-son terminology was used for the suzerain-vassal relationship.)

Both the image and son identifications of man tell us that man is a creature under his Creator-God. All the glory and honor of man's creation endowment as image-son was to be enjoyed by him not as an autonomous being but as a creature in the service of his Creator and to the greater glory of his God.

Thus, from the beginning the primary obligation of covenant life has been: "Thou shalt worship the Lord thy God and him only shalt thou serve" (Matt 4:10). The covenant servant-son must be what is called in Hebrew *tam*, "perfect," a term which, when used to express the obligation imposed by the covenant, denotes genuine, sincere religious devotion (cf., e.g., Gen 17:1; Job 1:1). The oath of covenant allegiance must come from the heart; the covenant servant must be truly loyal to his Lord. Fulfilling this primary commandment, man would regard his life as a stewardship and all his privileges as responsibilities, gifts from God to be used for God. He would recognize in the Spirit's gift of image-sonship a divine anointing to an historical mission as servant of the Lord. And he would remember that it is required of a steward first of all that he be found faithful.

"Thou shalt love the Lord thy God with all thy heart and with all thy soul and with all thy mind and with all thy strength" (Mark 12:30; Luke 10:27) – that is another formulation of the fundamental law of the original theocratic order, the first and great commandment. This love of God is the consecration principle come to consciousness as a religious devotion, a passion for the glory of God and the hallowing of his name. There is no incompatibility between this demand for love in the sense of a total and exclusive commitment in personal devotion and adoration to God, man's heavenly Father, and the obligation of obedience to the multiple prescriptions involved in the mission of developing the kingdom order and carrying forward the kingdom program of the covenant. It was indeed by obedience to the particular requirements of kingdom activity that man would express his love for his Lord. The meaning of the law of love in biblical covenants is illuminated by the usage of the term "love" in ancient treaties. In these texts it is faithful adherence to the directives of the overlord that is called love. When swearing allegiance to the suzerain the vassals at times declared: "Our lord we will love." And a vassal wishing to clear himself of suspicion of infidelity protests that he is the great king's servant and "friend" (literally, one who loves the suzerain). Love in the covenantal vocabulary was not a term for an affective attitude that was resistant to delineation in specific legal obligations. On the contrary, to love the suzerain meant precisely to serve him by obeying the particular demands stipulated in his treaty.

When Moses as mediator of Yahweh's covenant with Israel issued the demand: "Thou shalt love the Lord thy God with all thy heart" (Deut 6:5), he was echoing the ancient treaty stipulations, even in the qualifying expression "with all thy heart." That adverbial phrase appears in treaty texts describing how the vassal is to love the suzerain, particularly while engaged in battle in his behalf. That Moses meant by love what the political treaties meant by it is clear, for he at once equates this wholehearted love of God with the conscientious observance of all the words he was commanding Israel – the stipulations, the statutes, and the judgments (Deut 6:6; cf. vv. 1,2,17,20). Similarly, Jesus as mediator of the new covenant tells his disciples that the one who loves him is the one who has and keeps his commandments (John 14:21; cf. v. 14; 15:14; cf. 1 John 5:3). The same equation of love with obedience to specific prescriptions emerges when James points to Abraham's compliance with God's demand to sacrifice Isaac as the validation that he was in truth "the friend of God," literally, one who loved God, that is, a true covenant servant (Jas 2:21-23; cf. 2 Chr 20:7; Isa 41:8; CD III, 3-4).

Not a substitute for more precise precepts, neither is the biblical command to love God a summary of just one group of covenant obligations, as though covenant law might be divided into two types of duties, one of which would be man's duty to God and another (dealing, say, with man's relation to his fellow man) would not be part of his duty to God. All covenant stipulations are expressions of the will of God, the lord of the covenant. Whether they have to do with bringing tributary offerings to him or with living at peace with his other servants, or with waging war against his enemies, they all articulate the basic demand for that exclusive and total devotion the covenant servant owes to the Lord. The whole revelation of covenant law is an unfolding of our duty to God, our duty to love and serve God. And that law of the covenant is the law of man's image-sonship.

Viewed from the perspective of the imitation-of-God principle, the command to love God is one expression of that principle. Viewed from the perspective of the command to love God, the imitation of God is the way in which that commandment is to be fulfilled. There is a profound inner coherence between the covenant's paramount obligation of the love of God and its comprehensive norm of the imitation of God. For out of love's admiration and adoration of the Glory-beauty of God comes a constraining desire to reproduce the likeness of that glory. A parable of this is afforded in marriage love, a particularly full parable in the desire of the woman, the image-glory of the man, to bear to her beloved children in his likeness. And here again in this relationship between the law of the love of God and the norm of the imitation of God we can perceive the complete compatibility of the covenant's demand for personal love of God and its demand for obedience to manifold commandments. For the latter are simply specific applications of the norm of the imitation of God; they are a manual whose summary design is to direct man how to reproduce in himself on his image-glory level the likeness of the God he loves.

II. THEOCRATIC KINGDOM COMMISSION

Introduction

1. Cult and Culture Alike Religious: Unlike the stipulations of the later Decalogue-covenant, which are largely negative, curbing fallen man's sinful bent, the specific obligations promulgated under the creational covenant were (with one familiar exception) positive in form. There were mandates that defined man's role in the advancement of God's kingdom and there were ordinances that established the institutional structures of man's historical existence. These covenant stipulations were concerned with both the vertical and horizontal dimensions of covenant life. They dealt with man's cultural task, his commission with respect to his horizontal relationship to the world that was his environment and to all his fellow creatures. They dealt also with man's cultic role, his duties in his directly vertical relationship to his Creator-Lord. Man's theocratic commission involved a dual priest-king office.

We have already met with this two dimensional, cultural-cultic character of man's covenant life and service in the two aspects of his kingdom-home, the Garden of God. As a garden-paradise it would occupy man with the royal-cultural labor of cultivating its bounty and beauty. As a sanctuary of God it presented man with a cultic vocation of priestly guardianship. We have also seen the shape of this dual office-vocation in the niche assigned to man in the hierarchical consecration pattern of the account in which the creation event was revealed. Man is located in that account as king over all the created order of the six days, but his position is that of a vassal king, a priestly, tribute-offering king consecrated to the Great King of the seventh day.

We have observed too that though the cultic and the cultural-political are distinguishable dimensions of human functioning, they are integrated into an institutional unity by the theocratic principle of the covenant kingdom. Moreover, we have noted that since all the covenant stipulations are given by God, compliance with them in whatever sphere of covenant life is a matter of the servant's performing his duty towards God and so expressing his love for God. This unity of the royal-cultural and the priestly-cultic functions as alike a covenantal service rendered to the heavenly Suzerain prohibits any dichotomizing of man's life into religious and nonreligious areas. On the other hand, though man's total life and labor, his cultural and his cultic functioning, are religious, the distinction between the cultural and cultic dimensions, present from the beginning, did provide a formal groundwork for the sacred-profane distinction that afterwards emerged in the fractured postlapsarian world. With the exception of one or two notable situations, God's servants find themselves after the Fall in a common grace situation where their cultural functions are not holy but profane. Nevertheless, they recognize that even these profane functions are to be carried out under God's mandate as service to him for his glory and thus are thoroughly religious. Within the creation-theocracy (and in any redemptive reestablishment of that theocratic order) the cultural dimension is, as we have said earlier, cult-oriented; it is itself holy.

2. Special Revelation in Theophany and Word: Another introductory matter concerns the mode of revelation in the covenantal commissioning of man, and in particular the necessity of special revelation to supplement natural revelation in communicating the specific cultural and cultic requirements of the covenant.

According to the law of the image-son, God's own nature was the norm to be emulated by man and man knew God through natural revelation. Yet from the beginning God was also known to man through the special revelation of the theophanic Glory-Spirit. Accompaniment of natural revelation by this special revelation was the normal order of the day in the original creation kingdom. And since the knowledge of the nature of God was knowledge of the norm of man's life and being, this special theophanic revelation of God constituted a special revelation of law, present from the beginning. Moreover, the significance of this special revelation of law is enhanced by the fact that the Glory-Spirit was the particular point of reference in the creation of man as the image-son of God who must imitate his Father-Archetype.

Glory-Spirit revelation was not simply visual. The theophany site was an oracle. Verbal communication was a normal accompaniment of this divine Presence. From the beginning there was special word revelation of God's will for man, supplementing the disclosure of covenant obligations conveyed through both natural and nonverbal (i.e., epiphanic) special revelation of God. Such special word revelation met a need for specific information about the Lord's purposes and requirements beyond what was revealed in nonverbal fashion. For apart from these oracular communications man would not know the particular objectives of his historical mission as priest-king, nor would he know about a specific community structure like the family institution or a culture-shaping ordinance like the Sabbath, arrangements within which the Lord would have him live and carry forward the kingdom program. Special word revelation was necessary to advise man of the extent and limitations of his God-like authority with respect to other creatures heavenly and earthly, human and subhuman. A notable and obvious example of such a limitation that required disclosure by a special word from God was the focal probationary prohibition concerning man's use of the tree of the knowledge of good and evil. Man would also be dependent on special word revelation for his knowledge of the curse and blessing sanctions by which God was pleased to encourage compliance with the covenant stipulations and to discourage disloyalty. That is, there was a necessity of special verbal communication to convey divine "prophecy" as well as divine law.

A. Cultural Commission

1. Construction of the Kingdom City
The record of God's commissioning of man to his historical kingdom task (Gen 1:28) is part of the account of the creation of man in God's image. It comes in the fulfillment section of the fiat-fulfillment pattern. In the fiat section God is heard addressing the heavenly council, advising them of his purpose to create man with a royal glory like that of the Glory-council itself (Gen 1:26). Then the fulfillment section depicts God addressing the man and the woman he has created, now repeating to them his designs for mankind previously announced in the angelic assembly. Thus God sent them into the world on their mission as his anointed servants with a royal mandate to exercise dominion over the earth in his name. They were to fill the earth with their royal kind and they were to bring the earth under their rule. Through human procreation and by the various labors of their royal rule they were to produce a royal human race, a universal ruling community.

Created male and female, man was to multiply through sexual fruitfulness. In Genesis 1 the procreation mandate is formulated in simply functional terms. Genesis 2 adds the institutional (i.e., familial) aspect, so assigning human procreation to its proper context in the marital relationship. Mankind shares in sexuality with the other living kinds mentioned in the creation narrative, while differing in this respect from the angels, who are created a host but are not a race. Man is created not a host but one pair, a male and female, one flesh in their marriage union, who by multiplying themselves become a host that is also a race. This vital, genealogical process is the central motif of human history. Man himself is the chief end-product of human culture. Genealogy is the primary genre of human historiography. Even apart from the Fall the record of human history after its creation prologue could appropriately have borne the heading: "These are the generations of Adam."

Throughout the historical-genealogical process human life would continue to be "of the earth, earthy" (cf. 1 Cor 15:47), needing to be nourished out of the earth. And though the blessing of God was imparted, human effort was required. The procreation mandate was accompanied by the command to work. Man must labor to secure from his environment its life-supporting stores for his multiplying race (cf. 1 Tim 5:8).

Besides availing himself of the earth's hospitality man would have to protect himself from earth's inhospitable elements and moments. This is perhaps reflected in the language of the cultural mandate for its terms are vigorous. Man was to subdue the earth and rule its creatures. Human labor was to be an exercise of man's dominion and a march of royal conquest. Even if the verb *kabash*, "subdue," (Gen 1:28) does not mean precisely "conquer" in this instance (cf., e.g., Num 32:22; Josh 18:1), it at least has the force of bringing into subjection (cf. 2 Chr 28:10; Neh 5:5; Jer 34:11,16). Man was to overcome whatever resistance or recalcitrance he encountered in nature and win from it its supportive service. However, though described by so forceful a figure in Genesis 1:28, it was not intended that man's dominion over the earth and his appropriation of its resources should be twisted into a process of destructive exploitation. Indeed, for man to ravage and poison his world would be to turn it into an unmanageable monster, a savage master that would tyrannize him. And that would be contrary of course to the objective of the cultural mandate, which was to enhance man's royal majesty and advance man's reign over the earth. A balancing indication of the intent of man's royal commission is provided in Genesis 2:15. It appears there that man's subduing of the earth and bringing it into his service involved his serving (*'abad*) the ground.

Appropriation of earth's riches for the cultivation of mankind was to be achieved through man's cultivation of the earth.

Fulfillment of man's cultural stewardship would thus begin with man functioning as princely gardener in Eden. But the goal of his kingdom commission was not some minimal, local life support system. It was rather maximal, global mastery. The cultural mandate put all the capacity of human brain and brawn to work in a challenging and rewarding world to develop the original paradise home into a universal city. The kingdom city – such is the picture that emerges when the design of all that was envisaged in the assignments of procreation and royal labor is pieced together (including an element that will receive further attention presently). The citizens of the city would come into being through the process of procreation. Its physical-architectural form would take shape as a product of man's cultural endeavors. And the governmental dimension of the city was provided for in the community authority structure that was appointed as a further creation ordinance (the element that still must be taken up). The kingdom city is the aggregate and synthesis of the creational ordinances that defined man's cultural commission. The city is mankind culturally formed.

2. Community Polity

The cultural commission was not to be carried out in starkly individualistic fashion but as an institutional program. Covenant life and history were to unfold within a community structure, within the close and comprehensive societal bond of the family.

An institutional union was effected between the first man and woman by the marriage ordinance. They were, of course, one in generic classification as members of one of the "kinds" God created. They were male and female varieties of man-"kind", each individually a member of the image-of-God "kind" (Gen 1:27; cf. 2:18). Moreover, a special oneness in creational origins obtained in the case of the first human couple in that the woman was fashioned of flesh derived from the man (Gen 2:21; 1 Cor 11:8). "Bone of my bone, flesh of my flesh," was Adam's acknowledgement of this, repeated in his name-pun when he called her `ishshah`, "woman," because she was taken out of `ish`, "man" (Gen 2:23). But beyond such ontological unity was the legal unity constituted by the divine ordinance of marriage. This societal ordinance was not promulgated in the first instance by being separately prescribed and then applied to a human pair previously existing as unrelated individuals. Rather, the ordinance was introduced as part of the naming process that defined the meaning of God's acts of creation (cf. Gen 1:28; 2:24). Mankind was virtually created a family in that the first human pair was created not just male and female, but husband and wife. God's original bringing of the woman to Adam was a nuptial presentation (Gen 2:21-23). (It may be noted that Adam's acknowledgement of the woman is expressed in terminology subsequently used to describe family kinship: cf. Gen 29:14; Judg 9:2.) The marriage ordinance (Gen 2:24) was thus operative from man's very origins.

The legal-institutional nature of the union in which the man and woman were joined together by the marriage ordinance was covenantal. "Cleave" (*dabaq*), the key word used in Genesis 2:24, is used for the covenantal relationship in ancient treaties (cf. in biblical covenants, Deut 10:20; 30:20; Josh 23:8). More obvious is Malachi's expression, "wife of thy covenant" (Mal 2:14f.; cf. Prov 2:17). In their marriage relationship the first pair might see a creational parable of God's covenant with them, which was similarly a troth arrangement marked by commitments of obligation and promise. Though drawn from the social sphere rather than from nature, the marriage parable was, like the nature parables mentioned earlier, simply an available illustration of a feature of the covenant ready to be noticed, not an official symbol of covenant reality appointed for observance, like the sign of the Sabbath.

It was within this marital relationship of legal troth that the procreation function of the cultural commission was to be fulfilled. As the words of the marriage ordinance in Genesis 2:24 indicate, it was in this covenantal union that the man and the woman were to become "one flesh." Indeed, the entire covenantal kingdom program was coordinated with the institution of the family. The cultural commission was a family mandate, not alone in the sense that it was to be performed by mankind acting as a family unit but in the further sense that the perfecting of the family itself was the cultural task to be accomplished. We observed above that the objective of the kingdom program was to produce a royal human race, the citizenry of the kingdom city. We may now refine that by saying that the goal in view was the city of the royal human family, filling and ruling the earth. When, therefore, in the course of redemptive history the restoration of the original covenant order and program was being portrayed in the experience of the Mosaic covenant community occupying and filling, subduing and ruling a paradise land, the nature of that covenant community was familial. Whatever other elements were absorbed into it, the community's basic identity was that of the twelve tribes of Jacob-Israel. In fact, that tribal-familial model is retained to identify the covenant people even after the engrafting of the elect out of all the nations has taken place under the new covenant (cf., e.g., Rev 7:4ff.; 21:12).

The original covenant family was not without its divinely appointed government. As in any just society, so in the community in Eden responsibilities were accompanied by an appropriate authority for fulfilling them. The requirement for children to honor their parents later enunciated as the fifth stipulation of the covenant at Sinai was already applicable in Eden (even the positive, role-defining form of the fifth word of the Decalogue would be congenial to original covenant law). There too parental responsibility for the child must be balanced by a commensurate authority over the child.

Likewise, the care of the wife assigned to the husband in the marriage ordinance (cf. Eph 5:29) was attended by an appropriate marital authority (cf. 1 Pet 3:1-6; Titus 2:5). Recognition that the marital authority structure was already part of the creational ordering of human society is evidenced in the thinking of the apostle Paul when he accounts for it by factors in the biblical record of creation. He regards the woman's derivation from the man as significant for her functional subordination in the marital context (1 Cor 11:8). Finding in Genesis 2 the idea that the woman was created for the man and not *vice versa*, Paul sees that too as indicative of the man's marital headship (1 Cor 11:9). Another feature of the creation account by which the apostle's interpretation of the marital authority structure might have been supported is Adam's assigning to the woman her name (Gen 2:23; cf. 3:20). The subordination of the woman to her husband is compared by Paul to the subordination of mankind as image of God to the authority of his divine Author (1 Cor 11:7). Accordingly, the social parable of marriage was illustrative of God's covenant not simply as a troth arrangement but as an authority structure between the Father-Archetype-Lord and the human image-son-servant. Paul further expounds the man's headship as analogous to Christ's headship over his church (Eph 5:23,24). Hence it is conditioned by the principle of self-sacrificing love of the wife and is designed to be instrumental in the fulfilling of love's responsibilities to her (Eph 5:25).

Each family unit of the branching covenant people would exhibit the marital and parental authority pattern. The covenant institution as a whole would be the complex of these family authority structures. This is a principle of polity that has proven to be a constant in the determination of the form of the covenant, even under its various redemptive administrations. For throughout the Old and New Testament ages alike the parental authority principle established in the creational covenant has continued to be honored, so that those who own the covenant have the privilege and duty of exercising their parental authority to bring their children with them under the institutional rule of their Lord in his covenant.

A distinctive element in the government of the Creator's Covenant of Works with Adam was the feature of federal representation. Adam, father of all mankind, was patriarchal head of the covenant community in the sense that he acted in a representative capacity for all in his probationary response to the Creator's claims and demands (Rom 5; 1 Cor 15). In the process of redemption the federal principle figures once again with Christ as second Adam, but in this case federal representation coincides with election and is not coextensive with the holy covenant institution in its historically administered form.

Under the creational covenant the covenant family was the universal cultural authority structure, a royal family with proprietorship and dominion over its world environment. This governmental order was headed up in the patriarchal authority of Adam. As noted above in chapter two, such governmental structure at the human level was consistent with the theocratic nature of the covenant kingdom, for that human government was a vassal-authority that acknowledged the supreme authority of God as its absolute head. Man's kingly proprietorship of the earth was a stewardship for which he was accountable to the Lord God, the Great King. The polity of the covenant community was theocratic. God was in truth the ruler and protector of the family-kingdom of mankind. He was their ultimate father and they bore his surname, for he had created them his image-sons.

Because this universal family-kingdom was theocratic and culture and cult are institutionally integrated in a theocracy, cult and culture alike were functions of this family, which was accordingly a holy cultic-cultural structure. It was the original "kingdom of priests and holy nation" (Exod

19:6). All members of the covenant community had priestly as well as royal office.

In the case of the later application of the theocratic principle to the nation of Israel, over and above the general priestly identity of all the people there was a special office of mediatorial priest. This special Israelite priesthood was part of the messianic typology that dominated the symbolic system of the Israelite kingdom. In the design of redemption Christ was provided as a mediator-priest to meet the needs of men resulting from the Fall, and the Levitical priesthood was a prototype of that mediatorial priesthood of Christ. In the original sinless situation, however, there would have been no mediatorial priesthood. Adam had a special representative status in the probation-event, but with reference to continuing priestly vocation Adam's patriarchal status would mean no more than that he was *primus inter pares* in the universal royal priesthood of the original holy theocratic family of mankind.

3. Culture and the Imitation of God
The fundamental and comprehensive norm of man's life, the principle of the imitation of God that was inscribed on man's heart, received specific application in various concrete ways in the cultural commission. As God's image-bearer, man in his kingdom activities must follow the direction taken by the Lord in his works of creation and providence. Man's offices and functions in relation to the construction of the kingdom city were designed to be a human reflection of the authority and activity of the Lord God, Creator and Governor of the world.

One expression of the imitation-of-God principle is found in the very fact that man was called upon to be a worker, like the Worker of the six creation days. Man was commissioned to enter into and carry forward the work of God, furthering God's ultimate purpose of glorifying himself by developing the kingdom city as a reflector of the divine glory. Invited to be a fellow laborer with God – that is the dignity of man the worker and the zest and glory of man's labor. Jesus, the second Adam, affirmed his own adherence to the imitation of God principle in this particular respect when he said: "My father works until now and I work" (John 5:17).

God's work was creative, sustaining, governing; so too, on a creaturely level, was man's. God's original works of absolute origination found analogues in man's constructive and inventive activities, in his artistic creativity, and in his procreative functioning. As we have seen, Genesis 5:1-3 reflects specifically on the parallel between human procreation and God's creation of man by noting that in each case an image-likeness was produced. In man's cultivation of the earth, his nourishing and nurturing of his own young, his caring for and using, taming and domesticating the animals, in all the variety of his cultural laboring to subdue the earth, he was imitating what God did in his providential preserving and governing of the world as a place which through its fullness of provision supported man's bodily life and through its harmonies and its infinities answered to the deep call of the human spirit.

Along with the biological and technological aspects of human culture there was the social dimension. And here too, in this area of the personal, family bonds and community relations of the children of Adam and Eve, the imitation of God principle had its specific applications. God is love and that love of the Creator-Father manifested in all the good provision of creation and the tender care of protective providence was to be the law of life in the covenant family. Imitation of the divine norm would find social expression in mutual regard and solicitude shown in the manifold crisscrossing relationships and responsibilities of the family community – in the affectionate parental nurture of children, in the love of brother-neighbor as oneself, in the love of husband and wife (cf. again Eph 5:23-25). In this area man was also to imitate God by being a covenant maker and covenant keeper, faithful and true.

God's interpretive activity was another aspect of the divine work of creation that was to have an analogue in man's cultural program. One of the recurring motifs in Genesis 1 is God's naming of his creatures. In ancient texts, when deities give names to things they are assigning them functions and ordaining their destinies. Similarly, God's naming of the products of the six creation days was a sovereign defining of nature and determining of the purpose of things. And God summoned man to imitate him in this interpreting function of assigning names. God brought to Adam the birds and beasts to see what he would call them (Gen 2:19). Man's interpretive role would become of increasing practical importance as an instrument for gaining mastery of the earth in fulfillment of his cultural task, for more and more man's growing knowledge of his world would be the key to his power over it.

Stated in terms of cultural office, man's interpretive vocation was a call to the post of wise man-philosopher-scientist. This was not so much an office in itself as it was an adjunct of man's kingship. Wisdom's royal connections become obvious if we notice that an important aspect of man's interpretive-naming function was the judicial kind of classifying denoted by the knowledge of good and evil, that prominent element in man's image-likeness to the Glory-Spirit.

It was of utmost importance that man bear in mind the subordinate, vassal character of the royal office to which his wisdom role attached. Man's interpretive-naming was no more an autonomous activity than his kingship was an autonomous authority. Though his naming was God-like, it still was something imitative and secondary. It was not an original divine act of creational definition of meaning where there had not been meaning before. Man's role as wise man was rather one of discovering and explicating, of receptively reconstructing the meaning of the things already imparted to them by the Creator. An illustration of the interpretive function properly performed is provided by Adam when called upon to name the animals. God had already interpreted the animal kingdom as subordinate to man (Gen 1:28) and agreeably, in naming these creatures, Adam found no counterpart to himself (Gen 2:20, cf. v. 23). By thus doing his thinking and interpreting as one standing under God, he conformed to the law of the image-bearer and showed himself to be endowed with true human wisdom. The point we are making and illustrating here is the burden of the book of Proverbs. God's archetypal role in the sphere of wisdom and man's duty to apply the imitation of God principle in this area are effectively presented there by urging men to get (*qanah*) wisdom as the first or principal thing (*reshith*) and simultaneously declaring that God possessed wisdom (the same verb, *qanah*, is used) as the beginning (*reshith*) of his ways (see 4:7, cf. v. 5 and 8:22). Possessed by God from the very beginning, wisdom was the guiding principle that informed the whole process of creation (Prov 8:22-31). Hence, for man, true wisdom must consist in naming creation in conformity with the meaning-names determined and assigned by the creative wisdom of God, starting with the recognition of man's own creatureliness and of the createdness of the heavens and earth and all their hosts – beginning, that is, with the fear of the Lord, which is wisdom (Prov 1:7; Job 28:28; Ps 111:10).

Viewed broadly, the cultural commission was a program to actualize that dominion which was central to man's image-likeness to the Glory-Spirit.

Man's culture was to provide a human replica of the divine kingship manifested in the Glory-Archetype. Man was invested with a God-like authority and majesty and charged, in imitation of God, to perfect the consecration of the world to his royal use and honor.

According to the biblical representation, God's handiwork serves him as royal structures and majestic adornments. The cosmos is his palace; the heavens are stretched out as his royal tent (Isa 40:22). Or again, the luminary emblazoned sky is his robe as he covers himself with light (or the sun) as with a garment and so is arrayed with honor and majesty (Ps 104:1b,2; cf. 102:26). Incidentally, imagery of deities in star-studded robes was not uncommon in the ancient Near East. The products of the cultural labors of man, the princely son of God, were also to bear this royal character. He was to adorn himself with clothing as a manifestation of the royal glory of his person. Jesus thus refers to the royal robes of Solomon as "all his glory" (Matt 6:29; cf. Exod 28: 2,40). Though the first explicit references to clothing in the Bible are in the aftermath of the Fall where clothing assumes a remedial purpose, it would have had a proper place with positive purposes in a sinless culture. For besides providing for the public preservation of the private proprietorship of marriage in the privilege of unashamed nakedness (cf. Gen 2:25), clothing would have served as a means of securing man's royal dominion over the world by guarding him from the inclement in nature and as an expression of man's royal majesty by enhancing his personal glory (cf. 1 Cor 12:23). And as human culture proceeded from clothing to clothing's more complex functional extensions in house and vehicle and in the city, it was all to be in imitation of God's kingship, implementing man's dominion and exhibiting his majesty.

It was not just the divine royalty as displayed in God's cosmic handiwork that was being imitated in man's fulfillment of his cultural commission. Human culture was a creaturely replication of the royal glory of God as revealed in the theophanic Glory itself, the Archetype of both cosmos and man. Clothing, house, vehicle, city – all these expressions of human culture provide metaphors for the Glory-cloud formation that manifested the Spirit-Presence. It is presented in the Scriptures as God's luminous covering, as his palace, as his royal chariot, as the heavenly city. Thus, the pattern of the kingdom city which man was commissioned to build was revealed to him from the beginning in the royal theophany of the Glory on the mountain of God.

Yet another feature of man's cultural program which identified it as imitating the royal glory of God was its sabbatical form. This feature, to which the Scripture applies most explicitly the imitation-of-God principle, will be treated under its own heading.

4. Culture's Sabbatical Form

The imitation-of-God principle was to find embodiment in the over-all pattern of the history of man's kingdom labor in that this history was to correspond to the course of God's creational working as a movement from work begun to work consummated. Mankind's cultural endeavors were to move forward to and issue in a sabbatical rest. In fact, man was to come by way of these works at last into God's own royal rest (Heb 4:1ff.).

As human history has turned out, it is through Jesus, the second Adam, that God's people find their way into the realm of Sabbath rest with God. It is he who leads them into the true and eternal Canaan, the new Eden (Heb 4:8-10). But this redemptive accomplishment of the second Adam illumines the design of the program originally assigned to the first Adam. Like redemptive history, the history of the original covenant was to be characterized by an eschatological thrust and direction. It was to have a sabbatical structure. This eschatological-sabbatical nature which the history of man had from the beginning was a consequence of the very fact that man was created in the image of the sabbatarian Creator. Entering into the kingdom program as God's servant-son, man was to reflect the divine glory, advancing through his six days of work to the seventh day of completion, from kingdom development to a Sabbath of joyous shalom.

This over-all structural pattern of human history as a process moving from the cultural commission to consummation rest was stamped by God as a repeating design across the days of man's years. By his Lord's appointment man was to experience the passage of time not as an indefinite, undefined string of mornings and evenings, but as a succession of weeks. The history of God's creational activity was revealed as transpiring in a seven-day framework with sabbatical seventh and this pattern was to be imprinted as a recurring sequence on the days of mankind's earthly existence. Hence, the Sabbath was translated into an ordinance, according to which man was to observe every seventh day as a Sabbath. In the formulation of this Sabbath commandment, the imitation of God principle came to its most explicit expression in covenant law.

That the Sabbath was an ordinance of the creational covenant is indicated by the interpretation of Genesis 2:3 which the author of that passage (whether one is thinking in terms of the primary or the human author) provided in the Exodus 20 version of the fourth commandment. As the ground for the requirement to sanctify the weekly Sabbath, Exodus 20:11 appeals to Genesis 2:3, citing the fact that there at the beginning the Creator had sanctified the Sabbath day. It is especially by substituting the term "the Sabbath day" (which is clearly the ordinance of the Sabbath in the Decalogue context) for "the seventh day" of Genesis 2:3 that Exodus 20:11 shows that the subject changes in Genesis 2:3 from the divine seventh day of the creation week (the subject of Gen. 2:2) to the ordinance of the weekly Sabbath. Another indication of the transition in subject from God's archetypal Sabbath in Genesis 2:2 to the ordinance in verse 3 is the statement in verse 3 that God blessed the seventh day. For throughout the creation narrative, God's act of blessing has to do with things within the sphere of his creatures' experience, imparting to them fruitfulness, impregnating them with felicity. Moreover, the accompanying statement that God sanctified the seventh day must be understood as God's appointing the day as a sacred ordinance for man to observe and thus to secure the blessing residing in it. God's sanctifying of the seventh day ought not to be interpreted as God's own celebrating of the day by a holy resting (a divine keeping of holy-day as it were) because in Genesis 2:3 and emphatically in Exodus 20:11 the divine resting on the seventh day is distinguished from the divine sanctifying of the Sabbath, the former being cited as the ground for the latter. The appointment of the Sabbath ordinance thus affirmed in Genesis 2:3 will, of course, have immediate reference to the God's covenant with Adam, not to the Sinaitic Covenant and Sabbath as assigned to Israel, for such an incidental allusion to a ceremonial observance in a remote redemptive era would be altogether out of place at the climax of the drama of the creation of the original covenantal order, so simply and sublimely narrated in the Genesis prologue. Confirmation of the appointment of the Sabbath at man's beginnings is found in what Jesus said when affirming his lordship over the Sabbath (Mark 2:28; cf. Matt 12:8; Luke 6:5). By way of preface to this claim he declared: "The Sabbath was made for man, not man for the Sabbath" (Mark 2:27). In this virtual interpretation of Genesis 2:3, Jesus refers to the time of creational origins when things were being made and relates the Sabbath to man generically, not narrowly to Israel. Using the same terminology for the origin of the Sabbath as he does for the origin of mankind, he identifies the origins of the Sabbath with the same creational beginnings that are in view in the reference to the making of man. Agreeably, in asserting his authority over the Sabbath, Jesus' designation for himself was not son of David (cf. Mark 2:25f.) but the son of man, the second Adam (v. 28).

In carrying out the duty of Sabbath observance, man was culturally structuring time. This too was part of his cultural commission, along with the task of being an architect of space. And just as man's shaping of the world spacially was a sanctifying of the world to God inasmuch as the goal of this architectural labor was the holy temple-city, so man's forming of time into a sabbatical structure was a sanctifying of time to God because of all that the Sabbath signified concerning the holy divine Glory. All culture in its spacial-temporal fullness was cult-oriented; kingship was ancillary to priesthood.

For man to observe the Sabbath in obedient imitation of the paradigm of work and rest established by his Creator was an acknowledgment that he was the Creator's servant-son, a confession of God as his Father and Lord. As an ordinance observed by man the Sabbath was a sign of the covenant as a personal relationship and specifically it was a confessional sign of man's consecration to God. Sabbath observance was a recurring reaffirmation of man's covenantal commitment. This aspect of the Sabbath's meaning surfaces prominently when it is formally reinstituted in Israel. For the Lord identifies it as "a sign between me and you throughout your generations, that you may know that I, Yahweh, sanctify you" (Exod 31:13; cf. v.17), and he calls it a "perpetual covenant" (Exod 31:16), terminology also applied to circumcision, the sign of covenant discipleship (Gen 17:7, 13). And if a sign of man's discipleship, the Sabbath is, by the same token, the sign of God's lordship. If it is an acknowledgment by man that his own kingship is only a vassal-kingship, the Sabbath signifies the corollary truth that God is the Great King, sovereign over man and over the land that is man's royal realm, in stewardship. The Sabbath signalizes the theocratic order.

From man God-ward the Sabbath was a sign of consecration; from God manward it was a sign of consummation. In giving man the Sabbath ordinance the Lord made a covenantal commitment, promising that triumphant royal rest was to crown the genealogical-cultural history of the family of Adam, in their faithful keeping of the covenant. As the garden of Eden was a space-sign, a replica of the whole cosmos as God's dwelling, so the sabbatical week was a time-sign, a replica of the total history of man's fulfillment of the cultural mandate after the pattern of God's working in creation, with the Sabbath at the end of that week a promissory symbol of the hope of consummation. The Sabbath ordinance is covenantal privilege as well as covenantal duty, for it is always divine promise and divine demand together. In the ordinance of the Sabbath, covenant stipulation and covenant blessing-sanction were thus conjoined. To be like God was not just man's duty; it was his very beatitude.

Whether the Sabbath is viewed as God's promise of the consummation of the covenant order or as man's pledge of devotion to the covenant suzerain, it is always a sign of the covenant. In this primal sign the covenant receives comprehensive expression, for the Sabbath brings out the nature of the covenant as both personal relationship and historical kingdom program. For Israel the Sabbath was the sign of the covenant par excellence (Exod 31:16,17). That the Sabbath was appointed to the covenant community at the creation suggests that it is of perpetual validity, as long at least as that community experiences life and history as a succession of days. However, if we appreciate this essential connection of the Sabbath with the covenant, and especially if we recognize that the Sabbath is always covenantal promise and privilege as well as duty, we will avoid thinking of it abstractly as at any time after the Fall a universal ordinance of general application to the world at large. The Sabbath belongs to the covenant community exclusively.

Moreover, since the Sabbath is a sign of sanctification marking that which receives its imprint as belonging to God's holy kingdom with promise of consummation, the Sabbath will have relevance and application at any given epoch of redemptive history only in the holy dimension(s) of the life of the covenant people. Thus, after the Fall, not only will the Sabbath pertain exclusively to the covenant community as a holy people called out of the profane world, but even for them the Sabbath will find expression, in a nontheocratic situation, only where they are convoked in covenant assembly, as the *ekklesia*-extension of the heavenly assembly of God's Sabbath enthronement. That is, Sabbath observance will have to do only with their holy cultic (but not their common cultural) activity.

Sabbath observance is celebration of God's lordship, from whatever perspective it is viewed. Man observes it as a sign of consecration, a confession that God is Lord. In its symbolic import as a sign of consummation it speaks of God's sovereign authority over the world and his control of its history. Insofar as the ordinance recalls the seventh day of the creation it commemorates the enthronement of the Creator in the Sabbath-Omega phase of his royal majesty which had been manifested from the beginning in the Glory-Spirit. In Sabbath observance there is thus an imitation and celebration of the original day of the Lord that finds its ultimate expression in the final *parousia*-day of judgment and consummation. [On this theme, see further *Images of the Spirit*, chapter 4.] Accordingly, not late in redemptive history and as a modification of its previous meaning, but from its creational beginnings the Sabbath has been precisely and preeminently the Lord's day. By stamping this symbol of the day of the Lord across the days of man under the creational covenant, the Creator impressed on world-time the claims of his judicial sovereignty over it. History thus bore the image and superscription of the Lord of the Sabbath day and was thereby placed under tribute to render all its glory unto him.

As prophetic sign of the final day of the Lord, the Sabbath held before mankind symbolically the prospect of the divine judgment. Under the creational covenant, the proper purpose of the covenant was to bring man to the end of his historical labors in a consummation of kingdom blessings and agreeably the proper purpose of the covenant sign of the Sabbath was to point to and minister to a consummation of blessedness. But the Sabbath, viewed more broadly, symbolized the day of judgment generically, and since that judgment confronts man with the options of both blessing and curse verdicts, the generic significance of the Sabbath included both the dual sanctions of the covenant. The Scriptures reflect the curse option in the meaning of the Sabbath when they use the verb *shabath* in word-play to threaten the curse of the cessation of covenant blessings, like the possession of the kingdom or, most strikingly, the joy of the Sabbath itself (Isa 24:8 [cf. v. 5 for the reference to the covenant with Adam]; Hos 1:4; 2:11[13]; Ps 89:44[45]). In this respect, the Sabbath, continuing on into redemptive administrations of the covenant, is like its accompanying signs of circumcision and baptism. For these also symbolize the judgment of death generically, while pointing, as to their proper redemptive objective, to a faith-passage through the death-curse in Christ as the way to ultimate resurrection and consummate beatitude. (Note also the use of the same pun on the idiom of cutting, *i.e.*, making, a covenant to denote the curse of the cutting off of the covenant-breaker in the case of violations of both circumcision [Gen 17:14] and Sabbath [Exod 31:14]).

B. Cultic Ministry

1. Adoration and Consecration

No special revelation was needed to inform Adam that he had cultic obligations to perform, that is, that he was commissioned to priestly office. Through natural revelation God is known as One who is to be worshipped and thanked (Rom 1:19ff). Priestly adoration of the Creator would arise as the spontaneous response of Adam to the sense of deity within him and the revelation of the Godhead clearly seen in the creation around him.

Man would recognize that he was to be a personal temple of God, a living locus of the adoration of his Creator. He would accordingly present before the Lord the thoughts of his heart, his faith interpretation of the world and himself as a theocratic creation, or, more personally stated, his faith-commitment of the world and himself to his Father and Great King. He would present these meditations of his heart in the confessional, doxological word-songs of his mouth as acceptable priestly offerings.

Constrained by the sense of deity within, man's priestly-cultic response would at the same time be evoked and conditioned by the special revelation which was a normal accompaniment of natural revelation at the beginning. The theophanic Glory-Spirit on the mountain of God, which constituted Eden a sanctuary, would give a visible focus to man's priestly experience of the divine Presence and a local external orientation for his cultic ministry. And from this oracular source man would receive directives as to various particulars of his priestly duties in the Edenic sanctuary that could not be discovered from natural revelation.

Before man faced the world, sent into it with royal cultural commission, he was confronted with the Presence-Face of his Creator. Man thus began life as a priest before God, as a beholder of the divine Glory. Through such creative encounter God replicates his likeness in image-bearers, transforming them from glory to glory as reflectors of his Glory. Hence, in man's primal priestly vision of the Glory-Spirit he saw the Alpha-Paradigm and Omega-*Telos* of his existence as image of God. Here at the heart of man's vocation as priest we meet once again the life principle of the imitation of God.

Along with adoration, consecration belongs to the priestly office, both the positive dedicating of things to the holy Lord and, complementing this, the negative charge of keeping evil away from the sanctuary. (On the latter, see further under the Guardianship of the Sanctuary.) The priestly obligation of positive consecration followed from man's status as a covenant servant or vassal-king. For a vassal-king is a tributary of the great king, and when the great king is the Lord God, the payment of tribute is a cultic act, a priestly dedication of holy offerings. In the adaptation of the ancient suzerain-vassal treaty as a model for Yahweh's covenant with Israel, the customary annual trips to the royal court of the suzerain to pay the stipulated tribute become the annual pilgrimages of the Israelites to the temple with their offerings for the Lord.

The question arises whether an offertory ritual that was in some sense symbolic would have been appropriate to man's priestly ministry before the Fall. A more particular question would be whether such a ritual offering, if there were such, might have taken the form of animal sacrifice. On the latter, there would be no principial difficulty with the idea of such slaying of animals if one accepts the approach adopted in chapter 2 above in the discussion of death in the prelapsarian world. As for the more general question, the employment of symbolism in the cultus evidently had its ground and rationale elsewhere than in the exigencies arising from the entrance of sin. For in the midst of Eden's garden-sanctuary were the two trees with their special symbolic significance. There was also the symbolism of the Sabbath ordinance, signifying for one thing the very principle of consecration that would be expressed by priestly offerings.

Metaphorical relationships obtained between various aspects of the created order. There were natural analogies between the physical and spiritual realms. We have previously spoken of parables of nature and social parables in Paradise. Also in the unfolding eschatological movement of man's history there were in the earlier stages prototypical versions of the realities of the later world of the consummated kingdom of heaven. And by virtue of man's being made in God's Glory-likeness, human activity corresponded in certain ways to the divine. There were therefore various lines of analogy all around for human thought to draw upon in religious reflection and theological interpretation. Of course, the distinction must be recognized between mere presence of metaphorical potential for general conceptualizing and communication and the appointment of a particular symbolic ordinance to function as a sign in the worshipping covenant community. We have thus distinguished above between the marriage relationship and the Sabbath ordinance.

In any case, the Lord had introduced symbolism into the original cultic arrangements and therefore no objection to the assumption of external consecratory offerings before the Fall can be made on the grounds of their symbolic character. Neither is it decisive against that assumption that there is no record of the precept or practice of such sacrifice at that time. In the first generation after the Fall the biblical text mentions consecratory sacrifices as an acceptable cultic practice, without noting prior divine appointment (Gen 4:3ff.). Man's cultic service in Eden was given a local focus in the presence of the Glory-theophany and this sensory context and visible theophanic focus of man's priestly approach to God suggest the appropriateness of outward token offerings such as were prompted by and prescribed for human encounter with the same mode of divine Presence in the subsequent history of revelation.

Whatever we ought to conclude concerning the cultic presentation of token offerings of human labor in the practice of sinless religion, certainly man had from the beginning the priestly obligation to consecrate himself to the Lord God, a heart-offering proferred through the words of his lips (1 Pet 3:15; cf. Isa 8:12,13). And ultimately his priestly responsibility would be to deliver over the world subdued in fulfillment of the cultural mandate to the glory of his holy Creator Lord (cf. 1 Cor 15:28).

2. Guardianship of the Sanctuary

The Creator had prepared in Eden an earthly replica of his heavenly dwelling as the holy place where man would fulfill his priestly office. In the compact report given in Genesis 2:15 of man's obligations with respect to his garden-world a specifically cultic as well as a cultural assignment is included. In addition to tilling or cultivating the garden man was to "guard" it. He was to protect the Edenic sanctuary from profanation. Such priestly guardianship of the holy Presence is a basic function of sanctuary service, a negative kind of consecration. The cultic force of the verb "guard" in Genesis 2:15 is indicated by the use of the same verb *shamar* in Genesis 3:24 for the task of protecting the sanctity of the garden when that assignment was taken from man and transferred to others. In fact, in the narrative of the expulsion of man from the garden after the Fall both elements of man's commissioning mentioned in Genesis 2:15 are taken up, with the same terms used there for both of them employed again. Thus, fallen man was to continue to "till" the ground (Gen 3:23), though now outside the garden. (Were it not for this interpretive echo of the *'abad* of Gen 2:15, the latter might be understood in the cultic sense which it sometimes has, as, e.g., in

Num 3:7). However, man was no longer to "guard" the garden. The responsibility to guard the way to the tree of life was given to the cherubim with the flaming sword (Gen 3:24). Here *shamar* unmistakably signifies the maintenance of the sanctity of the garden, and the value of the appeal to the use of *shamar* in this passage is all the greater if the suggestion is valid that the narrative of Genesis 2:4-3:24 is chiastically arranged with Genesis 2:15 and 3:24 coming in the corresponding end-members of that structure (2:4-17 and 3:22-24 respectively). Elsewhere in the Bible, especially in passages dealing with the functions of the priests and Levites in Israel, the verb *shamar* occurs frequently in the sense of guarding the holiness of God's sanctuary against profanation by unauthorized "strangers"" (cf., e.g., Num 1:53; 3:8,10,32; 8:26; 18:3ff.; 31:30,47; 1 Sam 7:1; 2 Kgs 12:9; 1 Chr 23:32; 2 Chr 34:9; Ezek 44:15f., 48:11). A particularly interesting example is the charge given by the Angel of the Lord to the post-exilic high priest Joshua in the vision of Zechariah 3 (a vision that harks back to several motifs of the Genesis 2 and 3 narrative). Joshua's re-investment with the priestly robes symbolic of the Glory-image is accompanied by the words of recommissioning to sanctuary ministry: "You shall judge my house and guard (*shamar*) my courts" (v. 7). Noteworthy here is the judicial aspect of the priestly office.

The conclusion appears warranted, therefore, that Genesis 2:15 contains an explicit reference to the entrusting of man in his priestly office with the task of defending the Edenic sanctuary against the intrusion of anything that would be alien to the holiness of the God of the garden or hostile to his name. From subsequent developments it is evident that Adam's priestly charge was meant to set him on guard, as at a military post, against the encroachment of the Satanic serpent. In the Zechariah 3 passage, we see the messianic figure of the Angel of the Lord fulfilling this primal priestly duty. He judicially rebukes the malicious accuser, who in effect poses in God's holy presence as one of the cherubim guardians, as though he would defend the sanctuary against the sin-stained human priest. Back at the beginning, the challenge of Satan's unholy trespass was to precipitate the critical hour of probation when man, under the priestly charge to guard God's courts, was faced with the duty of pronouncing the holy judgment of God's house against the preternatural intruder.

This judicial-military function of the office of the guardian-priest is an important aspect of the whole course of judgment executed by agents of God's kingdom subsequently in redemptive history. It is in fact the essence of holy war. Israel's conquest and dispossession of the Canaanites was carried out in fulfillment of their status as a nation of priests who were commissioned to cleanse the land claimed by Yahweh as holy to him. The priestly character of this and other such holy war undertakings was accentuated by the prominent role which the special Levitical priesthood within priestly Israel was assigned in them (see, e.g., Josh 3:3ff.; 6:4ff.; cf. Deut 20:2ff.). Similarly, Messiah in his going forth in the great final judgment for the cleansing of God's cosmic temple, a judgment adumbrated in the temple cleansings recorded in the Gospels, is depicted in prophetic psalm and apocalypse as a priest-king leading a priestly army (Ps 110:3f.; Rev 19:11ff.). Within the present age of the new covenant the function of negative consecration belongs to the church, this ecclesiastical form of it being declarative and spiritual and not applicable outside the holy covenant community (cf. 1 Cor 5:12,13).

At the level of the individual's identity as a temple of God the priestly office involves this negative, protective kind of sanctification as well as positive consecration. The judicial-military aspect of the priestly guardianship of the personal temple of God is brought out in redemptive revelation by the injunction that the armor of God be put on to defend against the hostile, defiling incursions of Satan. Since putting on the divine armor is a variation of the metaphor of investiture with the priestly glory-robes, a major biblical symbol of the *imago Dei* [see further *Images of the Spirit*, chapter 2], the connection between priesthood and the image of God is again in evidence here. If the priestly privilege of beholding God is creative of the reflected image of God's Glory, possession of the dominion-glory of the image in turn equips for the priestly service of guarding God's sanctuary. Accordingly, the judicial as well as the ethical dimension of the *imago Dei* comes to expression in the triumphs of priestly guardianship of our personal sanctity.

3. Primacy of Priesthood
Priesthood is man's primary office. It was with the priestly experience of beholding the Glory of the Creator in his Edenic sanctuary that human existence began. And the priestly charge to guard the sanctity of that garden-sanctuary in the hour of satanic encroachment, the critical probationary task, was man's first great historical assignment. This cultic-judicial encounter with the evil one was to precede the pursuit of the royal cultural commission to expand the sanctuary-kingdom-house of God from focus to fullness.

Priesthood's primacy is not just a matter of historical priorities but of the teleological subordination of the kingly occupation to priestly-cultic objectives. In a theocratic context, kingship is an adjunct of priesthood, a middle stage between an initial priestly reception of glory from God and an ultimate priestly return of glory to God. In kingship the priest turns toward the world to reflect the divine glory on it in a representative exercise of the divine rule over creation. It is a vicegerency in God's holy name.

Properly performed in the sinless situation, the cultural commission would be cult oriented. Since the kingdom was theocratic, the kingdom-city man was to develop would be the city of God, having a cultic focus, yet in its entirety God's holy dwelling. The cultic orientation of man's cultural task becomes evident particularly when it is viewed as one of filling the earth with the fullness of mankind, the living temple of the Spirit. Designed to produce the community-cultus, the people-temple, man's royal culture was directed to the goal of man's engagement in his priestly-cultic vocation of the adoration of God.

The centrality of this cultic objective of human culture continues in the redemptive program. High points of Old Testament history are provided by the episodes of tabernacle and temple building. Israel in the wilderness dedicated its cultural possessions and skills to the construction of the tabernacle (cf. Exod 35ff.) and David consecrated the accumulated fruits of his kingly conquests and reign to the building of a house of God in Jerusalem (cf., e.g., 1 Chr 22). And in the New Testament, Messiah's final achievement is portrayed as the building of the city-temple, the New Jerusalem. [On this theme see further my *Structure of Biblical Authority*, chapter 3.]

Standing in sharp contrast to the theocratic principle of the subordination of culture to cult, was the prostitution of the cult to culture that took place in the nations displaced by Israel. In the pagan fertility cult of Canaan the ritual was conceived of as a magical technique calculated to manipulate the gods so as to promote increase in field and flock and family (so, according to the customary view, which, however, has been challenged). In ancient and modern religious theory and practice, prostitution of cult to culture takes all kinds of forms, gross and subtle. The prostitution of the covenant cult of the Lord whereby the church is turned into an idolized culture is depicted in the symbolism of the New Testament Apocalypse by the replacement of the holy bride with the figure of the Babylon-harlot.

Pursuit of the cultural mandate understood as a process of temple-building would be an act of imitating God. For God in his paradigm acts of creation formed the world as his cosmic temple. Indeed, man's world-temple building would be a producing of a likeness of the Glory-cloud itself, which was the revelation of the heavenly house of God and the archetype for all creaturely replication of the divine likeness. Similarly the producing of mankind itself as the people-temple of God would be imitative of God's original creating of man as the image of God (cf. Gen 5:1,2), a replica of the Spirit-temple.

It has now become clear that culture's orientation and subordination to the cult was not to be merely a matter of bringing various products of culture as offerings to the cult. Rather, to produce the cult itself, the cosmic-human temple, was the ultimate objective in view in the cultural enterprise. In the next chapter something more must be said to clarify the temple-building contribution of the historical process of human culture in relation to the divine, eschatological perfecting of the holy cosmic-human dwelling of the Glory-Spirit.

While stressing the fact that culture was to be oriented and subordinated to the cult, the observation may be in order that it was the cultural dimension of the cultic task under the creational covenant that distinguished the historical role of men from that of angels. Like men image-sons of God, angels have a cultic office. But they do not have the cultural function of producing their kind, for, as we have noted, the hosts of heaven were created such. Nor do these heavenly beings have the task of culturally developing their heavenly environment. Though they are involved in man's cultural history as agents of God in his providential working, this functioning in earth history is not by way of producing an angelic culture on earth but is rather a ministering in connection with the development of man's culture (cf. Heb 1:14). The cultural commission is then something distinctively human. Here, however, our chief concern has been to indicate that the royal-cultural task is ancillary to man's priestly-cultic vocation.

In this analysis of man's offices in the created order the prophetic office has not been mentioned, for that office among men belongs to the postlapsarian order. When it emerges it is found to be a reproduction of the royal priesthood of original man, but having as its peculiar characteristic a mediatorial standing and even a certain antithetical stance in relation to the covenant community for which there would have been no place before the Fall. [On this comment see further *Images of the Spirit*, chapter 3.]

Chapter Four

ESCHATOLOGICAL SANCTIONS

Balancing the review of the past presented in the historical prologue of ancient suzerain-vassal treaties was a section of sanctions pointing to the future of the covenant. They expressed the determination of the suzerain that his dominion should be irresistibly enforced and indefinitely continued in his ongoing dynasty. His promise of blessing and, even more, the curse of appalling desolation which he threatened against disloyalty were calculated to impress upon his vassals the wisdom of performing faithfully the obligations laid on them in the treaty stipulations.

Similarly, the future of God's covenant with Adam was revealed in the form of covenant sanctions. That the Creator's sovereign rule would endure was certain, but just how it would be ultimately manifested must be determined through a probationary testing of mankind. Eschatological destiny, the choice of eternal weal or woe, was set before man in the dual sanctions of the covenant.

Here in the blessing and curse sanctions of God's original covenant with man are the beginnings and essence of prophecy as we meet it throughout the Scriptures. What is central and pervasive in the concern and character of biblical prophecy is its profoundly religious purpose and its earnest ethical orientation and application. It does not cater to idle curiosity or to a lust for knowledge of secret things in the interests of an autonomous quest for control of human existence. By its very nature as a covenantal word it summons man to a life of loyalty to his Lord as it interprets the future in terms of the holy Creator's just judgment on his servants. First and last biblical prophecy has to do with man in covenant with God, with his present responsibilities as a servant-son and with his future accountability to the Lord.

Man's confrontation with the alternatives of the curse and blessing sanctions signalizes the condition of probation that obtained in the first phase of the covenant in Eden. Along with our examination of the precise nature of those sanctions as such, the promise of life and threat of death, we shall, therefore, include an account of the governmental principles operative in this probation and the specific means employed in administering it.

I. THE DUAL SANCTIONS

A. The Promised Blessing

1. Eschatology of the Image

Man's creation as image of God meant, as we have seen, that the creating of the world was a covenant-making process. There was no original non-covenantal order of mere nature on which the covenant was superimposed. Covenantal commitments were given by the Creator in the very act of endowing the man-creature with the mantle of the divine likeness. And those commitments were eschatological. The situation never existed in which man's future was contemplated or presented in terms of a static continuation of the original level of blessedness. For the God in whose likeness man was made is the consummating God of the Sabbath. This sabbatical aspect of the divine image was present in the image as imparted to man and it came to expression in the promise of consummation contained in the creational ordinance of the Sabbath. Blessing sanction promising a consummation of man's original glory as image of God was thus built into man's very nature as image of God. This eschatological prospect was in-created. It was an aspiration implanted in man's heart with his existence as God's image. That being so, to restrict man to the mere continuation of his original state of beatitude would be no blessing at all, but a curse. For it would frustrate man's longing to realize his in-created potential as image of God by disappointing his hope of entering into the Creator's Sabbath rest and thereby experiencing the perfecting of his likeness to the divine paradigm of the Glory-Spirit. The blessing sanction was, therefore, no artificial addition to the covenant but was already involved in man's God-like eschatological-sabbatical nature and was essentially nothing other than the perfecting of that nature.

Since this eschatological aspect of the *imago Dei* shapes the kingdom mandate assigned to man by setting the sabbatical goal toward which man's work must press forward, the covenant blessing sanction was intrinsic to the law of the covenant, being in fact present in the general stipulations of the covenant given before the special probation commandment. The blessing sanction may be identified then not only as the realization of the potential and promise of the *imago Dei* itself but as the successful completion of man's assigned historical mission of filling and subduing the earth, the process in which the *imago Dei* develops from glory to glory. Here again it becomes evident that the bare perpetuation of man's original measure of blessedness would actually have been a curse, not a blessing, for it would have amounted to failure in his endeavor to fulfill God's commission to be fruitful and to extend his dominion.

Perfecting of the *imago Dei* coincides with the attainment of the sabbatical goal of completing the construction of the temple of God as mandated in the kingdom commission. (See above, chapter three.) Identification of the blessing sanction with this sabbatical temple directs us once again to the creational origins of the revelation of that sanction. For the sabbatical temple is constructed according to the original divine pattern revealed on the mountain of God in Eden. The Glory-Spirit-temple was the archetype temple, the promise-paradigm and, more than that, the matrix of the Sabbath-temple of man in the Spirit. From this perspective too, then, it can be seen that the eschatological blessing sanction of the creational covenant, the Omega-hope of the covenant, was disclosed from the earliest beginning in the theophanic Alpha-Original of the human temple-image.

2. The Sacramental Tree

Another reproduction of the theophanic Glory-Spirit, a symbolic one, was planted by the Creator in the midst of the trees of the garden-sanctuary (Gen 2:9), and therewith another revelation was given of the offer of ultimate beatitude by which the covenant was sanctioned. In the wonder of the trees that God made, light is transformed into a tangible glory, a delight to the eyes, with fruit for food to nourish the life of man. And these lords of the plant world, these majestic by-forms of light, the Creator put to further use as earthly symbols of the heavenly Glory-light.

Two aspects of the theophanic Glory that reappear as elements in the replication of that Glory in man are judicial dominion and the light of immortality (cf. Rom 2:7; 1 Tim 1:17; 6:16; 2 Tim 1:10). The two special trees in Eden's sanctuary were designed to function as symbolic means in man's participation in those aspects of God's glory. In these trees the heavenly divine Glory was represented in an earthly form that expressed God's intention of making that glory available to man for his appropriation. How the tree of knowledge was to figure in the development of man's judicial likeness to God will be discussed below. Here we focus upon the tree of life as the sacramental seal of man's participation in the glory of immortality.

Certainly at the time of the Lord's pronouncing of sentence on man for his transgression (Gen 3:22) the tree of life possessed the special significance suggested by its name. But one can hardly suppose that it was only after the blessing symbolized by the tree had been forfeited that the Lord invested the tree with that promissory character or that he then first disclosed its significance to man only to taunt him about the unsuspected treasure he had lost. The absence of a reference to this tree in the recorded words of God to man before the Fall or in the words of Eve to Satan during the temptation can be simply explained in terms of the terse conciseness of the narrative and its immediate concern with the role of the tree of knowledge in this first stage of the probation process. That man had not eaten of the tree of life prior to the judicial pronouncement of Genesis 3:22 seems to be implied in that verse, especially by the "also". We are probably to assume then that man had previously been apprised of the symbolic import of the tree of life and accordingly realized that, though not it but the tree of knowledge was more specifically the forbidden tree in this special testing, nevertheless his partaking of the tree of life was reserved for an appropriate future time and purpose.

It was not life of the kind or at the level bestowed on man in creation that was signified by the tree of life but life consummated through eschatological transformation. This is intimated by the identity of the tree as a symbolic replica of the immortal Glory. It is also indicated by the relationship of the tree of life to the probation, particularly to the outcome of the probation. This tree is introduced in the narrative in conjunction with the tree of probationary testing, whose location in the midst of the garden it shared (Gen 2:9); it is mentioned again in connection with the consequences of the probation in Genesis 3:22, where it is regarded as a seal of everlasting life; and subsequently in revelation in the course of redemptive history it reappears in the context of the consummated glory of the restored paradise of God (Rev 2:7; cf. Ezek 47:7,12; Rev 22:2).

No mere endless existence was signified by this arboreal sign of the promised blessing of the covenant. Unending existence is a feature of the curse as well as of the blessing sanction. One thinks of how the fate of the wicked raised up to endless life in the lake of fire is called the second death (Rev 20:13-15; 21:8). Eternal life properly so called, the life signified by the tree of life, is life as confirmed and ultimately perfected in man's glory-likeness to God, life in the fellowship of God's Presence. Access to the tree of life and its fruit is only in the holy place where the Glory-Spirit dwells; to be driven from there is to be placed under judgment of death. Here again it is relevant to recall the identity of the tree of life as an earthly symbolic replica of the immortal Glory. Consummation of man's life and God-likeness, like their creation, is of God, the Alpha and Omega Glory-Spirit.

Clearly sounded through the blessing sanction was the call to covenant-keeping whereby man might maintain his enjoyment of the presence of God and so of his access to the symbol and the reality of eternal life. Piety and total prosperity were united in the creational order. More than that, the fullness of life, the true *summum bonum*, consisted in the religious life, the union and communion of man with God, the Source of life. This truth appears in redemptive history in Jesus' identification of himself as the resurrection and life of his people. Those united to him never die (John 11:26). That which is called death, and for others is death, is "the first resurrection" for believers, whom dying unites more closely to Jesus so that they live and reign with and in him (Rev 20:5,6). And the prologue of John's Gospel tells us that this redemptive identity and function of the Son of God stands in continuity with what was already true of him as the Logos in the beginning. "In him was life; and the life was the light of men" (John 1:4). The tree of life was, in a figure, the Logos, the life of man.

God the Logos as well as God the Spirit was revealed in the theophanic Glory in Eden. Theophany is necessarily trinitarian. He that has seen the Son has seen the Father, and similarly in beholding the Glory-Spirit man also beheld the Logos-Son. If then the trees in the garden were an earthly replication of the theophanic Glory, they were symbols of the Son as well as of the Spirit. In that the trees, while representing the Glory, also made that Glory available to man, both revealing and communicating the Glory to man, they gave particular expression to the mediatorial function of the Son. What is said of the redemptive office of the incarnate Logos in the Gospel of John includes counterparts to the aspects of the divine Glory represented by both of the trees. These two features of the divine Glory are brought together in the discourse of Jesus recorded in John 5. There he affirms that the Father has given all judgment to the Son to be executed by him (vv. 22,27). The Father has also given to the Son to have life in himself and to give it to whom he will (vv. 21,36). In the coming hour of the resurrection of life and the resurrection of judgment, this dual mission of the Son will be consummated in a judicial separation of good and evil (v. 29). The Son's authority to execute judgment corresponds to the judicial glory of God represented by the tree of the knowledge of good and evil and delegated through that tree to God's image-bearer, the son of man (cf. John 5:27). The Son's power to speak the vivifying word of eternal life to men (John 5:24) is a redemptive (resurrection) counterpart to the glory of "the Logos of life" who was with the Father in the beginning (1 John 1:1,2) in his capacity as the life of man, and that was the reality symbolically represented by the tree of life. Placing the tree of life before man in the garden sanctuary, the Creator-Logos invited man, coming in the worthiness of a keeper of the covenant, to partake of the sacramental fruit: "Take, eat; this is my life, offered to you."

3. Consummation of Glory

Bestowal of the proferred blessings of the covenant would occur over a lengthy span of history, including an extended semi-eschatological stage before the coming of the fully eschatological state of glory.

Obedience with respect to the tree of knowledge would qualify man to avail himself of the invitation of the Logos-Life to partake of the sacramental tree of life. By that sacramental communion he would be confirmed in the beatitude of the covenant; the promise of glorified life would be sealed unto him. He would experience Sabbath rest in the sense that he would be placed beyond the onus of probation; established by the Spirit in indefectible righteousness and holiness, no longer subject to a fall into sin and exposure to the covenant curse; and confirmed as the heir of the full-orbed, luminous glory of the *imago Dei*.

While the ethical glory of the *imago Dei* would at once be confirmed forever, the perfecting of the glory of dominion and the transfiguring realization of the physical glory would not be realized immediately. Though there would be at once a sabbatical fulfillment of rest from probationary work, entrance into the Sabbath as rest from and completion of the cultural commission of the covenant belonged still to the future. Ultimate attainment of the consummation of glory symbolized by the covenantal signs of the Sabbath and the tree of life would have been made secure but the actual consummation would await man's passage through a semi-eschatological stage of history devoted to the fulfilling of the assigned historical task of building the kingdom-city by filling and subduing the earth. Successful probation would have launched man on his way to the glorious destiny of God's Sabbath, but there was still the journey of the workdays to be traveled before the eternal rest-day was reached. That journey would, however, have been no wilderness trek such as mankind has experienced in the fallen world. A better image of the history leading to the assured eschatological goal would be that of the expansion of the settled community within the promised land, secure under the protection of the God of all the earth. It would be a history of the development of the holy kingdom from its original focus at the mountain of God in Eden to the global fullness mandated in the cultural commission of the covenant.

During this preconsummation earthly history the weekly Sabbath sign would point the way, indicating that the six days of genealogical-cultural work would eventually come to an end and man would enter with joy into the eternal seventh day of the Creator's Sabbath. The eternal state itself, when it was attained, would not of course be a mere perpetuation of man's original beatitude. In fact, the latter would, as we have noted, be no blessing at all in view of the eschatological hope instilled in man's heart as image of God and in view of the kingdom-program assigned to man with its ultimate objective of constructing the cosmic-human temple-city. In its ultimate form the covenant blessing must comprise the full actualization of the dominion that belonged to man as image of the Glory-Spirit, the dominion formulated as the objective of man's royal cultural commission.

According to the promise made to man in his endowment with likeness to the One revealed in theophanic Light, physical glorification was also contemplated in the blessing sanction. Here, and in our entire attempt to portray the heavenly hope of the covenant, disclosures of the eternal state provided in the biblical revelation of the consummation of redemptive history help us draw out the eschatological prospects that were intrinsic to the *imago Dei* and were signified by the Sabbath and tree of life. Caution is called for in exploiting this analogy because features peculiar to God's redemptive response to man's Fall are taken up into the nature of the heaven to which Christ brings his church. Nevertheless, the biblical identification of Jesus as the second Adam guarantees that his redemptive achievement fits into the basic eschatological framework that informed the covenant with the first Adam. Indeed, Christ's work is explicitly expounded by the Scriptures as a re-creation and perfecting of the *imago Dei* and as a bringing of his people into their Sabbath rest in the land of access to the tree of life. Hence, we may properly resort to the analogy of the eschatological glorification of Christ's redeemed people. They are assured that their present earthly bodies, designed for genealogical history, will be transformed into spiritual bodies suited for a state of existence in which earthly marriage has no place. This physical transformation belongs to the re-creation of the new mankind in the image of the incarnate Glory, the Light of man. By this analogy we can more readily perceive that the prospect of ultimate glorification was implicit in the nature of the first Adam as image of the theophanic Glory. Moreover, apart from such glorification the assigned objective of the cultural commission of the covenant could not be fully achieved. In postlapsarian history man's advancing technological control over his world is such that at the pinnacle of his lordship over nature man is thoroughly dependent on the culture he has produced; he is the servant of his machines. Even in a sinless world the ultimate in natural human achievement of mastery of the environment must leave man dependent on external technological contrivances for the very preservation of his life, not least in those situations, like the depths of the sea and space, to which his more advanced science would eventually bring him. Only through personal glorification could man be exalted to the royal freedom of access to the totality of his cosmic environment without the limitations of the hampering assistance of his technology. By glorification alone is the cosmos opened to man as a realm to be entered in joyous liberty in the unencumbered integrity of his own physical capabilities (cf. Heb 2:7-9a). And beyond the visible dimensions of the cosmos there is the heavenly dimension, a realm invisible to man in his normal present state. Certainly, glorification is necessary to unveil and open that realm of consummated glory to man's eternal enjoyment.

Heaven is not a human achievement; it is not the end-product of human culture. God created it in the beginning (Gen 1:1) and it requires a supernatural act of God to bring man into participation in the reality of heaven. The consummation of human earth history consists in the removal of man's limitation to the earthly. Or, positively, it consists in the transformation of man's perceptive capability and total experiential capacity with respect to the cosmos whereby he can apprehend the heavenly dimension(s) and particularly that epiphanic Glory, which, filling all, gives to the whole, from the perspective of human history, the character of a new heavens and earth. Glorification, by which man enters this Sabbath realm of glory, is as much a supernatural act of God as the original act of man's creation. Man's own historical cultural enterprise could take him only so far toward gaining a maximal creaturely mastery of the world. Only by an eschatological injection of divine creative power does man move past the days of his cultural working and come to the Sabbath enthronement in which his dominion over the world, under God, is perfected.

At the consummation man leaves behind the external culture he has developed through his earthly history. He then has no further need for the instruments he has devised to protect himself from whatever in nature has been inhospitable or to extend his influence over the world or to enhance the splendor of his person. Glorification has made all of this superfluous. Clothed in the luminosity of his transfigured nature, man has no need for his former man-made garments whether for beauty or protection, nor for the cultural extensions of clothing in the earthly architecture of the city. This divine investiture of men with the glory-light which is the perfecting of the *imago Dei* makes obsolete the fashions of human culture. Such too is the enduement of the glorified nature with the Spirit of power and knowledge that man has no need for his former cultural aids for the processing of information, communication and transportation. Man's external culture was intended to serve only a provisional purpose during man's preconsummation history. It was merely a temporary substitute for glorification, the real and permanent thing.

If we think of culture in terms not of things external to man but of culture's central product, the family of mankind itself, then there is a continuity of that which is produced during the historical process and that which is found in the eternal state. But the human contribution made in this multiplicative cultivation of the original earthly human couple into the maturity of the foreordained heavenly mankind would be that simply of secondary agency. And in the final episode of this cultural process, as in the first act of the creation of man, man would not be an active agent at even a secondary level. Glorification is the work of God. Glorified mankind is the divine culture, the metaculture beyond human culture.

Typological terminology may be applied to this relationship; historical human culture is prototype and the divine heavenly-glorified culture is antitype. We should remember too that the Glory-Spirit stands at the beginning of history as the archetype of all created glory. Scripture endorses such typological analysis by portraying the heavenly goal of redemptive history after the model of the cultural preformations of earthly history. Glorified mankind is depicted as the city of God, the fullness of the new heaven and earth, the ultimate realization of the cultural mandate. Prototypal culture performs its necessary function, then passes away at the advent of the heavenly antitype culture, which is not just a top-story superimposed on the earth-founded prototype but an eschatologically new reality through and through. And this metaculture, which renders all prototypes obsolete, comes down from heaven, from God, its Architect-Creator.

New Jerusalem is the name of the metaculture in biblical prophecy. The city of God at the goal of the redemptive process bears the distinctive impress of the specifically redemptive history that has led to it. Specifically, the antitype at the consummation of the new covenant is depicted in the mode of the typological model of it that was developed under the old covenant. But stripping away the peculiarly redemptive features, we are still left with the generic image of a city in the biblical vision of the consummation. The metaculture is a metapolis. Particularly, then, when it comes to the consummate cosmos, the ultimate eschatological blessing proferred in the sanctions of the creational covenant, Metapolis may serve as its name. New Jerusalem is a specifically redemptive version of Metapolis.

In an unfallen world, cultural history would have been a tale of one city only. Starting from Eden man was to work at constructing this one universal kingdom-city. Blessed by the Great King of the city, man would have prospered in that task and eventually the extended city might have been aptly called Megapolis. But such a worldwide community of the human family would have marked the limits of the cultural potential of earthly man. God himself must perfect the promise of the covenant by transforming prototypal Megapolis into antitypal Metapolis.

Metapolis is not just an enlarged Megapolis, but a Megapolis that has undergone eschatological metamorphosis at the hands of the Omega-Spirit. Nothing of earthly culture external to man enters Metapolis. Even man himself cannot enter it as mortal flesh and blood (1 Cor 15:50). Only as the glorified handiwork of God can man pass through the gates of the eternal city. Actually, to speak of glorified men entering Metapolis is to speak with a pronounced typological accent. For Metapolis is not a city that glorified man inhabits. It is rather the case that glorified man *is* Metapolis; in the redemptive dialect, the bride of the Lamb *is* the New Jerusalem (Rev 21:9,10). In the Metapolis enterprise materiel and personnel coincide.

"Yahweh-is-there" is another name for Metapolis (Ezek 48:35; cf. Rev 21:3; 22:3). The eternal city of glorified mankind in the Spirit is a temple of God's Presence. To produce this temple-cultus was the ultimate objective of man's cultural enterprise, as we concluded from an analysis of the programmatic stipulations of the original covenant. But from our analysis of the blessing sanction of that covenant we must conclude that whatever contribution of personal materiel ("living stones") is in a secondary sense supplied by human culture, it is the Lord God, the Alpha and Omega, who creates and consummates his Spirit-temple.

Scriptures' identification of the eternal city with the glorified church (Rev 21:9,10) is accompanied by its proclamation of a new heaven and earth (Rev 21:1) and thus intends, of course, no negation of the cosmic dimension of consummated creation. In Metapolis, glorified mankind is incorporated into the archetypal Spirit-temple with which, from the epiphanic flash of the absolute beginning, the cosmos has been integrated. Hence, Metapolis is at once the people-temple and the cosmos-temple, together consummated in the Glory-temple.

B. The Threatened Curse

Blessing belonged properly to the creational covenant. In its created condition that covenantal order was one of beatitude and the eschatological perfecting of that beatitude was its proper goal. Nevertheless, a threat of curse was included within the total disclosure of the terms of this covenant. "But of the tree of the knowledge of good and evil you shall not eat, for in the day that you eat thereof you will surely die" (Gen 2:17).

Something of the form of this death specter might be descried by way of analogy in the phenomena of death in the subhuman creation. We have suggested above that this was one of the nature parables the Creator had made available by which his spoken revelation might be illustrated. What was threatened in the curse could be ascertained in more of its human particularity, however, by way of antithesis to what was revealed in the promised blessing sanction. Death was failure to realize the eschatological potential of the *imago Dei* and the loss of all the glory of the divine likeness, ethical and regal, already bestowed in the creation of man. It was frustration of the hope of completion of man's historical mission beaconed by the covenant sign of the Sabbath. It was the denial of the consummation of life that was proferred in the tree of life. It was the loss of all these things, and it was their opposite.

The curse was the reversal of man's original and proper relationship to the world. He who should have exercised dominion over all the earth would be humiliated and tormented by the world. Instead of becoming a realm of cosmic freedom and luminous fulfillment, man's world would be turned into a prison of diabolical darkness, the very lake of fire prepared for the devil and his angels, as it is known to us from subsequent biblical revelation, which names it "the second death." It is to be observed that this "second death" does not involve what we know as physical death but on the contrary is something experienced by the wicked after they have been raised from the grave in the resurrection of damnation. Accordingly, the disembodied state we commonly identify as death was not contemplated in what was threatened in the curse sanction of Genesis 2:17. In fact, apart from the intervention of the program of redemption after the Fall, death as physical disembodiment would have served no necessary historical function. Death of that (mitigated) sort is the form that death assumes only as part of the common curse with which God afflicts fallen mankind while the judgment of the lake of fire is delayed during the time that the foreordained salvation-history is introduced and runs its course. Once this kind of death exists as a first kind of death experience for fallen mankind, the death-curse of the lake of wrath, which in the beginning would have been simply "death," comes to be distinguished as a "second" death.

Just as our analysis of the covenant blessing led to an exploration of the eschatological concept of heaven, so our analysis of the covenant curse turns out to be a matter of delineating the nature of hell. These are the primal subjects of biblical prophecy.

The severity of the curse answered to the gravity of the offense of covenant-breaking. In the ancient international treaties the terrible retaliation threatened in the curse sanction against the offending vassal had its rationale in the fact that the vassal's disloyalty to the suzerain was also an act of defiance against the gods by whom the covenant oath had been sworn. Closely associated with the curses in the treaty was a section in which the gods of the oath, individually named in long array, were invoked to witness the covenant ratification and so assume their role as supervisors and, in case of violations, as avengers of the covenant. With such surveillance no transgression of the stipulations could go undetected and, since any such offense constituted an impious challenge to the gods, it was not only foolhardy but deserving of the total destruction detailed in the curse sanctions. Under the Creator's covenant with Adam the character of covenant-breaking as a sin against deity was directly entailed in the divine nature of the Lord of the covenant himself. Disloyalty to the covenant

Lord was in itself disruption of the religious relationship and it is in terms of this alienation of man from his God that the curse sanction of death is, in the last analysis, to be perceived.

God's Glory-Presence was the executor of both the dual sanctions. Thus, in Israel's exodus history, the same Glory that functioned to bless Israel was the divine Agent to inflict God's curse on the Egyptians. The Glory-cloud was a protective shade to one, a bewildering darkness to the other. The Glory-fire was a guiding light to one, but to the other a blinding, consuming blaze. So it was from the beginning. The Spirit-Presence was the holy Sanctifier who made the garden a sanctuary. As Sanctifier he enforced the sanctions that maintained the holiness of God's house. Man's blessedness, his life, consisted in the Spirit's sanctifying him, fashioning him in the likeness of the Spirit, so that he might abide in joy before God's Face lifted up over him in holy beauty and in the benediction of peace. The curse would consist in the putting of another visage on the Presence-Face. Death would be the wrathful glare of the Glory that makes intolerable to those on whom it is directed the presence of the holy Glory-Spirit, the Breath of life.

It was then not simply that the punishment threatened in the covenant would be commensurate with the crime; the curse would take its shape from the nature of the offense. In sinning man would contradict the norm of the imitation of God, despise his likeness to the Spirit, repudiate the Face of Glory. The curse of death would deliver the sinner over to his hatred of the Glory-beauty of God, the hatred that makes him turn away from God's Face and separate himself from it. But to be thus separated from the vivifying-glorifying Spirit is to be cut off from participation in the divine Glory-likeness. And in the eyes of God, for creatures whom he has made in his image, men and angels alike, to lose the glory of the *imago Dei* is to perish.

II. PROBATION

A. The Probation Tree

In its original form as produced through creation the covenant order was already one of beatitude, but, as previously observed, this covenant contained the proposal of a special grant to man, the servant-son, for loyal service to his Lord. It offered an eschatological advance in kingdom glory conditioned on man's obedience.

If the Lord of the covenant were to fulfill his offer of confirming his servant in a state of blessedness, if man's entrance into the promised Sabbath were not to be delayed forever, the testing of man's obedience could not be endlessly prolonged. The arrangement could not be one of permanent conditionality. The testing must have temporal limits; that is, it must be a probation. And that being the nature of the necessity of the probation, its proper purpose was clearly not to put man in jeopardy of losing his beatitude but to bring him on the way to its consummation.

Another factor was present in the divine ordering of the covenant that required that the days of man's probation be shortened. This factor was the governmental principle of federal representation. Mankind was to undergo probation as a corporate whole represented by the first Adam, rather than on an individual basis. But the proliferation of responsible covenant servants before the issue of the probation had been settled would conflict with the operation of this principle of federal representation. The Lord, therefore, arranged that the probationary issue should be settled prior to such a development by bringing the test of Adam's obedience to a point of crisis where a prompt, decisive response was unavoidable. In view of the momentous consequences of the probation for all humanity, it was in any case a desideratum that the crucial testing should probe man's covenantal commitment at its most radical depths.

Two measures were introduced by the Lord to achieve this intensification of the probationary process. One was to add to the general obligations of the covenant a special proscription (Gen 2:16,17). If we call this the probationary stipulation, our intention is not to suggest that man's covenantal obligations and testing were reduced to this one requirement, but simply to indicate that this stipulation had a special function to perform in bringing the probation into concentrated focus for a radical decision. The second measure was to subject man to a direct satanic solicitation to disobedience. The two measures were not unrelated. Indeed, it is through an appreciation of their relationship to one another that we can best apprehend the meaning of the probation tree and the significance of Satan's role in the probation episode, and thus the nature of the probationary assignment.

Both in its form and substance the special probationary proscription was exceptional within the law of the covenant. Whereas the other stipulations were framed positively and set man forward on his cultural-cultic journey, the negative form of the special stipulation confronted man with a limitation on his way which he must not transgress. In its substance, this proscription introduced an exception into the pattern of consecration by which God had interpreted the world and man's place in it. Man's investment with dominion over the earth, according to which all earth's hosts were consigned to his use, was contradicted by this prohibition. Specifically, the probationary stipulation separated one tree from the realm of plants and trees that God himself had subjected to man and had defined as "for food" (Gen 1:29,30; 2:16) and assigned it the opposite meaning: "You shall not eat of it" (Gen 2:17). The prohibition removed the eating of the fruit of this tree from the category of good or lawful and sovereignly reclassified that act as unlawful.

In the probation tree man found himself face to face with the claims of absolute lordship. Restricting man in the exercise of his royal authority and privileges, the probationary commandment compelled him to acknowledge that his own kingship was that of a vassal-king, that the world was his only in stewardship. It demanded that in the naming-interpretive task, the wise man role that was ancillary to man's kingship, he must follow without question the direction of the Logos-Creator. Even when God addressed to him an apparently arbitrary word that constituted an exceptional instance within divine revelation, man must not assume an autonomous, critical stance over against his Lord, selecting for himself a canon within the canon of God's word. He was rather held responsible to recognize the canonical word at every point, to grasp it, and submit his thought and life to all that God said. The effect of this special probationary prohibition was to confront man head-on simply and solely with God's absolute authority and thus to face him inescapably with the demand for a clear-cut confession of his sovereign Lord. And in this way the test of man's covenantal loyalty was brought to its decisive issue.

To find the significance of the probation tree we naturally begin with its name, "the tree of the knowledge (or knowing) of good and evil" (Gen 2:17). Good and evil are viewed in this designation of the tree as opposites between which a choice is to be made (the usual usage where this pair is found in the Bible), not as an antonymic pair indicative of a totality (as is sometimes the case in ancient literature). Repeatedly in biblical usage the good-evil pair appears in the context of references to the ability to discern between things and especially to exercise a legal-judicial kind of discrimination (cf. Mic 3:1,2). The references are largely to the rendering of verdicts. "Good" and "evil" may at times even be legal terms used in pronouncing judgments (cf., e.g., Isa 5:20,23; Mal 2:17). In clear allusion to the probation tree, God identifies man's knowing of good and evil as an aspect of his likeness to God and angels (Gen 3:22). The same connection is recognized in Satan's perverse suggestion (Gen 3:5). Now, as we have previously observed, when the discerning of good and evil is elsewhere noted as a mark of likeness to God and his Angel or of the possession of God-like wisdom, the reference is precisely to a king engaged in rendering judicial decisions (2 Sam 14:17; 1 Kgs 3:9,28). The probation tree was the judgment tree.

God-like judicial prerogative was signified by the name of the probation tree and in the course of the probation this tree would be instrumental in man's exercise of the royal-priestly function of rendering judgment, the function inherent in his status as image of God. It would be by the appearance of the satanic agent at this judgment tree in the garden of God that man would find himself compelled to discern in judicial act between good and evil. Here man as priestly guardian of the sanctuary would be called upon to enforce the demands of God's exclusive holiness against the unholy intruder. It might seem strange that this tree should simultaneously signify something to do as well as something not to do, that along with the prohibition against partaking of its fruit it should also present the positive obligation to perform the work of judgment expressed in its name as the tree of the knowing of good and evil. Perhaps the explanation of this combination is in part that precisely when man was being exalted to the high authority implied in the requirement to pronounce judgment on heavenly beings it was opportune to remind him, as the prohibition compellingly did, of his subordination to the ultimate and absolute authority of God.

In the event, the negative and positive aspects of the probation tree would come together as the evil one centered attention in the encounter which transpired at the site of the tree on the prohibition concerning it. Refraining from the forbidden fruit and performing of the holy judicial function against the tempter were thus intertwined. It appears, then, that the name of the tree pointed not so much to something man would acquire as to something he must do. It referred not to knowledge of a certain kind that he might gain, but to knowledge in action, knowledge engaged in pronouncing judgment. At the same time this tree would be instrumental in an acquisition man would make. For by doing what was signified by the name of the judgment tree, man would advance in the glory of his judicial likeness to the Lord of the heavenly council. (According to Gen 3:22, in a formal sense this regal dimension of man's likeness to God came to intensified expression even when he rendered a false verdict). Thus, this tree would, like the tree of life, be instrumental in man's maturing participation in the *imago Dei*.

In the judicial encounter with Satan at the tree of judgment man was obliged to come to a crucial decision as to his own ultimate personal loyalty by committing himself to the side of good or evil in the conflict between God and Satan. And his choice between good and evil in the form of opposing covenant suzerains constituted a choice of good or evil in the sense of blessing or curse, life or death, for man himself. The tree of the knowing of good and evil was indeed the probation tree. By this tree it would be determined whether man, by faithfully fighting the Lord's battle in the war against Satan, should receive from his Sovereign approbation and the proposed grant of the kingdom. The whole covenant order ought not to be reduced to this one feature of the probation tree and the requirements centering in it as though this were the sum and total substance of the covenant. But the outcome of the probation crisis at the tree of judgment was decisive for the future of the entire covenant order. It was the hinge on which everything turned.

B. Covenant of Works

A principle of works – do this and live – governed the attainment of the consummation-kingdom proferred in the blessing sanction of the creational covenant. Heaven must be earned. According to the terms stipulated by the Creator it would be on the ground of man's faithful completion of the work of probation that he would be entitled to enter the Sabbath rest. If Adam obediently performed the assignment signified by the probation tree, he would receive, as a matter of pure and simple justice, the reward symbolized by the tree of life. That is, successful probation would be meritorious. With good reason then covenant theology has identified this probation arrangement as a covenant of works, thereby setting it in sharp contrast to the Covenant of Grace.

This standard Reformed analysis of the covenants with its sharp law-gospel contrast has come under attack from various theological quarters, including of late the broadly Reformed community. Indeed, it has been contended that in bestowing the blessings of his kingdom God has never dealt with man on the basis of law (i.e., the principle of works as the opposite of grace). Paternal love informs all such transactions and, so the argument runs, that fatherly beneficence is not compatible with the legal-commercial notion of reward for meritorious works, of benefits granted as a matter of justice. Appeal is made to the fact that man as a creature is an unprofitable servant even when he has done all that has been required of him in the stewardship of God's gifts. Or, stating it from the reverse side, man cannot possibly add to the riches of his Lord's glory for God is eternally all-glorious; everything belongs to the Creator. Hence, the conclusion is drawn that in the covenant relationship we must reckon everywhere with the presence of a principle of "grace" and, therefore, we may never speak of meritorious works. The rhetoric of this argument has gone to the extreme of asserting that to entertain the idea that the obedience of man (even sinless man) might serve as the meritorious ground for receiving the promised kingdom blessings is to be guilty of devilish pride, of sin at its diabolical worst. With respect to the over-all structuring of covenant theology, once grace is attributed to the original covenant with Adam, preredemptive and redemptive covenants cease to be characterized by contrasting governmental principles in the bestowal of the kingdom on mankind. Instead, some sort of continuum obtains. A combined demand-and-promise (which is thought somehow to qualify as grace but not as works) is seen as the common denominator in this alleged new unity of all covenants. (The following discussion of this radical departure from the classic law-gospel contrast reflects my studies "Of Works and Grace," *Presbyterion* 9 (1983) 85-92 and "Covenant Theology Under Attack," *New Horizons* 15/2 (1994) 3-5, critiques of the teachings of the Daniel P. Fuller-John Piper-Norman Shepherd school.)

Contrary to the sweeping denial of the operation of the works principle anywhere in the divine government, the biblical evidence compels us to recognize that God has in fact employed that principle. Indeed, the principle of works forms the foundation of the gospel of grace. If meritorious works could not be predicated of Jesus Christ as second Adam, then obviously there would be no meritorious achievement to be imputed to his people as the ground of their justification-approbation. The gospel invitation would turn out to be a mirage. We who have believed on Christ would still be under condemnation. The gospel truth, however, is that Christ has performed the one act of righteousness and by this obedience of the one the many are made righteous (Rom 5:18,19). In his probationary obedience the Redeemer gained the merit which is transferred to the account of the elect. Underlying Christ's mediatorship of a covenant of grace for the salvation of believers is his earthly fulfillment, through meritorious obedience, of his heavenly covenant of works with the Father.

Since the works principle is thus foundational to the gospel, the repudiation of that principle – in particular, the denial of the possibility of meritorious works where paternal love is involved (as it certainly is in the relation of the Father and the Son) – stands condemned as subversive of that gospel. What begins as a rejection of works ends up as an attack, however unintentional, on the biblical message of saving grace. Moreover, in the attributing of diabolical pride to the one who thinks to do something deserving of the reward of the kingdom glory there is, in effect, a blasphemous assault on the religious integrity of Jesus himself. For Jesus, the second Adam, regarded his works as meritorious. He claimed for himself the Father's glory on the basis of his having glorified the Father (John 17:4,5; cf. Phil 2:8,9). Here in the relation of Jesus with the Father, where we encounter pure religion and undefiled, the holy validity of the works principle receives divine imprimatur.

Also contradicting the contention that no divine covenants have ever been governed by the works principle is the irrefutable biblical evidence that the Mosaic economy, while an administration of grace on its fundamental level of concern with the eternal salvation of the individual, was at the same time on its temporary, typological kingdom level informed by the principle of works. Thus, for example, the apostle Paul in Romans 10:4ff. and Galatians 3:10ff. (cf. Rom 9:32) contrasts the old order of the law with the gospel order of grace and faith, identifying the old covenant as one of bondage, condemnation, and death (cf. 2 Cor 3:6-9; Gal 4:24-26). The old covenant was law, the opposite of grace-faith, and in the postlapsarian world that meant it would turn out to be an administration of condemnation as a consequence of sinful Israel's failure to maintain the necessary meritorious obedience. Had the old typological kingdom been secured by sovereign grace in Christ, Israel would not have lost her national election. A satisfactory explanation of Israel's fall demands works, not grace, as the controlling administrative principle. (See further discussion below.)

According to ample and plain biblical testimony, God has dealt with man on the basis of the works principle in covenantal arrangements within even redemptive history, and these arrangements of God the Father with God the Son and with his son Israel have been at the same time expressions of the most intense paternal love. Manifestly, paternal love and the legal justice of the works principle are not mutually exclusive but entirely compatible. The revulsion felt at the concept of meritorious works in divine-human relationship by those who reject meritorious human works in the avowed interests of making room for divine love is not attuned to the teaching and spirit of the Scriptures. In particular, it is inimical to a Scriptural theology of the Cross. We are obliged by the biblical facts to define works and justice in such a way that we can apply both the legal-commercial and family-paternal models to explicate the same covenants.

From the presence of the works principle in these other divine covenants it is clear that there can be no a priori objection to the standard view of the original Edenic order as a covenant of works. Moreover, the works-covenants already adduced are so related to God's covenant with mankind in Adam as to demonstrate the works character of the latter. This is particularly clear in the case of the works-covenant of the Father with the Son as second Adam. Correspondence in God's dealings with the two Adams is required by the very analogy that Scripture posits in its interpretation of the mission of Christ as a second Adam, succeeding where the first Adam failed. Adam, like Christ, must have been placed under a covenant of works.

Likewise, the identification of God's old covenant with Israel as one of works points to the works nature of the creational covenant. Here we can only state a conclusion that study of the biblical evidence would substantiate, but the significant point is that the old covenant with Israel, though it was something more, was also a re-enactment (with necessary adjustments) of mankind's primal probation – and fall. It was as the true Israel, born under the law, that Christ was the second Adam. This means that the covenant with the first Adam, like the typological Israelite re-enactment of it, would have been a covenant of law in the sense of works, the antithesis of the grace-promise-faith principle.

In the introduction to this discussion we mentioned factors which, according to those who reject the Covenant of Works concept, make it impossible that man could merit reward and compel us to attribute whatever blessings he enjoys to divine grace. Among the factors appealed to were some that obtained from the very beginning of man's existence, and before it. There was the nature of God, the eternal Creator, all glorious, all sovereign; the very thought of his further enrichment from any outside source is inconceivable. And corollary thereto was man's nature as a creature and the unprofitable character of the service that he might render, even when he had done his utmost.

Since these factors are always present in the religious relationship, they would – if they were valid arguments against the works principle – not only prove the creation covenant was not a covenant of works but negate the possibility of a covenant of works anywhere else. Therefore, the biblical teaching that there actually have been covenants of works shows that these factors do not in fact negate the operation of the works principle nor demonstrate the presence of its opposite, grace; no more so in the creational covenant than they do elsewhere.

Furthermore, though Adam could not enrich God by adding to his glory, it was nevertheless precisely the purpose of man's existence to glorify God, which he does when he responds in obedience to the revelation of God's will. And according to the revelation of covenantal justice, God performs justice and man receives his proper desert when God glorifies the man who glorifies him.

To be so rewarded is not an occasion for man to glory in himself against God. On the contrary, a doxological glorying in God in recognition of the Creator's sovereign goodness will become the Lord's creature-servants. But if our concepts of justice and grace are biblical we will not attribute the promised reward of the creation covenant to divine grace. We will rather regard it as a just recompense to a meritorious servant, for justice requires that man receive the promised good in return for his doing the demanded good. Indeed, if we do not analyze the situation abstractly but in accordance with the created, covenantal reality as God actually constituted it, we will see that to give a faithful Adam anything less than the promised reward would have been to render him evil for good. For we will appreciate the fact that man's hope of realizing the state of glorification and of attaining to the Sabbath-consummation belonged to him by virtue of his very nature as created in the image of the God of glory. This expectation was an in-created earnest of fullness, to be denied which would have frustrated him to the depths of his spirit's longing for God and God-likeness. Whatever he might have been granted short of that for his obedience would be no blessing at all, but a curse.

According to God's creational ordering it is a necessary and inevitable sequence, in preredemptive covenant as well as in redemptive history, that "whom he justified, him he also glorified" (Rom 8:30). Within the framework of this judicial-eschatological bonding of glorification to justification, once it has been determined on what principle justification operates under a given covenant, the principle governing the grant of eschatological blessings in that covenant has also been determined. If justification is by grace through faith, as it is under the gospel, glorification will not be by works. And if justification-approbation is secured on the grounds of works, as it clearly is in the preredemptive covenant, glorification will not be by grace. Bestowal of the reward contemplated in the creational covenant was a matter of works; it was an aspect of God's creational love, but it was not a matter of grace.

By clarifying the biblical-theological concept of grace we may further expose the fallacy of those who would inject the idea of grace into the analysis of the creational covenant, thereby clouding and indeed contradicting the meritorious character of the probationary obedience and the works-justice nature of the covenant. Grace lives and moves and has its being in a legal, forensic environment. In the biblical proclamation of the gospel, grace is the antithesis of the works principle. Grace and works could thus be contrastively compared only if they were comparable, that is, only if the term grace, like works, functioned in a forensic context. Grace does not exist then except in relation to the rendering of divine judgment on situations involving acts of human responsibility, acts of man as accountable to God for compliance with appointed duty.

Divine judgment may be by the principle of works or of grace but in either case the standard by which man is measured in the great assize is covenant law. In a judgment according to works, blessing rewards meritorious obedience and curse punishes the transgressor. In a judgment by the principle of grace, blessing is bestowed in the face of violation of stipulated moral-religious duty, in spite of the presence of *demerit*. (Divine justice will, of course, be satisfied whether it be a judgment of works or of grace.)

The distinctive meaning of grace in its biblical-theological usage is a divine response of favor and blessing in the face of human violation of obligation.

Gospel grace takes account of man in his responsibility under the demands of the covenant and specifically as a covenant breaker, a sinner against covenant law. Accordingly, the grace of Christ comes to expression in his active and passive obedience, together constituting a vicarious satisfaction for the obligations and liabilities of his people, who through failure and transgression are debtors before the covenant Lord, the Judge of all the earth. Gospel grace emerges in a forensic framework as a response of mercy to demerit.

Theologically it is of the greatest importance to recognize that the idea of demerit is an essential element in the definition of grace. In its proper theological sense as the opposite of law-works, grace is more than unmerited favor. That is, divine grace directs itself not merely to the absence of merit but to the presence of demerit. It addresses and overcomes violation of divine commandment. It is a granting of blessing, as an act of mercy, in spite of previous covenant breaking by which man has forfeited all claims to participation in the kingdom and has incurred God's disfavor and righteous wrath. It bestows the good offered in the covenant's blessing sanctions rather than the evil of the threatened curse even though man has done evil rather than good in terms of the covenant stipulations.

Because grace cannot be defined apart from this context of covenantal stipulations and sanctions and is specifically a response of mercy to demerit, it must be carefully distinguished from divine love or beneficence. For God's love, though it may find expression in gospel grace, is also expressed in the bestowal of good apart altogether from considerations of the merits of man's response to covenantal responsibility. Such is the goodness or benevolence of God displayed in the act of creation. This marvelous manifestation of love seen in God's creational endowment of man with glory and honor had nothing to do with human merit. Without prior existence, man was obviously without merit-rating one way or the other when the Lord creatively assigned him his particular ontological status, with its present good and eschatological potential.

We might speak of this creational act of love as unmerited, but it would be better to avoid that term. It is an abstraction whose use, whether for God's creational goodness or redemptive mercy is liable to considerable theological confusion. In the only situation where merit enters the picture (that is, in connection with human response to divine demand) there is either merit or demerit. In this situation of accountable response to covenant duty obedience brings merit and failure to perform the probationary task incurs demerit. There is either merit or demerit, but no "unmerit." Unmerited is not, therefore, a proper description of the blessings bestowed against an historical background of (unsatisfactory) exercise of covenant responsibility. And to speak of the goodness of God shown in the act of creation as unmerited is not apropros since there can be no thought of merit at all in that context.

Unfortunately, however, gospel grace has been commonly defined by the term unmerited. Then, when unmerited is also used for the divine benevolence in creation an illusion of similarity, if not identity, is produced. As a result the term grace gets applied to God's creational goodness. And the mischief culminates in the argument that since "grace" is built into the human situation at the outset, the covenant that ordered man's existence could not be a covenant of works, for works is the opposite of grace. If we appreciate the forensic distinctiveness of grace we will not thus confuse the specific concept of (soteriological) grace with the beneficence expressed in the creational endowment of man with his ontological dignity. We will perceive that God's creational manifestation of goodness was an act of divine love, but not of grace. And we have seen that the presence of paternal love in a covenantal arrangement is no impediment to its being a covenant of works.

Another form of the attack on the Covenant of Works doctrine (and thus on the classic law-gospel contrast) asserts that even if it is allowed that Adam's obedience would have earned something, the disproportion between the value of that act of service and the value of the preferred blessing forbids us to speak here of simple equity or justice. The contention is that Adam's ontological status limited the value or weight of his acts. More specifically his act of obedience would not have eternal value or significance; it could not earn a reward of eternal, confirmed life. In the offer of eternal life, so we are told, we must therefore recognize an element of "grace" in the preredemptive covenant. But belying this assessment of the situation is the fact that if it were true that Adam's act of obedience could not have eternal significance then neither could or did his actual act of disobedience have eternal significance. It did not deserve the punishment of everlasting death. Consistency would compel us to judge God guilty of imposing punishment beyond the demands of justice, pure and simple. God would have to be charged with injustice in inflicting the punishment of Hell, particularly when he exacted that punishment from his Son as the substitute for sinners. The Cross would be the ultimate act of divine injustice. That is the theologically disastrous outcome of blurring the works-grace contrast by appealing to a supposed disproportionality between work and reward.

The disproportionality view's failure with respect to the doctrine of divine justice can be traced to its approach to the definition of justice. A proper approach will hold that God is just and his justice is expressed in all his acts; in particular, it is expressed in the covenant he institutes. The terms of the covenant – the stipulated reward for the stipulated service – are a revelation of that justice. As a revelation of God's justice the terms of the covenant define justice. According to this definition, Adam's obedience would have merited the reward of eternal life and not a gram of grace would have been involved.

Refusing to accept God's covenant word as the definer of justice, the disproportionality view exalts above God's word a standard of justice of its own making. Assigning ontological values to Adam's obedience and God's reward it finds that weighed on its judicial scales they are drastically out of balance. In effect that conclusion imputes an imperfection in justice to the Lord of the covenant. The attempt to hide this affront against the majesty of the Judge of all the earth by condescending to assess the relation of Adam's act to God's reward as one of congruent merit is no more successful than Adam's attempt to manufacture a covering to conceal his nakedness. It succeeds only in exposing the roots of this opposition to Reformed theology in the theology of Rome.

The drift toward Rome is evidenced by the fruits as well as the roots of the views that repudiate the idea of merit and the law-gospel contrast. For blurring the concepts of works and grace in the doctrine of the covenants will inevitably involve the blurring of works and faith in the doctrine of justification and thus the subversion of the Reformation message of justification by faith alone.

Of a piece with the specific teaching that God's dealings with mankind in Adam were on the basis of the forensic principle of works-justice is the general biblical teaching that the rewarding of obedience and punishing of disobedience are foundational to God's government of the world, an expression of the nature of God as just. In the divine juridical order one's eschatological harvest is what he has sown as the Lord renders to every man according to his works (Rom 2:6-10; Gal 6:7). This law of recompense is positive as well as negative, for the verdict of justification and praise belongs to the doers of the law (Rom 2:13,29; cf. Heb 6:10). And in its distinctive, vicarious way of grace the gospel order honors this principle too.

On the approach that mistakenly contends that the presence of God's paternal love involves grace and so negates the possibility of meritorious works and simple justice, divine justice ceases to be foundational to all divine government. A negative, punitive justice may be recognized, as in the retribution against the wicked in hell, to which paternal love does not reach. But there is no place in that view for positive justice; those who advocate it must deny that the rewarding of doers of the law with life forms the reverse side of the negative justice which punishes the breakers of the law with death. They cannot consistently confess that justice is the foundation of God's throne (Pss 89:14(15); 97:2).

Marking this view that repudiates the works principle as a radical departure from classic Reformed theology is its drastic revision of the fundamental theological construct of federal-representative probation and forensic imputation. According to the biblical data, the probationary role of the two Adams called for a performance of righteousness that was to be imputed to the account of those they represented, serving as meritorious ground for justification and inheritance of the consummate kingdom. What was in view was not merely the transmitting from the one to the many of a subjective condition of righteousness but the judicial imputation to the many of a specific accomplishment of righteousness by the federal representative. That decisive probationary accomplishment involved the obedient performance of a particular covenantal service, and accordingly it is characterized as "one act of righteousness" (Rom 5:18).

This standard doctrine of probation and imputation is obviously not compatible with the position that disavows the works principle. On that position, a declaration of justification and conveyance of eschatological blessings in consequence of a successful probation, whether of Adam or Christ, would be an exercise of grace, not of simple justice. But if there is no meritorious accomplishment possible, the rationale of the imputation arrangement in general becomes obscure, if the whole point of it is not in fact lost. In the case of the gospel, if there is no meritorious achievement of active obedience on the part of Christ to be imputed to the elect, then this cardinal doctrine of soteric justification in its historic orthodox form must be abandoned.

Our finding is that under God's covenant with mankind in Adam attainment of the eschatological kingdom and Sabbath rest was governed by a principle of works. Adam, representative of mankind, was commissioned to fulfill the probationary assignment; he must perform the one meritorious act of righteousness. This act was to have the character of a victory in battle. An encounter with Satan was a critical aspect of the probationary crisis for each of the two Adams. To enter into judicial combat against this enemy of God and to vanquish him in the name of God was the covenantal assignment that must be performed by the servant of the Lord as his "one act of righteousness." And it was the winning of this victory of righteousness by the one that would be imputed to the many as their act of righteousness and as their claim on the consummated kingdom proferred in the covenant.

We conclude then that covenant theology has been biblically sound in its traditional formulation of God's original kingdom administration in Eden as the Covenant of Works. However, it is also the case that the redemptive order, though a covenant of grace in contrast to works when viewed from the perspective of God's covenantal offer of the kingdom to men, at the same time included as a foundation under that covenant of grace a covenant of works in the form of the eternal intratrinitarian counsel envisaging the Son as second Adam.

Chapter Five

COVENANT JUDGMENT

Later in biblical history we come upon another administration of God's kingdom featuring the principle of works. In the covenant mediated through Moses at Sinai it was arranged that Israel's enjoyment of the external typological kingdom awaiting them in Canaan should be governed by the principle of law, that is, works, the opposite of the gospel principle of promise. This works principle is elaborately expounded in the book of Deuteronomy, the treaty record of the subsequent renewal of the Sinaitic Covenant, just before Israel entered the land. At the climax of that renewal ceremony, the people, reminded of the claims of Yahweh upon them and summoned to choose between good and evil, life and death, reaffirmed their allegiance to their divine Lord (Deut 29). But Israel proceeded to violate their covenant oath repeatedly throughout their generations and the books that follow Deuteronomy in the Old Testament are the documentation of that tragic history of unfaithfullness on through the days of the judges and the kings. They relate also how the curses threatened against disobedience in the Deuteronomic treaty overtook the offending nation until, as their ultimate punishment, God drove the Israelites out of their holy paradise land into exile in the east. Banishment from Canaan came as the final result of a protracted legal process which God instituted against Israel, a covenant lawsuit he conducted through his servants the prophets. Warned over and again, Israel defied the prophets until God cut them off from the place of his sanctuary and blessing. Records of ancient international treaty administration attest to this same kind of legal process in which an overlord carries out his lawsuit against rebellious vassals through the agency of special messengers.

When we turn to the historical outcome of the covenant established at creation we find much the same story as we do in the case of the Sinaitic Covenant. Genesis 3 is also a tragic record of covenant-breaking, followed by a divine lawsuit and the execution of a curse, consisting in the expulsion of man from the sanctuary-paradise of God into a state of exile east of Eden. However, in the midst of the judgment curse, unexpectedly a divine word of grace and promise is spoken and a future opens up beyond the curse. There is, therefore, an epilogue to add to our account of the creational covenant, an epilogue about a new covenant. This new redemptive covenant occupies such a commanding position in the actual historical-eschatological unfolding of the kingdom of God that rather than speaking of it as epilogue to the original covenant, it would be more appropriate to speak of the latter as its prologue.

I. THE BREAKING OF THE COVENANT

A. Advent of the Antilord

With the coming of Satan the probationary history of the primal covenant reached its crisis phase. Abruptly, the Genesis 3 record tells us of one of the creatures God had made which proceeded to speak to Eve. Only if there were exegetical grounds for taking Genesis 3 as a whole as a religious allegory would a symbolic interpretation of the serpent commend itself. But such an assessment of the chapter would be gratuitous in terms of literary canons and it is disallowed in terms of the primary principle of biblical hermeneutics, for it would contradict the understanding of Genesis 3 (and of the broader context of the early chapters of Genesis) which is reflected unambiguously and in a variety of ways elsewhere in Scripture. There may, of course, be figurative touches even in straightforward prose accounts of historical events, but unless one refuses beforehand the possibility of the supernaturalism involved in the speaking serpent there is nothing in the Genesis 3 context itself that suggests a figurative understanding of the serpent. On the contrary, the matter-of-fact introduction of the serpent comparing it to the other wild creatures God had made indicates the intent of the text plainly: this serpent was one of the real animals to be found in Eden. Also, apart from the participation of an actual serpent in the temptation the pronouncing of judgment on the tempter in terms of a serpent (vv, 14f.) would be inexplicable.

It is equally plain from the total witness of Scripture, however, that the serpent was only the instrument of the prime agent of temptation, the devil (Matt 13:38,39; Luke 10:18,19; John 8:44; Rom 16:20; 1 John 3:8; Rev 12:9). Perhaps as illuminating a parallel as any to this phenomenon is the episode of Jesus' encounter with the demons in the region of the Gadarenes. These demons spoke through the possessed men among the tombs, then took possession of the herd of pigs driving them to mad destruction in the sea (Matt 8:28ff.; Mark 5:1ff.; Luke 8:26ff.). By some such kind of demonic body-appropriating, Satan entered the garden in Eden through the intermediary agency of the serpent. Why he should choose to approach in bestial form we may not know; certainly, like the demons who begged Jesus' permission to enter the swine, Satan's options were subject to the limitations of God's sovereign permission. Genesis 3:1 does point to a characteristic of the serpent that made it a suitable choice: it was more subtle (or crafty) than the other creatures. In the serpent's sinuous movement and camouflaged form, the insinuating, stealthy guile of the tempter found striking figurative representation.

In the devil's mission of temptation the objective was to forestall the erection of the kingdom-house of God as the consummate revelation of his power and glory and, as a corollary of that, to prevent man's attainment of permanent world dominion as vicegerent of God. The objective was, in effect, to desecrate and lay desolate the holy domain of God over which man had been set as royal-priest. Satan's strategy was to contrive to activate the curse threatened in the covenant sanctions and so utilize the very power of God to accomplish the objective of reducing the cosmic sanctuary to chaotic ruin. If man could be seduced into breaking the covenant, God as offended Lord and divine Avenger of the covenant would (so Satan might assume) terminate forthwith the kingdom program entrusted to his human image-bearers. It was, therefore, the immediate purpose of the tempter to effect the estrangement of the two parties to the covenant or, more particularly, to get man to forsake his allegiance to his Creator-Lord. And to persuade man to violate the basic covenantal demand for wholehearted devotion to the Lord God, Satan exploited the focal proscription. That strangely exceptional word that God had spoken was the most vulnerable point in the stipulated arrangements for it could plausibly be so misconstrued as to cloud man's confidence in the Lord's benevolence. The arrangement God had designed in love for man's greater blessing Satan would thus pervert with a view to man's undoing. From the perspective of this evil intent of Satan, the crisis of probation took on the character of a temptation.

The significance of the encounter of man with the antilord is not adequately apprehended if it is seen only as something introduced by the devil as an obstacle in man's way. There was also the purpose and the initiative of God in this event. It was according to the wise permission of the Creator that his earthly servant was subjected to temptation by a superior, malevolent intelligence. And as we have seen, in this confrontation in the garden, man, though in a sense put on the defensive and exposed to Satan's attack, was at the same time afforded an opportunity for positive action in fulfillment of his historic vocation. It was an occasion in which he might manifest his God-like nature and play a crucial role in transactions that transcended the earthly sphere and affected the history of heaven.

From the vantage point of God's purpose, Satan's advent in Eden with lying wonders and all deceivableness of unrighteousness is seen to be nothing less than a delivering over of the devil to man for judgment. The destiny of man to judge angels (cf. 1 Cor 6:2f.) is not a later addendum to the agenda but a primal assignment. Agreeably, authority to execute judgment is given to Jesus in his identity as the Son of Man, the second Adam. The first Adam was made in the image of God, a judge between good and evil, and when the devil entered the Edenic temple of God, in effect setting himself forth there as God, opposing and exalting himself above all, Adam was faced with the challenge to rise up in holy judicial wrath and cleanse God's temple.

When he placed the tree of the knowing of good and evil in the midst of the garden, God was already setting the scene for the judgment drama. And now God had brought the enemy, lured by his own wiles, to the judgment bar to be condemned, to Har Magedon, the mount of assembly, to be cast down to the Pit. The hour had come for the priest-king of Eden, robed in his God-like dignity, to declare the righteous judgment of his holy Lord. The blaspheming profane serpent must be trampled under foot. This was the task which, by the Creator's appointment, lay at the threshhold of man's historic mission. Let him consign the devil to the divine wrath and so have his part with God in the slaying of the dragon, and heaven would rejoice and human history could then proceed in serene triumph to its eschaton of peace. What we anticipate at the end of the ages as the final judgment would then have transpired at the beginning of history. Having thus begun with the clearing of the temple of God, history would have moved on to the cultural construction and eschatological completion of that temple. To slay the dragon and to build the temple-palace of the heavenly King – that was the pattern of the messianic mission of the son of man from the beginning. We should not be surprised, therefore, when we find that pattern widely reflected even in postlapsarian mythology. When man faced the draconic tempter at the judgment tree, the first great moment of his messianic challenge had arrived.

B. The Temptation and Fall

Various factors may have entered into the tempter's strategy of approaching the woman rather than Adam. Certainly in maneuvering Adam out of the position of primary response Satan was defying and subverting the structure of authority God had appointed for the human family. Moreover, there would be greater contradiction of this same divine institution if Eve could be induced to lead the family head into sin than if it happened the other way around.

By the whole manner of his approach the tempter conveyed a false impression of the situation. In reality, he had intruded where he did not belong and should have been on the defensive, but seizing the offensive he so confused the woman that she found herself engaged in apologetics, struggling to defend both man and God (or at least giving an appearance of the latter). It was Satan who had been brought to this place as an offender against heaven to be judged, but he right away assumed the role of judge. The arrogant boldness of his cunning appears most astonishingly in the fact that he turned man's attention directly to the judgment tree, the very object that called on man to pronounce the intruder's doom, and used it as the basis for a charge against the heavenly Judge.

"Did God actually tell you not to eat of any of the trees in the garden?" (Gen 3:1b). In the tempter's opening word he challenged the stipulations of God's covenant law. This insinuating question of fact was designed to undermine respect for God's authority. Explicitly he asked about the extent of God's prohibition, yet in such a way as to suggest the possibility that God's prohibition might be too extensive (so calling into question too God's goodness). Implicit in such a question was the assumption that a creature has the right to make an autonomous judgment about God. It therefore amounted to a denial of God's absolute right of command and his absolute lordship and so struck at the very foundations of the covenant order.

By pointing to the negative, prohibitory aspect of the special probationary command, Satan turned attention away from positive requirements that were entailed in the juridical significance of the probation tree or that were expressed in the general stipulations of covenant law. Duped by this diversionary tactic, man lost sight of his positive obligations in the areas of his priestly-cultic charge, his royal-cultural commission, and his family-community responsibilities. We find that in the process of their succumbing to temptation and breaking the covenant, sins of omission in these several areas by both Eve and Adam preceded their overt violation of the special proscription itself.

The insinuating challenge of the opening question, inciting to rebellion, unmistakably exposed the serpent as a hostile presence and an unholy trespasser in the sacred precincts of the garden and left no doubt as to the path of duty for the priestly guardians of God's courts. The faithful priest must hallow God's name and defend God's sanctuary. It was an obligation of the vassal in the ancient international treaties that if he heard seditious words spoken against his suzerain, he must report this and take military action against any rebellion that was underway. Similarly, man in the garden should have promptly opposed and denounced and expelled the blasphemous tempter. But he failed to discharge his solemn priestly duty. Moreover, for man to accept the serpent, viewed simply in its animal nature, as his peer, if not superior, among the orders of creation, was to fail to exercise his mandated dominion over the subhuman creatures. It was an abdication of his proper royal authority. And there was also failure to uphold the divinely instituted family authority structure. For her part, Eve did not turn to her husband as the one with the primary authority and responsibility in the crisis produced by the approach of the serpent-tempter in the sanctuary. We shall also be noting Adam's culpability in this same regard.

Satan's challenge to God's authority compelled man to choose between two masters. It was part of Satan's falsifying of the situation that he projected for himself the image of lordly benefactor. While he was getting the woman to separate in theory between God's interests and her own and to act in a spirit of self-interest over against the (insinuated) inconsiderateness of God, Satan managed to strike the pose of one who was himself concerned for man's best interests. At every turn he forced on man this choice between authorities. By approaching the woman and ignoring the man's headship he presented a different interpretation of the social structure from that given in God's covenant law, so compelling the woman and man to choose which authority they would submit to. That was also the effect of the very form of Satan's approach as a beast of the field with an assumed superiority over man and even God. Standing there at the tree of the forbidden fruit with this haughtily speaking serpent before him, man was faced with two exceptions to the consecration pattern of creation according to which all the world with its vegetable and animal kingdoms had been subordinated to man and consigned to his use. He was simultaneously under probation to accept obediently God's own exception, the forbidden fruit, and under temptation to accept Satan's exception, the creature of the field that would dominate man. By thus challenging God's law-order for the world with a different order of his own, Satan presented himself as a rival lord. And of course this challenge to God's authority was aggressively articulated in all that the satanic serpent said, whether in the opening insinuating question or the following blatant contradiction of God's threat. Failure to reject forthwith this usurping challenge of the antilord was failure at the ultimate level of the covenant's first and great command to love the Lord God with all the heart and to serve only him.

The woman's response to the tempter (Gen 2:2,3) must be faulted for leaving undone and unsaid those things she should have done and said. And in this failure to fulfill these positive duties her choice was already determined in favor of the idol-lord in the radical test of allegiance posed by his approach. In view of the lapse of loyalty to the Lord evidenced by her sins of omission, we are warranted in detecting some inkling of revolt in the words of her response. She corrected Satan's expansion of the probation prohibition by stating that it did not extend to all the trees, but then she apparently expanded on the divine proscription herself by adding the restriction about touching the tree. If so, she was probably venting a feeling of resentment that the special prohibition was arbitrary and unfair, a critical feeling which betrayed an assumption that she had rights the Creator had not sufficiently respected.

Pressing his advantage, the tempter shifted his attack from the stipulations of the covenant to its sanctions. He moved on from questioning God's norms for the present to challenging God's interpretation of the future. His outright contradiction of God's warning as to the deadly consequences of disobedience (Gen 3:4) was not so much a denial of God's knowledge as an assault on the divine integrity. Satan's claim was that God, because of a jealous reluctance to share his honor with others, had lied about the probation tree to prevent man from becoming like him in respect to the knowledge of good and evil (Gen 3:5). With subtle artistry the devil painted a complete falsehood, a total distortion of reality, portraying God in his own devil-likeness and representing himself in the guise of divine virtue and prerogative.

An appearance of reasonableness attached to the tempter's implicit recommendation that man should ignore the special proscription. He was able to suggest plausibly that besides being arbitrary in declaring unlawful something that was in itself altogether useful and desirable, the prohibition set an obstacle in the way of man's fulfilling his potential for and indeed his commission to the scientific enterprise. (Understandably, Satan slanted the significance of the probation tree towards the notion of the acquisition of knowledge, while obscuring the juridical function to which it summoned man.) A twisted half-truth was contained in the false prophecy of Satan that eating the fruit of the tree of knowledge would bring an increase in man's God-likeness – does not God himself afterwards affirm that such had been the result (Gen 3:22)? Satan's proposition would thus seem to be harmonious with the fundamental covenant norm of the imitation of God, as well as promotive of the ultimate objective of the perfecting of the *imago Dei* in man.

However, in Satan's approach to the *imago Dei*, the aspect of dominion-glory was misleadingly isolated from the ethical-glory of the image. His suggestion (a reflection of the kind of thinking that had prompted his own rebellion, the vanity of which he knew full well) was that the image-bearer's dominion over the world might be firmly established without his prior confirmation in holiness and righteousness and the love of God's truth. If that were so, the whole probation would of course be left without relevance or meaning. Another way of analyzing the fallacy in Satan's approach is to observe that he abstracted the norm of the imitation of God from the context of the total revelation of covenant law, as though the *imago Dei* could be cultivated in indifference to the absolute authority of God that was present in every word he spoke. Entailed in this was a suppression of the fact of the essential difference between God and man which, equally with the fact of their similarity, comes to expression in the identification of man as image-likeness of God. Satan represented man's advance in God-likeness as a matter of ascent up a monistic scale of being. Instead of promoting the fundamental norm of covenant law, Satan, by obliterating the Creator-creature distinction in his monistic blender, was attacking the unique and absolute sovereignty of the Creator-Lord, which was the foundation of the entire covenantal arrangement.

Although Satan had now blatantly accused the Creator, the One who is light and love, of being in fact darkness and hate, the woman did not react to the blasphemy with shock and abhorrence. Instead, she was attracted by the evil-spell. She gave credence to the tidings of the advent of the antilord come to liberate mankind from his vassalage under the malevolent oppressor, come to show him how to assert his innate rights effectively and how to develop his full potential from the level of humankind to godhood. In the woman's heart, Satan had replaced Yahweh-Elohim as covenant overlord. Forsaking the covenant of life, she had entered into a covenant with death, accepting the claim of the prince of death that in league with him there was immunity from death.

The woman's new religion was polytheistic. She idolized herself as well as Satan, for she arrogated to herself the divine prerogative of final judgment in discerning between good and evil and in defining the meaning of reality in general. Her new theology was evidenced in her assumption of a critical stance over against the word of God. In reaching a decision on the relative merits of conflicting legal and prophetic words of God and the devil, she did so on the basis of her newly liberated powers of reason, functioning autonomously without a pre-commitment to the absolute authority of the Creator as the God of truth. Presumptuously assuming divine right, she redefined the special, exceptional tree as a tree the same as all others, pleasant to the eyes and good for food (Gen 3:6a; cf. 2:9), and assigned to it a new name. By her fiat it was no longer to be the forbidden tree but the desirable tree – desirable (should the truth be told) to satisfy the lust of the flesh, the lust of the eyes and the pride of life. Then, further and more openly demonstrating her antifaith by her antiworks, she availed herself of the fruit of the desirable tree (v. 6b).

Partaking of this tree was also a confirmation of the woman's league with the devil. He had pointed to the fruit of the tree of knowledge as in reality the seal of the abundant life, inviting man to partake of it. This was, in Satan's reconstruction of the situation, the sacramental tree of his covenant, substituted for God's sacramental tree of life. Somehow Eve was able to assimilate into her new theology the devil's concept of this tree as a special tree, the sacramental means to divine wisdom, along with the interpretation of it as just another tree. And, in confession of her antifaith, she spurned the table of the Lord and accepted the invitation to eat of the sacramental tree of the prince of demons, so ratifying her pact with him.

Moreover, in her missionary zeal for her new religion, the woman presented the evil-spell to her husband and made a convert of him (Gen 3:6c). Whereas she had responded to the tempter at first with what had the formal appearance of being a defense of the Lord, she now unashamedly acted as the devil's advocate and apostle.

So appallingly successful had the devil's tactics been that the capitulation of Adam, whose fall as federal representative of mankind was the key objective of the temptation, transpired without a direct confrontation between the two principals. Satan could leave it to Adam's helpmeet to be the immediate agent in his undoing. We do not know for sure how long the temptation episode lasted or whether Adam was close by Eve during the whole process. If he witnessed her encounter with the serpent, he incurred guilt by failing to intervene and take the front place in direct opposition to the intruder, neither accepting Satan's contravention of the divine delegation of authority, nor allowing Eve to ignore it. Again, failure to step forward and directly challenge Satan would be a surrender of God's holy honor to the enemy in violation of man's priestly guardianship of the sanctuary. Adam was guilty of this kind of failure even if we were to suppose that he had not seen the serpent but was first caught up into the crisis at a later stage by Eve's approach to him as a promoter of the antifaith (by which point the serpent might have momentarily withdrawn from view). For in that case Adam would have confronted in the person of Eve herself an evil presence, one who must be repulsed and delivered over to God's judgment. What his obligation would have been under such a circumstance is illuminated by a stipulation in God's covenant with the Israelites. On them too was laid the priestly task of resisting the encroachment of apostasy into the holy community, the law insisting specifically that the instigator to idolatry, though a close kinsman or even "the wife of your bosom," must not be pitied or concealed but exposed and killed (Deut 13:6ff.). Our Lord's demand that his disciples be prepared for his sake to hate even loved ones (Luke 14:26) is the corollary of the primary obligation of God's covenant that man love him perfectly. Depending then on the particular scenario, the priestly duty left undone by Adam was either that of declaring judgment directly upon the devil or judging him indirectly through the judgment of his advocate, Eve. For Adam, as in the case of Eve, the sins of omission of which he was guilty represented a fundamental failure of his covenantal commitment to the Lord God. Inevitably such sins of omission on his part were followed by his committing of the more evident sin of consenting with the woman in her idolatrous revolt and participating with her at Satan's sacramental table (Gen 3:6a).

II. JUDGMENT DAY

God had brought Satan to the judgment tree to be damned. To man had been assigned the awesome role of standing as God's vicegerent at the place of judgment and consigning the great adversary to perdition. Man, however, had utterly failed in his messianic mission. He had declared good to be evil and evil to be good. He had broken his covenant with God and made league with the devil. But "be not deceived; God is not mocked; for whatsoever a man soweth, that shall he also reap. For he that soweth to his flesh shall of the flesh reap corruption; but he that soweth to the Spirit shall of the Spirit reap life everlasting" (Gal 6:7,8). The Lord God therefore came to the place of judgment in Eden to enter into a covenant lawsuit with his offending vassals. Moreover, Satan was not to escape through man's malfeasance. It was also the purpose of the Lord's juridical appearance that he should himself pronounce the devil's doom.

Another factor, all important, affected the particular character of the judicial sentences imposed on both man and Satan. According to the principle of justice expressed in the creational covenant the rebellious human vassals might have been consigned then and there to God's eternal wrath along with the devil. But the Metapolis mission was not to be aborted before human history had scarcely started. In eternal covenant with the Son, the Father in heaven had decreed that a new mankind should be redeemed out of fallen mankind and emerge at the consummation of redemptive history as God's holy temple, New Jerusalem. To make room for this history of redemption, the execution of the final judgment against men and demons must be postponed until a later hour. God's judgment on the covenant-breakers in Eden did not, therefore, assume the form of a final total curse, nor did his condemnation of Satan have the effect of casting him at once into the lake of fire prepared for him and his angels.

A. Parousia of the Glory-Spirit

1. The Spirit of the Day
Adapting the mode of his self-revelation to the judicial purpose of his coming the Lord approached the judgment-site in the awesome glory of his theophanic Presence. So he ever comes on the day of judgment, the day of the Lord, the day of the covenant servants' accounting before the Face of their Lord. It is that kind of fearful advent that is reported in Genesis 3:8. [For a more complete treatment of the translation and interpretation of this

verse, see chapter four of my *Images of the Spirit*, of which the following paragraphs are a short summary.]

The key phrase describing God's approach through the garden, traditionally translated "in the cool of the day," should be rendered "as the Spirit of the day." "Spirit" here denotes the theophanic Glory, as it does in Genesis 1:2 and elsewhere in Scripture. And "the day" has the connotation it often has in the prophets' forecasts of the great coming judgment (cf. also Judg 11:27 and 1 Cor 4:3). Here in Genesis 3:8 is the original day of the Lord, which served as the prototypal mold in which subsequent pictures of other days of the Lord were cast. Such a day is one of divine epiphany. The final such day is preeminently the day of our Lord's parousia, the day of his presence as the personal revelation of the Glory with the clouds and angels of heaven. Significantly, *panim*, face or presence, one of the biblical designations of the Glory-Spirit, is referred to in Genesis 3:8, and accordingly what is depicted there is nothing less than the primal parousia. On the original day of the Lord in Eden, God's parousia-advent was in the theophanic mode of "the Spirit (Presence) of the day (of judgment)."

Trumpeting the advent of the divine Presence — at Sinai, at Pentecost, at the parousia of Jesus, at every day of the Lord — is the fearful sound of the voice of the Lord, the thunderclap of the approaching theophanic storm-chariot. It was by precisely this arresting signal that the primal parousia was heralded. Alarmed by this sound of God's coming (v. 8a), the man and his wife sought escape (of all places) in the area of the judgment tree (v. 8b).

2. The Exposure

There is no hiding from the Parousia, no place to flee from the Spirit. By reason of the advent of the Spirit of the day, even the darkness is flooded with light (cf. Ps 139:7-12). No concealment was possible in the shadows of the trees of the garden of Eden.

Even before the judicial disclosures made in formal pronouncements of the Lord, a process of self-exposure and self-judgment on the part of Adam and Eve had already occurred. Theirs was the God-like vocation to discern between good and evil and no sooner had they sinned by judging God to be evil and the devil to be good than involuntarily, and more accurately, their own consciences delivered a verdict of evil against themselves. It took the form of a sense of shame over their physical nakedness (Gen 3:7a). What was not a source of shame within the husband-wife relationship established in creation (Gen 2:24,25) had become so in the altered relationship resulting from the temptation. In the course of the temptation they had repudiated their marriage as it had been defined in the creation ordinance. By their virtual act of divorce they had forfeited their privilege of sexual intimacy and hence their physical nakedness brought confusion and shame to them in their condition of alienation, compelling them to hide from one another's eyes by clothing over that nakedness (Gen 3:7b). (According to biblical and other sources, shameful nakedness has subsequently served at times as a legal symbol in official notification of divorce.)

If hiding from each other was an exposure of their unlawful severing of their marriage covenant with one another, their hiding from God (Gen 3:8) betrayed their guilty awareness of having broken the covenant with him. Judgment by parousia confrontation is a trial by ordeal in which the guilty person's own reaction is self-incriminating (cf. Rev 6:16). The attempt to conceal sin has precisely the opposite result of revealing it. For the guilty pair in Eden to flee in terror from the Glory-Spirit, in whose presence those faithful to the covenant find their ultimate bliss, was an open confession of their alienation and divorce from their holy Lord.

Their hiding from God under the covering of the trees, like their hiding from each other under the covering of leaves, pointed to a sense of shameful nakedness, in this case a spiritual nakedness which they felt before God's eyes. This nakedness resulted from their loss of the covering of righteousness, the garment of the beauty of holiness. They had lost the ethical glory of God-likeness which is the prerequisite to stand as priest before the Face of God and reflect the Glory of God. Whatever the half-truth of Satan's prophecy of increased God-likeness (Gen 3:5), the fact was that by rejecting God's holy commandment they had rejected and lost their original endowment with the image of God and had instead taken on a likeness to the devil. He was their newly adopted covenant father. The Genesis narrative conveys the point that man's nakedness signified a likeness to the serpent-Satan by means of a word-play on the similarity of the sound of the Hebrew word "naked" (Gen 2:25; 3:7) to that for "subtle," used for the serpent (3:1), the pun being made more obvious by bringing the two words into proximity in Genesis 2:25 and 3:1. In a more substantial way the same fact becomes evident in the reproduction of the subtle evil of the serpent in the pattern of man's behavior under divine interrogation. That love of the truth which is part of the spiritual glory of the *imago Dei* is nowhere to be seen in the defensive retorts of Adam and

Eve. The tempter's counsel had been urged and adopted in the name of advancing knowledge, but the consequence of man's disobedience of the word of God was an obscurant suppression of the truth. Finding it impossible to hide their persons from God's Presence and being constrained to submit to a process of judicial interrogation, they still persisted in their attempt to thwart the discovery of the truth. To hide the facts about their apostasy, they resorted to evasion, distortion, and deception, the tactics of the tortuous serpent.

In his order of procedure in prosecuting the covenant lawsuit the Lord honored the family authority structure he had instituted, the structure the tempter had subverted and the man and the woman had ignored. Accordingly, he directed the interrogation first to the man as the one with primary responsibility. Brought out of hiding and obliged to account for his self-concealment, Adam cited not his act of disobedience but its consequence, his nakedness (Gen 3:10), with the implication, most likely, that the fault was God's own since nakedness was man's created condition. When this evasion failed and God's next question (Gen 3:11) forced Adam to deal with his act of disobedience, he still avoided acknowledging his responsibility and even more explicitly laid the blame on God. He placed the proximate responsibility on Eve (so carrying further his repudiation of his wife), but appended an insolent insinuation about the ultimate source of the problem by observing that it was God who had given him this woman (Gen 3:12). When the focus of the divine interrogation turned to her, Eve too avoided confession of the truth. Switching quickly from devil's advocate to his accuser, she tried to dissolve her own responsibility in the guile of the serpent, and this too probably involved the perverse suggestion that in the last analysis God had only himself to blame, for (as the reader of Genesis 3 is reminded when the serpent is first introduced, v.1) the serpent was one of those beasts of the field which the Lord God had made. Thus, the process of judicial interrogation completed the full exposure of the fallen state of the man and the woman by eliciting a series of lying evasions and even recriminations against God himself. This dramatically displayed their loss of their former likeness to God and their assumption of the image of their new god, the great accuser and father of lies.

B. The Curse on the Serpent

When once the offense of the covenant servants had been laid bare, the Lord proceeded to deal with the serpent, taking up the judicial task in which man had proven derelict. Though he did not execute his final judgment against Satan immediately, the Lord did then and there at the judgment tree declare against him an irrevocable curse. The father of false prophets had contested the prophetic sanctions announced by the Lord of the covenant, the original true Prophet, but now he found himself being addressed by that same Prophet with a silencing judicial authority that could not be gainsaid.

No interrogation of Satan was necessary. The process of exposure that had led step by step to the serpent had uncovered ample evidence of the role that he had played in the Fall. There was of course the woman's direct accusation, but quite incontrovertible was the evidence of the devil's handiwork so terribly evident in the total response of the guilty pair. At once, therefore, the word of doom went forth: "You are cursed" (Gen 3:14). In the figurative depiction of this curse, the imagery is that of Satan's own chosen instrument: "Upon your belly shall you go; and dust you shall eat all the days of your life." If, from the viewpoint of physical analogy, the tortuous movement of the serpent had made it a suitable choice as the medium of Satan's approach for temptation, its prostrate position in the dust also supplied an appropriate image of him as the object of divine judgment. Satan's choice had been more apt than he would have preferred.

After the general description of the curse as a humiliating degradation of the utmost degree and of perpetual duration (v. 14), an intimation was added (the serpentine figure being continued) of what was to be the historical course of its execution: "I will put enmity between you and the woman, and between her seed and your seed" (v. 15). God would wrest the prey from the serpent's coils. The alliance Satan had secured with man, and with it the mastery over mankind, would not stand. God would overturn it, turning friendship into enmity. In Eve's accusation of the serpent that alliance had already begun to disintegrate. Satan's very success in reproducing such a striking likeness to himself in his human allies spelled the failure of their covenant, for devil-like deceit and falsehood are the contradiction of the commitment and truth that are of the essence of covenant. Satan, as liar, is by nature a contra-covenantal being, the antithesis of the covenantal Lord God, holy and true. The enmity that God was to effect between the woman and Satan was, however, to be of a far different and more radical kind than Eve had exhibited during the judicial interrogation. It would spring not from her likeness to the devil but from the renewal in her of the image of God. Enmity with the serpent would be only the reverse side, the repentance side, of her renewed (now saving) faith in the Lord. By virtue of her renewed love of God, she would hate the devil.

God's pronouncing of the curse of enmity was a declaration of holy war. Satan's peace of death must not be allowed to settle over the earth. The Lord had come, therefore, not to bring peace (at least not yet) but a sword, to turn history into a struggle that would issue at last in the final destruction of the devil's power. God's avenging counterattack would begin where Satan's assault began, with the woman. It would then continue unrelentingly through the generations of human history so that from the expanding family of man God would rally the holy army of the new mankind who were one with Eve in her divinely initiated hatred of the devil, a spiritual family of the woman which would continue to wage the holy war against the devil and his brood among men. That "her seed" (that is, the seed of the woman) is to be understood in this spiritual sense of the elect of mankind, sovereignly enlisted by the Lord in his army, follows from the fact that its counterpart, "your seed" (that is, the seed of the serpent), whether understood of men or demons, must be taken in some non-literal sense. This result then determines the interpretation of the serpent's seed as the company of reprobate men who persist in their devil-likeness, since the idea of reprobate men rather than that of the demonic hosts forms the appropriate counterpart to elect men. Such is the interpretation of the term evidently reflected in Jesus' identification of unbelieving Jews as children of the devil in the context of their boastful self-identification as "the seed of Abraham," the latter being an updated, more parochial version of "the seed of the woman" (John 8:44, cf. 33). This interpretation also underlies the apostle John's contrast between the children of God and the children of the devil in a passage rich in allusions to the Genesis 3 context (1 John 3:8ff.).

"He will bruise your head and you will bruise his heel" (Gen 3:15c). A climactic battle in the holy war is here envisaged, and the war's final outcome. On the eschatological horizon of the judgment-prophecy of the divine Prophet appeared the hope of a victory that belonged by God's decree to the army of the woman. God would crush Satan under their feet (cf. Rom 16:20). This victory prophetically announced in the curse on the serpent would be in the first instance, however, a victory not of the collective seed of the woman but of an individual. "He" is thus to be understood, as an individual counterpart to the individual "you." The latter points to the figure of Satan behind the creature of the field through whom he spoke, one who, unlike that particular serpent, would still be on the world scene at the distant historical time referred to. What is in view in the all-decisive battle is a judgment ordeal by individual combat, fought by a champion from each of the opposing armies. Mention of a wound to be suffered by the champion of the woman's army does not throw in doubt the decisive victory he was to gain for them. As an historical exposition of the absolute defeat of the devil affirmed in the curse of verse 14, verse 15 must reinforce that idea and such is certainly the intention of the contrast drawn between the blow inflicted on the heel of the woman's seed and the blow delivered to the head of the serpent. And just as all the seed of the woman participate in the victory of their champion, so the seed of the serpent, who share in the cause and nature of the devil, must share also in his destiny of defeat and doom. Here, beforehand, God's covenant curse was declared against reprobate men whose final judgment verdict, when it at last issues from the great white throne, inevitably echoes the curse uttered at the primal parousia: "Depart from me you cursed into everlasting fire, prepared for the devil and his angels (Matt 25:41; cf. Rev 20:10,15).

C. The Judgment on Man

1. The Common Curse

After the cursing of the serpent, the Judge turned to the human pair whose reaction to the divine ordeal in the interrogation phase of the lawsuit had exposed them as guilty of disloyalty against the covenant. In pronouncing his verdicts, the Lord followed the sequence in which guilt had been incurred in the temptation and Fall. Judgment, therefore, moved on from the devil, by whom the temptation was first conceived, to the woman (Gen 3:16) and then to Adam (Gen 3:17-19). Though the judgment addressed to Adam was in part more particularly oriented to men as distinguished in their life roles from women, much of it was more broadly applicable to man generically.

Covenant-breakers though they were, Adam and Eve were predestined to become God's covenant people once again through redemptive grace. Before long they were displaying faith and hope in the salvation promise contained in the curse of Satan (Gen 3:15). Nevertheless, the divine revelation addressed directly to them (Gen 3:16-19) did not have in view their personal identity as elect individuals; it rather contemplated the mankind that had been represented in Adam and in him had broken the covenant. God's judicial pronouncement was an official registering of his verdict against the generality of fallen mankind, publicly marking the transition from his original attitude of favor towards man to the wrath with which he now regarded the inhabitants of the earth because of their violation of his covenant. The whole manner of his approach testified to his displeasure with mankind as he announced the curse that would befall them. This curse was not, however, the ultimate curse of damnation against those who as individuals were to prove reprobate, but a temporal curse to be experienced by all men in common until the great separation would be effected at the final judgment.

"Unto the dust you shall return" (v. 19). By reason of the common curse the history of mankind would be turned into a history unto death. The ground man was to subdue would subdue him. Prefacing the statement of the ultimate effect of the common curse in verse 19 is the explanation: "for dust you are." It is not that the ground had a natural claim on man that required his return to the dust. Man's falling victim to death is not to be accounted for by his created nature; it is the wages of sin. The prefatory reference to man's physical nature simply indicates how, under the common curse, he can experience death (the first death) in the form of physical dissolution. The common character of this curse (experienced as it is by believers as well as others) is underscored by the recurrence of the statement "and he died" as a closing refrain in the treatment of the lives of even the long-lived patriarchs of the faith in the genealogy of Genesis 5 (cf. Rom 5:14).

A shadow would be cast by the inevitability of death over all man's earthly existence, making all his labors seem like a clutching at the wind. Considered apart from the redemptive purpose which was to unfold in the course of human history, that history would appear to be nothing but vanity. Moreover, according to the terms of the common curse pronounced by the Lord, death's ultimate frustration of man's efforts would be preceded by a blight of pain and sorrow on the whole genealogical-cultural process. The woman's function in procreation would be characterized by the travail of her childbearing and the sorrows of barrenness and miscarriage (Gen 3:16a). The man's task in the cultivation of the earth would become a wearisome, sweaty toil beset by vexation and disappointment (Gen 3:17b-19a). Though the specific word of curse (v. 17b) is directed against the ground, it is precisely with regard to its baneful impact on man that the cursing of the ground must be understood. (In the similar phraseology of Genesis 8:21, the cursing of the ground is the turning of the elements of nature into a weapon to smite man.) Scorning man's kingly dignity, the ground would bring him a tribute of thistles and a crown of thorns.

Under the common curse, humanity was to be troubled by social discord as well as by afflictions in the realm of nature. In the course of the temptation God's appointment concerning the marriage relationship had been transgressed by the man and the woman and their personal relationship would henceforth be disturbed by conflict. It was on this note that the word of judgment spoken to the woman concluded (v. 16b). Whether the problematic word usually rendered "desire" be understood of a desire of the woman to dominate her husband or whether it be translated "fealty" and understood in the sense of a feudatory submission of the woman to her husband, the statement certainly includes the idea that the man's proper original headship would become a tyrannical domination over the woman. (See Gen 4:7, where the same idiom has such a meaning.) That verse 16b is indeed concerned with the authority structure aspect of the marriage relationship is corroborated by the fact that the immediately following judicial word to the man begins with the charge that he had submitted to the direction of his wife (v. 17a). One particular personal relationship is spoken of in this judicial sentence, but the common curse would bring disharmony into the whole range of social relationships in the family of man in general, manifesting itself in all manner of oppression and injustice, in violence and the agony of war.

In sum, the common curse would turn human existence on earth into a struggle for survival, a perpetual conflict, a vain history unto death. Yet the common curse is not the curse of perdition pronounced on the serpent; it is rather a temporal curse, a curse on which restraint is exercised by the operation of another providential principle. To this other principle of common grace we shall return at a later point.

2. Expulsion from the Sanctuary

In order that the race's forfeiture of God's favor might be dramatized in a public historical act, the Lord drove the man and woman out of the place favored by his special Presence (Gen 3:23). In this episode they were once more dealt with in their capacity as representatives of the generality of mankind now fallen. Their removal from the garden openly marked the passage from the original normal state of beatitude under the Creator's favor to the abnormal state of the world under the common curse which had resulted from man's rebellion against the covenant.

In his zeal for the sanctity of his own holy Name, God had come to cleanse his temple and he made a thorough work of it. By their apostasy the priests of the temple had turned it into an abomination of desolation. In due course, the earthly paradise-sanctuary would be desolated, but without delay the apostate priests were cast out along with the false god they had allowed to stand in the holy place. Defiled and driven out, the former priests of Eden were now regarded as themselves potential intruders, against whom the sanctuary must be guarded. The priestly guardianship, originally assigned to man, was now committed to the cherubim (Gen 3:24).

Driven from his native homeland, the holy and blessed land, into a world profane and cursed, man is in exile on the face of the earth. His historical existence is a wandering east of Eden, a diaspora. Until the restoration of all things, the earth has taken on the character of a wilderness, lying outside the holy land of promise. It is a realm under the shadow of death. When the model of paradise and exile-wilderness is later applied to the typological history of Israel, the prophet Ezekiel depicts the Israelite diaspora under the image of a valley full of skeletons and he sees restoration from exile as a resurrection from the dead.

In the hour that God drove man into exile it was indicated that any future return to God's dwelling-place and the tree of life must involve a passage through the flaming sword of God's judgment, with which the new guardians of his sanctuary were armed. This message too is typologically conveyed in Israel's history, in the cultus so arranged that an altar with the sacrificial sword stood before the holy dwelling, itself bounded by representations of cherubim in the colors of flaming fire. By these striking circumstances of man's expulsion from Eden an additional ray of light was thrown on the prophecy of the suffering which the champion seed of the woman must endure in securing the victory in his great judgment ordeal.

REDEMPTIVE COVENANT IN THE OLD WORLD

"For as by one man's disobedience many were made sinners, so by the obedience of one shall many be made righteous" (Rom 5:19). There was a first man Adam and a first covenant of works. And for the redemption of the lost world there is a second and last Adam, the Adam from heaven (cf. 1 Cor 15:45-49), and another covenant of works. This second covenant was kept, this second man was obedient and his obedience under this covenant of works is the foundation of the gospel order. The redemptive program as well as the original kingdom order in Eden is thus built on the principle of works.

This second covenant of works is the eternal covenant, which we shall call "The Father's Covenant of Works with the Son." The series of temporal administrations of redemptive grace to God's people are subsections of what we shall call "The Lord's Covenant of Grace with the Church" (or, for brevity's sake we may use the traditional "Covenant of Grace"). Preeminently the Covenant of Grace finds expression in the new covenant, but it also includes all those earlier covenantal arrangements wherein the benefits secured by the obedience of Christ in fulfillment of God's eternal covenant with him were in part already bestowed during premessianic times, in each case according to the particular eschatological phase of covenant history.

Though interlocking, these two redemptive covenants, the eternal and the temporal, are nevertheless to be clearly distinguished from each other for they differ in several most basic respects. In the eternal covenant, (1) the Son is assigned the role of covenant servant; (2) the second party is the Son in his status as second Adam and thus, included along with him, the elect whom he represents, and them exclusively; and (3) the operative principle is works. Contrariwise, in the series of historical administrations of the gospel, (1) the messianic Son is Lord and mediator of the covenant; (2) the second party is the church, the community of the confessors of the faith and their children, including others beside the elect; and (3) the operative principle is grace.

In the Introduction above and in our introductory observations to Part I, Section A, we defended the propriety of the biblical theologian's applying the term covenant to arrangements not labelled *berith* (or *diatheke*) in the Bible. In the case of the intratrinitarian covenant, the justification for the covenantal designation is once again that the substance of a *berith* is found in the biblical intimations afforded us of the eternal counsel between God the Father and the Son. Commitment was there, and divine sanctioning – there if ever!

Jesus' life is portrayed as a mission. His very identity as Messiah involved commissioning and his messianic consciousness was revealed in statements reflecting his awareness of having been sent by the Father on a special mission with a commandment to obey (John 10:18), a righteousness to fulfill (Matt 3:15), a baptism to be suffered (Luke 12:50), and a work to finish (John 17:4). This special mission of the Son is interpreted in the New Testament within the context of various covenants. When the fullness of time was come, he was sent by God as one under law (Gal 4:4), as the Servant of the Lord prophesied by Isaiah (cf. Isa 42; 49; 50; 52-53), and thus as the true Israel, the true covenant servant that Israel failed to be. Indeed, covenant sums up the mission of the Isaianic Servant (Isa 42:6; 49:8). Or again, as we have seen, Jesus was sent forth as another Adam, to be the obedient covenant servant that the first Adam failed to be. Also, he was the image of God (2 Cor 4:4) and, as observed above, covenantal relationship was inherent in the first Adam's possession of that image.

The messianic mission performed on earth began in heaven: "For I came down from heaven, not to do my own will, but the will of him that sent me" (John 6:38). Jesus was sent forth from heaven to earth on a covenantal mission with covenantal oath-commitments from his Father. Messianic psalms reveal to us the eternal communion between the Father and Son, in which the Father covenants to the Son a kingship on Zion over the uttermost parts of the earth (Ps 2:6-9) and grants him by oath an eternal royal priesthood (Ps 110:4; cf. Heb 5:6; 7:17,21). Jesus, identifying himself as the divine royal Son of those psalms declared to his disciples: "As my Father appointed unto me a kingdom, so I appoint unto you that you may eat and drink at my table in my kingdom, and sit on thrones judging the twelve tribes of Israel" (Luke 22:29, 30). It is interesting that the verb translated "appointed" (*diatithemi*) is the verb to which *diatheke*, "covenant", relates. Indeed, this affirmation of Jesus stands in the context of his ordaining the sacramental seal of the new covenant, in association with his statement, "This is my blood of the new covenant" (Matt 26:28; Mark 14:24; Luke 22:20; 1 Cor 11:25). Hence, in this biblical passage we have the next thing to an actual application of the term "covenant" to the arrangement between the Father and the Son. A justifiable rendering would be: "My Father covenanted unto me a kingdom." On that same occasion, the Son of God in prayer recalled the Father's commitment to him in love before the foundation of the world, a commitment to grant him as obedient messianic Servant the glory he had with the Father before the world was (John 17:5,24). He presented his claim of merit as the faithful Servant who had met the terms of the eternal covenant of works by obediently fulfilling his mission: "I have glorified thee on the earth; I have finished the work which thou gavest me to do" (John 17:4). And then he made his request that the grant of glory proposed in that covenant now be conferred: "And now, O Father, glorify thou me with thine own self with the glory which I had with thee before the world was" (John 17:5). Jesus, the second Adam, standing before his judgment tree could declare that he had overcome the temptation to eat the forbidden fruit and that he had accomplished the charge to judge Satan, and, therefore, he could claim his right of access to the tree of life.

Heavenly commitments of the Father to the Son are reflected in words of covenant promise spoken by God to man. In the Abrahamic Covenant God promised to Abraham and his seed royalty and a mediatorship of blessing to all nations. And in the Davidic Covenant that royal seed of Abraham was identified as a coming son of David, concerning whom God swore that his throne should endure as the days of heaven, higher than the kings of the earth (cf. 2 Sam 7 and Ps 89). In the New Testament, Paul, expounding God's ancient covenant, quotes its promise and interprets: "And to thy seed, which is Christ" (Gal 3:16), and he identifies this descendant of Abraham, the Christ, as "the seed to whom the promise was made" (Gal 3:19). Jesus Christ was the one to whom God's covenantal commitment, given in promise and oath, was directed. Thus, both in the inner divine communication of heaven's eternity and in the revelation provided in the course of earthly history the Son of God received, along with his commissioning to redemptive suffering, his Father's covenantal commitment of a reward of kingdom glory.

Enough of the evidence has been cited to show that the biblical theologian will certainly want to identify these eternal commitments between the Father and Son as a covenant. Incidentally, since this arrangement between the Father and the Son, viewed as the second man, is the second half of the two Adams structure (cf. Rom 5 and 1 Cor 15), to demonstrate its covenantal character is also to corroborate yet further the case that has been made for identifying God's relation to the first Adam as a covenant – and, indeed, as a covenant of works.

Because God was pleased to constitute both the first and second Adams as federal representatives of a corporate humanity, the obedient performance of the obligations of the covenant of works administered to each of them would have the result that all whom they represented would receive with them the proposed grant of God's kingdom-glory. In the case of the first Adam all the predestined mankind that should descend from him was represented by him in his covenant of works and all would, therefore, have been beneficiaries, if he had kept the covenant. In the case of the second Adam, however, not all of mankind is elect in him and represented by him in his covenant of works and, therefore, not all men but only those who, by the sovereign election of divine grace, are in Christ are the actual beneficiaries of the eternal glory bestowed through the Covenant of Grace.

In the historical administration of the Covenant of Grace until the Consummation, membership in the covenant community is not coextensive with the elect. This is the case not so much because of the anomaly that some elect persons who belong in the visible covenant community might not unite themselves with it, but rather because numerous persons who are not elect, and not therefore "the seed of promise," nevertheless are part of the visible covenant community in this world. Some indeed are in it in terms of a legitimate application of the divinely appointed terms of admission; others, through various abuses. Not to be lost in these complexities of the historical administration of the covenant institution is the simple fact that this grace covenant is built upon the Father's covenant of works with Christ, the second Adam. It is by the obedience of the one that the many are made righteous in God's grace (Rom 5:19). Paraphrasing the words of Jesus already quoted: "As my Father covenanted to me a kingdom, so I covenant to you to participate with me in the glory of the royal court and dominion of God's kingdom" (Luke 22:29f.; cf. Matt 19:28).

Here in Section B of Part I we shall survey the earliest of the administrations of redemptive grace, culminating in the covenant with Noah (Gen 6-8). Then in Part II we will treat the remaining covenantal transactions recorded in the book of Genesis, particularly the Abrahamic Covenant, whose promises look ahead to fulfillment in two stages and at two levels under the old (Mosaic) and new covenants. The Bible, as Old and New Testaments, was designed to provide constitutions for these old and new covenants, and in these covenants, the conferral of the kingdom-grant promised in God's covenant with Christ takes place, in typological symbol under the old and in consummate reality under the new.

Chapter One

INAUGURATION OF REDEMPTIVE COVENANT

Back of the redemptive renewal of the covenantal community on earth stood the eternal intratrinitarian covenant as the necessary foundation for the restoration of God's covenant with men. Disclosures of this predetermined redemptive purpose were made in the course of the judicial proceedings following upon the breaking of the Creator's Covenant of Works with Adam. Intimations of this divine plan of salvation were given in the curse on Satan (Gen 3:15) and in the sentence pronounced against mankind (Gen 3:16-19). A divine act of symbolic sealing of God's redemptive intentions also occurred before the sentence of exile was executed (Gen 3:21). The Genesis 3 narrative of the judgment that terminated the original covenantal order in Eden is, therefore, at the same time the record of the inauguration of the new redemptive order of the Covenant of Grace.

I. RENEWAL OF THE COVENANT

A. Gospel of Redemptive Judgment

Here we return to God's curse on the serpent (Gen 3:15), emphasizing now those features in the passage that make it, surprisingly, as the church has recognized, the first disclosure of the gospel.

1. Messiah
As the Scriptures themselves plainly indicate, the individual seed of the woman, the champion of the woman's army who would vanquish Satan, is to be identified as the Messiah of Old Testament redemptive promise and prophecy. The portrayal of the mission of Christ in Revelation 12 may be singled out as rich in clear allusions to Genesis 3:15. In this vision a great dragon appears, identified as the ancient serpent, the devil (v.9). There is also a woman who gives birth to a son, and the passage speaks too about the rest of the "seed" of the woman (v.11). The history of the child born to the woman is described in messianic terms: he attains to the world-rule of the anointed Son foretold in Psalm 2 and fulfills the Daniel 7 vision of the Son of Man, for his encounter with the dragon culminates in his ascension to the throne of God (v.5), a victory celebrated as a coming of the salvation

and kingdom and authority of the Christ of God (v.10). As for the dragon-serpent, though he sets himself to devour the child (v.4), he is doomed to defeat. When the messianic son is caught up to heaven in triumph, Satan is cast down out of heaven into the prison of the abyss and at last into the lake of second death (v.9; Rev 20).

Though Satan's doom was already announced by God himself on the occasion of the *parousia* in Eden, that very announcement made known that the task of judging the evil one which was given to man at the beginning was still to be carried out by a son of man. It is true that the son of man in view in Genesis 3:15 would be one who is at times set forth in the Scriptures as the embodiment of the Glory-Presence, so that with reference to his defeat of Satan the Lord might have said to the serpent: "I will bruise your head." Nevertheless, he would be the woman's seed, a man. And the fact that Genesis 3:15 attributes to him as a dominant concern of his mission the judicial confrontation with Satan that was so central in the covenantal probation of the first Adam is indicative that this descendant of the woman would have the historical status of a second Adam, a new federal head in a new administration of God's kingdom.

Scripture's identification of Jesus as a second Adam is therefore another facet of its identification of him as the representative seed of the woman of Genesis 3:15. Particular mention may be made of the relevant data in the Gospel accounts of Jesus' temptation-encounter with Satan, where the parallelism of our Lord's experience to that of the first Adam is most pronounced. Once again there is the special presence of the devil with the same objectives and strategies as of old in Eden. He tempts again to break covenant with God and render allegiance to himself and it is again his seductive suggestion that the dominion and glory belonging to image-of-God status (peculiarly so in the case of the messianic Son of God) might be attained at the hidden expense of defying the authority of God as expressed in specific covenantal stipulations. By rebuking Satan and driving him away from the holy hill the second Adam performed the judicial assignment that had figured critically in the probation-temptation of the first Adam. The probation of Jesus, too, involved the accomplishment of a particular act of obedience; specifically, the gaining of a decisive victory over Satan. Further, in connection with the temptation of Jesus there is again found the presence of the Spirit and the angels. The acts of the Glory-Spirit and the angel attendants are now appropriate to the faithfulness displayed by Jesus in his probation and therefore contrast sharply with the roles they played in

Eden, but this very antithesis accents the fundamental parallelism in the two events. Against the first Adam, the angels stood as adversaries, preventing his return from the wilderness to the garden. Now they minister to the needs of the second Adam in the wilderness (Mark 1:12). Following the unsuccessful probation in Eden, the Glory-Spirit had appeared in terrifying storm-theophany to pronounce condemnation. Now, before leading Jesus to the temptation crisis, the Spirit appears in the theophanic form of the dove above the waters, evocative of the Creator-Spirit of Genesis 1:2 and bespeaking the divine favor. Again there is the heavenly *parousia*-voice (cf. Gen 3:8), but this time it utters a word of approbation, anticipating Jesus' triumph of obedience in the imminent temptation, where he would remain unswervingly on the way to fulfill his baptismal commitment to undergo the ordeal of redemptive suffering foretold of him in Genesis 3:15.

Coming as the second federal head, the Son of Man, whose origins were in heaven, would undergo probation in another covenant of works, the covenant which he made with the Father before he left heaven and for the fulfillment of which he came to earth as the seed of the woman. The covenantal commitments made in eternity in the intratrinitarian counsels must be fulfilled on earth in historical time. In the world of the generations of Adam and the woman the second Adam, as the representative of God's elect, must gain the reward of the covenanted kingdom for himself and for them, as had been decreed in Genesis 3:15. By his obedience in the earthly probation phase of his eternal covenant of works the champion of the woman's seed would open the way for the Covenant of Grace, whose proper purpose is to bring salvation to the rest of the woman's seed and to bestow on them the kingdom of the Glory-Spirit won by their messianic kinsman-redeemer. Indeed, in suffering the bruising of his heel the messianic seed would ratify this new covenant.

2. Grace

Essentially the same eschatological goal that is secured through the second Adam was already envisaged as the reward for a successful probation of the first Adam. In both cases the blessing sanction of the covenant consists in a consummation of the kingdom of God. But however similar with respect to the ultimate blessings offered, the new redemptive covenant administration differs from the creational covenant in that it is an administration of divine grace. It is a covenant of grace in distinction from works inasmuch as it bestows the grant of the kingdom of God on those who had forfeited their right to God's favor and so lost their hope of glory.

Consummation blessing must now come by way of reconciliation and restoration through God's forgiving, redemptive mercy. And since the grace of God operative in the Covenant of Grace is sovereign grace in Christ, the eschatological kingdom goal is not merely offered; its attainment is assured.

The promise of this redemptive grace was present in the curse on Satan in Genesis 3:15 as the implicit corollary of that curse. God's declaration that he would initiate enmity between the woman's seed and the serpent, severing the league man had entered into with the devil, was a promise of reconciliation and of the restoration of the covenant between the Lord and man. Thus, the curse of the bruising of the serpent's head would itself be an act of blessing, for through the crushing of Satan's power the community of the woman's seed would be rescued from the fierce hostility directed by the devil and his forces against them. Victory for the champion-seed of the woman meant the deliverance of the woman's army from the onslaught of the demonic hordes, deliverance from the power of death possessed by the devil (Heb 2:14). The judgment of the devil foretold in Genesis 3:15 would be a redemptive judgment, a work of judgment that was itself the means of procuring salvation.

Redemptive grace entails another kind of deliverance too, a redemption from sin and its penalty. The curse sanction of the broken covenant must be honored and the justice of the Lord of the covenant must be satisfied with respect to the company of the woman's seed as well as the seed of the serpent. It is for this reason that the prophecy of the victory of the messianic seed of the woman must contain the additional words: "You will bruise his heel." Suffering, the suffering of the curse to which all the rest of the woman's seed were liable, must be vicariously borne by the second Adam. Messianic prophecy is summarized in Scripture as the message of the sufferings of Christ and the glory that should follow (1 Pet 1:11; cf. Luke 24:25-27,44-47; Acts 26:22,23). In fact, without the sufferings to make atonement and deliver from sin there could not be the glory of the redemptive judgment against Satan. In Isaiah's prophecies of the messianic Servant, the sufferings that seem to threaten the success of the Servant's mission are eventually seen to be the very means by which he accomplishes his soteric purpose and achieves his matchless exaltation (cf. Rev 12:11). In the first messianic prophecy this interrelationship of Messiah's sufferings and glory is already observable. They are brought together in the figurative imagery, according to which it would naturally be in the act of trampling the head of the serpent that the woman's seed would suffer the wounding of his heel.

If it were not for God's concern to redeem a sinful people, the judicial triumph over Satan and his demonic hosts might have been accomplished as a simple exercise of divine power. The Son of God in the angelic existence-form known to us in biblical revelation as the Angel of the Lord, or Michael, might have led the legions of his angels against the dragon and his angels and prevailed in judgment against them (cf. Rev 12:7). But because it must be through the suffering of an atoning death that he destroyed the devil as a redemptive victory in behalf of his people, it was necessary that the Son of God partake of the existence-form of flesh and blood for the suffering of that death (Heb 2:14,15). He must become the seed of the woman as foretold in the mother prophecy. In his incarnate form, assumed so that he could make reconciliation for the sins of his people (Heb 2:17), he must not resort to the more than twelve angelic legions at his disposal, for how then should the Scriptures be fulfilled that the Christ must suffer and only so enter into his glory (Matt 26:53,54)? The sequence as well as the combination of visions in Revelation 12 is significant. Only after the son born to the woman had undergone the sufferings of the conflict with the dragon that issued in his ascension to glory (Rev 12:1-5) might Michael wage war and prevail against Satan (Rev 12:7ff). It is through the blood of the Lamb that the brethren are said to overcome their accuser (Rev 12:11).

Some of the details of the conflict symbolism in Revelation 12 can be traced back through Old Testament prophecies to the familiar ancient myths of hero-gods who battled draconic monsters. These myths are in turn perversions of traditions stemming from revelatory roots whose authentic version is presented in Genesis 3 (cf. above Section A, Chapter One). Later biblical revelation, in making use of details from the mythological version, does so in merely formal literary fashion, exploiting the culturally meaningful images without carrying over the mythological substance.

At this point it should be observed that the theme of the suffering of the hero-seed of the woman in Genesis 3:15 has its deviant derivatives in those myths in which the hero-god undergoes a death experience before subsequent revival and victory over the dragon-powers. As over against those who can find in Genesis 3:15 nothing more than an aetiology of the common abhorrence of snakes, the mythical tradition attests to reverberations in the ancient memory of man of the supernatural dimensions of the primordial event and prophecy. Both the serpent and the champion seed of the woman become divine figures in the myth. However, in the dragon of the myth Satan becomes the deified force of chaotic nature and the redemptive conflict becomes either a cosmogonic combat or the subsequent ongoing struggle of antithetical aspects of nature. The real human problem of man's sin against the Creator's covenant and the true nature of the suffering of the human champion as a redemptive sacrifice for sin are thus suppressed in this existentialized version of the myth-makers. In so falsifying the original divine prophecy, the myth-makers became part of its fulfillment, for they thereby exhibited their enmity against the faith of the woman's seed. They demonstrated themselves to be the seed of the evil one who in the temptation in Eden had also suppressed man's responsibility to God's covenant stipulations and reduced the meaning of human life to an ontological scramble up or down a cosmic scale of being.

To repeat an earlier observation, when a biblical passage (like Rev 12) adopts some of the imagery of this mythical perversion in its treatment of the theme of the divine warfare, the design is to call attention to the myth in order to take issue with it. The Bible exposes the falseness of the myth by taking these features obviously drawn from the myth and reinterpreting them by putting them and the conflict motif as a whole in their proper framework, the genuine historical framework of creation-fall-redemption.

3. Election
A happy ending was guaranteed in the redemptive program, even though it was founded on a covenant of works. Successful probation was assured in advance by the fact that the second Adam was the incarnate Son of God. While, therefore, the messianic seed of the woman was, like the first Adam, a federal representative of a people, he could also be presented to them as their surety, as the guarantor of the blessings of the covenant for them. Their victory over Satan and their inheritance of the kingdom of glory were certain because their champion must surely win the battle.

Moreover, this guarantee was given in spite of the conditionality that obtained by virtue of the necessity that the rest of the woman's seed fulfill their responsible part in repentance, faith and perseverance. No uncertainty as to the outcome crept in at this point because the grace that is operative in redemptive covenant is the sovereign grace of the God who keeps covenant. If the identity of the second Adam as the Son of God guaranteed that he would perform his part in that covenant of works made in heaven, then the fact that it was God the Father who promised him the reward of a people and kingdom in the Spirit guaranteed that that reward would be granted, that the promised people, the rest of the woman's seed, would come to Christ and share his glory. It was the Glory-Spirit, the Alpha-Omega executant in the creation of the cosmic temple at the beginning, who was given in the promise of the Father to the Son to raise up and consummate the living temple of Christ's people in a further exercise of that same sovereign creational omnipotence.

Genesis 3:15 announced that mankind would be divided by virtue of the separation of a people of God from the people of the devil and further that this separation, this "enmity", would be the result of God's own action: "I will put enmity." This declaration of a strictly divine initiation of the distinction between the two seeds, in particular of the separation of the one seed unto God in Christ, was a disclosure of God's sovereign election of a remnant people. It was this act of election that defined at once the design of the Son's work of atonement and his corresponding just reward from the Father. Implicitly included too was an assurance of the sovereign operation of the Spirit, infallibly effecting what the Father promised the Son in their eternal covenant. Because of the Father's faithfulness to his covenant promise, all those for whom the Son suffered the bruising of his heel would be given the requisite perseverance in faith by the Creator-Spirit and so come to heaven; because of the justice of God, none of those for whom the Son suffered the penalty of the broken covenant could suffer it a second time by descending themselves into hell. This is the gospel of sovereign redemptive grace which the Lord published in Eden. Proclaiming his own sovereign decree of election he prophesied in Genesis 3:15 the future that had been foreordained and guaranteed by the mutual commitments of the Father, Son, and Spirit in covenantal council before the world began.

B. A Seal of the New Covenant

God's words of judgment on man (Gen 3:16-19) were directed to the generality of mankind who would experience in common the curse pronounced. But Genesis 3:21 relates an episode in which the Lord dealt with Adam and Eve in their own individual identities as those who had heard the gospel of redemptive judgment in the judicial sentence against

Satan and had responded in faith. This shift in perspective takes place in verse 20, which breaks off the account of God's judicial words and provides an introduction to verse 21 by relating an act of faith on the part of Adam. It tells us that Adam in effect declared his confessional "Amen" to the Genesis 3:15 promise of restoration from death to life through the woman's seed. This he did by naming the woman "Life" (Eve). Verse 21 then narrates how the Lord responded to Adam's confession of faith by strengthening and instructing that faith further through a symbolic transaction in which he reaffirmed his redemptive purpose. Only after this did he proceed with the banishing of the representatives of the fallen race from the holy garden.

Shameful nakedness, though not the actual cause of man's alienation from God (as Adam had evasively claimed), was a symptom of man's fallen condition. Hence, by providing Adam and Eve with a covering for that nakedness the Lord signified to them (more directly and personally than he had in his words of judgment on the serpent) his intention to provide a remedy for man's alienation. It was only a symbolic sign, not the actual remedy for man's sinful condition, but it was indeed a sign that confirmed God's purpose to do what was necessary to cover man's shameful defilement and bring him out of hiding back into fellowship with his now reconciled God. The enduring quality of the material the Lord used to clothe Adam and Eve contrasted with the impermanence and inadequacy of their own attempted self-covering and thus signified that true salvation must come from the Lord.

A complex pun, artfully developed in the Genesis 3 narrative, points to the particular symbolic meaning of the clothing provided by the Lord. The term "naked" serves here as the center of a three-cornered word-play. We have previously noted that the narrative puns on the similarity of the sound of the words for naked and subtle, so indicating the likeness to the serpent taken on by man when he lost the likeness to God with which he had been invested at creation. It is now to be noted that the Hebrew word for naked is also linked to the word for skin (used for the clothing) by similarity of sound, if not by etymology. Within the framework of correspondences in this triangular word-play, in which man's nakedness connects on one side to the divine covering of skin and on the other to fallen man's likeness to the serpent, it would appear that the skin coverings, as the antithetical counterpart of the image of the devil, are to be understood as symbols of adornment with the glory of the image of God. (Compare the later use of animal skins among the tabernacle coverings that were symbolic replicas of the divine Glory.)

If then God's clothing of Adam and Eve was symbolic of investiture with the divine image, it will follow that this divine act should also be viewed as a renewed plighting of covenantal troth. (For a discussion of this point and particularly of the combination of the imagery of marriage troth and the clothing with God's image in the allegory of the Sinaitic Covenant in Ezekiel 16, see my *Images of the Spirit*, pp.50ff.)

We arrive at this same understanding of the Genesis 3:21 event as a sealing of covenantal commitment if we approach the episode from yet another perspective. We have seen that in the course of the temptation and subsequent interrogation the man and the woman had put asunder what God had joined together and that it was in fact their state of divorce that accounted for the shame that had come to attach to their nakedness. In that connection we observed that the condition of nakedness figures in biblical and extra-biblical legal symbolism as a sign of divorce. For God to cover the nakedness that publicized our first parents' state of divorce was to reunite them in marriage. In fact, quite apart from the situation of divorce, a man's spreading of a garment over a woman constituted a symbolic pledge of marriage. This fact is instructive at both levels of covenant ratification that we find ourselves dealing with in Genesis 3:21. At the level of the God-man covenant, God's covering the human covenanting party with a garment would itself (even apart from the identification of the skin-garments as symbolic of the *imago Dei*) symbolize directly God's renewal of his covenant with man (cf. Ezek 16:8). And at the human level, the covering of Adam and Eve with garments of skin would then serve, irrespective of the divorce background, as a marriage ratification ceremony. (The fact that the term for skin is singular might then be significant – the garments symbolic of their oneness being appropriately derived from one skin.) Thus recognized as the record of the remarriage of Adam and Eve, verse 21 forms the appropriate sequel to verse 20. Viewing verse 20 at the level of God's covenant with man, we have interpreted Adam's statement as a confession of faith. But obviously implicit in Adam's naming of Eve was also a resumption of their marital commitment to one another, and the ceremony of marriage described in verse 21 then follows after that in natural sequence.

If now Genesis 3:21 answers to verse 20 at two levels of covenantal engagement as a sealing of troth, it can hardly be doubted that these two levels are intended to be seen as sustaining a symbolic correspondence to each other, with the human marriage providing a picture of the divine covenanting. This symbolic interrelationship is corroborated by the fact that to confirm the marital reunion of the man and the woman was to correct the condition of divorce responsible for the sense of shame over nakedness which serves in the Genesis 3 narrative as evidence that man had broken his covenant with the Lord and which was indeed the concrete problem directly addressed by God's provision of clothing. Accordingly, in performing the ceremony of the remarriage of Adam and Eve the Lord was signifying through an eminently apt symbol his purpose to renew the divine-human marriage covenant.

Summing up, several lines of exegesis have converged on the interpretation of the act of clothing in Genesis 3:21 as a divine pledge answering to the faith-commitment of man described in verse 20. This symbolic ritual of mutual divine-human avowal of covenantal relationship was a ratifying of the redemptive covenant. Because of her whoredom the Lord had set forth the wife of his covenant naked, saying, "She is not my wife and I am not her husband" (cf. Hos 2:2,3). But now in forgiving grace he promised that he would betroth her to himself anew and forever (cf. Hos 2:19,20), acknowledging that she was his as she confessed, "You are my God" (cf. Hos 2:23; Deut 26:17,18).

Another feature of the remedy the Lord provided for man's condition of nakedness was that it had to be procured through a sacrifice of life Though the biblical text lays no emphasis on this and does not even mention the slaying of the animal specifically, the fact of the sacrificial death that took place inevitably arises in the reader's mind at the mention of the skin used for the clothing. This symbolic sealing of the gospel-promise of Genesis 3:15 thus echoes the latter's prophecy of the sufferings which the messianic seed must endure to secure the reconciliation with God and the renewal of the covenant. Viewing the clothing in terms of its derivation from an act of sacrifice, we cannot but regard it as a prophetic sign of the robe of righteousness the Savior obtains through his death to cover the sins of his people. This is entirely compatible with the interpretation of the clothing as a symbolic investiture with the *imago Dei* since righteousness is a component of that image and appertains, indeed, to the aspect of the image – its ethical glory – that has been most conspicuous in our interpretation of the clothing as symbolic of the divine likeness. When Adam and Eve left paradise they did so bearing a sign of restoration, a sign obtained by God's wielding the fiery sword of the cherubim against a sacrificial animal substitute.

Sacrifice was then a part of the earliest ratification of the Covenant of Grace as narrated in Genesis 3:21. In the postlapsarian situation, if the Lord is to enter into covenant with a people to bestow his holy kingdom on them, it is necessarily by sacrifice that this is done. Provision must be made to secure the fulfillment of the proper purpose of the covenant expressed in its redemptive promises before the Lord commits himself in covenant to those promises. Prerequisite to such covenant-making, therefore, is the sacrificial atonement whereby guilty sinners may become the forgiven, holy recipients of the covenanted glory. That is, the covenant of the Father and the Son as second Adam, with its requirement of obedience unto the death of the cross on the part of the incarnate Son, was foundational to the Lord's Covenant of Grace with the Church. Accordingly, the new covenant, the ultimate administration of that covenant, was ratified in the blood of Christ (Matt 26:28; Heb 10:29; 13:20) and it is this prerequisite role of Christ's atonement in the establishment of the new covenant that is prototypically expressed in the symbolic sacrifices by which the premessianic administrations of the Covenant of Grace were inaugurated from Genesis 3 onward.

II. REDEMPTIVE ESCHATOLOGY AND COMMON GRACE

A. Common Grace and Common Curse

If the gospel promise contained in Genesis 3:15 was to be fulfilled, final judgment must be postponed to make room for the kind of human history that was presupposed in the prophecy of the woman's seed and the great warfare with the devil and his seed. A confirmation of the divine purpose of salvation was in effect given, therefore, when the Lord pronounced a temporal, common curse rather than an ultimate judgment against the generality of mankind (Gen 3:16-19).

Though God's approach to man to pronounce judgment was of such a kind as would manifest his displeasure it was not an apocalyptic appearance in fiery wrath. The world order continued. The sun was not darkened; the heavens did not pass away; the earth was not consumed. Man was not totally abandoned to the power of sin and the devil; he was not cast into outer darkness. The positive benefits realized in a measure through this restraint on the effects of sin and the curse are not the eternal blessings of the holy, heavenly kingdom that come to the elect through God's saving grace in Christ, but they are blessings – temporal blessings that all men experience in common by virtue of their remaining part of the continuing world order. These common blessings are not deserved by mankind, but are a benefit enjoyed only by the grace of the Creator in his forbearance with those who have forfeited all blessing by their rebellion against him. A principle of common grace, a grace that provides benefits to the just and the unjust in common, thus informs the divine government of the postlapsarian world. This principle would subsequently receive more explicit formulation in divine revelation, especially in the postdiluvian covenant of God with all the earth. But it is clearly implicit in the pronouncing of the common curse in Genesis 3:16-19, for common grace and common curse are correlative to one another. The limitations of the common curse, which distinguish it from the postponed ultimate, unmitigated curse, are those imposed by the simultaneously operating principle of common grace.

Another benefit of common grace, besides the preservation of the natural order in a form that made a history of man on earth still possible, was the continuation, even though in modified fashion, of some important elements of the social-cultural order that had been established under the Creator's covenant with Adam. This too was implicit in the announcement of the common curse. Thus, in the curse upon the woman (Gen 3:16) it is assumed that the marriage institution would continue as a divine appointment for human society. Moreover, the blessing of the Creator would rest on the marriage relationship in sufficient measure for its function as the institution for the propagation of human life to be fulfilled. There would be barrenness and pain, miscarriage and abortion, but there would be children. In spite of the common curse, by virtue of common grace there would be the "book of the generations of Adam" (Gen 5:1). Again, in the curse on the man (Gen 3:17-19) it is presupposed that man's dominion over the earth would be continued and that here too divine blessing would be granted on man's labor to such a degree that human life would be sustained and cultural satisfactions realized. There would be thorns and pests, drought and famine, toil unto death, the destiny that seemed to mock the meaning of it all, but meanwhile there would be bread as the staff of life and wine to make glad the heart of man. And in man's settlements would be heard the sound of the forge and of music. The way the biblical narrative subsequently traces the significant beginnings of industry, the arts, and sciences in the Cainite communities (Gen 4:17ff.) underscores the commonness of common grace, the ungodly as well as the godly enjoying its benefits. Thanks to common grace, chaos would be averted; human life would retain societal structuring through the continuation of the institution of the family, afterwards supplemented by the institution of the state (Gen 4:15; 9:6).

Common grace was introduced to act as a rein to hold in check the curse on mankind and to make possible an interim historical environment as the theater for a program of redemption. By reason of the common curse there would be natural and social evils, destructive earthquakes in various places and devastating wars of nations rising against nations, so that man's civilization and man himself would be threatened with total extinction. But the restraining hand of God's common grace would temper the common curse until redemptive history had run its full course and the appointed hour of the final *parousia* had come.

B. The Holy and the Common

A further facet of the commonness that is in view when we speak of common grace calls for attention. This sphere is common not only in the sense that its benefits are shared by the generality of mankind, the just and the unjust alike, but in the sense that it is nonsacred. Particular emphasis needs to be given to the fact that the political, institutional aspect of common grace culture is not holy, but profane.

Significantly, when the Lord republished the cultural ordinances within the historical framework of his common grace for the generality of fallen mankind, he did not attach his Sabbath promise to this common cultural order. The ordinance of the Sabbath was not reissued in the revelation of the common grace order either in Genesis 3:16-19 or in the covenantal promulgation of it in Genesis 9. This withholding of the Sabbath sign from common grace culture is a clear indication of the secular, nonholy character of that culture. For to place the stamp of the Sabbath on a cultural program is to set it apart as holy to God, as a bearer of the divine name and of the promise of being crowned with consummation glory. Accordingly, in the postlapsarian context the Scriptures relate the Sabbath sign of sanctification and consummation to the redemptive program exclusively. The only culture on which the sabbatical sign is explicitly impressed is the theocratic kingdom-culture of Israel under the old covenant. (That does not mean that the Sabbath sign is not present in any form at all in the life of the covenant people when they are organized as a simple cultic community, as in patriarchal times or in the present church age.) By appointing the Sabbath as the sign of his covenant with the Israelite kingdom, the product of his redemptive grace, the Lord sharply distinguished Israel as a cultural-political entity from the common kingdom-cultures of the common grace world. The Sabbath given to Israel signified that God was sanctifying this redeemed nation to be peculiarly his own, uniquely identified by his holy name (Exod 31:13). And to separate and differentiate Israel from the common grace kingdoms of the earth as distinctively and uniquely the holy theocratic kingdom sanctified by and unto the Lord God was, of course, to identify those common grace kingdoms as nonholy, profane.

The Consummation, with its eternal holy Sabbath, does not come through the operation of the principle of common grace in history, as is signalized by the fact that the sabbatical time pattern, which gives symbolic promise of that Consummation, does not inform common grace activities and institutions. To be sure, the principle of common grace is put into the service of redemption. By making possible a general history common grace opens the way for holy redemptive history. Especially by providing for a genealogical history of mankind that should continue until all the seed of the woman had been born, and in particular the messianic seed, common grace contributes to the purposes of the kingdom program of God's special saving grace. But the contribution is indirect. The common culture that is the direct fruit of common grace is not itself identifiable with the holy, Sabbath-sealed redemptive kingdom of God.

Another way of saying this is that common grace culture is not itself the particular holy kingdom-temple culture that was mandated under the creational covenant. Although certain functional and institutional provisions of the original cultural mandate are resumed in the common grace order, these now have such a different orientation, particularly as to objectives, that one cannot simply and strictly say that it is *the* cultural mandate that is being implemented in the process of common grace culture. It might be closer to the truth to say that the cultural mandate of the original covenant in Eden is being carried out in the program of salvation, since the ultimate objective of that mandate, the holy kingdom-temple, will be the consummate achievement of Christ under the Covenant of Grace. On the other hand, the genealogical and earthly aspects of the original cultural mandate that were to constitute its preconsummation history are not part of the redemptive program *per se*. For example, even though it may be said that Christ, through the Spirit, begets the new mankind, this redemptive work of regeneration sustains a metaphorical, or analogical, not literal relationship to the genealogical function stipulated in the commission assigned to man in the beginning. The treatment of the great commission (Matt 28:18-20) by theonomic reconstructionists may be cited as a glaring instance of confusion in this fundamental area. Indeed, dominion theology as a whole represents the systematic outworking of their failure to understand the biblical concept of common grace culture. As brought over into the postlapsarian world, the cultural mandate undergoes such refraction that it cannot be identified in a simple, unqualified way with either the holy or common enterprises. Nevertheless, when dealing with postlapsarian functions and institutions, both common and holy-redemptive, it is important to recognize their creational rootage and the kind of continuities that do obtain between them and the terms of the original cultural mandate.

In the coexistence of the holy and common lies the peculiar character of the present world aeon. Such is the antithesis between the holy and the common that the perfecting of the universal theocratic kingdom at the consummation of the holy redemptive program terminates the common grace order. Meanwhile, the partial presence of that holy eternal reality is, from the perspective of common grace, an intrusion into the general world order. It is an eschatological intrusion if viewed as a proleptic realization of the consummate kingdom. It is a cosmological (specifically, heavenly) intrusion if viewed as a downward projection of the holy sanctuary-domain of God already existent above. (For a further discussion of this, see my *The Structure of Biblical Authority*, Part 2, Chapter 3.)

Intrusion of the principles and powers that characterize the eschatological judgment and consummate kingdom assumes a variety of forms, both realistic and symbolic. To cite the supreme instance, in the incarnation of the Son of God the heavenly world entered into earth history by way of personal divine presence. Thus, Christ's priestly ministry on earth is regarded in the book of Hebrews as a service of the heavenly tabernacle itself. Also, Christ's redeeming death was the first act of the Final Judgment and his resurrection was the actual beginning of the final resurrection. In connection with the personal presence of Jesus, the Lord from heaven, the restorative powers that will produce the eschatological cosmic renewal broke through beforehand in the form of miraculous healing as a prophetic earnest of paradise restored and perfected. Similarly, in the presence and operation of the Spirit the common grace order is penetrated by the reality of the heavenly-eschatological order, which is peculiarly and preeminently the order of the Spirit. To be in the Spirit is to be in the celestial realm of divine Glory. The work of spiritual renewal which the Spirit has been accomplishing in the elect from the woman on through all subsequent generations of her seed has been a continuing pre-experience of the reality of the everlasting life of heaven within this present common grace/common curse aeon.

As this last example shows, eschatological intrusion was a feature of premessianic times as well as of the present new covenant days, even though the advent of Christ inaugurated a distinctive epoch in the whole development. There was indeed under the old covenant a comprehensive (partly realistic, partly symbolic) projection of the heavenly-eschatological domain into earth history in kingdom form in the theocratic kingdom of Israel. Heaven came to earth in supernatural realism in the phenomenon of the Glory-Spirit revealed in the sanctuary in Israel's midst. The eternal cosmic realm received symbolic expression in the land of Canaan. As is shown by the sharp distinction between this holy, theocratic, Sabbath-sanctified kingdom of Israel and the kingdoms of the common grace world around it, the special Israelite manifestation of the kingdom of heaven was indeed an intrusive phenomenon in the common grace order. Appropriately, in connection with the symbolic kingdom-intrusion under the old covenant there were also in-breakings of the power of eschatological restoration in the physical realm and anticipatory applications of the principle of final redemptive judgment in the conduct of the political life of Israel, notably in the deliverance from Egypt, the conquest of Canaan, and the restoration from exile, though also throughout the governmental-judicial provisions of the Mosaic laws.

In messianic as well as in premessianic times the intrusion of the heavenly-consummate reality has been accompanied by symbols of various sorts. There have been prophetic typological symbols of the coming intrusion in the Son and there have been sacramental symbols of the already realized intrusion through the Spirit – holy signs all of the presence of another world-aeon within the historical order of common grace.

Recognition of the exceptional intrusive character of things holy within the common world is of vital importance in biblical hermeneutics, particularly in the interpretation of Old Testament legislation and prophecy. When interpreting laws, we must constantly reckon with the possibility that a particular stipulation of the old covenant was shaped to a greater or lesser degree by the unique intrusive nature of the holy-kingdom order which was regulated by that covenant. Since the intruded holiness of the heavenly kingdom extended to the Israelite theocratic structure as a whole, to its cultural as well as cultic dimensions, we always have the responsibility, whether dealing with laws of cultic ceremony or laws of community life, to distinguish which features of Israelite law were peculiarly theocratic (or typologically symbolic) and which are still normative in our present nontheocratic situation. In the area of institutional functions we must avoid the common fallacy of assigning to common earthly kingdoms the distinctive functions prescribed for Israel as a holy, confessional, redemptive kingdom. For example, we must not impose on the civil government the duty of punishing sins against the first four laws of the Decalogue as though they were civil offenses.

Similarly, the interpreter must take full account of these same factors in the treatment of the curse and blessing sanctions that are affixed to the stipulations of the old covenant and are the core of kingdom prophecy. For example, one must determine whether a particular divine guarantee of earthly good is not an intrusive feature of the life of theocratic Israel as prototypical symbol of the consummate kingdom of heaven and therefore not to be extended to individuals or nations within the nonholy, nontheocratic context of common grace. Thus, we will not misapply a text like Psalm 33:12, appropriating for some common nation the blessing it pronounces on the holy covenantal kingdom of God (cf. Deut 32:9). At the level of broad eschatological reconstructions, the biblical theologian who is aware of the intrusive nature of the holy within the common grace order will shun those premillennial and postmillennial views that posit a fulfillment of the kingdom prophecies in the form of a holy, specially protected and prospered, worldwide geopolitical institution before the advent of the world to come. Such a worldwide theocracy before the Consummation, he will perceive, would be a contradiction and indeed a premature abrogation of the common grace cultural order of this world.

Again, in this connection, it would be well to recall a point made above by way of introduction to the law of the creational covenant, namely, that all human activities are religious. In the postlapsarian world the people of God function in both the holy-cultic and the profane-cultural spheres and as they do so they are to be conscious of doing all things, whether in the holy or common spheres, as a matter of thankful obedience to God and for his glory and thus as a religious service (Col 3:17,23). Nevertheless, this religious integration of the believer's life as a comprehensive service of Christ does not mean that the distinction between holy and common spheres gets obliterated. On the contrary, it is precisely because of our religious commitment to obey the commandments of the Lord we love that we will honor and maintain this distinction which he has established in his covenant Word.

Chapter Two

PROPHETIC CULT IN THE CITY OF MAN

At the end of the days, Metapolis, eternal city of the Great King, will be revealed, a gift of heaven. From the cocoon within which it exists through the long ages of postlapsarian history, the covenant community will emerge in an apocalyptic metamorphosis-event as the new creation of God. The story of how that historical matrix structure first came into being after the Fall and was preserved through prediluvian times, a story entwined with that of the origin and apostate development of the city of man in the world wilderness, is compactly narrated in Genesis 4:1-6:8. Though it was all at another time and in another world, there is a profound correspondence between the circumstances of the people of God in that world-age and the situation of the church of the new covenant age. In fact, with regard to the form and function of the redemptive community and its relationship to the world and its institutions that ancient community offers a parallel in some respects closer to the church of our age than does the Israelite kingdom whose history, occupying most of the Old Testament, stands nearer in time to ours. Insight into fundamental aspects of the church's place within the interim world order today may, therefore, be derived from reflection on the biblical record of the covenant community in the world that once was.

About two-thirds of the first of the ten generations-sections composing the book of Genesis is devoted to the account of man's probation in Eden (Gen 2:4-3:24). The last third of that section (Gen 4:1-26) is an extremely condensed survey of the history of the world that then was from the Fall to the Flood. We shall begin this chapter by examining the picture drawn there of the world culture as it took shape among the fallen earthlings. That cultural structure, produced according to the principle of common grace, was the interim environment in the midst of which the community of redemptive grace and covenant was to exist and pursue its historical journey from paradise lost towards paradise regained. In the last part of the present chapter our attention will turn to the redemptive community and its distinctive place in the postlapsarian world. This theme is the primary subject of the second of the ten generations-sections, which begins at Genesis 5:1. The closing part of this second section of Genesis returns, however, to the rebellious development of prediluvian man outside the covenant line and that closing passage (Gen 6:1ff.) will also figure prominently in the treatment of the city of man, with which we start.

I. INTERIM WORLD STRUCTURE

When the course of events described in the early chapters of Genesis is compared with the reconstructions of mankind's cultural progress arrived at by historians of man's remotest past on the basis of the archaeological evidence at their disposal, certain questions arise that are of considerable interest but which fall outside our particular purview here. Our task is biblical theology and our present concern is with what the biblical revelation discloses concerning the religious character and direction of the interim world culture referred to above. Our comments on these other issues will, therefore, be confined to a couple of brief observations. First, with respect to the archaeological data it must be remembered how extremely scanty and fragmentary are the bits of information available for the vast stretches of earth history under scrutiny. Moreover, here and there hints have apparently been found of advanced culture, with a globe-spanning navigational capability, in a far more remote past than traditional evolutionary historiography has perceived. Second, from the side of the biblical text and its interpretation, we wish to insist that there is no warrant for regarding the Genesis 4 account of the over-all course of man's prediluvian technological history as a stylized picture, dependent on a culture belonging in literal terms to a much later time. To read the narrative that way is to treat it as something akin to allegory rather than as the history it actually is. Further, we must not fail to recognize that the facticity of the prediluvian culture as depicted in Genesis 4 receives a virtual endorsement from Jesus in his acceptance of the historical reality of the Noahic ark, the construction of which would seem to presuppose such a previous history of technological progress as Genesis 4 presents.

A. The City as Divine Ordinance

1. Promulgation of the Ordinance

The story of man's cultural advance quickly comes into focus in Genesis 4 as the story of the city. The whole career of Cain after he has been cursed for the murder of Abel and driven out into the land of Nod is related in one verse (4:17), stating that he had a son and built a city, naming the city after his son, Enoch, "Dedication". (If certain textual emendations of verse 17 are adopted, Enoch would be the builder of this city.)

In spite of the connections of the city here at its first appearance in the Bible with the rejected line of Cain, it is not to be regarded as an evil invention of ungodly fallen man. As developed and exploited by sinful mankind the city does indeed become the towering manifestation of man's revolt against God. But the city is not in itself a cursed contradiction of the divine order which might be supportively affirmed by those who wish to do so only by some dialectical sleight of hand. If we are to avoid giving such a dialectical warp to our theological interpretation of the city, nothing is more important than the recognition of the genuine historicity of the earliest chapters of the book of Genesis. For there we have the record both of an original, normal order when the city of God was mandated in the stipulations of the creational covenant and of the subsequent common grace order and its provision of the city, not now the city of God but the city in a form adapted to the abnormal situation following upon the Fall. We will consider these two cities as divinely appointed through creation and common grace ordinances, before surveying man's sinful distortion of the postlapsarian city and the judgment thereby incurred.

When we attempted in our account of the sanctions of the God's covenant with Adam to picture the eschatological goal set for man at the beginning, we observed that human history would proceed by way of a development of Megapolis and thence to the Metapolis of the Consummation. Human culture would take city-form. This was inevitable because the city is nothing but the synthesis of the several elements already present in the cultural program that man was directed to carry out. The couple in the garden was to multiply, so providing the citizens of the city. Their cultivation of earth's resources as they extended their control over their territorial environment through the fabrication of sheltering structures would produce the physical architecture of the city. And the authority structure of the human family engaged in the cultural process would constitute the centralized government by which the life and functioning of the city would be organized, under God. The cultural mandate given at creation was thus a mandate to build the city and it would be through the blessing of God on man's faithfulness in the covenanted task that the construction of the city would be completed. Whether, then, we examine the creational order from the perspective of the covenant's stipulations or the perspective of its blessing sanctions, the city comes into view. It is the sum of man's endeavors and the shape of his hope.

It was, therefore, plainly an act of grace and mercy when, after man in Adam had broken faith and covenant, God again appointed a city-structure for the benefit of the generality of mankind. This city would not be the same city that the Lord established at the beginning. That is, it would not be a theocratic, covenant city with an institutional integration of culture and cult. Such a holy temple-city would be provided through the redemptive program for God's elect. The city that fallen man would build would be a common city, temporal, profane, and it would exist under the shadow of the common curse. Nevertheless, that mankind in general should in measure be fruitful and their work productive, that they should not be abandoned to chaotic lawlessness, that there should still be an urban structuring of man's historical existence — this was, indeed, a good gift of the Creator's common grace.

The revelation of the common grace institution of the city was to come to its most complete expression (so far as the book of Genesis records the history) in the divine disclosure to Noah when mankind was beginning to make its way again after the judgment of the old world in the Flood. The appointment then assumed the form of a covenant, in which the city was a divine mandate and blessing (Gen 8:21-9:17). But the divine provision of the common grace city had been made known in the old world long before the Flood. Indeed, the disclosure concerning some of the necessary components of this common city took place immediately after the Fall. For as we have seen, implicit in the word of God's curse addressed to the generality of mankind at the judgment in Eden (Gen 3:16ff.) were intimations of the continuance of the marriage institution and of the task of subduing the earth. And shortly thereafter the foundation of the judicial authority structure of the city was established in a remarkable divine communication to the one who was to become the founder of the city of man. Genesis 4:15 records God's reply to a complaint-appeal of Cain and in this word of divine response we have the oracular origin of the city, or state. (On Gen 4:15 see my "The Oracular Origin of the State" in *Biblical and Near Eastern Studies*, ed. G. A. Tuttle [Grand Rapids: Eerdmans, 1978], 132-141).

Cain had just heard God's judicial curse against him for killing his brother and he cringed in anticipation of a fugitive existence in what he assumed would be a totally lawless world-wilderness. He complained that he found unendurable the prospect of a God-forsaken world abandoned to anarchical terror, a world from which the Judge of all the earth turned his face, paying no heed to rampant wrong or clamant cry for right. He lamented that in this world devoid of law and order he would be exposed to the unrestrained vengeance of the family of mankind, all of them seeking to avenge the blood of their brother Abel (Gen 4:11-14).

God responded to this complaint by correcting the false assumption that mankind was not to be under the control of any formal judicial system. In fact, the Lord took the occasion to promulgate an ordinance to the effect that there would be a divinely sponsored administration of justice among men. In particular, under the contemplated judicial order an act of murder was to be met with full divine vengeance. In the language of Genesis 4:15a, formulated in terms suited to the immediate occasion: "If anyone kills Cain, he will be avenged sevenfold." In verse 15b this asseveration of God is referred to as a solemn commitment, an oath that has been given to Cain (the text does not have in view any "mark" of Cain). Paraphrased the verse says: Thus the Lord gave Cain an oath assuring him that it would not be the case that anyone who came upon him would be free to kill him with impunity. God declared that the anarchical situation Cain had described would not actually obtain. God's face would not be hidden; it was rather his purpose to establish a judicial office to execute vengeance sevenfold, that is, complete divine retribution (cf. Lev 26:24; Ps 79:9-12). The subsequent actualization of the sevenfold divine enforcement of justice in a human agency is reflected in the designation of the human agents of judgment as "gods" (cf., e.g., Ps 82:6). Also, the Scripture identifies the state's avenging function as an execution of God's wrath (cf., e.g., Rom 12:19; 13:4).

The judicial order announced in Genesis 4:15 is, of course, identical with the authority structure of the city. In the Genesis 4 context, the oracular word to Cain concerning the order of sevenfold vengeance serves as a prelude to the account of the historical beginnings of the city (vv.16ff.). Genesis 4:15 is thus a virtual city charter. This is reflected in the way Lamech, tyrant king of the city, alludes to the terms of this text in his boastful apology for his reign (Gen 4:24).

2. Remedial Benefits of the City

The postlapsarian city thus had its original authorization in a divine pronouncement to Cain ordaining an order of law and creating through the principle of common grace a political structure in the formless void of the accursed wilderness. Soon thereafter a "city" (Gen 4:17), a settlement of separate families under a common territorial jurisdiction, came into being in the land of Wandering (Nod). Insofar as this city derives from the principle of God's common grace, it is to be viewed positively. Man may turn the city into something more dreadful than the howling wilderness, but that is another matter. As the provision of God's common grace, the city is a benefit, serving mankind as at least a partial, interim refuge from the wilderness condition into which the fallen race, exiled from paradise, has been driven. Certainly, according to the biblical record the original divine promulgation of the city was gladly welcomed by the one who became the human founder of the city, and again in the postdiluvian era the founders of the representative world-city of Babel were covetous of the cohesive benefits of the city.

Peculiar to the common grace city, in distinction from the original holy city of God, is the remedial role which is so prominent in the common grace cultural enterprise in general. Functions that would have been performed by the city apart from the Fall are now modified by being turned to the new purpose of offsetting, to an extent, the evils arising through man's sinfulness and as a result of the common curse on the race.

We have seen that even apart from sin man's culture, summed up in the city, would have had a protective function, sheltering from whatever was inhospitable in nature. But beyond such preventive purpose is the corrective, ameliorating function of the common grace city. It serves now not just as hospice but as hospital. Its societal dimension mitigates the fragmentation of the human family and the isolation of people thrust apart by the scattering impact of the common curse, the curse which doomed man to vagabond or even fugitive existence. The exile-curse would work relentlessly to drive man on in a restless vagrancy, exposed to wild terrain and tempest in an untracked world, but the city community would bring a measure of settled rootage and stability. Even for the extreme separation introduced into the human race by death, that ultimate common curse evil that separates the rising generation from preceding generations, the city supplies a kind of surface continuity at the burial place, the place of name monuments that retain deceased citizenry in the memory of the living. In contemplation of the cemetery we become acutely conscious of the limitations of the remedies afforded by common grace.

Involved in the remedial functioning of the common grace city are fundamental modifications in the original meaning of the city itself. As we have already noted, the city is now not just hostel but a center for medical help and in providing such euphemistic alleviation as it can for the curse of the separation wrought by death the polis undergoes a shading off into the necropolis. Such changes are observable in one aspect of the city after another. Its drawing together of resources, strength, and talent is no longer just a matter of mutual complementation of effort for greater efficiency in the task of subduing the world but becomes now a pooling of power for defense against the subjugation of the community by attackers; the city assumes the character of a fortress. No longer is it just a geographical center for commerce, a marketplace to expedite the flow of the abundance of the manifold fruits and products of man's cultural endeavors. Rather, as an administrative community it becomes a welfare agency burdened with the relief of those destitute by reason of the cursing of the ground and the general frustration of man's cultural efforts under the common curse, all aggravated by the selfishness of men themselves competing in an economy tending to disequilibrium.

Particularly significant in the altered identity of the common grace city is the corrective function now performed by it as a governmental structure. Positive regulation of societal order and direction of cultural endeavor must now be supplemented by an enforcing of justice through penal sanctions. As a major means used in his common grace to restrain the manifestation of man's depravity, God assigns to city government the responsibility to act as his agent for the protection of the community by repressing and punishing evil-doing. He appoints the city as the minister of the temporal sanctions of justice until the world comes to the hour of God's final judgment with its eternal sanctions. It has the authority to kill the body until the Judge comes who can destroy both body and soul in hell. Thus the city is invested with the sword, and so heavily preoccupied does it become with this enforcement of justice, with policing and punishing, that it is known in this present evil world as preeminently a judicial order. Its distinctive hallmark is that it bears the sword.

A formal, partial continuity obtains between the city of common grace and the city envisioned in the original cultural mandate, but the interim city is so different from the city that would have emerged in a sinless history that we distinguish it from the latter by calling it the state. As used here the term "state" corresponds to the broader application of it by anthropologists rather than to the restricted usage of it by political scientists for modern states with certain distinctive political features. The term "city" must do double duty. It must be used for the individual city, which may coalesce with the state in the city-state or exist as one of many cities within a state.

But "the city (of man)" will also be used here for the total phenomenon of world kingdoms or states throughout history.

3. Common Grace City and the Kingdoms of God and Satan

a.   Bestial but Legitimate: Abuses of the city result in urban malformations, like the slum, the ghetto, the gulag. But beyond the city's malaise of social-economic-political injustice is an evil more central to the concerns of biblical revelation. There is in the city a spiritual malignancy, the fatal consequence of the usurpation of the world kingdom by Satan and the prostitution of the city to demonic service. In the lurid exposé found in the apocalyptic mode of Scripture, the satanically perverted urban power structure is seen as a beast savagely turned against the citizens of the city who refuse its mark. The conflict thus depicted is not that of class struggle or racial strife. The victims are not those disadvantaged in things temporal. It is rather a matter of religious antithesis, an ancient diabolical enmity. It is against the redeemed of the Lamb that the controlling powers of the world kingdom direct their hellish hostility.

Yet, in the face of the bestial aspect assumed by the city and the ensuing religious warfare that rages within it, Scripture affirms the legitimacy of the city. One thinks of the historical context of Romans 13. The legitimacy of the city is affirmed not because the bestializing of the city is a relatively late historical development. As a matter of fact, the Beast-power is not just a phenomenon of the present church age. The founder of the city was himself the slayer of the first martyr-prophet. And Old Testament apocalyptic exposes the beast-nature of the world-kingdom in the days of Israel. Our positive affirmation of the city structure is not based on a mere chronological priority of positive to negative factors in the make-up of the city. It is due rather to the fact that fundamental structural legitimacy is a matter of divine ordinance, not of the nature of man's administration of the institution. The frightful religious tension of the city belongs to the story of the apostate direction taken by the city potentates and should not be allowed to obscure the character of the city as a structure founded on the common grace ordinance of the Creator.

Over against every tendency to identify the city at its essential core with those demonic powers that seize and manipulate the power structure of the state we must assert the biblical testimony to the goodness of this postlapsarian institution as an appointment of God's common grace, beneficial and remedial in its functions. This testimony contradicts not only the theological interpretation of the city that goes to the extreme of identifying it in its essential structure with the demonic powers. It also invalidates the kind of ethical scruple expressed in the decision of some who, conscious of their citizenship in another, heavenly city, would exclude themselves from a fully responsible role in the total valid functioning of the interim city and particularly would exempt themselves from the characteristic function of the city as wielder of the sword of justice.

b. Legitimacy Not Sanctity: In backing away from the mistake of identifying the city *per se* with the kingdom of Satan, we must beware of backing into the opposite error of identifying it with the kingdom of God in an institutional sense, an error equally serious and even more common. In the midst of the threatening world environment to which man is exposed through the common curse, the common grace city offers the hope of a measure of temporal safety, but it does not afford eternal salvation. It should not, therefore, be identified with the holy kingdom of God, which is the structural manifestation of that salvation. Failure to respect the boundary between the common grace culture, of which the city is an institutional expression, and the holy kingdom of God is an error that takes various forms within a variety of theological positions in other respects quite divergent from one another. With respect to this problem, special account will be taken here of a branch of the Reformed Kuyperian tradition, the tradition to which the present work is most indebted for its concern with the development of a biblical world-and-life view. We shall interact with the neo-Dooyeweerdian school and their application of the cosmonomic philosophy to the subject at hand.

Characteristically, members of that school have been critical of schematizations that distinguish between the city of man and the city of God. In particular, they would frown on the suggestion that the city of man is common, in the sense of nonholy. They believe that they detect a scholastic nature-grace dualism lurking in any such approach. But to dismiss every two-cities schema on the grounds of such a suspicion is too hasty and undiscriminating. Certainly in the form being advocated here the common city/holy city distinction is part of a total view of Christ and culture that recognizes and indeed emphasizes the full cosmic-creational character of the covenantal kingdom at last realized through the Covenant of Grace. Our contention is, moreover, that the identification of the common grace city as nonholy is not only systematically compatible with such a total world-view but that it is demanded by the specific relevant biblical data. The Scriptures compel us to distinguish between the kingdom of God as realm and reign and to recognize that though everything is embraced under the reign of God, not everything can be identified as part of the kingdom of God viewed as a holy realm.

We are in agreement with the neo-Dooyeweerdians when they account for the religious antithesis evident in the life of the city by treating it not in terms of the structural nature of the city but as belonging to the direction of the response given to the city-mandate in the fallen situation. By relating the religious antithesis to the directional aspect and not to the structural aspect, the institutional legitimacy of the city can be properly affirmed. Unfortunately, however, in a philosophical zeal for an abstract structural monism apparently, the neo-Dooyeweerdians commit themselves to a view of historical reality within which the Creator himself would not be allowed to respond to the Fall with appropriate modifications of the institutional structuring of the original creation. Specifically, he would not be free to introduce a structural dualism in which there coexisted legitimately both holy kingdom institution and non-holy institution. Or, stated in other terms, the cosmonomic philosophy does not seem able to do justice to the impact of historical-eschatological developments on the created world-order.

We must apparently assume that the neo-Dooyeweerdians are prepared to repudiate structural dualism anytime, anywhere in the divinely instituted order. Otherwise it is difficult to explain their out of hand rejection of any and all views that distinguish between the holy kingdom of God and a common sphere (including the state) not identifiable as God's kingdom as just so many examples of scholastic nature-grace dualism. But how fallacious such a stance is becomes manifest when the attempt is made to carry it through to the eschaton and apply it to the eternal abode of the damned. In dealing with the phenomenon we call hell it becomes evident how necessary it is to distinguish in God's kingly rule between holy realm and sovereign reign. Hell cannot be accounted for, certainly not fully, in terms of the apostate direction given to the creational order by Satan and his followers. The place of perdition is rather God's own ultimate structural response to the satanic rebellion. The lake of fire is the place prepared by the Creator for the devil and his angels and his human "seed" (Matt 25:41). And according to the biblical representation it is a place outside the gates of the holy city (Rev 21:8; 22:14,15). Though not even hell may be viewed as a realm beyond a presence of God in sovereign power and revelation of wrath, according to the conceptual model of the biblical imagery it is a realm outside the holy realm of the kingdom of heaven.   It is embraced within the Creator's reign (in a general, not redemptive sense, obviously), but it is not part of God's kingdom realm. Nor does the Creator's structural response to the satanic rebellion against his holy sovereignty wait until the Consummation. Scripture discloses the existence of an interim place for the restraining or imprisoning of demons. Surely this dark realm is no holy realm.

If philosophical theorizing is to remain under the control and correction of biblical revelation, the neo-Dooyeweerdian assumption that all creation can be identified in monistic fashion with the kingdom-realm of God must be abandoned. If our theology is not hampered by that assumption, we will readily perceive that it is too simplistic to appeal to the universality of God's rule as the reason for rejecting an analysis of postlapsarian culture that distinguishes between a common city and the holy city. If we listen to what the Word of God says specifically about the institutions in question, we discover that with the emergence of the religious antithesis, the Lord God, in the interests of his redemptive purposes, sovereignly revised the original structure of things, bringing into being within the arena of earthly history an interim world order which involved the holy/common distinction as one of its fundamental features. In particular, he established the institution of the state as a nonholy structure under the principle of common grace. The sphere of the state, though not exempt from God's rule and not devoid of the divine presence (indeed, though it is the scene of God's presence in a measure of common blessing) is, nevertheless, not to be identified as belonging to the kingdom of God or sharing in its holiness. We may not deny to the Creator his sovereign prerogative of creative structuring and restructuring and authoritative defining and redefining.   And least of all should we venture to do so in the name of honoring the universality of his kingly rule.

Appreciation is due to the cosmonomic philosophy for contributions it has made to the interpretation of the structure of created reality, but its canonization of a formal monistic schema for the creational structures has tended to render it impervious at certain important points to the instruction of the canonical Scriptures. It cannot accommodate in its world-view the Bible's conceptual modeling of the cosmos (as in the case of the apocalyptic depiction of hell as the outside realm) or the Bible's ordering of culture by specific ordinances (as in the case of the common grace instituting of the state). Thus, ironically, this world-view which dismisses the distinction between the common city of man and the holy city of God as a form of nature-grace scholasticism itself falls under suspicion of being a new scholasticism by according in practice a hermeneutical priority to philosophical speculation over perspicuous biblical revelation. It may be added that though the perspectivalist method of doing theology is critical of the cosmonomic philosophy, it too is beset by this same hermeneutical problem, as evidenced for one thing in its handling of this very subject of the theology of the state.

Conclusion: Summing up then, the meaning or essential identity of the postlapsarian city is not found in identification either with the kingdom of Satan or with the kingdom of God. Nor is it to be explained in terms of a dialectical seesawing between the demonic and the divine. This divinely appointed institution exists within the sphere of common grace, which is the corollary, the counterpoise, of the common curse. The fundamental shape of the city is the resultant of the interplay of these two correlative principles of divine action, a divine wrath and a divine grace that restrains that wrath according to the measure of sovereign divine purpose. Such is the biblical conceptual framework for defining the basic meaning of the city.

4. State Functions and Limitations

Under the present heading no attempt is made to survey the state's total sphere of authority and activity. We shall simply be taking note of certain basic factors relating to its historical origins as a common grace institution which provide guidelines for the determination of the state's proper province. Because of the ever urgent necessity of guarding against the undue expansion of the domain of the state, it will be our special concern to point out the limitations of the state's role in society.

a. Complementarity of Family and State: Unlike the originally mandated temple-city of the family of Adam, the postlapsarian city does not encompass the totality of the life and activity of humanity within its assigned jurisdiction. All societal organization does not get absorbed into the state. In the divine reordering after the Fall the several aspects and functions of the original city were distributed among several nonconcentric authority structures that replaced the one original universal kingdom. Only a segment of the total complex of functions belonging to the original city was committed to the state, and then only with modifications.

Along with the institution of the state in this common grace realignment stands the institution of the family, with its own share of the redistributed functions and its own sphere of authority. As reconstituted under common grace, the family is not identical with the original family. There is, indeed, a certain continuity of form and function between them. The common grace family is still structured by the marriage ordinance and it continues to be the institution for procreation and the primary institution for the nurturing of children and the cultivation of the world. But unlike the pre-Fall family of Adam, this reconstituted family *per se* is not the covenant community, not the kingdom people. Though not designated by a different name comparable to the term "state" used to distinguish the common grace city from the pre-Fall city, the common grace family confronts us with another instance of the general truth that the cultural enterprise under common grace cannot be simply identified as *the* (original) cultural mandate. There is continuity but with a difference. However, our chief concern in the present context is to observe that the presence, alongside the state, of this other institution of the family with its own allotted functional domain constituted a delimitation of the scope and the sovereignty of the state.

Within the common grace era the family, of course, precedes the state. The latter could not emerge in the postlapsarian world until the simple, undifferentiated family of Adam and Eve had multiplied and subdivided into a number of sufficiently distanced families. Illustrative of the development is the history of Cain. His early crime of murder was not punished by human society, evidently because only the undifferentiated family existed when the crime was committed and, according to the divine wisdom, it was not appropriate that the simple family should execute internally the penal sanctions of retributive justice. That is a task for the state, and, as we have seen, God revealed to Cain his purpose to establish the state to perform it. Meanwhile there was a stage in which the family existed prior to the rise of the state, as the anomalous judicial treatment of Cain attests.

When, presently, the state came into being it was then as a complementary institution alongside the previously existing family within the common grace order. From this biblical datum of the complementarity of family and state as alike institutions of the same common grace order, the two assuming between them the full compass of cultural functions given at creation (adapted now to the new order), we derive our basic orientation for determining the proper responsibilities of the state in society. Clearly the state was not introduced to challenge the previously existing family, whether by usurping its God-given functions or in any way undermining it or eroding its sphere of authority. By reason of its prior presence as a discrete sphere of sovereign responsibility established by God, the family set bounds on the sphere of the state's functioning. At the same time, the family presented the state with positive obligations, namely, to recognize, protect, and preserve the rights and role given to the family as an associate common grace institution. The state was to provide a supportive framework for the life of the family. Likewise the family was in turn to recognize and honor the state in its God-given task. The public and private institutional spheres each defined the other's limits.

Besides being supportive of the family, the state was to perform a role supplementary to that of the family. On the state would devolve various responsibilities in the public domain that would arise as a connecting tissue between separate family cultural entities. And in the area of the interrelationship of individual families in the cultural task the state would have a governmental role. In part, these functions of the state would involve merely conservation, maintenance, regulation of common procedural conventions – the sort of thing that would have appertained to human government before or apart from the Fall. But central to the state's supplementative role would be a function discontinuous with the pre-Fall government. Specifically and emphatically in the Scriptures the state is charged with responsibility in the matter of rights and their violation, that is, with the maintenance of justice within human society, particularly by way of punishing violations of rights, even to the point of executing capital punishment for violation of the right to life.

b. Social Duty and Utopian Delusion: Another role of the state that emerges from its complementary, supplementative relation to the family is that of substituting for the family in a limited area of family responsibility by way of exception and emergency. The state has a special responsibility for those among its citizens who are without a secure means of subsistence within the family structure, people like the fatherless and widows, to use the classic biblical examples. Such dependents without competent family providers or defenders fall in a space between the more fully functional family units, much like the terrain that occupies the space between private properties within the territorial bounds of the state, and like such lands these dependents become a public responsibility. They are to be cared for by the state, substituting for the family.

What we would thus deduce from the complementarity of family and state as jointly bearing the responsibilities of the cultural task under common grace has been argued from other biblical evidence. This evidence is not as abundant as is often supposed, for not a little of the customary argumentation involves misapplication of the texts cited in support of the thesis. We have urged caution in appealing to the Israelite theocracy to establish norms in a nontheocratic situation. So, in the present instance, one must not try to determine the duty of the civil magistrates in the matter in question too simplistically, as if it were necessary merely to observe what were the obligations of the Israelite king or community in general towards the widows and orphans, the poor and the aliens. For example, provisions made in the Mosaic law for restoring to impoverished Israelites their lands within the tribal allotments are not to be carried over to the ordinary state, because they found their rationale in the peculiar character of the Israelite theocratic land as typological of the eternal-cosmic theocratic land to be inherited by the people of God in the eschaton. Nevertheless, the general obligation of the Israelite king to see to it that persons otherwise not adequately protected or provided for should enjoy fair treatment in judicial proceedings and should receive the daily necessities of life is evidently to be understood as the duty of all kings. A passage like Daniel 4:27 would seem to support that conclusion. Certainly, in the literature of the ancient nations special concern for the poor and helpless is regarded as the hallmark of the ideal king. And if specific, direct biblical evidence is sparse, there is, on the other hand, nothing that would contradict the thesis of the state's marginal and limited role in substituting for the family, the conclusion which, as we have suggested, is a proper deduction from broader theological considerations relating to the historical origins of that institution.

Moreover, the Lord God, who designed and established the family and the state, is emphatically portrayed in the Scriptures as himself a King who is the father of the fatherless, intervening in behalf of those bereft of paternal support; who upholds and provides justice for the widow, gives food to the hungry and preserves the sojourner; who is the helper of the helpless (cf.,e.g., Pss 10:14,16; 27:10; 68:5,6; 146:7-10; cf. Ps 72). Surely, he will not have failed to give expression to this compassionate concern when, in his perfect wisdom, he was, as Lord of heaven and earth, devising the institutional structures entrusted with social responsibilities under the common grace order.

In the Lord's structuring of the church as the institutional embodiment of his redemptive grace under the new covenant, this divine concern for dependents who lack normal family support is once again clearly in evidence. The mission of the diaconal office is designed precisely for the likes of the widows in the household of faith. In this ministry, the church, like the state, substitutes for the family. Of course, the family character of the church goes far beyond this function, in ways not true of the state. For not only is the New Testament church as a whole set forth in Scripture under the image of the family, but the church family in the Spirit is the new family of mankind which ultimately will replace the common grace family and constitute the restoration of the original holy family-city structure of the creation order. At this point, however, what is to be particularly observed is how harmoniously comprehensive is the over-all scheme of God's surrogate family arrangements as he manifests his compassion for all the helpless. Between them, the common grace institution of the state and the redemptive grace institution of the New Testament church (or earlier, the Israelite theocracy) are responsible for the relief of all the needy who are without regular family resources. The state is responsible for all its disadvantaged citizens. For the state to perform this surrogate family role for the benefit of Christians and others alike is altogether consistent with its nature as a common grace institution. On the other hand, the Scriptures direct the flow of the church's benevolence (in distinction from its evangelistic mission) within the channels of the household of faith. And this is once again in complete accord with the church's nature as an institution identified with the covenant people exclusively.

As legitimate recipients of both the common and special grace arrangements, the needy among God's people have a double institutional provision made for them by their heavenly Father. And the covenant people as a whole, as responsible members of both church and state, have a two-fold opportunity of imaging in charitable ministry the love of their Father in heaven.

The state's supplementation of the family in a function that belongs primarily to the family must remain just that – supplementation, a secondary and exceptional role. When the state expands the bounds of its limited, marginal, substitute-family assignment by assuming responsibilities where the family itself is prepared to fulfill its God-given primary responsibility, the state is guilty of an act of usurpation and contradiction of the divine order. For the state thus to move towards the suppression of the family is to repudiate the very grounds and purpose of its own existence, which are found in its origin as a supportive institutional companion to the previously existing family within their shared framework of common grace.

To put the matter more positively and broadly, it is a concern of the state that all its citizens should enjoy a certain viable position in society, preserved and protected from deprivation and depredation, where they can carry out their God-assigned responsibilities as individuals in their families and in other associations. Here again the limits of the biblical warrant are to be respected. Regard for those limits compels us to challenge the suggestion that it is the state's obligation or prerogative to exercise its constraining authority to effect a more or less egalitarian distribution of the power of production, if not of actual material goods, as though this were a natural, inalienable right that all men can claim. Those who assume that such a right exists have taken their cue from pagan humanism rather than from the biblical doctrine of man.

Fallen mankind has no rights but those God is pleased to give as an act of grace, common or special. Moreover, divine grace is sovereignly bestowed. This is true of common grace as well as saving grace. The latter is given to those chosen according to God's own purpose in Christ Jesus. Common grace is conferred in varying measure, again according to God's sovereign will; as it comes from God to men in their fallen sinfullness it is not of works or debt or right of claim. In its unequal distribution of cultural talents and treasure, common grace is not even apportioned according to the consideration of whether or not a person is a recipient of redemptive grace, but simply in accordance with God's sovereign pleasure. Scripture does not recognize that anyone has a right to complain of supposed injustice in the distribution of divine grace.

As for the responsibility that God has imposed on the state to endeavor to secure for its citizens a certain protected place, this might be spoken of from the citizens' viewpoint as a God-given right which they possess vis-à-vis the state, to be claimed from the state. However, as we have observed, the Scriptures provide no warrant for the notion that God has appointed the state to level off the differences resulting from his own sovereign giving and withholding of common grace. And if equality in material prosperity is not a God-given right that citizens may claim from the state, then for the state to employ its coercive powers with the aim of achieving or closely approximating an egalitarian distribution of wealth would not be satisfying a just claim and therefore, would not be a performing of justice. Indeed, such state action would be in conflict with what the Scriptures stipulate concerning impartiality in the judicial process. Along with the Scripture's insistence that the poor be given a fair hearing in court is its demand that judgment must be rendered in righteousness, the poor man not being favored over the rich in his lawsuit (see the requirement in Exod 23:3 and Lev 19:15, which is surely applicable to the state as well as to the Israelite theocracy). No matter if the thief is poor and his victim rich. Justice requires that the stolen property be returned to the one who has legal right to it and that the guilty be punished. Would there not be an intolerable tension in the Bible's teaching concerning the state's role in administering justice if the state, which is obliged to honor the right of the richer citizens to the protection of their property against theft, including theft by the poor, were simultaneously required to honor an alleged right of its poorer citizens to as much of the property of the rich as was needed to eliminate the distinction between rich and poor? If the state were to take coercive action in the name of such a supposed demand of distributive justice to effect an egalitarian situation, it would in fact succeed only in making itself guilty of the flagrant injustice of plundering some of its own citizens.

Definite limits are imposed by the Scriptures on the state's function of intervening in behalf of its weaker and poorer citizens. Such action is to be taken by the state only to secure to its citizens that essential protected place, economically and socially, which they can claim as a right vis-à-vis the state, and only when the cause of those who are to be thus assisted would not have adequate advocacy and promotion apart from the state's intervention. Such limitations follow from the fact of the establishment of the state as a common grace institution supplementary to the family, the latter being the institution with the primary role in this area. Or again, the restriction of the sphere of operation of the common grace institution of the state to the boundary situation where the harsher effects of the common curse are being experienced is consistent with the fundamental nature of the common grace principle itself as designed to be merely a control on the common curse, mitigating the severity of its effects.

Though it serves to keep a rein on the extreme effects of the common curse and to restrain the expression of the evil within man, common grace does not eliminate these evils. It is not redemptive. Accordingly, the state as an institutional embodiment of common grace is not designed to provide ultimate and complete solutions for malfunctioning society. Sin, which is the root of society's evils, and death, the inevitable destiny which overshadows the existence of mankind, are overcome only through the redemptive principle and program of God's special, saving grace in Jesus Christ. Functional objectives that belong to this program of redemptive grace are not to be attributed to the common grace institution of the state. Justice is the concern of the state, not justification. Its role is not eternally redemptive but only temporally remedial, and even that only with respect to the essentials of human needs and the excesses of societal malfunctioning.

Apostate mankind in constructing the city of man is ever inclined to transgress the common grace boundaries of the state by projecting on it Utopian expectations in lieu of accepting the hope of the redemptive restoration of the kingdom of God, offered through Jesus Christ. What a baneful disservice it is, therefore, on the part of biblical theologians when they confuse or even merge the Christian eschatological hope with pagan, humanistic Utopian ideals by appropriating the terminology if not the concepts of the kingdom of God and redemptive deliverance from bondage and oppression and prostituting these to the promotional portrayal of social-economic causes related to temporal political institutions. (In this connection we may note again the hermeneutical muddle entailed in simplistic appeals to features in the life of theocratic Israel to determine the functions of the common grace state.)

c. **Transgression of Cultic Boundary:** At the beginning of this section we made our point about the limitations of the state's agenda by noting that it was only one of several institutions among which the functions of the original city-family were divided after the Fall. We have dealt particularly with the division of the cultural task (in modified form) between the state and the family, both of them common grace institutions. It is also to be observed that the cultic function of the original city-family and indeed the very identity of that institution as the holy covenant people of God has been assumed since the Fall by still another distinct institution, this one not another common grace institution, but the holy covenant community which is the organizational embodiment of the Covenant of Grace. Here then is a further bound that has been set, limiting the province of the state. Religious confession, cultic activity in general, appertains to the sphere of this holy covenant institution, not to the state. The common grace institution of the state was designed to provide for a pragmatic cooperation in the political task between the woman's seed and the seed of the serpent. To fulfill that purpose, the state had to be a non-confessional, a-religious institution. (The question of the relationship of the family to the covenant community is discussed elsewhere.)

Every form of state participation in religious confession, whether through constitutional affirmation, official pronouncement, public ceremony, or the like, is a transgression of the boundaries set in the divine ordering of the distribution of cultural and cultic functions among the institutions of the postlapsarian world. Such cultic activity on the part of the state, if it is not in confession of the living God, is, of course, idolatrous. But even if it is in acknowledgment of the God of the Christian faith, it is guilty of a monstrous confusion of the holy kingdom of God with the common, profane city of man. (Direct engagement of ancient Near Eastern kingdoms with the Israelite theocracy and its agents produced a typologically special situation, which imposed on the civil magistrates thus involved special demands that do not obtain otherwise, just as the theocracy itself constituted a special situation for the Israelite king, so that his involvement with the theocratic cultus is not normative for the rulers of common earthly kingdoms.) Also forbidden to the state in its exclusion from undertaking the cultic functions of the covenant community is the role of executing the discipline of the covenant cultus. For the state to employ its coercive powers and sanctions to compel formal participation in covenantal cult and confession, as by enforcing compliance with the first four laws of the Decalogue, is a disastrous perversion of the nature of both the redemptive kingdom and common grace kingdoms. On the other hand, the state is not to hinder the holy covenant institution in the fulfilling of its peculiar mission, much less persecute or suppress it. Rather, the common state is designed by God to provide a supportive framework for the life and mission of God's covenant people, in keeping with the fundamental purpose of common grace to make possible a general history within which God's redemptive program might unfold.

B. Apostate Malformation of the City

1. City of Man
Human history since the Fall is a tale of two cities.

The city of God, the Metapolis offered to man at the beginning in the prophetic sanctions of the creational covenant, is again offered as the final goal of the process of cosmic redemption. It is promised as the crowning achievement of Christ, the redeemer-king. Towards it the people of the covenant wend their historical way as pilgrims in a wilderness. For a while, late in the ages prior to the Incarnation, God provided in the midst of the world wilderness a sign of the eternal city in the form of the Jerusalem-centered theocratic kingdom of Israel. It was not possible to reproduce perfectly the character of the original theocratic-family community of Eden in the midst of a common grace/common curse world. Nor was this Old Testament theocracy long preserved. Only as a typical sign did it stand for a while, pointing to the city that was to come down out of heaven having the glory of God at the eschatological re-creation. In the New Testament age, even before the eschaton, the city of God is in one sense already a present reality. It is currently a heavenly reality, the heavenly Jerusalem where Christ, the king of the city, is present amid the innumerable hosts of angels and the saints whose rest is won (Heb 12:22ff.). Moreover, even the redeemed of Christ who are still on earth already have their ultimate citizenship and their hidden life of the Spirit in that invisible celestial sphere. But in terms of public visibility in this world, that city is yet to come. At present it is perceived only by eyes whose range of perception has been faith-sensitized to receive rays issuing from the otherwise invisible borders of the light spectrum (Heb 11:1).

Over against the heavenly city stands the other city, mundanely present and visible to all. Although the term "city of man" used for this other city marks, in the first place, the contrast between human political government as an interim product of common grace and the city of God as a holy eschatological kingdom produced by redemptive grace, "city of man" also carries a negative religious charge insofar as it connotes the apostate character borne by this city in its development under the hand of fallen mankind.

Apostate men misuse the state to reassert the rebellion against the Creator which was the essence of man's original covenant-breaking. They do this by their cultic dedication of the state to false gods and by their exploitation of the state for their own aggrandizement in their self-proclaimed autonomy. The literal expression of the first abuse was more characteristic of the ancient pseudotheocratic state, while the second deviation predominates in the modern secular state. Both varieties are idolatrous (the modern perversion of the secular state too even if it publicly professes atheism). The idolatry involved in both is a worship of man (the ancient pseudotheocracy too even if it was formally devoted to superhuman beings). For in both cases human autonomy is assumed over against the living God, and this is tantamount to an assertion of deity. The story of the city of man is one of the turning of the culture of man into the cult of Man.

Twice in the Genesis narrative we see this pattern of apostasy developing towards a blatant self-deification of the city-king in a violently tyrannical reign of might. It happened first in the history of the old world and then again in the postdiluvian resumption of the city of man.

2. Dynasty of Cain

Ominous for the future of the city of man, and especially so for the people of God in their relation to that city, is the story of its founding. For (according to the Masoretic text of Gen 4:17) the establishing of what is evidently to be regarded as the first city is ascribed to the one who had slain the first martyr. Cain's murder of Abel was not the upshot of a merely social or civil disagreement. It was in the cult, at the altar of worship, that enmity had broken out. Cain's hatred flared when the Lord exposed the hypocrisy of his act of worship. It was because he was still in league with the deceitful serpent that he could not be accepted at the sacred place. Cain's quarrel was with the Lord God, and with Abel as the one accepted by the Lord. This violence was an erupting of the predicted conflict between the serpent's seed and the seed of the woman. Ominous indeed that the spiritual source at the origin of the city of man was the spirit of Cain, devilish and antichrist.

By virtue of God's common grace, restraint was applied to curb the apostate spirit that was thus present in the city of man from the outset, lest its demonic potential escalate too quickly. In the brief biblical account of the history of this city the positive benefits provided in God's grace are clearly in evidence. The city was a refuge within whose security the family of Cain was able to continue generation after generation (Gen 4:17,18). In it was found the stimulation and cooperative enterprise and the accumulation of knowledge, skill, and resources that proved conducive to notable progress in those industries and arts that minister to the physical and aesthetic needs and pleasures of man (Gen 4:19-22).

Meanwhile, however, the very name of the city was a reminder of its inner spirit of autonomy, passed on from its founding father to its ruling dynasty. Cain dedicated the city to himself in naming it Enoch (Dedication) after his son, who was his image and his continuing memorial in the earth. (On the reading of Gen 4:17 that makes Enoch the city builder, he names it after himself, or his son.) The obsession of the city builders with making a great name for themselves is a major theme in the biblical delineation of the history of the city of man. This lust for a name was not simply the expression of a sense of need for self-identity, nor merely a desire for fame widespread in space and enduring in time. It was rather a heaven-defying quest for a name which boasted of human autonomy and self-sufficiency, a name intended to replace the name of man's Creator-Father, the birthright name man had despised. Within this name-lust were the seeds of man's ultimate self-idolatry and the blasphemy of the man of sin (2 Thess 2:3,4).

Cain's genealogy in Genesis 4 leads to Lamech (vv.19-24). Set as it is in the context of the story of the city founded by Cain, this genealogy is to be understood as naming some of Cain's royal successors. It is a dynastic list. Agreeably, at the climax of the list Lamech is depicted as engaged in that function of avenging wrong which belongs peculiarly to the special kingly office and authority God had appointed.

Lamech's performance of his royal duties travestied the office. From Cain to Lamech evil had increased in the city dynasty. Godlessness was ever more rampant and wanton. More than Cain, Lamech manifested alienation from God. Though his reign was outstanding for its harvest of cultural achievements, made possible by God's common grace (vv.20-23), he showed contempt for God's common grace ordinances. He perverted God's family ordinance by practicing bigamy (v.19) and he betrayed the divine trust of his kingship by turning the institution appointed to maintain justice into a tyrannical agency for his own personal vengeance (4:23). Disdainful of the just measure of life for life, eye for eye, wound for wound, bruise for bruise (Exod 21:23-25), he boasted of taking a life to avenge a bruise.

It has been plausibly assumed that the intention of the narrative in associating advances in the use of bronze and iron with Tubal-Cain (Gen 4:22) is to attribute to this prince in Lamech's court the invention of the sword. In that case, the instrument of death which is henceforth the identifying symbol of the state was at Lamech's disposal. This product of the forge of Tubal-Cain was not the first sword that figured in human history. Lamech was probably familiar with the primeval tradition of a fiery sword wielded by God's court-guardians in Eden. But the fire-forged sword in his hand seemed more real than any such flaming swords of paradise. Armed with the weapon of Tubal-Cain, Lamech scorned the protection of the divine order of justice which his ancestor Cain, fearful of being left to his own resources for self-protection, had so gladly received. Lamech judged himself to be more competent than God to achieve vengeance: "If Cain is avenged sevenfold, Lamech will be avenged seventy-seven fold" (Gen 4:24).

What a remarkable act of common grace it had been that, after the Lord had been obliged to assign cherubim agents to employ the sword to bar sinful man from his sanctuary, he had nevertheless entrusted a sword to these very offenders to be used by them as agents of his justice in this world. The spectacle presented by Lamech is thus that of man clutching the instrument of authority given him for his good by God in merciful divine forbearance and waving it insultingly in the face of God. Lamech's boastful arrogance was a trampling of the divine charter of the city under foot. In his contemptuous assertion of superiority over God in the execution of vengeance, man's name-lust vaulted above the heavens and became a claim to super-godhood.

God's sword, despised by Lamech as inferior to his own, was going to surprise mankind with its versatility and power. It would assume the form of flood instead of flame, and with this water-sword God was going to "cut off" Lamech's whole breed from the earth (Gen 6:17; 9:11). The self-styled super-gods and the true God would cross swords and in the duel God's water-sword would assuage the fire of Lamech's blade and snuff out the breath of his nostrils. Then it would be seen how falsely Lamech had named himself when he identified himself in terms of the completeness of divine sevens, rather than with sixes, the number of man (cf. Rev 13:18).

But before the Genesis narrative relates this final outcome of the matter it turns in chapter 5 to its central theme, the history of the covenant line descending from Seth. Recapitulating the period of the old world from this perspective, the author brings the genealogy down to Noah and the generation of the flood. And then at the beginning of chapter 6, just before narrating the judgment of the old world, he reverts to the climactic developments in the city of man that provoked the wrath of the Almighty and brought down the devastating deluge. (On Gen 6:1-4 see my "Divine Kingship and Genesis 6:1-4," *Westminster Theological Journal* 24,2 (1962) 187-204.)

3. Cult of Divine Kings

The account of the *bene ha'elohim*, "the sons of the gods," in Genesis 6:1ff. completes the portrait of the dynasty of Cain begun in Genesis 4. A phrase that brings out the connection of the two passages is "(from) upon the face of the earth" found in both 4:14 and 6:1,7. The phrase is indicative of their common concern with broad developments in human history. It is the story of the city of man in general that is resumed in Genesis 6 in order to trace it to its catastrophic conclusion in the deluge judgment.

This relationship between Genesis 4 and 6 is decisively proven by their common content. That Genesis 6 is once more concerned with the theme of human kingship gone awry is independently demonstrable. Our argument will not be circular, therefore, if we already make use of the royal identity of "the sons of the gods" as we proceed to describe the thematic unity of Genesis 4 and 6, even though this thematic continuity is in turn being appealed to as constituting a powerful confirmation of our interpretation of "the sons of the gods" as kings.

It is then to be observed that Genesis 6 treats again of those same aspects of the royal court that are mentioned in the Genesis 4 record of Lamech's reign: the royal marriages and children, and the exploits for which the royal family and rule were famous. Furthermore, it is precisely the sins of Lamech's court noted in Genesis 4 that characterize the court and reign of "the sons of the gods" in Genesis 6. There is in both instances the same abuse of the divine ordinances of common grace. In Genesis 6, the perversion of the ordinance of monogamous marriage assumes the form of the royal harem: multiplying wives, these kings took "all that they chose" (6:2). Again, in Genesis 6, the office for the administration of justice is exploited as a tool for the acquisition of power and the royal rule becomes a reign of terror as these mighty dynasts fill the earth with violence (6:4,13). Most significantly, once again in Genesis 6 the ultimate offense of the evil monarchs is a Lamech-like blasphemous boast of deity. Whether Lamech was himself one of the deity-claimers of Genesis 6, perhaps the most infamous of them all, or whether Genesis 6 describes in summary fashion a further, final stage in development of the spirit of Lamech's kingship, Genesis 4 and 6 are clearly of one piece. Their common theme is the history of the city of man founded by Cain.

What is singled out in Genesis 6:1ff. as the final, intolerable affront of human kingship against the Lord of heaven is, as we have noted, the claim to deity made by the earthly rulers. This astonishing claim came to expression in the titulature by which these mortal kings named themselves, the divine self-designation, which the biblical author then took over from their own blasphemous mouths to denote them: "the sons of the gods." The final words of Genesis 6:1-4 underscore the fact that the main target of the indictment of mankind in this passage is their lust for a name, which had culminated in the assumption of the name of "gods" by the royal house of the city of man. For the account concludes with a reference to the members of the royal court as "the men of the name" (v.4, literally). The ideology of divine kingship thus focused upon in Genesis 6 was widespread in the ancient world. According to traditions attested in dynastic lists, divine figures were numbered among the rulers of the city-kingdoms in the prediluvian world. Moreover, in the extra-biblical texts, as in Genesis, kingship featuring "divine" figures served as a bridging theme between creation and flood.

In addition to the positive evidence presented here for our interpretation of Genesis 6:1ff., brief note may be made of weaknesses in alternative views. Contradicting the identification of the *bene ha'elohim* as nonterrestrial beings, whether divine or demonic, is the exclusive attention paid to man, and to him as a creature of flesh, in God's verdict on their sin (v. 3). For the traditional view that the *bene ha'elohim* are Sethite men who sin by marrying ungodly Cainite women, one difficulty is that the daughters of men in verses 1 and 2 are clearly women in general. A more serious problem is the inability of this view to explain why the offspring of such religiously mixed marriages would be *nephilim-gibborim* (v. 4), evidently characterized by physical might and military-political dominance. For example, Nimrod, king of Babylon, belonged to the category of *gibborim* (Gen 10:8-10). While problematic for the traditional view, these mighty princes of Genesis 6:4 confirm our interpretation of their fathers, the *bene ha'elohim*, as kings.

The continuity of Genesis 6:1-4 with the preceding narrative at a fundamental thematic level becomes evident on our interpretation of "the sons of the gods" with its conceptual combination of the ideas of divine sonship and kingship. For the theme of man's role as possessor of the glory of royal dominion as an expression of his identity as image-son of God is a major interest of the history from Genesis 1 onwards. Later on in the Scriptures human rulers, those who especially reflect this judicial aspect of God's glory, are called "gods" (cf. Pss 82:6; 138:1; Exod 21:6; 22:8,9,28[7,8,27]). In view of this usage it is possible that we should translate the designation of the kings in Genesis 6:2,4 "the sons of God", rather than "the sons of the gods". In that case, by calling attention to the heights of the nobility properly appertaining to the office they occupied, the narrative would accent by means of ironic contrast the depths of the ignoble malfeasance of these tyrants. Even on this view of it, the use of this striking title at this point in history should be regarded as having been suggested to the narrator by the kings' own idolatrous self-designations. But on either view of the translation of the phrase, its use in Genesis 6 to denote kings who boasted of divine kingship was, in context, hardly abrupt or isolated.

In its continuity with the preceding narrative, Genesis 6 more particularly takes up again the theme of the satanic perversion of human kingship and the godlikeness to which it gave expression. Back in Eden it was by the prospect of becoming like God with respect to the royal function of knowing good and evil that the tempter had lured man into breaking his covenant with the Creator. Surely the same inspiration impelled the kings of Genesis 6 to take the truth of their godlikeness, involved in their appointment to serve as ministers of God's justice, and to twist it into a claim of their own godhood. Their contemptuous denial of the living God of heaven can be directly traced to a diabolical source. Possibly we are even to understand that these titans of old were demon-driven. Indeed, this is how the demonic dimension should be incorporated into the interpretation of the passage if one concludes that 1 Peter 3:19,20 and Jude 6 refer to the involvement of demons in the episode recorded in Genesis 6. That is, demons should not, then, be substituted for the human kings in the reconstruction of the event but rather the demonic element should be kept in subordination to the fundamental reality of the earth rulers' revolt against heaven. It could be accounted for in terms of the phenomenon of demon-possession in the experience of "the sons of the gods," or of some such extraordinary working of demons through them (cf. 2 Thess 2:9). In that case, Satan will have intruded himself into the history of the world that then was both at its outset and at its culmination through acts of preternatural entry into other creatures.

God's condemnation of "the sons of the gods" mocked their claim to deity by confronting them with their humanity in all its fallen propensities and its debilitation. With a touch of ridicule, the contrast of the balancing phrases "the sons of the gods" and "the daughters of men" sets over against each other the kings' claim to be gods and their very human carnal desire for human women. And the Lord's verdict directly contradicts their pretensions to divinity by describing them as "man" in all the frailty of his nature as "flesh" (v.3). In the context, in the sequel of judgment which this divine verdict declared should overtake mankind at the end of 120 years (v.3b), the term "flesh" is used repeatedly for mankind and in such a way as to emphasize man's animal-like mortality. Man, in seeking to participate in the status of immortal deity, succeeded only in getting reduced to the fate of the mortal beasts (cf., e.g.,Gen 6:12,13,17,19). This striking motif of God's mockery of the divine aspirations of human kings by the deflating reminder of their mortality is found again elsewhere in the Bible as prophetic judgment encounters the recurring phenomenon of the divine kingship ideology. Isaiah tells the avowed heaven-scaling king of Babylon, who thought to make himself like the Most High, that the depths of Sheol await him with derisive greetings (Isa 14, especially vv.9 ff.). And the word of the Lord through Ezekiel meets the assertion of the king of Tyre that he is a god with the prediction that his boast of deity will be silenced in the face of death at the hands of violent assailants (Ezek 28, especially v.9). It is characteristically in connection with human kings that we find in Scripture this motif of God's derision of self-deification by mortals, and this is then yet another confirmation of the interpretation of "the sons of the gods" in Genesis 6 in terms of such royal pretenders to deity among the rulers of the city of man.

As the story of the city of man in the world that then was draws to a close we see a state that has monopolized governmental powers, not tolerating any other sphere of sovereignty such as family or institution of religion. All culture and cult have been brought under the domination of the absolutized rule of the divine king. The city of man has become an idolatrous theocracy in which man has assumed the position of deity. For the cultural enterprise thus to produce a cultus was formally in accord with the design of human history prophetically projected under the creational covenant. In actual fact, the theocratic cultus of "the sons of the gods" was the diametrical opposite of the eschatological goal that had been set in man's original cultural commissioning. It was an anti-God cult, the diabolical antithesis of the purposed formation of mankind as the cult of the Creator, the sanctuary-community of God's Presence.

Satan had thus worked the same kind of deception with respect to human kingship in the postlapsarian world as he had earlier in the matter of Adam's kingship. In each case man had been lured into a formal realization of what God had prescribed, while disregarding and flagrantly violating the ethical-spiritual stipulations that were integral to the divine mandate. Adam thought to advance his royal godlikeness through a means contrary to the law of God and contradictory of the Lord's Godhood. And afterwards in the city enterprise, man's pseudo-attainment of the cultic end of culture was by way of disobedience to the word of God's law and rejection of his lordship. In the cultus thus produced, God was defied and man was deified. The logic of the program suggested by the tempter had worked itself out in history from the ungodly godlikeness of Adam to the godless godhood of the cult of Man.

Beyond this transformation of the city of man into the temple of Man, the god-king, earth's revolt against the Creator could not go — an idolization of power, full of corruption and violence (Gen 6:5,11,12); a regime that dehumanized the mass of men and women by brutal oppression; a demon-ridden beast-power that doubtless persecuted the people of the saints of the Most High, perpetuating that enmity of the seed of the serpent against the seed of the woman that had been manifested by the founder of the city of man, the slayer of martyr Abel. Tyrannizing all, the self-proclaimed god-king sat enthroned in the city's royal holy of holies, a living image of the dragon between mighty princes in bronze armor, brandishing iron swords (mightier for vengeance than golden cherubim with flaming swords — such was the dynastic boast). The old world had reached a man of sin stage, and the man of sin is the son of perdition. But those who dwelled on the earth continued to marry and give in marriage and build houses, and fear the son of perdition. They knew not the hour. They could not read the signs in the heavens and discern the deluge in the gathering clouds.

II. THE REDEMPTIVE COMMUNITY

The entire age of the old world, traced once in Genesis 4, is surveyed again in Genesis 5:1-6:8, the second of the book's ten generations-sections. This time the line of Adam through Seth occupies the center of the stage. The narrative had in fact returned in the closing verses of the first section (Gen 4:25,26) to Adam and the new beginning marked by the birth of Seth, the son whom Eve saw as another seed appointed to her by God to replace Abel whom Cain slew.

It is only the mainstream of the covenantal line as that arose and continued among the Sethite descendants of Adam that is treated in any detail at all. The existence of numerous other lines receives barely passing mention, this in the form of the recurring notation that the several patriarchs begat other sons and daughters. Moreover, as previously noted, even in the main line of descent from Seth to Noah, which is the chief concern of the Genesis 5 account, the genealogical listing is not complete but selective only. A long world history is telescoped in this brief genealogical record, and the longer the time involved, the more remarkable it is that the distinctive covenantal movement delineated here adhered for so extended a period to one particular continuous ethnic branch of mankind.

A. Identification as People of Yahweh

The distinctive characteristic of those who are listed in Genesis 5 is clearly that they are God's people. In the literary pattern of the book of Genesis an account of the community of faith regularly follows a section devoted to the rejected line. The several extra episodic details interspersed in the genealogical formulary of Genesis 5 all contribute to this picture of the Sethite line as the channel of faith and godliness in that ancient age. Though fully explicit covenantal terms are not employed in the narrative until we come to Noah at the end of this genealogy, the covenantal identity of the Sethites is disclosed when they are first introduced. This takes place in the transitional verses at the end of Genesis 4, where the narrative returns from the brink of the flood judgment to the first generation of human history.

Genesis 4:26b relates that the Sethites identified themselves as those who belonged to the Lord, as Yahweh-people. Such is the meaning of the statement rendered in AV: "then began men to call upon the name of the Lord". The use of this expression in Isaiah 44:5 is illuminating: "This one will say: I belong to Yahweh. This one will take the name of Jacob. This one will inscribe his memorial: (I am) Yahweh's. (This one) will surname himself Israel." In this poetic A.B.A.B form, the second and fourth lines are synonymously parallel, as are the first and third lines. Accordingly, the second line, which contains the idiom in question from Genesis 4:26, means that someone identifies himself by a particular surname (cf. Isa 45:3,4). It obviously does not mean that God's people were supplicating Jacob. The prophet describes the covenantal confession that will be made when God pours out his Spirit on the descendants of his servant Jacob

(44:1-4). They will identify themselves as Israelites, the people belonging to Yahweh, the people under the covenant lordship of Yahweh. The idea of identification with and by God's name is also conveyed by a passive variation of the expression used in Genesis 4:26. For this, see, e.g., Deuteronomy 28:10; 2 Chronicles 7:14; Isaiah 43:7 (cf. v.1); 63:19; 65:1; Daniel 9:19.

The aspect of subordination to the person whose name one takes, already evident in the passages cited, is present elsewhere too in the usage of this idiom. It expresses the classification of people under a notable ancestor (Gen 21:12; 48:5,6; Isa 48:1; 65:15); the submission of a city under its conqueror (2 Sam 12:28); the coming of the wife under the legal protection of her husband (Isa 4:1); the owned status of a person's property (2 Sam 6:2; 1 Kgs 8:43; and 1 Chron 13:6, all referring to the ark and temple of the Lord, a relationship involving more than simple proprietorship; cf. also Ps 49:11 [12]); subservience under the rule of a lord (Isa 63:19); and the consecration of a site to God by an altar or banner that bears his name (e.g., Gen 21:33; 33:20; 26:25; Exod 17:15).

Specifically, the overlordship of Yahweh that is in 'view in the passages where a people is identified by his name is that of the covenant suzerain. The contexts contain explicit covenantal references and identification with the name of Yahweh is explicated by formulae traditional in God's covenants. One such equivalency is taking hold of God (Isa 64:7[6]), a familiar idiom for affirming covenant relationship in the Bible and in the ancient international treaties. (See Isa 27:5; 56:2,4-6; cf. 1 Kgs 9:9; Isa 4:1). For other covenantal associations of the expression under study see, e.g., Psalms 99:6-8; 105:1,8ff.; Zephaniah 3:9; cf. Psalm 79:6; Jeremiah 10:25. For its use referring to commitment to the Lord in a new covenant context see Acts 9:14,21; 22:16; Romans 10:13; cf. Joel 2:32 (3:5). Association of this naming idiom with such expressions of covenantal commitment suggests for it the particular meaning of recognizing and invoking God in covenant oath as divine witness and judge.

Of special importance are passages where the people's acknowledging that Yahweh is Lord through the act of surnaming themselves after him is matched by a divine response acknowledging that the people are indeed God's special covenantal possession. This reciprocal acknowledgment of Yahweh as Lord by Israel and of Israel as his people by Yahweh expresses the core of their covenant relationship. Such an act of mutual acknowledgment is cited in Deuteronomy 26:17,18 by way of a concise summation of the covenantal transaction for which the substance of Deuteronomy served as treaty text. The terminology for the acknowledgment used in this passage is unique but it is apparently a semantic equivalent for the naming formula under survey, various forms of which appear elsewhere in Scripture in allusion to the same covenantal relationship in view in Deuteronomy 26. (See Ps 89:26-28[27-29]; Isa 43:1,6,7,10; 63:8-19; Zech 13:9.) In terms of this mutuality of identification whereby the covenant people bear the surname of Yahweh, their name, Israel, becomes identified with God's name, a truth much exploited by those who intercede for Israel's prosperity (e.g., Dan 9:19) and, indeed, a fact which the Lord clearly indicates is foremost in his own reckoning as he deals with Israel, whether in the curse of the covenant or in covenant restoration (e.g., Isa 48:9-11; Ezek 39:7,25).

The natural connection between bearing the surname of Yahweh and acknowledging God as Father-Creator (and receiving God's reciprocal acknowledgment as his son) becomes explicit in the relevant contexts (see Ps 89:26,27: Isa 43:1,6,7; 44:2-4; 63:16; 64:8; cf. Eph 3:14,15). In view, then, of the previously observed coalescence of the family image of father and the political image of lord within the covenant concept, we can more readily understand how the idea of a people bearing the surname of Yahweh was an expression of their covenantal relationship to him. God's covenantal authority is regarded in the Bible as implicit in his status as Father-Author-Creator. Incidentally, an implication of this for covenant theology is that from the biblical viewpoint the creation record is in the very nature of the case a covenant record.

To name oneself after Yahweh and so acknowledge Yahweh as Creator-Father and covenant suzerain is to claim the protection due to a true vassal-son. In judicial situations it is a matter of invoking God's intervention as legal protector. Hence, the common translation of the naming idiom of Genesis 4:26 as "call upon the name of the Lord" is at times most appropriate. For example, in Isaiah 64:7 the phrase appears in a context where the Lord is reminded that he is "our Father and potter" (v.8), and it is lamented that he has hidden his face from his people (legal terminology for withholding judicial action). In verse 7a, as an immediate parallel to the naming idiom it is said that the people fail to take hold on God, a figure for acknowledging lordship, as noted above, and one which, in the biblical context, would evoke the specific imagery of taking hold on the horns of the altar as a means of claiming refuge under God's wings (1 Kg 1:50f.; 2:28; Isa 27:5; cf. Isa 4:1; Rev 2:13). An illustration from the military sphere (another situation of divine judgment) is found in Psalm 20:5. In the hour of battle others place their confidence in horses and chariots (v.7) but God's army sets up a standard that identifies them by the name of Yahweh, and in so doing makes petition for his protection (cf. v.1; see also Prov 18:10). According to the Qumran War Scroll, the banner of the whole congregation would bear the inscription: "Army of God."

Returning to Genesis 4:26b, support for understanding this in terms of naming oneself by God's name is found in the fact that the immediate context, to which the opening "then" (`az̧) of verse 26b points, is concerned precisely with assigning names to people – Seth, Enosh (vv.25,26a). Indeed, in the case of Eve's naming Seth, the explanation refers to the original redemptive promise of covenantal renewal (Gen 3:15), the first word of which (the key verb of divine initiative) is the one Eve relates directly to the name Seth (Gen 4:25; cf. also Gen 3:20; 4:1; 5:28). Genesis 4:26 tells us then that in the period after the Fall it was in connection with the birth of Seth and the emergence of his family that covenantal witness was heard anew as a people began to take form on earth who identified themselves as the people of Yahweh.

This statement stands as the counterpart to Genesis 4:17 in the Cainite history. In contrast to the Cainite name-lust, the theme which begins in 4:17 and culminates in the account of the kings' blasphemous ascription of deity to themselves (Gen 6:1ff.), Genesis 4:26 sets the covenant confession of the Sethites, proclaiming Yahweh's sovereignty and acknowledging themselves to be his servants, dependent on his redemptive promise. The covenantal naming of Genesis 4:26 is also placed in contrast to the more closely preceding verse 24. Whereas Cainite Lamech scorned divine avenging (v.24), the Sethites sought the face of Yahweh for his judicial protection by their covenantal appeal to his name.

The terrible gap produced by man's breaking of the creational covenant was bridged by God's grace, providing for a continuance of a community of God's people on earth. A remnant of mankind appeared who laid hold on God in covenantal confession: Yahweh is our Lord, our heavenly Father, and we are his covenant protectorate. In the world wilderness a Sethite banner was raised, reading: Yahweh is our surname.

B. Covenantal Polity

1. Cultic Community

Until the fullness of time, when the coming One should perfect and so conclude altar sacrifice, the visible earthly altar held a central place in the community of redemptive covenant. So it was with the Sethite people of God in the prediluvian age. Martyred Abel, for whom Seth was the divine replacement, had been altar-oriented in his lifetime. At the altar he had by faith offered to Yahweh acceptable tribute from his cultural endeavors (Heb 11:4). The altar focus of the Sethite line of Genesis 5 becomes apparent again in the life of Noah at the end of that line. The construction of an altar and renewal of the cult of the Lord was Noah's immediate concern upon emerging from the ark after the flood (Gen 8:20). This episode, placing the altar at the climax of the history of the covenant community of Seth and at the commencement of the community of the line of Shem (cf. Gen 11:10), displays the continuity of the altar as an identifying feature of the prediluvian and postdiluvian covenant communities.

Another indication of the establishment of the altar in the midst of the Sethite line is provided in Genesis 4:26. We have interpreted the naming formula of that verse in terms of these Sethites identifying themselves with the name of Yahweh. However, it was also observed that covenantal avowal and legal petition for God's protection were related ideas. Now the locus of such acts would be the altar of the Lord. Further, this naming formula of Genesis 4:26 is conjoined in several passages in Genesis with the record of the building of altars or the installation of other symbolic cultic objects (Gen 12:8; 13:4; 21:33; 26:25). Moreover, it was customary to give to such cultic installations names expressive of their dedication to God. For example, Jacob erected an altar at Shechem "and called it El-Elohe-Israel" (Gen 33:20). See also Genesis 21:33; 22:14; 28:19; 35:7,15; Exodus 17:15; Joshua 22:34; Judges 6:24; 1 Kings 7:21; 1 Chronicles 21:26. The assigning of such a specific theophoric name might also be in view even where the narrator employs the more general statement that an altar was built "unto Yahweh" (Gen 8:20; 12:7; 13:18; 28:19) or "in the name of Yahweh" (1 Kg 8:32). Perhaps the naming formula under study might itself refer on occasion to the dedicatory naming of a sacred object, rather than to some other act of worship performed at the cultic site. Might that be the point in Genesis 21:33, which says that Abraham planted a tamarisk tree at Beersheba "and called there on the name of Yahweh El Olam"? Relevant too is the observation made in a previous discussion that the site selected by the Lord for his altar is referred to as the place where he puts his name or makes it dwell (e.g., Deut 12:5,11), or as the place he designates for the memorializing of his name (Exod 20:24). Accordingly, the characterization of the Sethites of Genesis 4:26 as the bearers of the name of Yahweh may be taken as an indication that the altar of the Lord found its place among them.

Altars among the Sethites attested to the presence there of the holy assembly of the Lord. This sacramental link between the heavenly Lord of the covenant and his earthly servants was their identifying nucleus as a special covenant community. By its presence in their midst the people of the altar were constituted a priestly fellowship, a cultic congregation. Generation after generation this distinctive altar-centered institution was the manifestation of the spiritual temple, the priestly people-house of God, in process of redemptive formation and destined to stand complete at the end of history, filled with the divine glory and filling all in all.

2. Familial Form

Patriarchal altar communities are family affairs. This is reflected beyond the prediluvian history in the accounts of patriarchal times later in Genesis and in the book of Job. The sphere of the altar is the sphere of the patriarchal family. Participation in the altar is one with membership in the covenant family. In the case of the prediluvian altar-assembly of Genesis 5, the altar family was that of Seth. Not that the cultic community might simply be equated with that ethnic line, as though they were coextensive. It was, however, a distinction of the Sethites that the covenant line flourished among them. Whereas the genealogy of Cain is a dynastic list of royal tyrants, the genealogy of Seth features a series of priestly patriarchs in the continuing community of God's covenant people.

Actually then, Genesis 5 is not so much the history of the Sethites *per se* as it is the history of the covenant institution. Viewed from this perspective, the fact that the history is cast in genealogical form takes on special significance as a disclosure of the organizational form of the covenantal cultus. The literary genre itself advertises the familial structuring of the cultic community. We thus learn that from the very beginning of redemptive history the constituency of the holy congregation of God's people in its historical existence and continuance followed along family lines. Though the family in its reinstitution under common grace is not as such the holy covenant community, nevertheless in connection with the faith-commitment of parent-householders particular families are brought into the covenant as the Lord honors the family authority structure in determining the constituency of the covenant community. (This is not saying, of course, that election to eternal salvation was necessarily involved in this family connection.) This is a constant principle of covenant polity, even in the administration of the church under the new covenant. Understandably, the genealogical genre yields to the missionary narrative in the historiography of the New Testament. But the familial principle of covenant polity is found to be playing still, as anciently, its vital role. Along with global missionary expansion, genealogical continuity is still fundamental to the church's ongoing life.

That the history of the altar-community is presented in Genesis 5 in the framework of a Sethite genealogy does not mean (we have noted) that the prediluvian covenant community must be identified with the Sethites inclusively or (we may add) exclusively. On the one hand, though there was an ethnic continuity of the covenant community along the line traced in Genesis 5 from Seth to Noah, we should not assume that all the peoples referred to as descending from Seth (cf. Gen 5:7,10, *etc.*) were within the covenant relationship to the Lord. On the other hand, it is not certain that prediluvian history witnessed a restriction of the people of God over an extended time to one ethnic stock, as in the age of Old Testament Israel. The analogy of the genealogical record of the line from Noah to Abraham (Gen 11:10ff.), illuminated by the subsequent Genesis narratives, suggests that the worship of the true God would have been preserved here and there within some of the non-Sethite branch-lines of Adam (cf. Gen 5:4), conceivably even among the descendants of Cain. However, such other lines of the covenant people will have lacked permanence, for there was an almost complete disappearance of true religion by Noah's day (allowing for possible qualifications of this, pending settlement of the question of the extent of the deluge judgment). By the last stages of prediluvian times, the covenant family tree was reduced to the line that led from Seth to Noah. Though the true faith had not been restricted to this line through the entire history of the old world, it was in this line that the covenant found ethnic continuity from Seth to the Deluge, and through that world catastrophe into the world that now is.

Comparing the form of the prediluvian covenant community with that of the new covenant community will bring out how fully the former was a familial structure. The family authority principle does function in the determination of the membership of the New Testament churches, but ecclesiastical polity is dominated by a separate system of authority vested in special officers so gifted by the Spirit. This arrangement of special offices gives a distinctive organizational form to the individual churches. It also provides a network of authority that links the separate churches, constituting a comprehensive unifying authority structure for the covenant community over-all. The altar-communities of the various patriarchal families treated in the book of Genesis were not connected by such a network of special officers. They were thus more simply and thoroughly familial in form. Not only was each altar-assembly bounded by the family, but the natural family authority structure served as the authority structure for the family in its identity as a cultic community. Though the family patriarch assumed a leading role at the altar, there was not a special, restricted priestly office. The covenant family as a whole was a holy priesthood, calling on the name of Yahweh.

3. Nontheocratic Community

The distinctive nature of the prediluvian covenant polity may also be clarified by comparison with the form assumed by the Israelite community under the Mosaic Covenant. Israel was like the Sethite community of Genesis 5 in that it was, essentially, family-bounded and it was organized about an earthly altar. But unlike Israel, the prediluvian altar-family was not a theocratic kingdom.

At some stage of its history such an altar-family might establish their own political commonwealth. An altar to God's name would then exist within this political territory and the political ruler might also be the officiating patriarchal priest at the family altar. As an example of this kind of situation in the later patriarchal era one thinks at once of Melchizedek, both king of Salem and priest of God Most High. Among the Genesis 5 patriarchs Noah might have played a similar dual role. We know he officiated at the Lord's altar in his family and, if extra-biblical tradition concerning the flood hero is correct, he was the king of his city. However, any such political structure would still have been merely a common grace institution in which those who were citizens, including their ruler, happened to be simultaneously, but distinguishably, members of the cult of Yahweh. It would not have been necessarily or properly even a sacred society (cultic state or nationalized cultus), employing the political power to enforce the altar-religion. Much less would that kind of nonintegral association of cultus and political institution constitute a theocracy.

As for the altar erected in the midst of such a people, it would have stood as a testimony to the general lordship of Yahweh over his creation and it would have pointed to the eschatological coming of his eternal cosmic kingdom (ideas we shall return to presently) but it would not have laid claim to a specific temporal domain, then and there, as a prototype of the coming kingdom. In this respect it would have differed from the Israelite altar in the land of Canaan, a land possessed in fulfillment of particular covenant promises to Abraham and claimed by the altar as a special holy kingdom, sanctified to the name of Yahweh. The presence of the altar in the prediluvian nation would not, therefore, have imparted a theocratic identity to it, as did the altar in Israel.

Inevitably, the legitimate altar of the Lord raised up at the beginning in the midst of God's covenant people was countered by idol-altars erected by other groups. When such a group was a political state, its altar-dedication to its national god would give that nation the character of a theocracy – a pseudo-theocracy challenging the sovereignty of the Lord. The theocratic aspect would be most evident when the divine kingship ideology was present. Such developments of the state were in contradiction of its common grace design. Even in the case of a nation where the altar-commitment of the people as such was to the Lord, the common grace charter of the state demanded that such a nation not be treated in theory or in political praxis as a theocracy. The close conjunction of the political establishment and the visible, earthly altar within a relatively small domain might tend to blur the perception of the distinction between the common state and the holy cultus of the Lord in that situation, but every definitive feature of a theocracy would have been missing. There is nothing to suggest that the Lord made a special covenant with any such nation comparable to the Mosaic Covenant with Israel, defining and claiming that particular domain as his own holy kingdom. There is no evidence that the Lord commissioned any such people to build him a royal temple where his Glory-Presence dwelled as God-King, providing special direction and protection, guaranteeing temporal blessings for cultic fidelity. We have no reason to think that God appointed any such kingdom to be, like Israel, an earthly typological symbol of the eternal theocratic kingdom. In spite, then, of Israel's having an earthly altar, while the new covenant church as an earthly institution is no longer organized about a visible altar, the prediluvian altar-communities of Genesis 5 resembled the church of the new covenant, structurally, more than they did theocratic Israel.

C. Mission of the Covenant People

Introduction: The altar-families that constituted the Lord's redemptive community had, as such, distinctive functions, priestly and prophetic. But when the covenant institution embodied itself in the structure of these families, they did not thereby cease to exist as common grace families with the functions belonging to such. Individual members of these families had all the cultural responsibilities that had been appointed to the generality of mankind under common grace. Stated from the point of view of office and privilege, they participated with all others in the enjoyment of a measure of kingly dominion over the subhuman creation and, as occasion afforded, they also occupied the special office of kingship in the common grace political order.

For the covenant people to participate in the common political enterprise with noncovenant people was entirely in keeping with the genius of the city of man as a common grace arrangement for the pragmatic cooperation of all mankind in cultural endeavor. God's prediluvian people must adopt towards the political order where they resided, even when Cainite dominated, the same stance that was advocated by the apostle Paul for the New Testament saints in the Gentile world (1 Tim 2:2) and, earlier, by the prophet Jeremiah in his instructions to the Israelites in their exile existence in the world-wilderness (Jer 29:4ff.). They were to be cooperatively constructive and exhibit towards the city of man an attitude of prayerful solicitude for its peace.

To assume such a stance is not to confuse the city of man with the kingdom of God. In the light of God's redemptive disclosures to his people they are to perceive that the purpose of all common grace structures and programs is the ancillary one of providing a field of operation for the history of God's kingdom of saving grace. They should not then fix any false hopes on the future of the city of man. God's prophetic word heard in the midst of his prediluvian people became indeed an increasingly urgent warning of the imminent doom of that city. While, therefore, they were to have a breadth of world-view informed by the programmatic purposes of the common grace cultural mandate, it was important that they also possess a depth of historical insight into the mystery of iniquity developing within the city of man and that they keep alive an eschatological vision of the realization of creation's cultural goal in the distant coming of an eternal city as the final fruitage of the mystery of redemptive grace, revealed to them and working in them. Accordingly, though they must not neglect their part in building the common city, they were also to fulfill with eager hope their distinctive covenantal mission. Though full citizens in the city of man, they were faithfully to maintain within it their altar to the name of Yahweh and remember that they were also citizens of his yet unseen heavenly city.

1. Priestly Function

Inherent in the covenant community's altar-centered form was a priestly vocation. This did not involve the formal establishment of a priestly office within the community with specialized officiants, apart from the natural family leadership. There were no priests acting representatively for others who lacked priestly status. The altar itself in the midst of the community pointed to the heavenly dwelling of the Lord and was a sacramental sign of his presence, but it was not an earthly house of God with a prescribed continual cultus to be maintained. It was rather a place of occasional, perhaps regular (possibly sabbatical), religious resort for the members of the altar-family. Here they came to render worshipful service to the Lord in consecratory tribute and expiatory sacrifice, and in confessional praise and petition.

a. Sanctification of Culture: Called to priestly mission by the altar, the Sethite saints were engaged in the priestly sanctification of culture to the Lord. Man himself is the chief product of the cultural process and the fundamental aspect of their sanctifying of culture was, therefore, the sanctification of themselves to God. They were to be building themselves up as a holy temple of God. Theocratic Israel was involved in the building of the house of God at the symbolic level. They had to construct tabernacle and temple as a habitation of the Glory-Presence. But the Sethite people of God were engaged in building only at the reality level of the people-house of God. Ultimately, such building of God's spiritual sanctuary is God's own doing by his Spirit. Yet there is an instrumental role assigned to the covenant community in the edification-cultivation of this living holy structure through a ministry of the means of grace according to the Spirit's varying provision "at sundry times and in divers manners."

This priestly mission of sanctifying culture by way of building the living people-temple of God took a different direction for the prediluvian covenant community than it does in the great commission given to the church. Like the Sethite covenant community, the church too operates in temple building only at the reality level of the people-temple (cf. Eph

2:21,22; 1 Tim 3:15; 1 Pet 2:5). The symbolic divine dwelling-places that were erected by the Israelites serve the church of the new covenant only as conceptual models for its understanding of itself as God's dwelling-place. But unlike the prediluvian priestly mission, the church's great commission sends it outwards to the ends of the earth. The presence or absence of the local, earthly altar coincides inversely with the presence or absence of the expansive, missionary dimension of the covenantal function of building the holy house of God. So long as it is local, earthly, symbolic, the altar concentrates the building function centripetally on the edification of the local altar-community. It is only when the focus of the community moves from such an earthly, local altar to the heavenly, universal altar, as it does in the new covenant established through the priesthood of Jesus, that the building of the living temple becomes correspondingly a missionary, centrifugal project. Certainly, nothing in Genesis 5 hints at a missionary lengthening of the cords of the covenantal tent. By this absence of a missionary dynamic in the covenant community of the world that then was, that world-age is shown to be, like the entire premessianic age, an earth-altar age.

We have considered the priestly mission of sanctifying culture as it comes to expression in the building of the holy people-house of God, but what would it entail with respect to the common city of man? Positively, it must be recognized that the whole life of God's people is covered by the liturgical model of their priestly identity. All that they do is done as a service rendered unto God. All their cultural activity in the sphere of the city of man they are to dedicate to the glory of God. This sanctification of culture is subjective; it transpires within the spirit of the saints. Negatively, it must be insisted that this subjective sanctification of culture does not result in a change from common to holy status in culture objectively considered. The common city of man does not in any fashion or to any degree become the holy kingdom of God through the participation of the culture-sanctifying saints in its development. Viewed in terms of its products, effects, institutional context, *etc.*, the cultural activity of God's people is common grace activity. Their city of man activity is not "kingdom (of God)" activity. Though it is an expression of the reign of God in their lives, it is not a building of the kingdom of God as institution or realm. For the common city of man is not the holy kingdom realm, nor does it ever become the holy city of God, whether gradually or suddenly. Rather, it must be removed in judgment to make way for the heavenly city as a new creation.

An apparent, not real, exception to the purely subjective nature of the sanctification of common culture by God's priestly people arises in connection with the presence of the earthly altar among them. For from the fruit of their cultural activity they presented at the altar token offerings expressive of the priestly dedication of themselves, their life, labor, and possessions to the Lord. Thereby they changed the status of these objects from common to sacred, symbolically. This exceptional cultic-symbolic sanctification of such token cultural items actually underscores the common status of the saints' cultural productivity as a whole, the common status from which the tokens utilized in cultic symbolism were distinguished in their becoming sacred. The merely token character of the objective altar-sanctification of culture by the prediluvian altar-community can be appreciated by contrasting with it the sanctification of theocratic Israel's culture. The latter was symbolically set apart in its totality (land and all) as the sacred realm of God's royal Presence. A sanctification phenomenon in the life of the church, corresponding in its limited character to its prediluvian counterpart, is the setting aside of the sacramental elements from the common lot to be used as holy liturgical symbols. Here in the New Testament situation again, this exceptional symbolic instance simply sharpens our perception of the objectively common status of the over-all cultural contribution of Christian people, an objective commonness that continues to obtain in spite of its having been subjectively sanctified by them.

In concluding this analysis of the cultural functioning of the prediluvian covenant people in terms of the concept of holiness, we return to the area of the familial form of that covenant community. It was observed in the introduction to this section on the mission of the covenant people that the Sethite families under study did not cease to function as common grace families upon becoming a covenantal altar-family. And it has just been argued that the cultural productivity of these families retained its common status, even though in spirit consecrated by the godly to the Lord. In keeping with all this it may be said that as families reproducing themselves they were part of the common cultural program of filling the earth that had been assigned to mankind under the common grace order. Simultaneously, however, something "holy" also resulted from this same process.

We are here confronted by the biblical data with another kind of sanctification of culture, involving another variety of holiness. There is the spiritual holiness of the saints, sanctified unto the Lord by his Spirit. And there is the symbolic holiness of tokens cultically dedicated to God. But there is also the formal holy status of belonging to the membership of the covenant community. Cultural products (*viz.* children) issuing from the reproductive functioning of the people of God have this covenantal brand of holiness because covenant membership is, by the Lord's appointment, determined in part by the principle of parental authority. This is the point of 1 Corinthians 7:14 (cf. Rom 11:16). The cultural process in the form of the procreative marriage union is covenantally sanctified when at least one of the parties possesses covenantal holiness, and consequently the child born of that sanctified union has the status of covenantal holiness. Here then for the prediluvian as well as later covenant families was a further distinctive aspect of their priestly task of sanctifying culture.

b. Confessional Witness: The altar was the site to which the priestly community resorted to call on God's name in praise and petition. A testimony to the Lord was, however, given by the very existence of the altar itself. The act of building the altar and perpetuating there the name of God which was identified with the altar was a confessional witness. As a public monument set up in the midst of the city of man, the altar's witness was a witness to the world. The missionary principle was thus present in these early altar-communities even though not yet implemented by an outward thrust in extension of the covenantal witness.

Altar building was a confession of God's sovereignty over his creation and a claiming of the world for him. Thus, Noah's erecting of the altar on the new earth freshly appeared from the waters after the flood was a confessional claim that the earth is the Lord's and the fullness thereof, the world and they that dwell therein, for he is the One who founded it over the seas and established it above the deeps (Ps 24:1f.). In their identification with the altar of the Lord these covenantal families stood over against the denizens of this world as a legal testimony, a witness sign planted by the Creator of heaven and earth, staking out his claim to ultimate sovereign ownership of the world and its nations.

Implicit in the altar identity of these covenant people was the summons, abeyant for the present, to undertake the priestly mission of the holy war of Yahweh. For the time being, the Lord was pleased to preserve the common order on earth. The altars were not declarations of holy war, not proclamations of God's immediate intention to transform the earth into a holy theocratic domain. Their confessional witness to the world was accordingly a call to turn from idols and render covenantal allegiance to Yahweh. Nevertheless, they were a prophetic warning of the coming day of his power when the decree would go forth to enforce his sovereign claims over the earth. Then his altar-people must assemble to him, a priestly army in the splendor of holiness, to fulfill the sacred charge of the guardianship of the sanctuary, to follow him in the battle of the great day, cleansing the world of the servants of the idols and sanctifying it to him as a universal holy domain. The Yahweh-congregation thus posed a threatening challenge to those kings of the earth who took rebellious counsel together against the Lord and his anointed, the promised champion of the woman's seed, who should come and slay the serpent.

Until the time arrives for that divine judgment on the unbelieving world, the presence of God's altar at the center of his covenant people marks them as a martyr community. Martyr in a twofold sense. They are martyrs in the proper meaning of that word – they are witnesses for the Lord their God. But from Abel on (cf. Gen 4:2-8) to be a witness-martyr is also to be a martyr in its customary sense. Faithful witness leads to martyrdom, to suffering, even unto death, at the hands of an unreceptive, unrepentant, hostile world. Such is the dual martyr mission of the people identified with God's altar.

2. Prophetic Function

Besides the priestly witness given by the godly Sethite succession in their identity as an altar community of Yahweh, a witness in the prophetic mode arose among them, that is, a witness in the form of a declaration of the word of the Lord. From the Genesis account we learn that at least on occasion divine revelation came to particular individuals within the cultic congregation, so qualifying them to perform the prophetic function of the community.

a. Prophet Figures: Before turning to these individual prophets, we shall take note of the parental naming acts recorded in the Sethite history (Gen 4:25; 5:29; cf. 3:20; 4:1). Names assigned to children are interpreted by the parents in terms of the covenantal relationship with its promises and hope. It may be questioned whether these parental interpretations are anything more than uninspired readings of their situation, not necessarily to be regarded as free from misunderstanding or miscalculation. Whether or not inspired utterances, they are certainly indicative of the outlook of faith that characterized these godly Sethites in contrast to the rebellious posture of the Cainites. It is clearly the intention of the biblical account to draw that contrast, as we can see, especially, from the circumstance that it is a Lamech in each line to whom a climactic statement is attributed, the two statements breathing out diametrically opposite spirits (Gen 4:23,24: 5:29). Incidentally, the narrative further invites comparison of these two Lamechs by associating each with the number seven; Cainite Lamech boasts of vengeance seventy and sevenfold and Sethite Lamech's life-span is seven hundred seventy and seven years. It should also be observed that there are indications in these naming episodes that the community of the Sethite faithful had the historic vocation of transmitting the covenant tradition with the oracles of God embedded therein, for in the explanations given for the names familiarity with those oracles is displayed.

Enoch and Noah are the two figures in the Sethite line who definitely perform the distinctly prophetic office. The New Testament, reflecting in part noncanonical tradition whose trajectory moved through late Jewish apocalyptic circles, presents both of these men as engaged in a prophetic mission of witness and warning. Enoch, according to the book of Jude, prophesied of the coming judgment of God against blasphemous sinners (vv.14,15). Noah, according to Peter's second epistle, was a herald of righteousness to his rebellious and doomed generation (2 Pet 2:5; cf. 1 Pet 3:20; Heb 11:7).

One not-so-obvious basis for this prophetic identification of the role of Enoch and Noah is discernible within the Genesis narrative itself. Each of them is there said to have "walked with God" (Gen 5:22,24; 6:9). The Hebrew expression is unusual; in fact, this precise combination of verbal form (*hithpa'el* of *halak*) and preposition (*'et*) appears nowhere else in Scripture. This verbal form with other prepositions is used with both men and God as subject to denote the maintaining of covenantal relationship through the fulfilling of the appropriate roles therein (e.g., Gen 17:1; 24:40; 48:15; Lev 26:12; Deut 23:14; 2 Sam 7:7). The walking with God attributed to Enoch and Noah ought then, if it does not have the more specific meaning suggested below, at least be understood as fidelity to covenant, rather than piety in a more general sense. But this verbal form is also used to describe persons engaged in a judicial mission. In Genesis 3:8 it portrays God's investigatory scrutiny of his sanctuary in Eden as he entered into judgment with Satan and fallen mankind. In Zechariah 1:10,11 and 6:7 it describes agents of God's heavenly council on missions of judicial surveillance and of actual judgment among the nations. It is also used of

Satan's malicious probings about the earth with a view to presenting accusations in the heavenly court (Job 1:7; 2:2). In 1 Samuel 12:2 the prophet Samuel and the king of Israel are the subjects of this verb, which seems to describe their acting as judges over Israel. Job 22:14 is another passage in which this verb describes God engaged in judicial surveillance (on this passage, see my comments in *Images of the Spirit,* p.102). Perhaps in Leviticus 26:12, Deuteronomy 23:14 and 2 Samuel 7:7 the idea is again more precisely that of God's presence in Israel by way of judicial superintendence. At the center of all this judicial activity, it will be noticed, is God's heavenly council and, significantly, that is the place where the prophets of Israel received their commissioning and from which they went forth on their judicial mission to Israel and the nations. (Of possible bearing on the interpretation of Enoch's walking with God is the fact that in what appears to be a Mesopotamian version of the Enoch tradition, Enmeduranki, seventh figure in prediluvian king lists, is said to have been admitted to the assembly of the gods and shown mysteries.)

It therefore appears that Genesis 5:22,24 and 6:9 portray Enoch and Noah as prophet figures, who had access to the counsel of the heavenly court and who shared with the Lord God in his judicial oversight of the earth, acting as messengers in the publishing of his decrees and judgments. They participated with the Lord ("walked with" him) in that judicial process which he initiated in Eden (Gen 3:8) and continues to conduct throughout history as Judge of all the earth. Confirming this interpretation is the fact that their walking with God is closely connected in the biblical record with statements presenting them in a distinctly prophetic role. In Genesis 5:24 Enoch's walking with God is prelude to his translation into heaven, which has its counterpart among the prophets of Israel in Elijah's rapture into the heavenly council in the Glory-chariot. And the statement that Noah walked with God in the introductory summary of the third generations-section of Genesis (6:9) soon finds its explanation in the coming of the word of God to Noah, declaring the divine verdict on the world and foretelling the imminent judgment (vv.13ff.). What we are plainly told in these accompanying statements about the lives of Enoch and Noah clearly fits the pattern of later prophet-messengers of the Lord engaged in the judicial administration of his covenant. Whatever one decides, then, about the meaning of their walking with God, these other disclosures of their prophet-like experiences firmly establish their prophetic identity and role.

b. Divine Lawsuit: As we have followed the trail of judicial walking marked at Genesis 3:18 and 5:22,24 and 6:9 we have found that the Lord himself initiated this lawsuit process against mankind for their breaking of the creational covenant and afterwards raised up from the midst of the community of the Covenant of Grace prophets to represent him in his continuing prosecution of that lawsuit. The target sphere of the message of the Sethite prophets was the world at large. In this respect they differed from the Israelite prophets who, though they had a secondary mission to the nations, yet, because they functioned within a theocratic kingdom arrangement that did not obtain in the prediluvian era, were primarily concerned with the people already within God's covenant. A resumption of a stronger focus on the world occurs in the Word-mission of the apostolic church. Indeed, the world-focus now becomes not simply a matter of the orientation of the message but of a missionary movement carrying that message out among the nations.

Rebuke of mankind's defiant disobedience and warning of coming divine judgment were the notes most loudly sounded in the proclamations of the prophets Enoch and Noah. At the same time, an offer of deliverance was entailed, for the prophetic warnings served as a summons to repentance. With respect to this two-sided witness, with its threat of God's curse and its offer of God's favor and blessing, there is continuity throughout redemptive history in the prophetic approach of God's people to the world. Only in relative emphasis on one or the other of the two elements would there be a difference from time to time, the gospel coming more and more to the fore in the postdiluvian history.

God's lawsuits against the prediluvian world and against Old Testament Israel followed similar courses, proceeding through periods of divine forbearance and warning to an ultimate visitation of divine wrath. In terms of this parallel it may be said that Enoch and Noah occupied positions in the prediluvian lawsuit analogous to those of Elijah and John the Forerunner respectively in the judicial administration of the old covenant. In the epoch beyond the united monarchy, Elijah introduced the warning stage, while John brought the final ultimatum to Israel when the true, messianic kingdom was at last at hand.

Like Elijah, Enoch appeared at a time when the challenge against the Lord had become acute and had to be met by the counterchallenge of God's lawsuit. The proportions which the human revolt had reached by Enoch's day are evident in his prophetic words of condemnation of the ungodly: Their offense consisted not only in unjust acts against man but in proud words spoken against God, the kind of blasphemous boasting that emanated from the courts of "the men of the name" (Jude 15). Also, if the Lamech of Genesis 4 does not stand at the very end of the prediluvian history, it might be conjectured that since both Enoch and Cainite Lamech are the "seventh" in their respective lines, the intent might be to associate their eras. In that case, it would be the alarming aggravation of man's idolatrous arrogance in Lamech's reign (compare developments under Ahab in Elijah's day) that was the occasion for the vigorous prosecution of the lawsuit introduced through Enoch. And, of course, the Enoch-Elijah correspondence is confirmed by their sharing, alone of mankind, in a translation experience that brought them deathlessly into the heavenly council, from which the prophetic lawsuit was directed.

Enoch prophesied of an advent of the Lord in his Glory, with his heavenly armies, for universal judgment (Jude 14). The epoch of the world that then was would end the way the epoch in Eden ended, with a personal coming of the heavenly Judge in the thunder of the storm, amid angel-agents of judgment (cf. Gen 3:8). That primal *parousia* had set the pattern for subsequent comings of the day of the Lord. For the ungodly who rejected Enoch's warning, the advent day he foretold would come as darkness and death. Yet it was not without the promise of deliverance for those who found grace in God's eyes. Out of the death-waters a remnant would emerge through a justifying resurrection into a new world. Of this, Enoch's personal life experience bore witness. His deliverance from death by direct translation into heaven was at once a divine validation of the heavenly authority of the prophetic word he had spoken and a prophetic sign of deliverance from the ultimate death-curse of the broken covenant, a deliverance open to those who, responding in faith to his prophetic call, found reconciliation with the Lord.

Persistent failure to respond with repentance to the witness of God's prophet Enoch probably resulted in the world that then was being subjected in increasing tempo to the calamities of the four horsemen (cf. 1 Kg 17:1ff. for Elijah's day). In the Mesopotamian flood tradition, the final catastrophe is preceded by a series of plagues. Possibly it is a background of intensified natural disasters that is reflected in the reference to "the ground that the Lord has cursed" in the explanation of the name given by the Sethite Lamech to his son Noah (Gen 5:29). By such warning judgments the Lord reenforces the demand of his prophetic word that men repent if they would escape the coming day of wrath.

Noah's prophetic activity is described in 2 Peter 2:5 as a heralding of righteousness in the face of the world of the ungodly. According to the probable meaning of 1 Peter 3:19,20, Noah performed his prophetic preaching as the mouth of the Spirit of Christ, that Spirit-Presence from whom all the true prophets were sent forth in the judicial administration of God's covenant. Late in the lawsuit process though it was when Noah prophesied, his days were still a time of God's patient waiting, according to 1 Peter 3:20. The plea for repentance was, then, still present in Noah's preaching, perfunctory as it might now have become and fruitless though it proved.

However, like John the Forerunner, Noah did mark the very last stage of God's lawsuit, when the breaking forth of God's wrath was imminent. Such is the thrust of the divine disclosures to Noah in Genesis 6:3,5ff. and 11ff., which formed the content of his prophetic witness to his contemporaries. The end of all flesh on earth – and mankind too was flesh – had been decreed (Gen 6:13). As man had multiplied, so had evil (Gen 6:1,5); as man had filled the earth, so had lawlessness (Gen 1:28; 6:11,13). The axe was laid unto the root of the tree; the deluge waters would cut off apostate mankind from the earth. In fact, the verdict in Genesis 6:3, like the verdict on the Amorites made known to God's prophet Abraham (Gen 15:13-16), specified the number of the years until iniquity was ripe for judgment. The lawsuit that God's Spirit had been prosecuting through his prophets would not be indefinitely prolonged (Gen 6:3a). Developments among "the sons of the gods" were bringing the longsuffering of God to an end. There were just one hundred and twenty years to judgment.

The above interpretation of Genesis 6:3a assumes that the verb is *din* and that that verb may have the sense of engaging in legal process (cf. Eccl 6:10, where not only is the verb similarly used but the contextual concern is again with "man" in his mortality over against the Almighty). This third reference to God's Spirit in Genesis thus resumes the theme of the judicial activity found at the second reference to him as "the Spirit of the day" who was "walking" on judicial patrol in Eden (Gen 3:8; cf. Gen 1:2 for the first reference). We have now found that the key terms for the Spirit-prophet's judicial activity in both Genesis 6:3 ("Spirit") and Genesis 6:9 ("walking") hark back to Genesis 3:8. These two verses in Genesis 6 are thereby linked to each other, the effect being to tell us that it was in the course of Noah's participation with God in his judicial oversight of the world (v.9) that he learned of the heavenly council's decree that the Spirit's lawsuit with man would not go on forever but be limited to one hundred and twenty more years (v.3). Incidentally, it would also now appear from this understanding of Genesis 6:3 that 1 Peter 3:19,20 reflects the distinctive Spirit concept of the Genesis narrative itself when it speaks of a prophetic preaching by Christ in the Spirit-mode back in Noah's day. This then becomes an additional consideration in favor of that exegesis of 1 Peter 3:19,20. (Was the prefacing of "preached" by "went" in v.19 possibly influenced in part by the terminology of the prophetic going to and fro of Gen 3:8 and 6:9?)

Conclusion

The fundamental disclosure of Genesis 5 is that the Lord, in faithfullness to his soteric purposes and promises, established a community of the faithful and sustained it throughout the long history of the world that then was. Eventually, the preservation of God's altar people required an almighty redemptive intervention in the form of the deluge judgment. For by Noah's day the covenant community was perilously close to extinction. To account for the reduction of that community to a remnant family of eight souls we must evidently envisage a cancerous process of spreading defection from the faith. In this respect too the old world history serves as a paradigm of the eschatological course of the world that now is. According to the prophetic indications in the New Testament (cf., e.g., 2 Thess 2:3,9-12 and the Babylon-harlot of the book of Revelation) the development of the city of man to the final Beast-stage of the man of lawlessness is attended by massive apostasy. Similarly, the emergence of the idolatrous cult of the god-kings of Genesis 6 had as its concomitant the almost total disappearance of the covenant institution that had once flourished among the Sethites. We must assume then that the lawsuit warning of the Sethite prophets had been addressed to those apostatizing from the community of the Covenant of Grace as well as to the ungodly world persisting in the rebellion against the original covenant in Eden.

A chosen few through sovereign grace continued to surname themselves Yahweh-people with integrity. During the reign of terror of the god-kings, their confession of allegiance to the Lord God could only be viewed as subversive of the claims of the pseudotheocratic state. The altar-community would thus come increasingly under the pressure of persecution, which would then have been one important factor accounting for their diminishing ranks. It was the problem of such a fiery trial in the church of his day that the apostle Peter was dealing with in the context of his appeal to the paradigm history of the prediluvian world (cf. 1 Pet 3:12,14; 4:14,16). About the camp of the Sethite remnant, where a standard was raised bearing the name of Yahweh, the encompassing coils of the serpent tightened and from the altar the cry for judicial intervention went up to heaven: "O Lord, how long?".

Chapter Three

SIGN OF KINGDOM CONSUMMATION

Introduction

Once the antichrist stage is reached in the development of the city of man, divine judgment is not long postponed. So it was in the eschatological pattern of the prediluvian world. After the apostasy and the appearance of the sons of the gods, history hastened to the judicial intervention of God in the Flood, whereby the world that then was perished and a remnant community was redeemed.

The outstanding importance of the Flood is reflected in the expansive literary treatment accorded it in Genesis. The account of the Deluge dominates the narrative of the history from the Fall to Abraham, this single event (6:9-8:22) being given about as much coverage as all the millennia from Adam to Noah (4:1-6:8) or from Noah to Abraham (9:1-11:26). The momentous nature of the flood judgment is also indicated by the particular position of the flood narrative within the ten-fold sectioning of the book of Genesis; for it occupies there the climactic third section of the first triad. In both this triad and the one that follows (sections four through six), the third section records an epochal covenant, with Noah and with Abraham, respectively.

Though regarding it as of great importance to maintain that fidelity to the Scriptures requires that the Flood be recognized as a genuinely historical event, and one of vast scope, we will not here be entering into the discussion of its precise geographic extent.. Our present interest in the Flood is as a covenantal transaction and as a typological drama that prefigured major aspects of the Consummation: redemptive judgment, cosmic re-creation, and the perfecting of the kingdom.

But first, a prefatory review of the literary structure of the flood narrative will prove useful. This narrative does not comprise the entire third generations-division of Genesis (6:9-9:28), but is best taken as extending from 6:13-8:22. Seven sections can be discerned within the flood narrative proper, distinguished and delimited by a succession of seven distinctive themes arranged in a chiastic (more specifically, a delta-type) pattern of correspondences. The first (6:13-22) describes the building of the ark and the corresponding seventh (8:20-22) tells of the building of the altar. Or, in a word, the theme of the first is construction and the theme of the seventh is consecration. The second section (7:1-5) narrates the embarkation; and the corresponding sixth (8:15-19), disembarkation. The third section (7:6-12) depicts the *mabbul*, the 40 days flood proper, marked by the ever-increasing waters, while the corresponding fifth section (8:1-14) records the decreasing of the waters and drying out of the earth. The central and climactic fourth section (7:13-24) recounts the prevailing of the judgment waters as they overwhelm all the world outside the ark.

Though identified primarily by their distinctive themes, these sections are also marked off by certain opening-closing, or terminal, patterns. The first two sections begin with a divine command (6:13 and 7:1), and end with Noah's obedience (6:22 and 7:5). Similarly, section six opens with God's command (8:15) and ends with the obedience of Noah and all in the ark (8:18,19). Sections three and four begin with a date (7:6, cf. 11 and 7:13, cf. 11) and close with a summary time reference, to 40 days (7:12) and to 150 days (7:24). Section five starts with a striking statement of the turning point reached in the flood event when "God remembered Noah" (8:1) so that the waters hitherto increasing began to decrease; and this section closes with a date formula and the summary conclusion that the earth was dry. The seventh section opens with the statement of Noah's building an altar of consecration (8:20), his act of covenantal response to the covenant fulfilling divine remembrance (8:1). God's acceptance of the sacrifice closes this final section (8:21,22). It seems preferable to see the flood narrative proper ending at 8:22 rather than including 9:1-17 along with 8:20-22 in the final section. The covenant announced in the opening section (6:18) has been fulfilled by 8:22, while 9:1-17 records a different, subsequent covenant. At the same time, it should be recognized that when it comes to the broader integration of the flood narrative proper with the remainder of the third generations-division of Genesis, 8:20-22 performs a double role, concluding the preceding flood narrative but also introducing the following account of the common grace covenant.

A remarkable feature of the author's literary artistry appears in the structuring of sections two through four especially (although the device continues on, in a reverse form, into the following two sections). This is of particular importance because the data in view have often been seen as clumsy repetitions resulting from inept redaction of supposed multiple source-materials. What we observe is that there is a progressively rising structure as we move from the second to the third to the fourth sections, each successive section reincorporating the substance of the one, or two, preceding sections, not without significant supplementation (cf. 7:16b). Entrance into the ark is the theme of section two. Section three repeats this entrance theme (7:7-9) before adding its own distinctive theme of the 40 days *mabbul* (7:10-12). Then section four builds up to its distinctive theme by repeating both the entrance theme of section two (7:13-16) and the 40 days *mabbul* theme of section three (7:17a), only then adding as its top story, and as the peak of the entire flood narrative, the description of the prevailing of the waters in fulfillment of God's announced judicial purpose (7:17b-24). There is thus a literary heightening from a one- to a two- and then a three-level structure, and this rising and peaking literary form structurally mirrors the physical scene it is describing, with the continual increasing of the waters to their mountain covering crest.

The ascending movement of sections two through four is reversed in sections five and six, the decreasing literary structure of these sections now matching the historical scenario of the abating waters. Section five deals with two of the three topics included in section four, or rather with their reversal, namely, the cessation of the *mabbul* (8:2; cf. 7:11) and the end of the prevailing of the waters over the ark (8:4; cf. 7:17) and over the mountains (8:5; cf. 7:19). Then section six takes up only one of the three themes of section four, the one not found in section five, namely the entrance into the ark; for its theme is disembarkation, the counterpart to entrance (8:15ff; cf. 7:5; 7:7ff.; 7:13ff.). The chiastic correspondence between sections two and six and between sections three and five thus extends beyond the nature of the distinctive theme of each to the number of their themes, sections two and six dealing with just one theme each, and sections three and five with two each. Over-all there is a movement from both terminals of the narrative upwards toward the central fourth section, which, with its three sections, stands as the pinnacle of the delta-structured composition.

I. REDEMPTIVE JUDGMENT

A. Antichrist Crisis

The enmity between the serpent's seed and the woman's seed was that of rival claimants for the ultimate possession of the world (cf. Matt 4:8ff.; 1

Pet 1:4; 2 Pet 3:13; Rev 11:15; 12:10). By Noah's day the tension of this contention over the inheritance of the earth had reached the breaking point.

That the serpent's seed should enjoy even a temporary place on earth and be in a position to assert their claim at all was of course due only to the forbearance of the Creator-Lord, "not willing that any should perish but that all should come to repentance" (2 Pet 3:9). It was only because of God's merciful common grace arrangements that the unjust shared common status with the just in the temporal blessings of the world. They, however, were not about to accept this common grace interpretation of the historical situation. To do so would mean to convert, to abandon their own pretensions to autonomy and acknowledge the sovereign proprietorship of Yahweh over the earth and all its peoples. But their rejection of the principle of commonness went beyond refusal to make thankful acknowledgment of God's permission to enjoy common privilege with the godly in things mundane. Aspiring to world dominion and assuming the name of gods, they would not deign in their self-bestowed status as gods to extend common grace to those who did not bow before them. They would not grant to the servants of the rival deity, Yahweh, a common portion with themselves and their devotees on the face of the earth.

Coexistence with the cult of Yahweh was not consistent with the logic of the culture-cult of the serpent's seed. By raising an altar in the name of Yahweh, the godly were staking out a claim of world sovereignty for him, and by surnaming themselves by the name of Yahweh they were claiming the eventual inheritance of the earth for themselves as the children of the Lord of all creation. That was intolerable to the idolatrous ideology of the Cainite god-kings. An absolutized earthly monopoly of power, a deified here-and-now state, cannot be content with filing its claims in common court with competing claimants and waiting for adjudication by somebody else hereafter. Suppression and elimination of the rival claimants was the logically inevitable policy of such a regime. The precedent had been set by the founder of the dynasty in the slaying of martyr Abel and, as we concluded above, with the increasing tempo of mankind's rebellion against heaven (the main theme of Genesis 4 and 6:1ff.) the hatred of Satan's brood for God's children must also have intensified and reached a crescendo under the demon-driven, self-deified dynasts.

It is this diabolical reversal of the principle of historical commonness that precipitates the end of the historical process. When the Devil's seed repudiate common grace by refusing to the woman's seed a common place with them on earth, they in effect foreclose on God's common grace to themselves. Coexistence is the *sine qua non* of their own historical existence. By axing common grace they cut off the branch they are sitting on.

When therefore the remnant people of Noah's household were on the verge of being driven from the face of the earth, their covenant Protector could delay no longer to respond to their appeal (cf. Ps 94). God's name was identified with those eight souls (1 Pet 3:20). They represented the possibility of the continuance of the hope of mankind's salvation on into the future to its final messianic accomplishment. It was time for the Judge of all the earth to come quickly. The day of the Lord was at hand, the day for him to render a verdict and settle the case of the rival claimants for the world inheritance, the day when the Lord takes action and his people rejoice in him (Ps 118:24). The precise hour of the last great day is known to the Father alone (Matt 24:36), but the logic of the eschatological times which the Father has put within his own authority (Acts1:7) is exhibited in the prefigurative pattern of the days of Noah (Matt 24:37ff.).

B. Judicial Ordeal

1. Dual Verdicts
Trial by judicial ordeal was the procedure God employed in settling the disputed inheritance of the kingdoms of this world. This procedure is known to have been common in judicial practice in the ancient world. It was a technique by which the court sought to ascertain the judgment of the gods. The ordeal test assumed a variety of forms, like combat between the adversaries or individual exposure to an elemental power like water or fire. Through the ordeal test the divine verdict was registered, clearing the innocent and condemning the guilty, as the god either delivered from the ordeal element or delivered into its power. In some forms of ordeal, the process would serve both to declare guilt and to execute the offender. One familiar variety, the river ordeal, stood clearly in the formal tradition of the Deluge. The Deluge was the archetypal water ordeal.

Commenting on the parallel of the Flood to the Last Judgment, Peter calls particular attention to the ordeal elements employed. He notes that the final ordeal element will be fire instead of water (2 Pet 3:5ff.). In the imagery of some biblical ordeal contexts the water and fire blend, as in the river of fire flowing from God's throne (Dan 7:10). In the judicial ordeal between Israel and Egypt, the most notable of the Old Testament types of the Final Judgment other than the Flood, both ordeal elements were involved, not only the waters of the sea but the fire of the Glory-cloud (cf. the comments on 1 Cor 10:1,2 in my *By Oath Consigned*, p.68). In the exodus judgment event, as in the Deluge, the ordeal elements performed their dual functions of vindication-deliverance (in behalf of Moses and Israel) and condemnation-destruction (against pharaoh and Egypt). Germane here is the observation that the New Testament identifies both the Deluge and exodus ordeals as baptismal events (1 Pet 3:20f.; 1 Cor 10:1f.). Accordingly, baptism is to be understood as a passage through the judgment-ordeal waters of death.

Hebrews 11:7 brings out the judicially discriminating nature of the deluge judgment as an ordeal with dual verdicts: "By faith Noah being warned of God of things not seen as yet, moved with fear, prepared an ark to the saving of his house; by which he condemned the world, and became heir of the righteousness which is by faith." "The world," ungodly mankind, perished in the ordeal waters. Thus the God of the ordeal at once invalidated their world claims and executed the punishment for their sins against him and his people. In their own idol-name they claimed the earth, but the Judge of the earth decreed: "I will destroy them from the earth" (Gen 6:13, cf. v.7 and 7:4), because through them the earth was filled with violence. So the ordeal waters prevailed over them and condemnation, dispossession, and destruction together befell them in one day.

Those who are in the right are divinely enabled to overcome the ordeal power so that they emerge with a verdict in their favor. In the deluge-ordeal, God provided godly Noah with the plan for deliverance, secured his family in the ark, remembered them at the height of the crisis, and piloted the ark to rest on the far side of the flood. Brought safely through the ordeal, they were, by their resurrection-emergence from the waters of death (cf. 1 Pet 3:21), declared justified in the sight of God, heirs of righteousness and inheritors of the world-kingdom.

2. Redeemed Remnant

The flood-ordeal was a redemptive judgment. Its character as a salvation event is all the more pronounced because this ordeal-adjudication of the controversy over world inheritance came as God's response to the plea of his remnant community, crying out in the straits of persecution. Viewing the flood waters as the ordeal medium by which the people of God were declared justified, Peter says they were saved by means of the water (1 Pet 3:20). But the ordeal waters were the means of salvation for the godly in the further sense that they were rescued by these waters from the hands of those bent on their annihilation. By accomplishing the overthrow and destruction of their enemies, the deluge saved the righteous from the fiery persecution that threatened their very existence as a remnant-witness to God's name on earth.

The existence of the remnant of eight souls just before the flood manifested the continuity of the covenant community, enduring by God's grace and faithfulness in the face of persecution and expanding apostasy. But as a result of their passing through the experiences of deliverance from persecution and of preservation through world cataclysm and continuance on into the new world beyond it, their remnant-identity took on new overtones. The remnant were now the saved, the survivors. Alone of mankind they remained to perpetuate humanity in general as well as to carry forward covenantal-redemptive history in particular. And in that they emerged alive from mortal combat, the remnant were also now overcomers, victors.

C. Day of the Lord

Additional features of the final redemptive day of the Lord that were typologically represented in the flood-event are theophany and the gathering of the elect.

1. *Parousia*

From the primal day of the Lord in Genesis 3 to the last great judicial advent, the days of the Lord are *parousia* days, days of God's presence in supernatural intervention and special manifestation. The flood history is not without intimations of the Lord's advent "as the Spirit of the day" (cf. Gen 3:8). Noah, of course, received repeated special revelations in his walking with God before the flood-event and in the course of it. Most suggestive of theophanic presence is the narrative detail that after Noah and all the others had entered the ark, "Yahweh shut him in" (Gen 7:16b). This statement appears in the third occurrence of the entrance theme, at the beginning of section four. The narrative of this supplementary detail of the entry motif is made the more effective by its postponement to this later point in the account, for here the notice of this unusual act of divine protection comes in immediate connection with the description of the unleashing of the overwhelming peril.

Isaiah clearly alludes to the Genesis 7:16 episode in the midst of the climactic scene in his "little apocalypse" where he is celebrating God's final deliverance from death and Satan (see Isa 26:20). Once the relationship of the two passages is recognized, they become mutually illuminative. Both turn out to be dealing with the enclosure of God's people in a passage through death that proves to be a refuge from the outbreaking of God's wrath against the world. Isaiah encouragingly depicts the death of the saints as an entering into an inner chamber where they may shut the doors about themselves (the same terms as used in Genesis 7:16 for the entering of the ark and the closing of the ark door about Noah) and have a hiding-place until the indignation has passed by. Prominent in the Isaianic treatment of the divine conquest of death is the Glory-*parousia* of that day of Yahweh, and, we may assume, the prototype occasion of the Flood also witnessed an appropriate revelation of that divine presence.

In fact, the thundering storm clouds of the flood may themselves be regarded as an extended manifestation of the Glory-cloud of the Lord God, riding over the earth in judgment (cf. my comments in *Images of the Spirit*, p.101). A description of the thunderstorm in terms of the voice of the God of glory in Psalm 29 leads to the affirmation that "Yahweh sat enthroned from the flood (*mabbul*), yea, he sat as king from everlasting" (v.10). The psalmist evidently perceived the royal Glory-presence in the phenomena of the flood – and linked it further with the revelation of the Glory-Spirit at the creation (cf. Gen 1:2). As we shall note again below, the Genesis flood narrative itself suggests the connection with the Spirit (*ruach*) over the waters in Genesis 1:2 by its mention of God making the wind (*ruach*) to pass over the waters at the critical juncture described in Genesis 8:1.

2. Gathering of the Elect

A constant concomitant of redemptive Glory-*parousia* in the visions of the prophets is the gathering of the elect out of the doomed world into the sanctuary of God's presence and kingdom. This harvest-gathering into the Lord's heavenly garners is the definitive rendering of redemptive verdict in behalf of the saints. And such a gathering is associated with the *parousia* of the Flood. Indeed, it is in the gathering of the covenant family into the ark-kingdom that this prominent feature in the eschatological pattern of redemptive judgment first appears (though earlier adumbrated in some respects by the rapture of Enoch).

The triple narrating of the gathering-entrance theme (in sections two, three and four of the flood narrative) is indicative of its paramount importance as the critical judicial-redemptive act of God at his advent in Glory to subject the world to its judgment ordeal. Even in the coming of the animals to Noah to be brought by him into the ark, the gathering hand of God himself should be discerned. That the Lord himself is the Gatherer-Savior is plainly indicated by the climactic statement that the entry into the ark was completed by his own direct act of shutting the occupants securely in.

The day of the Flood was the day of the redemptive vengeance of Yahweh. As Lord of the earth he took judicial action in behalf of his people, exercising his rightful authority in defense and vindication of those under his protection. (For the idea of the divine vindication of the servant of the Lord in a context rich in Deluge-inspired imagery, see Psalm 18.) Such judicial discrimination between two groups of mankind strictly according to their religious status before God with a view to the redemption of God's own people is distinctive of the Final Judgment. Wherever such religiously discriminatory redemptive judgment appears in the course of history prior to the Final Judgment (as at the Flood or the exodus, and elsewhere in connection with the earthly kingdom stage of the covenant community) it is an eschatological intrusion contrary to the "normal" procedures of the era of common grace. In these typological instances, those who are redeemed and vindicated are the covenant people. They are thus sharply distinguished from the world as "holy" unto the Lord, even if all who thus partake of the typological salvation do not necessarily belong to the ultimately elect company who enter the eternal kingdom. As provisional annulments of the principle of historical commonness, these typological judgments point to the ultimate termination of the present interim history and the introduction of the eternal state characterized by an absolute discrimination between those who love and those who hate God.

II. RE-CREATION

Peter interprets the deluge-judgment as an act of re-creation, boldly making it the division between two worlds, the transition from the heavens and earth that were of old to the heavens and earth that now are (2 Pet.3:5-7).

There are some obvious parallels in the physical realities of the flood and the original creation events, each proceeding from a phase of unbounded waters to a habitable world. But before elaborating on this parallelism as to historical scenario we shall note some literary correspondences between the biblical accounts of the two events.

A. Literary Parallels

In some interesting ways the style and structure of the flood narrative recall the literary form of the creation account in the Genesis prologue. Apparently a conscious purpose was at work in the constructing of the Genesis 6-8 narrative to bring out the nature of the flood episode as a virtual second creation event.

According to certain extra-biblical flood traditions the duration of the event was seven days. Significant periods of seven days appear within the history of the Flood as chronicled in Genesis, but in all the episode takes about a year. However, although the imagery of a week of days is not used in Genesis as a figurative framework for the total deluge process, we have seen that the Genesis flood record, like its creation record, does have a sevenfold structure. And as in the Genesis prologue, the seven sections in the flood account do not represent separate successive time periods but are rather distinguished each by its own topic.

Moreover, chronological recapitulation of a preceding section in a later section, which has been noted as a feature of Genesis 1, is found again in the flood account. Thus, section four covers 150 days (7:24), the first 40 of which recapitulate the 40 days of the flood proper described in section three (7:11,12; cf. 7:17; 8:3,4). And section five begins chronologically where section three ends, 40 days into the 150 days of section four (8:1-4), so that the first 110 days of the eleven-month period covered in section five overlap the closing 110 days of the period dealt with in section four.

Like the seven days of Genesis 1, the seven divisions of the flood account contain two triads, with a unifying theme for each triad and with cross-correspondence between the three individual units of the two triads, plus a key seventh section. The theme of the first triad is the entrance of the ark-kingdom into the judgment and the theme of the closing triad is the re-emergence of the ark-kingdom in the re-creation. The key seventh part occupies the middle position as the fourth in the series of seven sections.

Its theme is the judgment of the world, which was the central reality of the flood event. It records the decisive execution of the dual ordeal verdicts, telling how the ordeal waters prevailed over all, destroying everything outside the ark, while those within the ark alone remained alive (7:23).

Thus, the climactic peak section stands in the center flanked by the two triads, producing an A.B.A´ structure (whereas in Genesis 1 the structure is A.A´.B, with the seventh climactic section preceded by the two triads). The chiastic principle in the flood account extends beyond the general positioning of the triads on the two ends about the key middle section. As we have observed, the thematic parallelism between the several members of the two triads is also arranged chiastically so that the matching members are the first and the seventh, the second and the sixth, and the third and the fifth.

Another major feature of the Genesis prologue with a counterpart in the flood narrative is the fiat-fulfillment format of the six day-stanzas that relate God's creative working. In the flood account, fiat-fulfillment takes the form of command-fulfillment (or obedience), though virtual fiat-fulfillment is also present. And here again, as in the Genesis prologue, the pattern extends through the first six sections of the record, but not into the seventh, which, with its consecration motif, is the thematic equivalent of the sabbath day of the creation narrative. We have observed above that the first two sections and the sixth begin with God's commands to Noah and close with the acts of obedience to those commands. By virtue of the repetition of the entry theme of section two in sections three and four the command-obedience scheme involved in the entry theme finds explicit expression in these two sections also (see 7:7-9 and 7:13-16). Further, the physical events which constitute the distinguishing topics of these two sections, the coming of the *mabbul* itself in section three and the prevailing of the waters in section four, are very much a matter of fiat-fulfillment. For the *mabbul* comes (7:10,11) in execution of God's declared purpose (6:17a) and decretive announcement (7:4a). And the waters prevail to the destruction of all life outside the ark (7:21-23) in fulfillment of God's word prophetically declared (6:7,13,17b; 7:4b). Again, section five has a virtual fiat-fulfillment pattern. For it opens with a statement of God's intention and his initiating act (*i.e.*, his making a wind to pass over the earth), and it continues with the realization of the divinely purposed effects, namely, the abating of the waters and the coming of the ark to rest (8:1-14).

One more point of literary parallelism. The theme of re-creation, as it comes into specific focus in the closing triad of the flood record (*i.e.*, sections five through seven), begins in a manner strongly evocative of Genesis 1:1,2. God is named as the author of the fontal action and the creatures who are the objects of that action are described in terms of comprehensive totality (8:1a; cf. 1:1). Then the water-covered earth is referred to and the creative reordering of the formless void is attributed to the *ruach* (wind) of God in movement over the waters (8:1b), compelling comparison with Genesis 1:2, where the creative structuring of the cosmos is attributed to the *ruach* (Spirit) of God hovering over the deep-and-darkness. (See the discussion of Gen 1:2 above and note the appearance of the same motif in the Exod 14:21 account of Israel's crossing of the sea.)

B. Cosmological Correspondence

We turn now to the correspondences between the creation and flood as physical-historical events. To trace these will also inevitably be to suggest further literary parallels between the records of the two events (though now with respect to content rather than style and form).

In his reading of the deluge episode as a re-creation of heaven and earth, Peter centers his attention on the way the flood waters, overflowing the earth, transformed its appearance into something much like its deep-and-darkness stage early in the process of its creation (Gen 1:2a). The merging of the waters of the heaven above and the deep below in the flood (Gen 7:11; 8:2) constituted a return to the intermixture of the two that obtained when earth was yet a primeval chaos, "without form and void." Another feature of the correspondence in the historical circumstances of the creation and flood at the stage in view in Genesis 1:2 and 8:1 respectively is the *ruach* phenomena. We have noted this as a striking point in the literary parallelism of the narratives, but these phenomena were indeed historical actualities, and as observed above, the two forms of *ruach* were related modes of divine manifestation.

As the sequel to that *ruach*-over-the-waters phase of the flood there followed a series of incidents reminiscent of the creation history. The effect of the restraining divine action on the flood waters was, according to Genesis 8:2, a reestablishment of the two distinct water sources, above and below, a result that matches the work of the second "day" of creation, described in Genesis 1:6,7. The next development noted is the emergence of the land, first the mountain tops (8:3-5), then the lower land, with evidence of vegetation (8:6-ll). That corresponds plainly to the third "day" of creation, with the bounding of the seas, the appearance of the dry land and the bringing forth of plant life on it (1:9-12). Possibly, Noah's removal of the covering of the ark (8:13), representing the heavens in the cosmic symbolism of the ark (see below), with the resultant full disclosure of the actual canopy of heaven once more after the year in the ark, is to be perceived as a parallel to what is recounted under "day" four in Genesis 1:14ff. concerning the production and functioning of the luminaries in the firmament of heaven. Certainly what came next in the flood history corresponds to developments depicted in "days" five and six of the creation narrative (1:24-31): the emergence from the ark onto the dry land of the living creatures of all kinds (described in language echoing the creation story), thenceforth to multiply on the earth, and the reappearance of the nuclear human family, the sole representatives of mankind in the new world beyond the flood (8:15-19). In a most realistic sense the reduction of mankind to Noah's family was a return to mankind's creational beginnings. The situation even called for a new issuing of a cultural mandate, with a fresh charge to the human family to multiply and overspread the emptied earth (9:1; cf. 10:32). In that connection there is another element that recalls the original creation of the order of nature, namely, God's confirmation of the day-night sequence and the cycle of the seasons in the new world come forth from the waters (8:22).

Finally, the closing scene of the flood narrative finds the Lord taking pleasure in a world consecrated to him by his priestly image-bearer (8:20f.) and this is clearly the equivalent of the Creator's original seventh "day" (2:1-3). As noted, the fiat-fulfillment (or command-execution) pattern, the pattern of the work days, does not extend into this seventh section of the flood account. Reckoning of time by weeks is prominent in the chronological notations throughout the account and it is possible that we are to think of the consecration episode as actually falling on a weekly sabbath. Curiously, the seventh section closes with the verbal cognate of the noun "sabbath" in a statement assuring the future constancy of the order of nature (8:22).

Conclusion: Whether or not we accept a geographically universal interpretation of the extent of the flood, we must recognize that the whole central movement of history as traced in the Old Testament was interrupted by the flood. That much at least is needed to account for Peter's cosmic exposition of the event (2 Pet 2:5; 3:6f.). Beyond all other premessianic symbolic prototypes of the final coming of the kingdom through redemptive judgment ordeal, the Flood anticipatively suggests the cosmic dimensions of that last judgment as a world cataclysm necessitating re-creation.

In his reference to the Flood, Peter's main interest in the event is as an instance of divine judgment ordeal, which serves warning of the final day of the Lord that is coming upon the world (2 Pet 3:10-12). But he does not fail to observe that the antitypical world dissolution will, like its deluge sign, be the occasion of a re-creation: "Nevertheless we, according to his promise, look for a new heavens and a new earth, wherein dwelleth righteousness" (2 Pet 3:13).

III. KINGDOM CONSUMMATION

A. The Ark as Cosmic House of God

Though the ark served an instrumental purpose as the vehicular means for the deliverance of God's people from the judgment waters, it was at the same time a representation of the kingdom of God. More specifically, it was a symbol of the consummated kingdom of God, the kingdom beyond the Final Judgment typified by the flood waters. True to the nature of the eschatological order of the re-creation, the ark did not present the picture of a simple restoration of the kingdom to its primeval paradise condition. Rather, it symbolically portrayed the kingdom as a cultural-urban structure, at last brought to perfect completion. The ark was a capsulated city of God. It was a prophetic type of Metapolis.

As we have seen, Metapolis is a royal temple, the house of God. It is the final eschatological manifestation of the Creator's cosmic house of heaven and earth, which was typified by Israel's microcosmic tabernacle and temple. What is now to be observed is that the design of the ark suggests that it too was intended to be a symbolic representation of God's kingdom in this cosmic house form. For the ark, however seaworthy, was fashioned like a house rather than like a sailing vessel. All the features mentioned in the description of the ark belong to the architecture of a house: the three stories, the door, the window. And more specifically, these architectural features of the ark match up with features in creation's cosmic house as that is figuratively envisaged in various biblical passages, including the flood narrative itself.

The three stories of the ark correspond to the three stories of the world conceptualized as divided into the heaven above, the earth beneath, and the sphere under the earth, associated especially with the waters (cf. e.g., Exod 20:4; Deut 4:16ff.; Rom 1:23). Possibly the idea of three such zones is reinforced by the animal lists which classify the creatures in the ark as birds of the heaven, cattle and beasts of the earth, and the creeping things of the ground (Gen 6:7,20; 7:23; 8:17; cf. 7:14,21; 8:19). The third category, the creeping things, might have special reference here to burrowing creatures whose subterranean world would then have been substituted for the sphere of the waters under the earth as the lowest level of the ark-cosmos. Or does the narrative intend the correspondence of the first story of the ark to the waters under the earth to be suggested simply by the fact that this lowest part of the ark was actually submerged under the waters of the flood?

Clearly, the window of the ark is the counterpart to "the window of heaven," referred to in this very narrative (7:11; 8:2). Appropriately, the window area is located along the top of the ark, as part of the upper (heavenly) story. One is naturally led then to compare the door of the ark with the door that shuts up the depths of the sea, holding back its proud waves. (For this cosmological imagery see Job 38:8-11.) Precisely such a restraining of the mighty surge of waters was the function of the door of the ark, once the Lord had secured it about the occupants of the ark at the outset of the deluge. Together, the window and door of the ark mirrored the two cosmic sources of the flood waters, the window of heaven, opened to unleash the torrents of the waters above the earth, and the door of the deep, unbarred to let the waters beneath the earth break loose.

Another indication of the cosmic house symbolism of the ark is that it is God himself who reveals its design. Elsewhere when God provides an architectual plan it is for his sanctuary-house, whether tabernacle or temple (Exod 25ff.; 1 Chron 28:19; Heb 9:5; cf. Ezek 40ff.; Rev 21:10ff.). As the architect of the original creation, who alone comprehends its structure in all its vast dimensions (cf. Job 38), God alone can disclose the pattern for these microcosmic models. When we look at the revelation of the design of the ark in this light we perceive that the architect and builder of the eternal temple-city (Heb 11:10) is providing plans for a symbolic, prophetic copy of that heavenly sanctuary, the final objective of man's cultural history.

Parenthetically, it is of interest that the house-identity of the ark is reflected in the pagan refractions of the flood tradition. Thus, the hero in the Mesopotamian tradition is instructed by the protecting deity to transform his house into a vessel. The reeds of which his house was composed were to be appropriated for the construction of the craft by being applied over a wooden framework and covered with pitch (cf. Gen 6:14, where, incidently, *qnym* should probably be read "reeds" rather than "rooms"). In one passage (*Gilgamesh Epic* XI, 95) the vessel is designated by a term used for large buildings, like temples.

Straying a bit further—since, in Near Eastern mythology, creation history and redemptive history suffer a confused fusion, it is tempting to see in the Canaanite Baal-Yamm cycle some deviant reflections of the flood tradition, along with its generally recognized "creation" motif. In the Mesopotamian tradition the flood-hero is immortalized after his encounter with the waters and is located at the northern confluence of the waters, the abode of the gods beyond the waters of death. One wonders if, in the suggested Canaanite mutation, there is a conflation of the flood-hero with the storm-god who succumbs to Death, ally of Yamm, the sea-god, but emerges again. Baal's death and resurrection would then be a mythological variant of the experience of Noah and the other ark occupants. In that case (and returning to our subject), the theme of Baal's palace-temple building after his conflict with the Sea might be related to the ark-house strand in the flood tradition. The special emphasis on the window of Baal's palace would then provide an interesting parallel to the window in the ark as cosmic-house.

B. The Ark Occupants as Glorified Mankind

Central in the make-up of the city are its citizens. New Jerusalem, the consummated city of God, is identified with Christ's bride-people (Rev 21:9,10). In the case of the typological kingdom-city in the ark, the human occupants of the ark, as well as the ark itself, afforded a sign of the final, perfect realization of the city mandate in the consummated order.

According to that mandate man was to exercise dominion over all the creatures and subdue the realm of nature. Agreeably, the scene within the ark was one of man in control of the subhuman orders of life. Gathered there were the representatives of the two major orders, the vegetable kingdom and the animal kingdom, each in the rich variety of its many kinds, and all under the supervisory rule of the royal human family of Noah. Man's mastery of the world found expression in the ark that he had built. By means of the ark man surmounted the threatening violence of the mighty waters and winds, the elemental forces of nature at the chaotic extreme of its power. This achievement of mastery was a sign of what man's physical glorification will ultimately do for him, when, transformed into the likeness of his glorified Redeemer, he transcends his former dependence on the order of nature and his vulnerability to its disorders. Appropriately then, while man had his part to perform in the building of the ark, it was God, the One who will supernaturally accomplish the eschatological glorification of the new mankind, who designed the ark, revealed its pattern, gathered its occupants, personally enclosed his people within the ark, and guarded and guided it securely and triumphantly through the world cataclysm into the new world.

Resurrection is introductory to redemptive glorification. And the experience of the survivors in the ark portrayed this resurrection prelude too, inasmuch as in a sign they underwent a baptismal passage through the sea of death and came forth from their burial-chamber (cf. again Isa 26:19-21), delivered from the power of the last enemy. As the overcomers in an ordeal battle that was the great prototype of the Final Judgment, as those who were in the symbolic drama of the Deluge victors over death and triumphant rulers over nature, the ark-community was a sign-pledge that a redeemed people of God would be brought through the ultimate cataclysm of the Last Judgment, gathered unto God through resurrection and rapture, re-created through glorification as the new mankind in Christ Jesus, and crowned as co-heirs with him to reign forever with him in the eternal city-kingdom.

C. Sabbath Consecration of the Kingdom

Theocratic culture is cult-oriented. To build the theocratic city is to build the temple in which culture's sanctification to the Creator is realized. Man, crowned with glory and honor by creative investiture, is a priest-king under covenant to consecrate the labors of his six days to the Lord of the Sabbath. This ultimate Sabbath-consecration of the kingdom of God, the

Consummation's goal of goals, was also symbolically anticipated in the closing cultic episode of the Deluge prototype.

The kingdom that was consecrated to God by the ark-community was a kingdom that God had brought to the state of Sabbath-consummation. The coming of the ark to rest in the seventh month after it had accomplished its task through the course of the flood was the beginning of the Sabbath for the kingdom in the ark. The Hebrew term for this resting in Genesis 8:4 (*nwh*) involves a play on the name of Noah, who was so named with a view to the relief from toil that he should bring (Gen 5:29). It is the term used in Exodus 20:11 for God's sabbatical resting on the seventh day of creation and in Isaiah 25:10 for the coming to rest of the Glory-Spirit ("hand") on Mount Zion at the Consummation-Sabbath. Frequently, this verb is used for the Lord's leading Israel to repose in the sabbath-land of Canaan. One such passage is Isaiah 63:14, where it is the Glory-Spirit who brings them to this rest. We are reminded in surveying the usage of *nwh* that the Sabbath original is found in the reality of the Glory-Spirit-temple, the paradigm of the visible heaven-earth temple. Now since the ark, as a microcosmic house of God, was, like the tabernacle and temple, an image-replica of the Glory-Spirit-temple (see my *Images of the Spirit*, pp.39ff.), the picture we have in the bringing of the ark to rest by the theophanic Spirit is that of the Spirit perfecting his likeness in an image-bearer by bringing it to share in his own Sabbath.

Anticipated in the Genesis 8:4 statement of the ark coming to rest, the Sabbath theme has its main exposition in the seventh section of the flood narrative (Gen 8:20-22). This section deals with the sabbatical consecration of the creation kingdom in the ark to the Creator Lord and is thus, as noted above, the counterpart here to the seventh day-stanza of the creation record.

The distinctive altar-identity and priestly office of the holy community in the ark came to expression in Noah's building an altar unto Yahweh (v.20a). In the token form of representative animals offered on the altar as burnt offerings (v.20b), Noah consecrated to God the consummated kingdom in the ark. By this offering the priest-kings of the theocratic ark-kingdom consecrated themselves to God, making doxological confession that they were servant-kings in the kingdom-house of the Lord and that their Creator-Vindicator was King of kings. This perfecting of human kingship in the ritual of priestly consecration pointed to the priestly act of the coming royal Son, who, when all things have been subjected to him, will deliver up the kingdom to God, even the Father, subjecting himself to him who subjected all things to him that God might be all in all (1 Cor 15:24-28).

God accepted the offering up of the kingdom in the ark and looked with sabbatical satisfaction on his work of creation consummated through redemptive re-creation (Gen 8:21). All was now in confessed subjection to him as he sat enthroned in his cosmic temple amid the praises of his redeemed people. Here was a new revelation of the glory of the divine sovereignty, in that sense a coronation, constituting, along with the consummation and consecration of the kingdom, the fullness of the Sabbath of the Glory-Spirit.

IV. COVENANTAL GRANT

A. The Covenant of Genesis 6:18

From the outset God's dealing with the family of Noah in the deluge event was presented explicitly in terms of covenantal commitment. The Lord announced: "I will establish my covenant with you" (Gen 6:18a). Two interrelated questions arise with this earliest occurrence of the word *berith*, "covenant," in the Bible. First, where in the sequel do we find the realization of the promise of this covenant? Does Genesis 6:18 point to the postdiluvian covenant described in Genesis 9, or was the covenantal promise of Genesis 6:18 fulfilled within the flood event itself? If the latter answer is accepted, as it should be, we then face the second question: Does Genesis 6:18 have in view a previous covenant (not hitherto explicitly given the *berith* label) which was now to receive fulfillment in the deluge judgment? Or is the *berith* referred to in this verse the covenant just being made with Noah's household – and if so, does the governing verb (*hqym*) denote the initial ratification of the covenant or its subsequent execution?

One of the lines of evidence leading to our answer to the first question is supplied by an examination of the position of Genesis 6:18 in the literary structure of the flood narrative. The verse comes within the first of the seven sections (6:13-22). This section has a command-fulfillment pattern. Thus, the Lord, disclosing his judicial purpose, instructs Noah as to the role he must perform (6:13-21) and Noah obediently carries out the assignment

(6:22). The divine commissioning of Noah is divided into two balancing parts, verses 13-16 and verses 17-21. Each of these begins with a statement of God's intention to destroy all flesh from the earth (vv.13 and 17). This is followed in each case by the actual directives. In the first part the instructions deal with the construction of the ark (vv.14-16); in the second part, with the ark's occupants and provisioning (vv.18-21). Placed at the beginning of the latter set of instructions, the verse 18 statement of God's intention to establish his *berith* with Noah's family thus stands as the counterpart to verse 14 at the beginning of the former set. That is, the covenant of verse 18 is thus identified with the arrangement stipulated in verse 14 for the building of the ark by which the remnant should be saved from and through the judgment ordeal. This conclusion is supported by the fact that the verse 18 statement of God's purpose of establishing his covenant with Noah's family is contrasted with the immediately preceding announcement in verse 17 of his purpose of destroying all flesh by a flood. Moreover, the verse 18a *berith*-statement is elaborated upon by the immediately following directive for Noah and his family to enter into the ark of salvation (vv.18b-21).

In the light of the literary structure of the passage there is no room for doubt that the covenant of Genesis 6:18 is a covenant of salvation, whose promise was realized within the historical episode of the flood judgment, and not in any arrangement subsequent thereto. In particular, the postdiluvian covenant delineated in Genesis 9 is not referred to in Genesis 6:18. It was not a covenant of special redemptive grace. It was not made with the holy covenant community, promising them the kingdom of salvation, but was rather a common grace arrangement made with mankind in general, indeed, with all the earth. (Further analysis of this postdiluvian, common grace covenant will be given at its appropriate place below.)

This interpretation of the Genesis 6:18 covenant as one that had its fulfillment in the course of the Flood itself is further confirmed by the statement that introduces the account of God's bringing the ark to rest: "And God remembered Noah" (Gen.8:1). The verb "remember" (*zkr*) employed at this key point is a term which in the covenant vocabulary describes the one who is actively mindful of covenantal commitments and proceeds to carry them out (see, e.g., Gen 9:15f.; Exod 2:24; 6:5; 32:13; Lev 26:42,45; Pss 98:3; 105:8; 106:45; 111:5; cf. Luke 1:72). What was presented in Genesis 6 as divine purpose is recounted in Genesis 8 as execution of that purpose. At both places in the overall narrative there is a statement about the perishing of all flesh (6:17 and 7:21-24, respectively) which is immediately followed by the exception, the salvation of the remnant in the ark (6:18 and 8:1ff., respectively). In this literary pattern, the divine remembering of Genesis 8:1 corresponds to the divine covenanting of Genesis 6:18 as fulfillment to promise. Genesis 8:1 thus identifies the covenant of Genesis 6:18 as a soteric commitment that found its accomplishment within the history of the Flood itself.

We must now ask what precisely is the referent of the word *berith* in Genesis 6:18. Conceivably it could refer to the whole previous course of the revelation and administration of saving grace, beginning at Genesis 3:15. But the fact that it is Noah who is the specific object of covenantal remembrance in the midst of the salvation-event that fulfils this covenant (Gen 8:1) suggests that it is rather the particular promise of salvation given to Noah that is referred to by *berith* in Genesis 6:18. The promise of Noah's deliverance from the threatened destruction of mankind had been clearly implied in the disclosures made to him prior to that occurrence of *berith*. For those disclosures had acquainted him, as one who found favor in God's sight, not only with God's purpose of world judgment but with the means of escape for the remnant (Gen 6:13-17). Certainly, when the hour or crisis came, that particular promissory commitment was fulfilled in the experience of those in the ark.

The verb *hqym*, of which *berith* is the object in Genesis 6:18, is not used for the initiating or ratifying of a covenant but for the performing of previously assumed covenantal obligations or promises (see e.g., Gen 26:3; Exod 6:4; Lev 26:9; Deut 8:18; 29:13; 2 Kgs 23:3; Neh 9:8; Jer 29:10; 34:18; Ezk 16:60-62). It has to do with the enduring validity or even perpetuity of a covenant (see e.g., Gen 9:9-17; Exod 6:4,5; Ezk 16:60). Accordingly, *hqym* in Genesis 6:18 does not describe the inauguration of the *berith* but expresses the assurance given by the Lord when disclosing the covenant that he would subsequently honor and fulfill the covenantal promise of salvation. The covenant establishing or fulfilling denoted by *hqym* in Genesis 6:18 is the same as the covenant remembering spoken of in Genesis 8:1. It describes God's intention, while the later remembering is the honoring of that intention.

Now although *berith* in Genesis 6:18 does not refer to the promises of kingdom blessings as previously given in earlier disclosures of the Covenant of Grace, this covenant with Noah did provide for a fulfillment of those previous promises. What the Noahic remnant experienced in the ark was not the ultimate fulfillment, only a type thereof. But it did represent in typological sign the ultimate kingdom reality that was in view from the beginning of redemptive revelation as the eschatological goal. After the Flood, in the history of the world that now is, there was a recurrence of this pattern which finds previously covenanted kingdom blessings being provisionally fulfilled at a preliminary level, typological of the ultimate eschatological fulfillment. The relationship of the mission of Moses to the Abrahamic Covenant was similar to that of the mission of Noah to the previous administration of the redemptive covenant in the Sethite covenant community. Through his servant Moses, God brought Israel into possession of the kingdom promised to Abraham, Isaac, and Jacob – not the heavenly kingdom itself of course, but Canaan, the typological figure of that consummate kingdom. In the Lord's announcement of this objective at the commissioning of Moses (Exod 6), the same verbs of covenant establishing and remembering that figure as key terms in the flood narrative are, not surprisingly, found again. The Exodus 6 passage begins with God's self-identification (v.2) and a reference to his dealings with the patriarchs (v.3), somewhat after the manner of the opening preamble and historical prologue of an ancient treaty. Then follows the Lord's declaration that he is going to "establish" the covenant he had made with the patriarchs by fulfilling the promise of the kingdom-land (v.4). Elaborating on this, the Lord says he is now "remembering" his covenant with Abraham, Isaac, and Jacob (v.5; cf. Exod 2:24). That is, he is about to redeem the Israelites from the tyranny of the Egyptians (vv.6,7) and to vindicate their claim to the kingdom-land against the rival claims of the Canaanites (v.8).

Both the old and the present worlds thus witnessed a typological coming of the kingdom and in that sense an establishing of God's covenant with its kingdom promise. This parallel brings out the similarity of the age of the patriarchs in the line of Seth and that of the patriarchs in the Abrahamic succession. Both were times of holding the covenant promises in faith until the day of judgment and kingdom inheritance should come, as it did with the covenant-establishing missions of Noah and Moses.

In all this, divine covenants are seen functioning as instruments of kingdom administration. By his covenants the Lord orders the kingdom, defining kingdom privilege and program, stipulating obligations and promising blessings. Divine authority undergirds these covenants and divine sanctions enforce them. They are exercises of God's sovereign lordship. Expressive of this, God calls his kingdom-covenant to Noah "my covenant" (Gen 6:18). The kingdom belonged to God as the Creator-King and therefore the covenant by which that kingdom was administered – defined, regulated, bestowed, sanctioned – was God's covenant.

Bestowal of the holy kingdom realm was the purpose in view in the covenant of Genesis 6:18. It was not just an ordering of the world of common grace under the general providential rule of the Creator, in the manner of the covenant of Genesis 9. The covenant fulfilled in the ark was rather one of the series of redemptive covenants particularly concerned with a special people sanctified unto the Lord, to bear his name as his own sanctuary-community and to receive the kingdom inheritance. Once again in evidence in this climactic episode of the administration of the redemptive covenant in the world that then was is that same identification of the holy covenant community with the natural family structure that was observed throughout the earlier history of the Sethite covenant community. As later events strongly suggest, not all the members of Noah's household were the elect seed of the woman (cf. Gen 9:22,25). Only at the Consummation when the Lord God has brought the covenant community, along with the world at large, under judicial scrutiny and exposed those who are not truly his, removing them from the company of those who receive the kingdom forever, will the circles of covenant and election at last converge and coincide. The consummating of the kingdom in the ark was still only at the level of typological sign, and the circle of the covenant household in the ark was apparently larger than that of the eternal election in that generation. But meanwhile Noah's household did indeed constitute the distinctive holy community on earth and as such it did serve to make the point adequately in the typological symbolism of the flood judgment that the Final Judgment will be informed by the principle of radical spiritual discrimination.

B. Noah, Grantee of the Covenant

1. Covenantal Grant for Faithful Service

The Genesis 6:18 covenant with Noah might be identified more precisely as a covenant of grant. That is the kind of covenant that ancient rulers gave to meritorious individuals for faithful service to the crown. Such grants had the character of a royal charter or prebend. They might guarantee to the grantee his special status, or bestow on him title over cities or lands with their revenues, or grant to territory under his authority exemptions from customary obligations. In our introductory comments on the Creator's

Covenant of Works with Adam we suggested that that covenant was comparable to the proposal of a grant in which a great king offered to give favored treatment to a lesser ruler on the condition of his assuming and performing the obligations of loyal service as a covenant vassal. Although Adam was created with the status of covenant servant, he was under a probation which proposed a special eschatological grant for covenant-keeping. Noah, unlike Adam, is viewed as a covenant servant who has already demonstrated his fidelity. He therefore receives not just the proposal of a grant but the actual reward, which the Lord was in fact in the process of bestowing in making this covenantal disclosure with its directives concerning the ark, the means of salvation and kingdom realization.

In Genesis 7:1, Noah's reception of the kingdom grant is clearly attributed to the integrity of his covenantal conduct. He and his household were to enter the ark and escape the world catastrophe, "because", as the Lord declared, "I have found you to be righteous before me in this generation." This word of divine approbation repeats the assessment of Noah as "righteous" and "perfect" given in Genesis 6:9b, immediately after the generations-formula in verse 9a, which serves as the heading for this third section of the book of Genesis. Much the same sequence is found in the book of Job where Job is introduced in the opening verse as "perfect and upright" and then this evaluation is repeated in Job 1:8 as a statement spoken by the Lord. The description of Noah in Genesis 6:9b as genuinely loyal to his covenant Lord provides the explanation beforehand for the exceptional treatment to be accorded to him in the midst of the world judgment announced in the following verses (Gen 9:10ff.; cf. vv.17,18).

This same contrast between Noah and the rest of the world had already been expressed in Genesis 6:5-8, the closing verses of the preceding generations-section of Genesis. God found the evil of mankind insufferable and decreed their destruction (vv.5-7), "but Noah found grace in the eyes of the Lord" (v.8). Genesis 6:8 makes the same point as Genesis 6:9b and 7:1. Noah was spared and blessed because, as a true and faithful servant, he met with God's approval. Obviously the idea is not that Noah is to receive God's blessings even though he had shown himself to be no different than the rest of corrupt mankind whom God had determined to destroy. The regular meaning of the expression "to find grace in the eyes of somebody" is to be approved of as deserving of favorable treatment. It does not mean to be favored as an act of mercy in spite of one's ill deserts. (See, e.g., Gen 39:4; 50:4; Num 32:5; Deut 24:1; Prov 3:4; cf. Luke 2:52.)

It is, of course, the gospel truth that God's dealings with Noah found their ultimate explanation in the principle of God's sovereign grace. This covenantal grant to Noah came under the Covenant of Grace whose administration to fallen men deserving only the curse of the broken creational covenant (and Noah too was one of these fallen sons of Adam) was an act of God's pure mercy in Christ. Wherever enmity has been reestablished between man and Satan it has been due to sovereign divine initiative (Gen 3:15). There is no reconciliation with the Creator, no renewal of love for him or genuine confession of Yahweh as covenant Lord that is not in the last analysis due to God's restorative power operating in forgiving grace. What is said in Genesis 6:8 is consistent with that but that is not the point that is being made in this verse. It rather refers to a covenant grant bestowed on Noah as one whose loyal service received God's approbation. The terms used to describe Noah's loyalty and obedience in Genesis 6:8 and the following biblical narrative are the Hebrew equivalents of the standard terms applied to the loyal recipients of rewards in the extra-biblical royal grants.

2. Type of the Messianic Servant

The covenant of grant given to Noah is one of several such divine dispensations in the premessianic era of redemptive history. Wherever we encounter such a bestowal of the kingdom and its honors on the basis of the good works of the grantee, the question naturally arises as to the consistency of this with redemptive covenant's promises of grace. In all such cases the key point to observe is that the opposing principles of works and grace are operating in different spheres or at different levels from one another. For these works-arrangements all involve a situation where there is a typological representation of the messianic king and kingdom, superimposed as a second distinct level over a fundamental level that has to do with the eschatological kingdom reality itself. Now at that basic underlying level, where it is a matter of the individual's gaining entrance into the eternal heavenly kingdom, not just a symbolic prototype thereof, sovereign saving grace is ever and only the principle that governs the inheritance of kingdom blessings. It is at the other level, the level of the superimposed typological stratum, that the Lord has been pleased on occasion to make the attainment of the rewards of the kingdom dependent on man's obedient performance of his covenantal duty. Since, then, the introduction of the works principle in such covenantal arrangements affects only the typological overlay and not the underlying stratum of ultimate redemptive-eschatological reality, these works-grants assume their ancillary place harmoniously within the administrations of the Covenant of Grace. And grace thus remains at all times the constant principle of eternal salvation.

Most familiar of the instances of the introduction of a works principle in a premessianic redemptive economy is the Mosaic Covenant. According to the emphatically and repeatedly stated terms of this old covenant of the law, the Lord made Israel's continuing manifestation of cultic fidelity to him the ground of their continuing tenure in Canaan. This was not then one of the covenants of grant; it was not a matter of Israel's being given the kingdom originally in recognition of past meritorious conduct. But this case of the old covenant is relevant in the present context as another notable example of the pattern which finds the principles of works and grace operating simultaneously, yet without conflict, because the works principle is confined to a separate typological level. Paul, perceiving the works principle in the Mosaic law economy, was able to insist that this did not entail an abrogation of the promises of grace given to Abraham, Isaac, and Jacob centuries earlier (Gal 3:17), precisely because the works principle applied only to the typological kingdom in Canaan and not to the inheritance of the eternal kingdom-city promised to Abraham as a gift of grace and at last to be received by Abraham and all his seed, Jew and Gentile, through faith in Christ Jesus. The pedagogical purpose of the Mosaic works arrangement was to present typologically the message that felicity and godliness will be inseparably conjoined in the heavenly kingdom, or, negatively, that the disobedient are forever cut off from the kingdom of the eschaton.

In the case of the covenants of grant, the message to be conveyed through the introduction of the works principle did not so much concern the nature of the messianic kingdom, but rather the role of the messianic king. The biblical data indicate that the Lord was pleased to take the exemplary obedience of certain of his servants and to constitute that a typological sign of how the obedience of the coming messianic Servant of the Lord would secure the kingdom and its royal-priestly blessings for himself and for his people. Abraham and David were recipients of such covenants of grant as rewards for faithfulness. Phinehas was another (cf. Num 25:11-13). Each of these individuals had personal hope of heaven only through God's grace in Jesus Christ, only as a gift received by faith alone. But the conspicuous faithfulness of their lives in general or of certain specific acts of outstanding service they performed was invested by the Lord with typological significance so that they, with reference to a typological manifestation of the kingdom, pointed to Christ as one who also was under a covenant of works and received the grant of the kingdom for the obedient fulfillment of his covenantal mission.

Common to all the displays of obedience that were rewarded with grants of the kingdom in a typological form may be discerned the motif of victory in the holy war against Satan and his earthly forces and followers. Actual military combat is at times involved. The promise of great reward to Abraham in Genesis 15:1 comes on the background of his warrior role in the conflict against the forces of the kings from the east (Gen 14). And the dynastic grant promised in the Davidic Covenant (2 Sam.7) follows David's victorious campaigns against the enemies of God's people and his capture of Zion as the site for God's sanctuary (2 Sam 5 and 6; cf. 7:1). It is as if these servants of the Lord had been confronted, like Adam, with a probation-mission, challenging them as guardians of God's sanctuary to enter into judgment against the Adversary. By their valiant exploits in faithful performance of their mission they typified beforehand the obedient second Adam's salvation-victory in his judicial combat with Satan and his hosts.

These other covenants of grant will be discussed further below, particularly the case of Abraham and his double role, serving as the great example of justification by faith, and yet, with respect to the typological phase of the kingdom, viewed as the recipient of a divine grant based on his obedience, a grant which God honored in bestowing the typological kingdom on the Israelites. Hence, though Israel's original reception of the typological kingdom under the Mosaic Covenant was not a grant bestowed on the ground of the Israelites' past performance, it may be construed as the carrying out of the Lord's grant to Abraham for his accomplishments of faith.

It is this same covenant of grant pattern that is found in the history of the world before the Flood in the mission of Noah. The notable service in view in the special typological kingdom grant made to him would presumably be his courageous prophetic stand for the name of God in the face of the apostasy and the blasphemy of the world rulers of his age. Noah's subsequent obedience to God's directive to construct the kingdom-house of God in the form of the ark would have been a supplementary extension of the faithfulness that was the ground for his reception of the kingdom grant. As in the other cases we have discussed, we must keep in mind the typological level of the kingdom that was secured by Noah's righteousness if we are to perceive the consistency of this works-grant with the grace principle that was operating at the permanent, fundamental stratum of the Covenant of Grace. The flood judgment was but a type of the messianic judgment and the kingdom in the ark that was granted to Noah as the reward for his good works was only typological of the messianic kingdom. Therefore, this covenant of grant to Noah was not in conflict with or an abrogation of the grace of the redemptive covenant that had been revealed to the Sethite community of faith and, of course, continued to be operative in the sphere of eternal realities in the days of Noah and his covenant of grant. Far from conflicting with the gospel of grace, the administration of the grant to Noah subserved the revelation of the gospel. For Noah functioned in that typological situation as a prefiguration of the Messiah, whose obedience, rewarded with exaltation and kingdom glory, provides the ground for God's grace-gift of redemption to his people. The covenant of grant to Noah, type of Christ, reminds us that the works principle is foundational in the program of redemptive grace in that the many are made righteous only by the obedience of the One, the One who by virtue of his perfect righteousness found favor in the Father's eyes.

3. Surety, Mediator, Savior

As the righteous servant whose obedience God reckoned as the ground of his household's deliverance and blessing, Noah was a type of Christ as the surety for the salvation of his church-family. There is always a difference between the type and the antitype but nowhere is the disparity more apparent than when the element of righteousness is involved. Certainly the absolutely rigorous standard used in judging the righteousness of Christ was not applied in the suretyship of Noah. The approach in the case of Noah was much the same as in God's judging of Israel's covenantal obedience as the ground of their kingdom tenure under the old covenant. As we have observed, the typological objective in the case of the Israelite kingdom was to teach that righteousness and prosperity will be conjoined in the consummated kingdom. For the purpose of keeping that symbolic message readable, persistent wholesale apostasy could not be allowed to accompany possession of the promised inheritance. But, on the other hand, the pedagogical point of the typological arrangement could be satisfactorily made, in a positive fashion, in spite of the inevitable imperfections of the people individually and as a nation. In meting out the blessings and curses of the Mosaic Covenant, the Lord applied the standard of symbolical appropriateness or typological legibility. With such adequacy Noah's exemplary righteousness pointed to the perfect righteousness of the messianic king himself. While the disparity between type and antitype might seem even more acute here than in the case of Israel as sign of the messianic kingdom corporately, the typological principles and symbolic standards are essentially the same in the two cases.

Besides the difference in the standard of righteousness applied in the suretyship of Noah and Christ, the Noahic typological analogue had certain other limitations. Christ is a federal representative whose righteousness is imputed to those he represents. Elsewhere in history that kind of representation and imputation were involved only in the case of the first Adam. Also, central in Christ's achievement of righteousness for his people is his sacrificial obedience in giving himself an offering for their sins, once for all, the sure ground of an unfailing intercession which avails for salvation unto the uttermost for those who come unto God by him. Such is the distinctly priestly setting of Christ's identification as "surety of a better covenant" in Hebrews 7:22 (cf.9:15). But whatever the limitations of the portrayal, inasmuch as God designated Noah's righteousness the ground of the covenant of grant, the guarantee of the bestowal of the kingdom in the ark, Noah did indeed provide a type of Christ as the surety who guaranteed the accomplishment of the promises of the new covenant.

Noah also affords a typological likeness of Jesus as prophet-mediator of the new covenant. For he came as messenger of the heavenly council to the remnant community with the revelation of the divine grant and so inaugurated this special covenant of kingdom fulfillment.

In the mission of Noah we also see prefigured the work of Christ as the savior-king, the One who delivers from the judgment wrath and rescues from the Satanic powers, the royal victor who raises up the sanctuary-house of God. At the exodus, the building of the tabernacle-sanctuary was for Moses a separate enterprise after the victorious conflict with the dragon of Egypt in the sea of judgment. Similarly, the construction of the Davidic-Solomonic temple followed as a separate sequel to David's victories over the encompassing enemies of Israel. But in the mission of Noah, who "prepared an ark to the saving of his house" (Heb 11:7; cf. Gen 6:22), these two things came together. In preparing the ark as the means of salvation from the divine judgment and of liberation from the oppression of the serpent's seed, Noah was also constructing a symbolic cosmic house of

God, a typological figure of the consummated kingdom, the goal of the covenant.

PART II

THE KINGDOM IN THE WORLD THAT NOW IS

Part I was divided into Sections A and B in order to underscore the radical change involved in the transition from the preredemptive to the redemptive era that occurred within the history of the world that then was. Such a distinction does not arise in the history of the kingdom in the world that now is, the period dealt with in Part II. This period from the outset falls within the redemptive era. The main distinction to be made within it is that between the covenant of common grace and the covenant(s) of redemptive grace, a distinction which also appeared in the organization of Section B of Part I. The postdiluvian common grace covenant will be the subject of Chapter One of Part II. In Chapter Two we shall examine the continuance of the Covenant of Grace in the new world from Noah to Abraham, observing the prophetic presence of the people of God in the midst of the city of man bent on its rebellious course to judgment at Babel. The final two chapters will be devoted to the Abrahamic Covenant.

Our analysis of the ten-sectioned structure of the book of Genesis suggested an arrangement into two sets of three followed by two pairs. The two triads that comprise the first six generations-divisions of Genesis correspond to each other in their inner structure. Both survey the general history of the city of man in their first section, then trace the elect line in the second section. And each triad in its climactic third section records an epochal divine covenant with man.

We have already dealt with the third section of the first triad (which begins at Gen 6:9), or at least with its account of the covenant of salvation fulfilled by the Lord God through the course of the Deluge. That covenantal event was the culmination of the history of the world that then was and brought that world age to an end. Since, however, that event was not simply an act of climactic, world-terminating judgment but was at the same time an act of re-creation, this third generations-section of Genesis, while the climax of the first triad, also serves as an introduction to the history of the world that now is. Besides narrating the creational beginnings of the present world found in the deluge-event, this third generations-section also contains the record of another covenant and of a programmatic oracle (see Gen 9) which provide foundational context and prophetic perspective for the subsequent history recorded in the remainder of Genesis and indeed in all the rest of the Bible. Here in Part II of our analysis of Genesis we will therefore be returning to that third division of the first triad in order to present the background it affords for the history of the kingdom in the world that now is.

The fourth generations-division of Genesis (10:1-11:9), like division one, sketches within a genealogical framework the developing world of mankind, following on a divine promulgation of the common grace order (Gen 9). Division five (Gen 11:10-26), like division two, traces in genealogical format the continuing line of the covenant community, now the line of Shem. And division six (Gen 11:27ff.), like division three, tells of a covenantal grant of the kingdom of God after a culminating episode of human defiance in the city of man (Gen 11:1-9; cf. 6:1-4). The two pairs that comprise the last four divisions are similar to each other (and to the first two divisions of each of the triads) in that each devotes one section to the rejected line (Ishmael and Esau) and a second section to the elect succession (Isaac and Jacob). These four sections are an extension of the sixth, for (especially in sections eight and ten) they relate the confirmation of the Abrahamic Covenant to the other two patriarchs, Isaac and Jacob. Psalm 105:9,10 (cf. 2 Kgs 13:23) reflects this view of Genesis 12-50 as a unified period – the period of the covenant God made with Abraham, even his oath to Isaac, which he confirmed to Jacob for a law, to Israel for an everlasting covenant. It thus appears that the Abrahamic Covenant stands at the midpoint in Genesis, the last five generations-sections being devoted to it, and the first five to the pre-Abrahamic history.

Chapter One

COVENANTAL RESUMPTION OF COMMON GRACE

What transpired in the Flood was a sign of the consummation of the kingdom and the finalé of redemptive history. Yet it was only a sign. Though the deluge judgment terminated the world that then was, it did not inaugurate the world to come. It rather introduced the world that now is, another phase in the interim world-order of genealogical history. Hence, the ark-kingdom not only played its role as an eschatological sign, but served the historical purpose of bridging the watery chasm between the former and present worlds. The redeemed remnant in the ark symbolized glorified mankind brought through the final cataclysm as the heirs of the eternal kingdom, but they were also the living continuation of the human race in general (as well as the covenant community in particular), carried through the Deluge into postdiluvian history. While the Flood as a sign of redemptive judgment prophesied the end of common grace, the Flood as an inner-historical episode marked a transition through which the world-order of creation in the common grace mode was re-creatively perpetuated beyond the world that then was into the world that now is.

This fundamental continuity of the postdiluvian order with what had gone before is manifested in the way religious-political developments after the Flood repeat the pattern of prediluvian history. The same division of mankind into the two rival companies delineated in Genesis 3:15 occurs again, with apostate forces turning the city of man in a direction offensive to the Creator. This repetition in the historical pattern is reflected in the repeating literary pattern of the book of Genesis, the arrangement of the second triad of generations-divisions matching that of the first triad.

Our topic in this chapter is the covenantal reestablishment of the common grace order after the Flood (a transaction that is narrated along with the Flood itself in generations-division three).

I. COVENANT CONFIRMATION

Most of the third generations-division of Genesis (6:9-9:28) is taken up with the flood narrative (6:13-8:22). The remainder is devoted to a record of the renewal of common grace arrangements and to an oracular overview of the future course of redemptive history. It was noted above that Genesis 8:20-22, the final section of the flood narrative, does double duty, serving also as the first section of the account of the postdiluvian covenant of common grace. The latter extends from Genesis 8:20 through 9:17 and is arranged in an A-B-A pattern. The introductory (8:20-22) and concluding (9:8-17) A-sections, which deal with the stabilized order of nature, bracket the central B-section (9:1-7), which presents regulations concerning the cultural domain of the nations of mankind.

In the concluding A-section (9:8-17) the revelatory transaction at the Noahic altar is formulated in specifically covenantal terms. It is identified as God's *berith*, which he will remember and maintain, and it is sealed with a covenantal sign. Since the opening A-section (8:20-22) contains the same guarantee of a stabilized order of nature that is formulated covenantally in 9:8-17, its contents too come under that same covenantal identification. So too, we are bound to conclude, does the B-section, embraced as it is within the covenantal framework of the A-sections. The fact that the cultural program of mankind dealt with in Genesis 9:1-7 is already implicit in the reference to seedtime and harvest in the previous A-section (8:22) is a further indication of the integration of the central B-section with the adjoining covenantal framework.

As we shall be observing in more detail below, this covenant is not an administration of redemptive grace but of common grace. It did not bestow the holy kingdom of God on an elect, redeemed people. The revelation of this covenant came to Noah and his family and the covenant is said to be made with them, but they are addressed here, as were Adam and Eve in the disclosure of common grace and curse in Genesis 3:16-19, not in distinction from but as representative of the generality of mankind. In fact, the second party in this covenant includes beyond mankind in general the other living creatures of the earth, dependent all for survival on the promised stability of nature (cf. vv.10,12,15-17). Indeed, this covenant is even described as one made between God and "the earth" (v.13). It is concerned immediately and directly with the continuance of the common interim order of mankind and his culture. Its sign, the rainbow, is not, like circumcision or baptism, a rite performed by and upon a peculiar people set aside from the rest of mankind as a seal of their distinctive status as covenant members. It is instead something effected by God in the natural world, visible to all, consecrating none. It does not produce the holy kingdom realm that is in view in the program of redemption. It rather defines a provisional world order under God's general kingly governance.

This postdiluvian covenant of common grace was substantially a resumption of the prediluvian interim order. Conceivably then the point being made when God says he will confirm or maintain (*hqym*) his covenant (Gen 9:9,11,17) is that the prediluvian common grace arrangement was covenantal (even though not specifically so designated hitherto) and the present covenantal transaction was a confirmatory continuation of that previous covenant. (Cf. the discussion of Gen 6:18 above.) That was in any case the truth of the matter. But more likely what is referred to by *berith* in Genesis 9:9,11,17 is the promised world order as just described in Genesis 8:20-9:7. For the covenantal formula (*hqym berith*) is introduced there in immediate connection with the assurance of the unbroken extension of the promised regularity of nature (with the associated cultural order) through all subsequent generations. More particularly, this formula is conjoined with the giving of the rainbow sign, that distinctive new feature of the just-beginning postdiluvian phase of the common grace order, the pledge of the uninterrupted continuance of this new phase until the Consummation. According to Genesis 8:21,22, God first formed "in his heart" the covenantal purpose to establish this postdiluvian order with its guarantee against another flood-scale catastrophe prior to the Final Judgment. Then, having made this covenantal heart-commitment, he revealed it to man with the assurance that he was now and henceforth determined faithfully to maintain this covenanted world-order (Gen 9:9,11,17).

Based, as it was, on commitments divinely sanctioned and sealed with heavenly sign, this postdiluvian arrangement exhibited the essential features necessary to qualify for the designation *berith*. In this case, the commitments were unilaterally divine. Regulations governing mankind's conduct were included, but no commitments were exacted from man on which the continuance of the covenant itself or individual membership therein might be dependent. Indeed, God determined to establish this covenantal order in spite of the inveterate evil of mankind (Gen 8:21). Though not immediately directed to the establishment of God's kingdom-realm on earth but rather to the ordering of the world of common grace, it was, like all the divine covenants of Scripture, a sovereign administration of God's heavenly reign.

II. THE ORDER OF NATURE

The parallel A-sections have as their matching theme God's providential ordering of nature in the world that now is. They present the divine commitment to prevent another return to virtually the chaos of the unstructured earth of Genesis 1:2, such as occurred in the Flood, or positively stated, as in Genesis 8:22, to preserve the ecological system in its fundamental structures and cycles – day and night, summer and winter, seedtime and harvest – until the appointed end of this world. It is this divine commitment that is constitutive of the covenant. In Genesis 9:11 and 15 the *berith* is directly identified with God's promise that the waters shall not again become a flood to destroy all flesh. This commitment to the permanent maintenance of the earth as a stabilized life-support system is the covenant in its essential character as a divinely sanctioned commitment. It is with this definitive commitment that the disclosure of the covenant begins and concludes, the covenantal regulations for man's observance being placed within this identifying framework.

Highlighting the equation of the *berith* with the commitment concerning the order of nature is the stated design of the special sign of the covenant, which is to bring this commitment into remembrance. Appropriately, the appointed sign, the pledge of divine faithfulness, is a natural phenomenon (9:12-17). In the biblical record of the covenant this sign is introduced in the center of the concluding A-section (9:12,13), flanked by two chiastically matching pairs. Each member of the outside pair (vv.8-10 and v.17) contains a formula of divine speech and a statement about God's confirming his covenant with all flesh on earth. The members of the inside pair (v.11 and vv.14-16) contain the constitutive covenant promise. In the second members of these two pairs, after the introduction of the covenant sign in the center verses, the topic peculiar to each one is related to that sign.

Probably, the rainbow sign appeared to Noah at the time of the revelation of the covenant, as a kind of ratification event. Its subsequent sporadic appearances were to be the occasions of continual covenantal remembrance on God's part. This arching color-spectrum in the heavens is designated by the word for the archer's bow. The war-bow is mentioned in God's arsenal of wrath, particularly when he is viewed as advancing in the judgment-storm, dispatching his arrows of lightning (cf., e.g., Deut 32:42; Pss 7:12[13]; 18:14[15]; 64:7[8]; 77:17[18]; 144:6; Hab 3:11; Zech 9:14).

However, in the sign of the rainbow the bow is not raised vertically and drawn taut in the face of the foe but is suspended in the relaxed horizontal position. There are Near Eastern representations of kings, first seen engaged in battle, then returning in peace, with the state-god of the storm depicted above in stance identical to the king's in each case. In the battle scene king and god hold bows fitted with arrows and full drawn, while in the peace scene their bows hang at their side, loosened. Accordingly, the designation of the rainbow as a battle-bow may best be interpreted as suggesting the picture of the divine warrior with his weapons laid aside, turning from the path of judgment against rebellious mankind, prepared now to govern them with forbearance for a season.

Provision of the measure of natural order necessary for the continuing historical existence of man and his cultural development was a gracious gift to be fully appreciated. But the limitations of the promise of this common grace covenant must be recognized too. Under the terms of this covenant man was not to enjoy conditions of nature at the more idyllic original level of Eden's paradise depicted in Genesis 2:8-14, certainly not consistently so, always and everywhere. Man would in fact continue to experience the common curse laid on nature after the Fall, whereby one by one in their ongoing generations men succumb in their battle with the earth and return to the dust. And if the blessings of the natural creation provided in the postdiluvian covenant did not constitute a restoration of the world of Eden, still less can they be identified with the consummated order of nature prophetically portrayed as the goal of the Covenant of Grace.

Like the natural blessings guaranteed in Genesis 8:20ff., the promised natural felicity to be enjoyed by the redeemed in the new heavens and earth is at times set forth in specifically covenantal formulations (cf., e.g., Isa 11:6-9; 65:17-25; Ezk 34:25-27; Hos 2:18[20]). But comparison of these redemptive covenants made with nature and the Genesis 8:20ff. covenant brings out the striking differences between them. The pictures of the world to come achieved through redemption contain dimensions of natural beatitude that go far beyond the mere continuity of a stable order of nature. The covenant of Genesis 8:20ff. does not promise the restoration-consummation of the paradise order envisaged as the goal of redemption. It does not produce the everlasting perfection of the blessings of nature but merely provides for a partial and temporary limitation on the infliction of the curses of nature. The sign of the Sabbath, prophetic symbol of consummated cosmic blessing, is conspicuously absent from it. It does not culminate in the new heaven and earth; on the contrary it is terminated by the final cosmic cataclysm, which it only for a while postpones.

From this radical difference in their prospects concerning the order of nature it is obvious that the covenant of Genesis 8:20ff. is not to be identified with the Covenant of Grace (specifically, as administered in the Gen 6:18 covenant). Identification of the two has been mistakenly argued on the ground that the postdiluvian covenant, like the redemptive covenant, has a creational aspect: it concerns the realm of nature and wildlife and has ordinances appertaining thereto. But such a vague, oversimplified appeal to a shared world-of-nature aspect will not do. It blurs vital distinctions and ignores pronounced differences. The fact is that the specific character of the nature provision of the covenant of Genesis 8:20ff., a provision merely for the postponement of the final creational curse not for the consummation of the blessings of nature, contradicts any identification of this covenant with the covenant of Genesis 6:18 or with redemptive covenant in general and demands that it rather be distinguished from all such administrations of saving grace and separately classified as a covenant of common grace. To do otherwise is to introduce hopeless confusion into one's biblical-theological analysis and the resultant world-and-life view.

We have just been observing that the natural order of the common grace covenant of Genesis 8:20ff., measured against the eternal world of the re-creation which is in view in the redemptive hope, is a temporary, interim arrangement. It continues only "while the earth remains" (Gen 8:22). But it is also important to do full justice to the permanence of this covenantal order within the stipulated parameters. Indeed we find later on that when the Lord wishes to illustrate the unfailing perpetuity of certain redemptive provisions, the best temporal analogy available is this relative permanence of the ordinances of nature in the postdiluvian covenant of common grace (Isa 54:9,10; Jer 33:20-26; cf. 31:35-37). The continuance of this covenantal arrangement right up to the Consummation is an integral feature of the rainbow-sealed promise which is the constitutive commitment of the covenant. Hence the covenant itself is an "everlasting covenant" (9:16); it will be maintained "for perpetual generations" (9:12). This permanence of the covenant as long as the earth remains, so emphatically expressed in both the A-sections of the covenant record, necessarily characterizes the regulations for human conduct set within that framework. They are part of that covenantal order coextensive with the world that now is, and as such they too remain in force until the final judgment on this world and the arrival of the world to come. Therefore, when considering the application of these cultural directives in our age, we may not suppose that they became obsolete with the dawning of the new covenant stage in the history of redemption. Our basic assumption must be that they are still normative, and if in any particular we conclude that the analogy of Scripture indicates otherwise, we must be prepared to accept the burden of proof in demonstrating that.

In brief then, God gave guarantee by solemn covenant, confirmed by rainbow-sign, that earth history would not suffer another interruption on the epochal scale of the disruption that terminated the old world. Until the time of the Consummation the devastating impact of the common curse would be so tempered by the common grace of God that the new postdiluvian world was assured of relative stability in the order of nature and its regular cycle of life-supporting processes.

Here again we see the correlation of creation and covenant. The original creation fiats were at the same time covenant fiats. Simultaneous with the creation-word of existence ("let there be") was the correlative covenant-word of name-meaning ("and he called"). So too the diluvian creation was covenantal. As an eschatological sign of the ultimate re-creation, the beginning of the eternal world, it belonged with the redemptive covenant of Genesis 6:18. But as the actual historical reestablishment of the interim order of this world it was covenantally formulated in the common grace covenant of Genesis 8:20ff. This latter correlation is reflected in the way the apostle Peter weaves the two together in 2 Peter 3:5ff. Expounding the concept of the Deluge as re-creation, he echoes the postdiluvian covenant in his interpretation of the world produced out of the flood waters as one which was to be preserved in God's forbearance, yet reserved for final judgment (2 Pet 3:7-13).

III. THE CULTURAL PROGRAM

A. General Regulations

The central B-section of the covenant record (Gen 9:1-7) contains stipulations that regulate mankind's cultural functions and institutions. They resume the terms of the common grace world order prescribed in prediluvian times, as recorded in Genesis 3:16-19 and 4:15. This fact demonstrates conclusively that the covenant of Genesis 8:20ff. is one of common grace, and not to be confusingly identified with the series of redemptive covenants whose distinctive grant of the holy salvation-kingdom to an elect people of God it quite lacks.

Matters more implicitly or negatively expressed earlier (cf. especially Gen 3:16-19) are formulated more explicitly and positively in Genesis 9. Indeed, the disclosure of these cultural prescriptions is introduced as an act of divine blessing: "God blessed Noah and his sons and said to them" (Gen 9:1). This recalls the original promulgation of the cultural commission to Adam and Eve: "God blessed them and God said unto them" (Gen 1:28a). The parallel extends to the contents of the blessing included in the two passages: creative fruitfulness in the propagation of the race, dominion over the earth and its creatures, and provision of sustenance (cf. Gen 1:28b-30). The Genesis 8:20ff. covenant thus occupies a position at the beginning of the new world beyond the Flood comparable to that of the original revelation of the cultural mandate in Genesis 1 at the beginning of the old world. Yet it is not a simple reinstituting of the creation ordinances but a revision of them in the common grace mode. An outstanding example of this modification is the provision for the institution of the state, absent from Genesis 1 but prescribed in Genesis 9, in resumption of the common grace arrangement of Genesis 4:15. The postdiluvian covenant thus corresponds to the Genesis 3 and 4 disclosures of the common grace order in the old world after the Fall. Evidenced by this double role performed by the covenant of Genesis 8:20ff. in the postdiluvian situation is the fact that there is both continuity and discontinuity between the creational kingdom program and the common grace cultural order.

Within the central B-section (Gen 9:1-7), as in the over-all record of this covenant, arrangement of the material is concentric. The passage begins (v.1) and closes (v.7) with the family function of multiplying and filling the earth, while the middle verses (vv.2-6) are concerned with the governing function to be exercised by mankind by virtue of their dominion over the subhuman creation (vv.2-4) and the special judicial authority vested in the state (vv.5,6).

This arrangement reflects the foundational status of the family, for the family in its assignment to fill the earth with mankind is placed first and last as the framework within which the state then finds its place as an ancillary institution. We are thus reminded that the primary cultural purpose in all human history is the reproduction of man himself and thereby of the image of God.

Man's dominion over the animal realm is described here (v.2) as a covenant of human lordship decreed by God. The noun *mora`* in the phrase "the fear of you" is used at times with respect to God himself (Isa 8:12,13; Mal 1:6). Obedient reverence is due to him as a concomitant of his establishing his covenant lordship (Mal 2:5). Similarly in Deuteronomy 11:24,25, God's imposing the fear (*mora'*) of Israel on the promised land is equivalent to their sovereign possession of it. The noun *chath* in the phrase "the dread of you" is used particularly for a divinely instilled kind of fear (Gen 35:5). One such instance possibly alludes to Genesis 9:2. In Job 41:33(25) the leviathan is said to be a creature whom the Creator made "without dread" in the face of all man's weapons and devices (cf. Job 41:1ff.). An exception to the general rule (cf. Jas 3:7), leviathan exhibits no inclination to submit to man as a covenant vassal (Job 41:4). In the light of this usage we conclude that Genesis 9:2 declares man to be endowed with the God-like dignity of covenantal lordship over the creatures of the earth.

No interval of time separates the divine re-authorization of the state (Gen 9:5,6) from the reestablishment of the rest of the common grace cultural order, such as we find in the prediluvian revelation of these matters (cf. Gen 3:16-19 and 4:15). For the state had meanwhile become a fixed feature of the common order and is accordingly included from the outset in the prescriptions for the postdiluvian resumption of that order. It had been demonstrated in the world that then was how hideously mankind could pervert the authority of the state and its power of the sword. Nevertheless, the urgent need, voiced by Cain, that called forth this common grace institution not long after the Fall (Gen 4:15) still existed after the judgment of the Flood. And though the state would inevitably turn bestial again and eventually produce the blasphemous, persecuting "little horn" power, God established it anew by formal covenantal stipulation in the postdiluvian world.

The original Genesis 4:15 formulation of the appointment of the state, even as to grammatical construction, is drawn upon in its renewal in Genesis 9:5,6. Conspicuous again is the problem of murder, and again murder is regarded as a Cain-like act of fratricide: "at the hand of every man's brother will I require the life of man" (v.5). After verse 5 declares the liability to judgment, verse 6 authorizes the human community to punish the crime with the sword, taking life for life. Highlighting the talion principle of commensurate punishment is the chiastic arrangement of verse 6: "(A) Whoever sheds (B) the blood (C) of man, (C´) by man (B´) his blood (A´) shall be shed." By their structural pairing the B-members convey the requirement of blood for blood retaliation. That it is the human community in the form of a duly constituted politico-judicial body that is in view in the provision of Genesis 9:6 is clarified by the total canonical elaboration and application of the matter (cf., e.g., Rom 13:1ff.; 1 Pet 2:13,14).

The authorization in Genesis 9:6a for this ultimate prerogative of man's common grace endowment with dominion is accompanied by the statement that he is the image of God, the likeness and vicegerent of him who exercises absolute dominion over all (v.6b). In Genesis 1:27-30 man's identity as image of God is stated first (v.27a) and then the significance of that is expounded in terms of man's investment with the God-like glory of dominion (vv.28-30). In Genesis 9:2-6 the dominion is set forth first (vv.2-6a) and then man's image-of-God status is cited at the close as the explanation of his magisterial appointment (v.6b). Actually, man is also characterized as God-like at the beginning of Genesis 9:2-6 when, as we have noted, the phrase "the fear of you" is used of him (v. 2). The underlying theme of this middle portion of the covenant as a whole might then be summed up as the outworking of man's image-of-God status in his cultural life within the modified conditions of common grace, or somewhat more concretely, in his civic role within the city of man.

B. Special Regulations For God's People

For the people of God there were some special questions as to the adaptation of certain of their practices to the projected common grace order. Though not of immediate relevance to all who were involved in the common order, it was appropriate that these matters should nevertheless be addressed within the stipulated terms of this covenant. For after all, God's people too are part of that common order. Moreover, this disclosure of the covenant of common grace was being made directly to them and therefore would hardly ignore issues of peculiar concern to them.

These special questions related to food, particularly to the eating of animal flesh, questions which arose because of the symbolic import that attached to animals in the use made of them within the cultus established by redemptive covenant. Coverage of these matters (Gen 9:3,4) comes at the structural center of the telescoped series of concentric patterns in Genesis 8:20-9:17. The subject of man's dominion over animals (9:2) leads to the topic of animals serving as food (9:3), and that to the prohibition of eating the life-blood (9:4), which leads to the matter of shedding man's lifeblood and the judicial response to murder (9:5,6). In this sequence the dietary issues (9:3,4) are transitional, linking the treatment of the two areas of man's dominion, general (9:2) and institutional (9:5,6).

Not only are the restrictive dietary regulations dealt with in Genesis 9:3,4 directly relevant only to the redemptive community, but they are not applicable even to God's people at all times. In fact, Genesis 9:3 removes a previous restriction, one which was later reimposed in the Mosaic era and then once more removed in the New Testament period. On analysis, this restriction is found to have had application only within theocratic phases of the organization of the redemptive community. The prohibition of Genesis 9:4 was a more continuous but not permanent regulation, being limited to the continuance of a legitimate earthly altar.

1. Discontinuance of Clean/Unclean Distinction
In Genesis 9:3 permission is given to eat all kinds of meat: "All the moving things that live shall be food for you; as in the case of the plants I give you all (the living creatures)." Verse 3b might be translated: "even as the green plants I gave you everything." This would then be a reference to an original appointment in Eden. As argued above, the eating of animal flesh was indeed permitted from the beginning. That, however, does not seem to be the point being made in Genesis 9:3b. It rather takes account of a limitation that had subsequently been imposed on the permissible varieties of animal flesh but was now being eliminated again in the postdiluvian common grace order. Such a limitation had occurred in the theocratic organization of the covenant community in the ark during the Flood. We come upon a distinction there between clean and unclean animals in the Lord's instructions to Noah about the ark. When this clean/unclean distinction appears as a feature of the Israelite theocracy, it serves to call attention symbolically to the distinction between the Israelites, whose sanctification was externalized in their outward separation to God in his sanctuary-kingdom, and the nations outside that holy theocratic realm. A similar separation of God's covenant people was effected in the ark-theocracy and it was similarly signalized at that time too in the symbolism of the distinction between clean and unclean animals. Moreover, since,

when we find this distinction in the Israelite theocracy, it is applied to the dietary area, it should also be understood as having dietary relevance in the Noahic theocracy. This will then help to explain the purpose of the additional clean animals brought into the ark beyond the basic pair for the postdiluvian replenishing of the earth (Gen 7:2,3; 8:17). We know that they were intended in part to provide for the burnt-offerings sacrificed by Noah at the conclusion of the deliverance (Gen 9:20). But they were also to serve as food. As is thus clearly assumed, the eating of animal flesh had been proper all along, but the holy community in the ark-kingdom was restricted in its selection of meat to clean animals. When, however, the flood had passed and the temporary theocratic ark organization was disbanded, the rationale for the clean/unclean animal symbolism disappeared and therewith the dietary regulations based upon it. This was recognized and registered in the postdiluvian covenant when things were being returned to the common grace order that obtained prior to the temporary period of the theocracy in the ark. God said (paraphrasing Gen 9:3): "I give you permission to eat all kinds of meat again, without clean/unclean distinctions, just as it has always been permissible to eat all kinds of green plants without distinction."

We find precisely this same change in dietary regulations being made at that later juncture in redemptive history which found God's people once more in transition from a theocratic to a common culture, that is, when the Israelite theocracy was being terminated at the founding of the church of the new covenant. Acts 10 narrates that Peter was informed through a vision that the regulatory distinction between clean and unclean meats was abrogated and that he proceeded to apply this heavenly disclosure to the broader cultural distinction according to which theocratic citizens were distinguished from the people of other nations as clean from unclean (Acts 10:28). The theocracy was about to pass away and the people of God, as to their cultural life, were to become part of the common generality of mankind. The opening of the way to table fellowship with the Gentiles was an index of the common character of the society to which the saints would henceforth belong in this world, joining with unbelievers in common political, economic, and other cultural endeavors and institutions of all sorts.

Such a fundamental shift in the divine structuring of the cultural order as is evidenced in Acts 10 must clearly have an extensive bearing on the Christian's assessment of his obligation to cultural regulations in the Mosaic legislation. This is obviously so with respect to Mosaic prescriptions in which the clean/unclean distinction figured and especially those in which the classification of nontheocratic culture and persons as unclean was a factor. By dealing with the illustrative instance of unclean meats and the related issue of table fellowship, Acts 10 establishes a broad hermeneutical principle that must be constantly reckoned with in the study of Christian ethics.

2. Continuance of Restriction on Blood

Although the termination of the temporary ark-theocracy phase of the culture of the godly abrogated the clean/unclean meat distinction (Gen 9:3), it did not annul the prohibition against the eating of flesh with the blood thereof: "Flesh with its blood, its life, you shall not eat" (Gen 9:4). The rationale behind this prohibition lies in the presence of the earthly altar of the Lord, and the end of the theocratic kingdom in the ark was not the end of the earthly altar phase of redemptive history. The altar arose at the beginning of that history in the covenant community of Seth and it was to continue until Christ performed his priestly service at the antitypical, heavenly altar. (As to the precise terminus ad quem, see further below.)

Here again a symbolic feature in the redemptive cultus accounts for a special stipulation in the cultural sphere. It was the significance of blood in the altar ritual that mandated the prohibition against the ingestion of blood. Some have suggested that the sacredness of all life accounts for the Genesis 9:4 prohibition. But the notion that all life is "sacred" is not a biblical conception and indeed savors rather of some sort of animistic mysticism, whether crude or more sophisticated.

The meaning of the lifeblood in verse 4, like the significance of the clean/unclean distinction in verse 3, must be understood in the light of the more ample data provided when this matter later appears in the Mosaic legislation. From the Levitical ordinances we learn that the life-value of the animal's blood derives from its symbolic role in altar sacrifice (especially, Lev 17:10-14). In that symbolic context the blood of the sacrificed animal is appointed as a ransom-equivalent for human life, human life that is forfeit through sin to the just wrath of God (Lev 17:11). Within the sphere of influence of the altar a distinction arose in the use of animal lifeblood like that which obtains in the taking of human life. To take a man's life for one's own satisfaction is murder; but to take a man's life in the divinely ordained administration of justice is to act as a minister of God. Similarly, to use the lifeblood of animals as a symbolic satisfaction of God's justice on the altar was to give the life to God to whom it was forfeit, according to his cultic appointment, whereas to devote that blood to oneself, as by eating it, or to devote it to an idol was to be guilty of a murderous shedding of lifeblood, an offense to be punished by being cut off from God's people (Lev 17:4). It is this symbolic equivalency of animal blood and human life that explains the conjunction of the ordinances in Genesis 9 against the ingestion of animal blood (v.4) and the shedding of man's blood, with the appended means of satisfying justice in case of violations (vv.5,6). Or, to put it the other way, the conjunction of these ordinances in Genesis 9:4-6 corroborates the rationale given above for the prohibition against animal blood.

It may be parenthetically noted that the prohibition, though finding its explanation in the symbolic significance of the blood of animals sacrificed on the altar, was also extended to nonsacrificial animals eaten by the altar-community (Lev 17:13; cf. Deut 12:16,23; 15:22,23). By performing the required procedure for disposing of the blood of animals slain apart from the Lord's altar, one would be guarded against the temptation to offer the blood to demons (cf. Lev 17:7) and reminded of Yahweh's claim on all areas of man's life.

The Mosaic legislation on this issue indicates then that the explanation of the life-value of blood is not mystical but forensic. Moreover, it shows that what is in view is a symbolic value introduced by special revelation, not just the natural property of blood by virtue of its critical physiological function. In this connection we may note that the preferable translation of Leviticus 17:11 is "the life of the flesh is the blood," rather than "is in the blood" (cf. Lev 17:14).

Since the whole rationale of the Genesis 9:4 prohibition is found to be in the sphere of the earthly altar, we should expect that the obligatory force of this ordinance would be coextensive with that sphere and would not extend outside it or beyond it temporally. And such is in fact the conclusion to which we are led by the Mosaic legislation on the matter and by the apostolic disposition of it in the church of the new covenant. In these canonical directives enforcement of the prohibition against the ingestion of blood is consistently subject to limitations. We find that the sphere of the altar, that is, the range of applicability of the blood-prohibition, varies in extent according to various organizational factors in the history of the altar community, but is never universal. And at last, this sphere of the altar ceases to exist at all. Thus, the prohibition was not at any time intended as an ordinance to be observed by all mankind.

During the period between the covenantal inauguration of the theocratic order of Israel at Sinai and their taking possession of the promised land, the sphere of the altar was the wilderness encampment with its supportive environs. Within those bounds even the resident alien was subject to the prohibition under discussion (Lev 17:10,12,13). This does not imply, however, that non-Israelites in general were similarly obligated. No more so than the inclusion of resident aliens in the restrictions of the day of atonement (Lev 16:29) meant that all non-covenant peoples wherever located had the privileged duty of observing that holy day. Indeed, when Deuteronomy legislated for the period following upon Israel's gaining possession of their land, it exempted even the resident aliens within Israel, as well as the foreigners outside, from obligation to one aspect of the ordinance of animal blood. Deuteronomy 14:21 stipulated that meat suspect of not having been properly drained of its blood, though not to be eaten by the Israelites, inasmuch as they were holy (Lev 20:25,26), might nevertheless be given to resident aliens or sold to foreigners. Certainly God's law would not condone complicity on the part of the Israelites in the Gentiles' violation of a divine ordinance binding upon them. It follows that this regulation did not obligate the non-Israelite. It did not obligate the resident alien in Israel even though he was bound to observe the basic prohibition against blood. And the foreigners in the world at large were not obligated by this marginal feature dealt with in Deuteronomy 14:21 (cf. Lev 17:15) because they were not under the prohibition against blood at all.

It also becomes apparent from this Deuteronomic legislation that as the organizational shape of the altar community changed (in this case from wilderness encampment to settled domain in Canaan) the altar's sphere of influence (as expressed in the application of the prohibition against blood) was not always obvious. It might require special divine specification. Such was the case once again in the new circumstances faced by the council at Jerusalem described in Acts 15.

This council came at a transitional stage in the history of the altar. The earthly altar was being phased out. In principle it was already obsolete because the true heavenly sanctuary was now the site of the ministry of Jesus, the true and final priest. Moreover, as the prophetic word of the

Lord had announced, the earthly altar was doomed soon to disappear in judgment. But until that prophecy was fulfilled in the fall of Jerusalem in 70 A.D., the altar retained a certain legitimacy. This was evidenced by the continuing relationship sustained to it by the apostles of the Lord (cf. Acts 18:18; 21:23ff.). Though the new covenant was inaugurated, the old covenant order was to continue for a short while longer. What then were the bounds of the altar's sphere of influence in this unprecedented situation, particularly with respect to the Gentiles now entering into God's covenant? That was the next question on the agenda of the Jerusalem council once it had settled the basic question of the Mosaic law's relationship to justification. And the council's conclusion was that these Gentiles, at least those associated with the churches of the Jerusalem-Antioch axis and its more immediate missions orbit, were included in the sphere of influence of the continuing altar.

Genesis 9 and Acts 10 and 15 represent two very similar turning points in the history of the covenant community. In each case God's people were moving from existence within a theocratic organization into the world of common grace. And in each case two questions posed by this change received essentially the same answers.

The first question concerned the nature of the cultural life of the righteous in the common grace situation. On both occasions we find that their culture underwent transformation, ceasing to be holy kingdom culture and taking on a common, profane character. Disclosure of this change took the particular form of permitting believers to participate at common table with unbelievers, permission conveyed by answering in the negative the question of the continuing validity of the divisive distinction between clean and unclean food that had obtained in the holy culture of the erstwhile theocracy (cf. Gen 9:3 and Acts 10).

The second question concerned the cultus of the godly within the common grace framework. More specifically, it concerned the altar, which would continue to exist in the new situation, and its effect on the cultural-dietary matter of eating animal flesh with its blood. On both occasions we find that the continuing altar was still to have the special cultural consequence of disallowing the ingestion of blood (Gen 9:4 and Acts 15). In view of the basic parallel in these historical situations, with their agreement in principle on these peculiar problems of cult and culture, it is surely proper to appeal to the evidence of the decree of Acts 15 in dealing with the question of the range of application intended in the Genesis 9:4 prohibition. According to Acts 15, some Gentile believers along with the Jewish Christians within a certain orbit were to observe this dietary restriction, so honoring the continuing earthly altar. But, as we know from Paul's handling of this matter in churches of his own founding farther afield (cf., e.g., 1 Cor 8:4ff.), the Jerusalem council's decree did not contemplate Gentile believers of the total church community, let alone Gentiles outside the church. Here then is further and decisive evidence that the Genesis 9:4 proscription was not intended to be of general, universal application. This altar-oriented cultural precept was always limited in application to the sphere of altar influence, which, though somewhat variable in its precise delimitation, always excluded the world at large. And, of course, even if the Genesis 9:4 prohibition had been universally applicable until 70 A.D., the fact that it was oriented to the earthly altar would then mean that subsequent to the final elimination of that altar in the divine judgment of the old Mosaic order that prohibition has not been binding anywhere. At the present time it is not an obligation for either non-Jews or Jews, unbelievers or believers.

Movement of the covenant community out of a theocratic domain into a common grace setting does not, of course, desacralize the redemptive cultus, with or without an earthly altar. Thus, after the conclusion of the initial period, when it overlapped with the briefly prolonged old covenant altar community, the Christian cultus of the new covenant continued to possess a distinctive and exclusive holiness in the midst of its common culture context. Hence, while the cultural table became common (Acts 10), the holiness of the cultic table of the Lord was strictly maintained (1 Cor 10:16-21; 11:25-29; 2 Cor 6:14-16; cf. 2 John 10).

Having now noted the limitations on the applicability of the regulation of Genesis 9:4, it would be well to go back for a moment and address the question of what relevance this might have for the continuing normativeness of the adjoining statute in Genesis 9:5,6 concerning the state's use of the sword. Some hastily conclude from the juxtaposition of these regulations that the authorization of capital punishment becomes obsolete along with the prohibition against the ingestion of blood. But, as is generally recognized, laws of permanent and temporary obligation stand side by side elsewhere in biblical legislation. Our hermeneutical approach may not be simplistic in sorting out such laws. We must take account of all the relevant factors in each individual case in order to determine the intended range of application. Now, as for Genesis 9:4-6, the covenant of which it is a part emphasizes, as we have observed above, the permanence of its stipulated order as a whole, and this creates a presumption in favor of the permanence of particular stipulations within it. In the case of the regulations in Genesis 9:3,4 this presumption is offset by their special nature as appertaining to the people of God and their cultus, particularly to their changing situation with respect to theocratic organization and altar. But the basic presumption of permanence is not thus contravened in the case of the legislation of Genesis 9:5,6. It does not have a narrower orientation to the community of faith. On the contrary, the rationale of the state's infliction of capital punishment is founded here in the broadly human consideration of man's nature as image of God (v.6). Moreover, the provision of Genesis 9:5,6 does not originate in this context but is a renewal here of the divine appointment made quite apart from the redemptive cultus, being indeed originally disclosed to Cain (Gen 4:15). Further, the analogy of Scripture (cf. e.g., Rom 13:4) points to the continuation of the Genesis 9:5,6 provision into the current age.

Concluding Summary: In revelation given at the altar of the remnant from the Deluge, the charter of the city of man was renewed in solemn covenant. This covenant was concerned with natural life, not with religious fellowship, though it did take account of certain implications of the presence of the redemptive cultus for the common cultural area. It was an interim arrangement governing the earth only through genealogical history. Its benefits were not the redemptive blessings of God's eternal kingdom. Its penalties were not the eternal or directly inflicted judgments of God but temporal judgments administered through the state as authorized judiciary.

This covenant of common grace must, of course, be subsumed like all things under the universal reign of the King of heaven. Its establishment, with the determination of all its terms, was by God's sovereign decree. But its administration was not to be directly productive of the kingdom of God as holy realm. On the other hand, in the coherence of God's counsel, the objective of this covenant was to subserve the divine purpose and program of redemptive covenant and thereby, indirectly, the coming of the holy kingdom.

By this common grace covenanting God re-established the witness of a universal natural revelation to his everlasting power and divinity and his present longsuffering forbearance (Rom 1:20; 2:4,5; 2 Pet 3:7,9), a matrix for a second universal witness (Rom 10:17ff.), the witness of special redemptive revelation presenting the gospel-call to all the nations of the earth to find blessing in the messianic seed of Abraham. In short, the common grace covenant of Genesis 8:20-9:17 was designed to provide the historical order and set the world stage for the renewed program of redemptive covenant, particularly as that was to receive distinctive formulation in the Lord's covenant with Abraham (Gen 12ff.).

Chapter Two

REDEMPTIVE COVENANT IN THE NEW WORLD

The first triad of generations-divisions in Genesis does not close until a prophetic forecast has been recorded outlining in broadest strokes the future course of biblical history. This oracular pronouncement (Gen 9:24-27) will be our first topic in this chapter. Then, moving into divisions four and five (Gen 10:1-11:26), we will trace the ominous developments in the kingdoms of this world and the continuing presence of the community of the godly, particularly in the line of Shem.

I. ORACLE OF KINGDOM JUDGMENT

A. Noah's Oracle and Genesis 3:14,15

Noah's oracular utterance in Genesis 9:25-27 occupies a position in the biblical narrative comparable to the great primal prophecy of redemptive history in Genesis 3:14,15. Each of these programmatic declarations comes at the beginning of a world age and suggests the shape of the future of redemption down to messianic times. Each is recorded in close association with a foundational disclosure about the interim world order of common grace (Gen 3:16-19 and 8:20-9:17, respectively) and each is followed by narratives about developments first in the city of man (Gen 4 and 6 and Gen 10 and 11, respectively) and then in the community of faith (Gen 5 and Gen 11:10-26, respectively). In these narratives we find the beginnings of the fulfillment of what has been foretold in the oracles. The oracles thus prove to be indexes of the major themes to be developed in the following biblical history.

The relationship of these two oracular pronouncements is even closer than has been indicated in the above comparisons. Noah's oracle is actually a resumption of the primal oracle of the Lord, both in function and substance. Genesis 3:14,15 is God's curse on Satan and his followers among mankind, a declaration of conquest to be executed at last through the messianic champion of the seed of the woman. Genesis 9:24-27 is a renewal of that history-shaping curse with its correlative promise of the triumph of the redemptive community. Salvation as victory in the conflict with the dragon and his forces is the common theme of both oracles. Only as to their immediate position and particular perspective within that history of the coming of God's kingdom do they differ. Genesis 3:14,15 contains no intimations of the division of premessianic history into its prediluvian and postdiluvian phases. Its prophetic overview moves quickly to the climactic encounter of Christ and Satan. The focus shifts in Noah's oracle. Delivered after the historical division marked by the Flood, it portrays the ongoing spiritual warfare in the lineaments of the upcoming Abrahamic Covenant, centering on the typological history of Israel, the distinctive form that was to be assumed by the redemptive program in the era leading to the messianic triumph of the kingdom.

Various links between the contents and occasions of these two prophetic utterances underscore their relationship. Genesis 3:15 foretold the development of the spiritual antithesis between the children of God and the children of the devil. The episode that called forth Noah's curse was one which found that antithesis in evidence among the sons of Noah. Ham is depicted as behaving in a manner that exposes him as one of the serpent's seed. For in the Fall of man Satan had contrived to bring Adam and his wife into a condition of shameful nakedness and it is, accordingly, likeness to the devil that is betrayed in Ham when he maliciously aggravates the shame of his drunken father's nakedness (Gen 9:20-23). At the same time, Shem and Japheth by their loving concern to cover Noah's nakedness emulate the love of the Lord in the Genesis 3 situation in his providing garments to hide the nakedness of Adam and Eve (Gen 3:21). The seed of the woman spoken of in Genesis 3:15, those redemptively renewed in the likeness of their heavenly Father, were thus also present as part of the setting of Noah's oracle. But particularly significant for the connection between Genesis 3:14,15 and Genesis 9:25-27 is the fact that it was similar acts of malice on the part of Satan and Ham, each involving the exposure of nakedness, that elicited these pronouncements (cf. Gen 9:24).

As judgmental responses to such offenses, both of these oracles were primarily curses. In the case of Noah's oracle, its basically curse character is demonstrated by its placing the curse on Canaan first (v.25) and then repeating that curse at the close of the following two blessings on Shem and Japheth (vv.26,27). What is of critical importance, however, for the interpretation of Noah's oracle is not any mere formal similarity of Genesis 9:25-27 to Genesis 3:14,15 in terms of the curse genre but rather its concern with the same realities as that primal prophecy. From the situational correspondences that have been noted it is evident that both curses are directed against agents of evil in the spiritual warfare of the Lord and the seed of the woman versus Satan and his seed. And by the same token, the blessings that are pronounced are those which are correlative to those curses and thus are spiritual. That is, they belong to the sphere of redemption, not to the social-political world of common grace. They are the blessings of the holy kingdom of God realized in the history of God's redemptive covenants with his saints. To find the application of these curses and blessings in the general history of the world is interpretation that ignores the literary-canonical context. That context demands that the curse pronounced in this oracle be understood as one of exclusion from the kingdom of salvation; and its blessings, as those of participation in the redemptive covenant and kingdom.

B. Canaan Cursed

"Cursed be Canaan" (Gen 9:25a). Between God's curse on Satan (Gen 3:14) and this curse on Canaan there is a series of curses that involve man and the ground (Gen 3:17; [cf. 5:29]; 4:11; 8:21). In these, the ground itself, rather than man, is mentioned as the immediate object of the curse (3:17 and 8:21), or the curse on man is at least said to be "from the ground" (4:11). In contradiction of man's proper dominion over it, the ground would show itself hostile to man in the execution of these curses. The common, temporal curse, to which common grace is correlative, is in view in Genesis 3:17 and 4:11. Genesis 8:21 refers to the curse of the Flood, a typological intrusion of the principle of final judgment. Like the curse referred to in Genesis 8:21, the curse on Canaan in Genesis 9:25 belongs to the sphere of redemptive judgment. It is akin to the curse on the serpent-Satan (Gen 3:14) in both form and meaning. Each of these curses is so formulated that the curse falls directly on the doomed person: "Cursed are you"..."Cursed be Canaan." And each concerns the ultimate issue of exclusion from the beatitude of the kingdom of God.

Genesis 9:25 is thus a declaration of reprobation with respect to Canaan. "A servant of servants will he be to his brothers" (Gen 9:25b) expresses this rejection of Canaan over against the election of his brothers, just as the similar idiom of subservience used in the contrast between Esau and Jacob signified the reprobating hatred of the elder brother and the elective love of the younger (Gen 25:23; cf. Rom. 9:12,13). The enmity instituted between the seed of the woman and the seed of the serpent in the curse of Genesis

3:14,15 would come to striking historical expression in the antithesis between Canaan and his brothers.

Canaan is mentioned in the curse rather than Ham, his father (cf. Gen 9:22, which anticipates this). And actually the particular historical events that were to constitute this curse involved the much more remote descendants of Ham, the Canaanite inhabitants of the promised land (cf. Ps 78:51). Similarly, the blessings pronounced on Shem (v.26) and Japheth (v.27) contemplate equally remote historical developments in their lineages. The only difference is that in the case of Ham it is explicitly indicated at once which particular line descending from him should experience what is foretold in the oracle. In all three cases the oracle envisages a specific episode or development in the history of a limited segment of the descendants of the party named. In no case is a destiny decreed that applies to all the descendants of that party. Not all Canaanites are reprobate. Not all Semites and Japhethites enter the kingdom. In each case, however, there was to be in some branch of the genealogical line in question a particular, notable experience of the predicated curse or blessing.

By naming Canaan rather than Ham in the curse a pun was introduced. The curse of servitude was suggested by the very sound of the name Canaan (whatever its etymology), for the verb *kana'* (in the Hiphil) means "subdue." It is used for God's subjugation of the Canaanites under the Israelites at the time of their entry into their promised inheritance (Deut 9:3; Judg 4:23; Neh 9:24). And that conquest is the actual event in which the curse on Canaan took effect. Israel's warfare against Canaan was not just another skirmish in the secular round of wars and rumors of wars but a redemptive intervention of God, appropriating the promised land for his holy kingdom realm on earth. The conquered Canaanites are to be seen as representatives of the serpent's seed, crushed under the heel of the redeemed people of the Lord in a typological act of judgment pointing to the Final Judgment.

C. Shem Blessed

Shem means "name" and the blessing on his line consisted in their becoming the bearers of God's name. There is again the wordplay. This benediction on Shem assumes the form of doxology: "Blessed be Yahweh, the God of Shem" (Gen 9:26). As God sovereignly differentiates between the woman's and the serpent's seeds, he identifies his own name and cause with the former by entering into a covenant relationship with them, in which they are adopted as his chosen, holy people and they confess him as their God, calling on his name, acknowledging him as Father and thereby surnaming themselves after him. This was the hallmark of the covenant community in the line of Seth (Gen 4:26) and the line of Shem is proclaimed their successors by Noah's doxological blessing, uniting them with the name of God.

Noah's promised blessing began to work itself out in the period from Shem to Terah, the father of Abraham. For this Shem-Terah line was the covenant line, as is indicated by the position of its genealogy (Gen 11:10-26) in the pattern of generations-divisions in Genesis. But it was surely in the Lord's covenantal calling of Abraham, descendant of Shem through Eber, that the blessing of Shem's line had its definitive realization. Indeed, Scripture records a benediction in which the doxology-benediction of Noah on Shem's line is applied specifically to Abraham. When Melchizedek declared Abraham, the Eberite, "blessed of God Most High," immediately conjoining with this benediction the doxology, "blessed be God most High" (Gen 14:19,20; cf. v.13), he was clearly echoing Noah's oracle. And it was, of course, with the Abrahamites that God's name became identified. In terms of the Abrahamic Covenant the Lord is known in Scripture as the God of Abraham, Isaac and Jacob. And subsequently he is identified as the holy one of Israel, the Abrahamite nation whose distinctive glory it was to be entrusted with the revelation of God's name in the divine oracles (Rom 3:2), to receive the covenantal adoption and the Glory-Presence, the theophanic Name, and to bring forth at last the Christ, the name of God incarnate (Rom 9:4,5).

Though involving the new covenant era, the focus in Noah's blessing on Shem (Gen 9:26) is on the premessianic stage of the Abrahamic Covenant. It was in that age that the Semites, in the form of the Israelites, were the dominant people in the administration of God's redemptive covenant. Further, their history witnessed a fulfillment of the blessing on Shem as the direct corollary of the execution of the predicted curse on Canaan (as in Gen 9:26). For the Canaanites' curse of being dispossessed was, of course, the reverse side of Israel's blessing, the blessing of inheriting as sons the kingdom-realm which had been claimed by their Father-God and promised to them in the Abrahamic Covenant. According to that covenant, in giving the Abrahamites a great name and making them a great nation, God would bless those who blessed Abraham and curse those who cursed him (Gen

12:2,3). Noah's oracle anticipated this when, in effect, it placed the Abrahamic Covenant in the center, on the one side preceded by the cursing of the Canaanites who cursed the Abrahamites, and on the other side followed by the blessing of those Japhethites who would come to bless the name of the seed of Abraham in whom all the nations of the earth would be blessed, for he would be the seed of the woman who would crush the serpent's head.

D. Japheth Blessed

In the blessing of Japheth (Gen 9:27) the focus of Noah's oracle moves beyond the stage of the Mosaic Covenant and the ethnic particularism of its concentration on Israel to the messianic age and the church's universal embrace of the nations. Japheth's descendants were eventually to have entrance into the covenant which would have been almost exclusively confined to the line of Shem in the days of the old covenant.

The imagery used to convey this union of Shem and Japheth within the covenant of God is adopted from the occasion of the oracle. Together these two brothers had entered the tent of their father to perform their godly act of love. Hence, the covenant is imaged as a tent-dwelling, which they will occupy together. In fulfillment of the blessing on Shem, Israel under the old covenant already dwelt in the covenant tents. Noah's prophetic prayer for Japheth proceeds to the prospect that Elohim (just identified as the covenant "God of Shem," v.26) would open the dwelling-places of Shem for Japheth so that he too might reside there. The two clauses of the blessing develop this one image, with the object of the verb in the first clause (i.e., the tents) supplied only in the second clause. That verb, *pathah*, seems to mean, "open wide." Thus in Proverbs 20:19 it refers to lips opened in speech. (The meaning "enlarge" is assumed for *pathah* in a prevalent misinterpretation of Gen 9:27a as a reference to the extensive geographic spread of Japhetic peoples.) The choice of the rare verb *pathah* for "open" instead of the usual *pathach* was evidently in the interests of securing a wordplay again on the name of the person involved. The result is: May God *yapht* (open, *i.e.*, the tent) for *yepheth* (Japheth).

This destiny found in Japheth's name was realized in the apostolic mission to the Gentiles, most particularly in Paul's mission to the Greeks, whose own traditions traced them back through Hellen and Prometheus to Iapetus. Noah's figure of the opened tent is possibly reflected in the missionaries' report of their penetration of the Gentile world with the gospel, rehearsing how God "had opened a door of faith unto the Gentiles" (Acts 14:27; cf. 1 Cor 16:9). And midway between Noah and Paul, Isaiah had prophesied this expansion of the covenant community among the Gentiles by the use of similar tent imagery, urging Israel to extend the curtains of her habitation in anticipation of the numerous children she would yet welcome there, when her seed possessed the nations (see Isa 54:1-3, noting the explicit reference to the Noahic context in vv.9,10, and cf. Isa 26:2; 60:11-14).

The tendency of interpreters to drift away from the contextually established concern of Noah's oracle with the sphere of redemptive history is probably most prevalent in the treatment of Japheth's blessing. This mistake is made by many who acknowledge the genuinely prophetic character of the oracle as an utterance of Noah, as well as by those who assume a later, Israelite origin for it, whether as a fierce, warlike expression of Israel's purpose in the course of their struggle for the mastery of Canaan or as an aetiological rationale for their dominance once it was attained. Commentators comb the history for occasions when Japhetic nations attacked or ruled Canaan, especially for episodes in which such a nation and Israel might be construed as acting in concert against Canaanites. One interesting suggestion connects the oracle with the Genesis 14 episode in which Shem (Elam) and Japheth (the Goyim under Tidal) control Canaan (the cities of the plain). Actually, Genesis 14 records a situation formally quite contrary to the oracle, for it relates how the representative of Shem specifically in view in Noah's blessing, namely the Hebrew Abraham, was allied with the accursed Canaanites in a successful operation against the mixed Semitic-Japhetic forces from the east. But the basic fallacy in all such views is their attempt to relate the curses and blessings of Genesis 9:25-27 to events in general history and to relationships and developments within the common grace sphere. Noah's oracle deals with the outworking of the primal messianic prophecy of Genesis 3:15, with the spiritual warfare of the ages, with election to and exclusion from the redemptive covenant. And thus properly read it emerges as an astoundingly rich and profound and farseeing vision of the future of the kingdom of God.

II. THE KINGDOMS OF THIS WORLD

How the international landscape of patriarchal times emerged in the course of the genealogical development of the ark-remnant is the subject of the fourth generations-division of Genesis (10:1-11:9). This account of the generations of Noah (10:1) may be viewed as a setting of the historical stage for the working out of the destinies of Shem, Ham, and Japheth revealed in Noah's oracle (9:25-27). From this broad perspective the table of nations is an introduction to the history of redemption which unfolds in all the rest of the Bible. But it may also be viewed in relation to the covenant of common grace in Genesis 8:20ff. From this angle, which concentrates on the Babel episode (11:1-9), it is a resumption of the theme of the city of man and particularly of the spirit of antichrist looming again (cf. Gen 6:1-4) in these postdiluvian beginnings. Before looking at Genesis 10:1-11:9 as a prelude to the story of the city of God, we shall consider it from the perspective of the city of man.

A. Focus and Fullness

The spiritual-historical dynamics of these postdiluvian movements of mankind and the ensuing covenantal calling of Abraham will be better understood if we back up for a moment and review the structure of the city according to its original character and in its postlapsarian development. The holy city under the creational covenant may be analyzed in terms of its created focus and its mandated fullness. God's epiphany as Glory-Spirit on the holy mountain in Eden, the historically localized manifestation of the heavenly Presence, was the central focus of the theocratic city. As created, the city had a vertical, cosmic axis at its center; its focus was the mountain of God, extending from earth to heaven, its feet in the garden and its head crowned by the Glory of the celestial temple, theophanically unveiled.

Fullness (what we called Megapolis earlier) was to be achieved according to covenantal mandate by an expansive movement out from the center, appropriating the earth by cultural structuring, incorporating it to its utmost circumference into the temple-city. This fullness of the circle of the city was to be attained without loss of focus or of the coherence of the whole. Beyond the fullness of Megapolis was the consummated city of Metapolis, the city transfigured by the opening up of its heavenly dimension to human perception. The heavenly dimension was in evidence from the beginning at the focus of the city in the form of the Spirit epiphany on the mountain of God, but this was only a provisional metaphor of the heavenly Glory. In Metapolis there is a cosmic diffusion of the theophanic heavens from the focus throughout the fullness of the city, so that no longer is the human experience of the heavenly vision available only at the mountain in Eden but everywhere in creation men worship in Spirit, the true, eternal heavenly dimension (John 4:21-24). For the Glory of the Lord fills the earth as the waters cover the sea (Hab 2:14). The focal axis becomes the cuboid fullness of the heavenly dimensioned holy of holies, which is Metapolis.

With the Fall the coherence of the whole in its common central focus was fractured. Indeed, the focus entirely disappeared, and with the loss of the vertical cultic axis the identity of the city changed from the city of God to the merely horizontal city of man. A kind of fullness was still mandated, but the process was launched by an act of expulsion from the holy focus. It therefore had the character of a curse, the curse of dispersion. Though this cultural expansion retained through common grace an aspect of blessing in the form of fruitfulness and dominion in measure, the fullness it produced was not the unity of holy Megapolis but the diaspora of the profane nations of the Gentiles, a world divided.

What is needed to achieve the fullness of the city as originally projected is the reintroduction of the focus. This transpires in the process of redemption and is a spiritual transaction, a matter of the reconciliation of the holy God with fallen men. To accomplish this redemptive restoration requires the Incarnation, and the Incarnation, while providing for the fulfillment of the messianic mission of salvation from sin, at the same time is the creation of a new focus, a new and permanent manifestation of the Glory-Spirit in the incarnate Son. In the new holy city, redemption-built, the process of attaining the fullness is achieved as a reversal of the dispersion process that followed the Fall. It has, therefore, the character of a regathering to the new focus. In the redemptive city of God focus and fullness coalesce in the Spirit-union of the church. For the church as Christ's body is his "fullness" and he, the head and focus of the church, is the one who "fills all in all" (Eph 1:22,23; cf. 3:18,19; 4:13; Col 1:19,20; 2:9).

A typological picture of the New Jerusalem, the fullness of the focal Christ, was provided in the old Jerusalem with its focus in the temple-dwelling of the Glory-Spirit on mount Zion and with its fullness in the tribes of Israel extended through the land. Moreover, in the later regathering of the Israelites from their exile dispersion to the re-established temple focus in Jerusalem there was a prefiguration of how the fullness of the heavenly city comes about through a final regathering of the redeemed of mankind's diaspora from the ends of the earth. The typological significance of this Old Testament model, and therewith its value for the clarification and enrichment of our conception of the eschatological cosmic reality, is evidenced in subsequent biblical revelation by the use of that model to portray the eternal city.

But before the Lord established Jerusalem in Canaan as his typological city, the focus for the gathering and regathering of his redemptive community Israel, the ungodly postdiluvian city-builders had presumed to solve on their own the problem of mankind's accursed dispersion over the face of the earth. Genesis 10:1-11:9 deals with this theme.

B. City of Man as Pseudo-Focus

1. Diaspora of the Nations

Genesis 10 exhibits the two-sided nature of the interim world, the field of operation of both the mutually tempering principles of common curse and common grace. On the one hand, Genesis 10 reflects the common grace blessing pronounced in Genesis 9:1, ordaining that man multiply and fill the earth, for it records the genealogical increase of the Noahic lines and their successful penetration of the earth in all directions (cf. Acts 17:26). Yet this expansion is portrayed under the aspect of the common curse, as a centrifugal expulsion toward a fractured fullness, without cohesiveness because of lack of focus. The language of scattering (9:19) and dispersing (10:18) is used for this general overspreading of the earth, the sort of terminology used for the judgment curse on the Babelites (11:9, cf.4). Further, as presented in Genesis 10 the result of this development was not the unity of an ecumenical family but schisms of all kinds. The term *parad,* "divide," (10:5,32) accents this breakup of Noahic humanity into separate families, tongues, lands, and nations (10:5,20,31). Over-all, the picture is that of a diaspora of mankind, a postdiluvian continuation of the exile of Adamic humanity from the focal Presence in the garden of God (cf. Gen 3:23f.; 4:16).

2. Babel's Ascent to Heaven

Appended to the broad survey of Genesis 10 is the representative, local episode of Genesis 11:1-9. Here the emphasis shifts from the outward aspects of man's worldwide expansion to the inner spirit and religious character of the movement. In this respect too postdiluvian history resumed the prediluvian pattern. For Babel was a revival, with crusading fervor, of the ideology of the city of man earlier adopted by the dynasty of Cain and the sons of the gods (Gen 6:1-4).

The account of Babel's founding, like that of Cain's city, begins with a reference to expelled mankind wandering in the east (Gen 11:2; cf. 4:16). A fractious sense of annoyance with the accursed fate of being scattered over the earth is sounded in the rallying cry to build the city (Gen 11:4), reminiscent of the complaint of Cain (Gen 4:14). In response to Cain, God had appointed the common grace city as an interim measure to exert a centripetal force, offsetting in part the outward thrust of the common curse and so ameliorating to a degree the fragmenting, isolating bane of dispersion. But a cohesive structure of this legitimated kind was not enough for the Babel builders. Impatient with the partial, temporal provision of the city of common grace, they lusted for something more. They aspired to a more ultimate solution to the oppressive problem of the loss of spiritual-cosmic focus, the problem they felt existentially, whatever they did or did not acknowledge about its historical origin and religious rootage. In their proud unbelief they spurned God's promised restoration of the true focus and fullness as an act of saving mercy and grace, purposing in an incipient spirit of antichrist to become themselves the creators of a cosmic focus. "Come, let us build ourselves a city and tower with its top in the heavens, and let us make ourselves a name, lest we be scattered over the face of the whole earth" (Gen 11:4).

So they conspired to erect the mythic sacred mountain of the divine assembly and thus re-create the central axis between earth and heaven. The *migdol,* "tower," of Genesis 11 is not to be taken as a lofty fortification (cf. Deut. 1:28; 9:1), for military concerns are absent from this context. It is rather to be understood in terms of those ancient staircase-mountain structures, the ziggurats, which are frequently described as having their top in the heavens and bear names like "the house of the mountain," "the house of the link between heaven and earth," and "the house of the foundation of heaven and earth" (thus, the ziggurat at Babylon). It is the literary tradition of these ziggurats that is strikingly reflected in Genesis 11, though with sarcastically polemical purpose.

The biblical Babel narrative is no mere adaptation of the Mesopotamian ziggurat tradition, lacking in historical facticity. On the contrary, Genesis 11:1-9 is the record of an actual event. And the ziggurat ideology, which is attested in the account of the founding of Babylon with its temple-tower in the Enuma Elish and in the various inscriptions concerning the building and rebuilding of ziggurats, originated in that Genesis 11 event. In fact, the ziggurat ideology represents the historical continuation of the inner apostate spirit of the Babel enterprise. At the same time, the Mesopotamian Babel tradition suffers from the radical distortion of mythologization. What was a revolt against the living God that was frustrated by his judgment is turned into a glorious achievement, a work of heavenly beings in honor of the deity Marduk. Also, in the mythological version the construction of the city-temple-tower by the gods is projected into the dimension of creation-event. Characteristically, the mythologizing process obliterates the sharp line of demarcation between the original creation and the later situation resulting from the Fall. Previously we observed how the theme of the conflict and victory over the dragon, which actually arises in connection with God's redemptive response to the Fall (Gen 3:14,15), becomes an aspect of the creation of the world in the mythical treatment of that theme. Similarly merged in pagan mythology are the sequentially separated events of the Creator's production of the Edenic mountain-focus in the normal, prelapsarian world and the postlapsarian apostate human scheme to recover the lost cosmic center. In all such recasting of historical reality there is a guilty suppression of the ugly fact of man's violation of his covenantal troth to his Creator and a devilish attempt to identify the abnormal conditions of man's fallen state with the pristine order that came from the hand of God. By this tactic the satanic assault of sinners on heaven is camouflaged as a noble quest by an innocent, victimized mankind aspiring to transcend its existential predicament.

In their oblique way, the Mesopotamian traditions of the origin of Babylon and ziggurats attest to the nature of the Genesis 11 event as a human effort to do the divine work of establishing the cosmic focus. Babel was an idolization of man. Inspired by the spirit of human autonomy and omnipotence, the Babel builders would soar above their geophysical entrapment. By the resources of their scientific genius they would master fusion and remove the sting of fission from their experience of fullness. Babel was the anti-city, the diametrical opposite of the city of God, which is the creation and gift of God, its altar an altar of plain earth or unhewn stone because it must be holy and man's technological processing would defile it (Exod 20:25; cf. Heb 11:10; Rev 21:2,10). Made-by-man was Babel's trademark: "Come, let us make brick...Come, let us build" (Gen 11:3a,4a). In building their pseudo-focus-city they were exploiting the common grace city, perverting the legitimate cultural product into an idol-cultus. What was ordained as an interim measure merely to provide historical space for the program of the eternal city they reinterpreted as the actual eschatological *telos*. Turning the city of man into the temple of man, they projected a tower-mountain that should open the way for them to the heights of the immortals. Gathered into the unity of this rival focus-city, they would preempt the eschatological gathering promised at the consummation of the redemptive city of God.

"There" (*sham*, v.2) at the place they chose in *shin'ar* (v.2), they determined to establish the foundation-platform of their mutinous mountain and to launch their temple-pinnacle into the "heaven" (*shamayim*, v.4) of the gods, so making themselves a "name" (*shem*, v.4). Sound plays tie things together: the project to its purpose, the foundation to the heaven-summit, and all to the quest for a name. The old temptation to be like the gods entrances the builders. They covet an immortal name.

Immortality of a kind may be pursued through begetting, but they sought it by building. Elsewhere in biblical history we read of others who built monuments to serve instead of descendants as memorials to keep their name in existence (cf. 2 Sam 18:18; Isa 56:5). In Genesis 11 this idea is suggested in a further instance of assonance: the subject, *bene*, "sons of (men)," adjoins the verb, *banu*, "built" (v.5). Genesis 4:17 uses the same wordplay and association of ideas, relating that Cain became a city builder (*boneh*) and named the city after his son (*beno*). For their name monument the Babelites aspired to build the mountain of the heavenly assembly, thinking to secure thereby access to the divine realm and to gain a name among the gods. "The sons of men" would perform the creative wonder of raising up the cosmic mountain in order to become "the sons of the gods." In grace God had bestowed on Shem the blessing of bearing his name (*shem*), but the Babelites despised Shem's redemptive blessing and grasped after the name-identity of deity as their own autonomous prerogative, to be seized by their own imperial power. Here is the blasphemous ideology of Genesis 6:1-4 rearing its head in the postdiluvian world.

The ideological similarity of the Genesis 6 and 11 episodes becomes clearer if the figure of Nimrod (Gen 10:8ff.) is associated with the Babel enterprise. That the biblical narrative does intend to identify him with the Genesis 11:1ff. event can be argued from the identification of both with "the land of Shinar" (10:10; 11:2) and, of course, from the mention of Babel at the head of the list of cities that constituted "the beginning of his kingdom" (Gen 10:10). While Nimrod's role in Genesis 10:10 might be construed in terms of conquest, the northward extension of that "beginning" is described specifically as a constructive activity (v.11), namely, as the building (or rebuilding) of various cities in the Assyrian area (cf. Mic 5:6). Now this city-empire builder, who is evidently connected with the Babel episode, is one in whom the spirit of the prediluvian "sons of the gods" lived again. Like those ancient dynasts, Nimrod is called a *gibbor* (10:8). His heroic might was displayed in hunting prowess (10:9), the reference probably being to Gilgamesh-like exploits against beasts that threatened his domain (cf. Gen 9:5), rather than to military campaigns. Incidentally, among the activities of the gods enacted in the Mesopotamian cultus was their participation in the royal hunt. Indeed, pretensions to deity in the tradition of the divine kingship ideology of Genesis 6:1-4 may conceivably be hinted at in the echo of the divine *reshith*, "beginning," of Genesis 1:1 in 10:10. That might also be the point when Nimrod's mighty exploits are described as "before (or like, or in the face of) Yahweh" (*lpny yhwh*), though the phrase might also identify Nimrod's royal office as a judicial agency of the Lord God (see 1 Sam 2:29,30,35; 12:7; 15:33; cf, Gen 4:15; 9:5,6). Claims to deity by Nimrod possibly lie behind the mythological tradition that the gods built Babylon with its stagetower for the majesty of Marduk. (Some have argued the equivalence of the names Marduk and Nimrod.)

To the entire commune of the Babel-conspirators the Lord himself applied an expression elsewhere used for God, and God alone. He declared that, unimpeded by problems of communication and coordination (Gen 11:6a), they would be unstoppable in the accomplishment of their every purpose (Gen 11:6b). Compare the similar language in Job's confession of God's omnipotence (Job 42:2). Already at Babel man was attempting a re-creation of the mountain-link of heaven and earth, an anti-God scheme, satanically conceived. They thus exhibited a godlike potential for execution combined with a devil-like dedication to evil. This was an intolerable combination, threatening as it did to produce prematurely the ultimate manifestation of the mystery of iniquity, which precipitates the final judgment of the world.

3. Heaven's Descent on Babel

According to ziggurat doctrine, the deity was expected to descend upon the tower. Babel's tower was favored with a divine descent, not however such as they would have preferred. Ironically, it was an advent of the God of the Flood whom they thought by their tower to defy. The challenge of their "Come, let us build...unto heaven" (v.4) was answered in his "Come, let us go down and confound" (v.7). By noting the necessity of the Lord's descending, the narrative intimates with a smile that the mountain-tower had not made it all the way up to the strata of the court of the gods after all.

Yahweh's coming is described as a judicial inspection, a coming down to take account of what was going on and to deal with it (v.5). In Genesis 18:21 this terminology is used for God's descent to judge Sodom and Gomorrah (cf. Exod 19:20). The plural form, "let us go down" (Gen 11:7), points to the presence of the angel attendants of the heavenly council, customary agents of God's judgments (cf. Gen 18:2; 19:1; Exod 19:20). This advent was very much like the primal *parousia* in Eden (Gen 3:8). Then the Lord had judged mankind to be defiantly intent on an illicit seizure of immortality (Gen 3:22), which he prevented by driving the offenders out into exile and diaspora existence. At Babel he again found men guilty of conspiring to carry out just such unlawful intentions and again countered with the curse of dispersion, effected this time by frustrating their dialogue and so unglueing the bonds of their ecumenical union.

The would-be creators of a new cosmic focus did not attain the success of Sabbath rest. They did cease from their labors, but it was the restless, unfulfilled cessation of failure. The Babylonian creation myth boasts of Marduk and his fifty great name-titles, recited by the heavenly host in celebration of his achievement of world order, with its center in temple-crowned Babylon. That is the kind of name the historical builders of Babylon coveted (Gen 11:4), but they are mocked as having won instead the inglorious name of "Mixed-up, Confusion" (a pun on the sound similarity of Babel to *balal,* "mix, confuse"). Their memorial tower was destined to become a forgotten ruin. Dozens of other ziggurat structures were built all over Mesopotamia to the north and south of Babel, but the very multiplication of them attests at once to the failure of the Babel-tower to be the ultimate, decisive achievement of the one cosmic focus and to the shattering, dispersive impact of God's judgment on Babel.

In the days of God's typological city, Jerusalem, Satan stirred up the sea of the nations and revived the Babylon of Nimrod in the land of Shinar. The vainglory of the city founders was heralded again in the boast of the head of gold: "Is not this great Babylon, which I have built for the royal dwelling-place by the might of my power and for the glory of my majesty?" (Dan 4:30). And the idolization of this city of man as the cosmic center of heaven and earth was imaged in Nebuchadnezzar's vision of the cosmic tree, focal gathering point of all creation and, like the ancient mountain-tower, reaching unto heaven (Dan 4:10ff.). Inevitably the claim of Babylon must clash with the claim of Jerusalem to be the true mountain of God and navel of the earth. In the succession of the kingdoms standing in the spiritual tradition of Nebuchadnezzar's Babylon and symbolized by the idol-beasts of the book of Daniel (chapters 2 and 7) there arose the little horn from the Seleucids, archenemy of God's holy city and people (Dan 8:9ff. and 11:21ff.). He was a prototype of the antichrist power of the messianic age, the little horn from the fourth beast (Dan 7:8 and 11:36ff.), the dragon-like agent of Satan that issues the final challenge against the city of God, evoking the day of wrath. Back at the Babel of Genesis 11 this evolution of evil had its ominous beginnings in the postdiluvian world. But the Satanic movement was at that point kept from premature efflorescence by God's frustrating judgment of the babel of tongues.

What befell the Babel project was a particular instance of the developments which were taking place everywhere in the world (as summarized in Genesis 10), the dispersion of the sons of men and the emergence of linguistic and national divisions. At Babel, however, the curse aspect of this centrifugal thrust was accentuated. The divisions were effected there more abruptly than elsewhere and by a more direct divine intervention. The scattering from Babel was an immediate judicial response appropriate to a more concerted and concentrated implementation of the apostate ideology infecting the city of man. But just as the general multiplication of mankind recorded in Genesis 10 had a two-sided curse/blessing character, so the Genesis 11 episode involved an exercise of the principle of common grace as well as an aggravation of the common curse. For God's judgment on Babel was in effect a restraint on the accelerating antichrist movement. By thus impeding the momentum of the mystery of iniquity, the Lord provided for a respite before the ultimate eschatological crisis, the time of the pseudo-parousia of the man of sin and his pseudo-gathering of the nations, which brings on the world's final judgment. This delay of judgment made room for a further common grace history and thereby for the maturing of God's redemptive program for mankind and its fruition in the advent of Christ and the achievement of the true focus and fullness of the eternal city of God. In the accomplishing of this redemptive goal the dispersive effects of the diversification of tongues would be reversed. A pure language would be restored and there would be a regathering of the new mankind to receive a name of praise (Zeph 3:9,20).

III. THE COMMUNITY OF THE BLESSING

Genesis 10 was viewed in the preceding section in relation to the program of the city of man as regulated by the common grace covenant of Genesis 8:20ff. and as represented in the misdirected venture at Babel (Gen 11:1-9). In this section we will observe how the common grace order, as surveyed in Genesis 10, subserved in its indirect way the program of redemption. This will involve our noting how the fourth generations-division in Genesis (10:1-11:9) sketches world developments in such a way as to point ahead to the fulfillment of the Noahic oracle of Genesis 9:25-27. Since our particular interest here is in the unfolding of the redemptive blessing on Shem and the continuing presence of the community of the godly in the interim world, we will also be taking account of the genealogical history of the fifth generations-division (Gen 11:10-26), which leads from Shem to Abraham.

A. Noah's Oracle and Genesis 10:1-11:26

An indication of the programmatic role of Noah's oracle for the composition of the table of nations is the place it occupies between two introductions to the latter. Genesis 9:18,19 is the first introduction. This passage near the close of the third generations-division is not a repetition of the statement concerning Noah's descendants at the beginning of that section (6:9,10; cf. 5:32), but an anticipation of the declaration about the descendants of the sons of Noah in Genesis 10:1, the heading of the fourth generations-division and the second of the two introductions to the descendants of Shem, Ham, and Japheth. Genesis 9:18,19 speaks of these three sons of Noah as those from whom the whole (population of the) earth stemmed, the theme of Genesis 10:1ff. Note also the use of the similar verbs of scattering in this introduction (9:19) and in the closing summation of Genesis 11:9 (cf. 10:32). Treatment of the theme of the overspreading of the earth by the three Noahic lines, thus introduced for the first time in 9:18,19, does not follow at once but waits while the oracle of Noah is inserted (9:20-27), so that it then becomes necessary to introduce it a second time in 10:1. Meanwhile, Genesis 9:18,19 serves more immediately as an introduction to the oracle passage (9:20-27), being obviously tailored to that additional function by its reference to Ham as the father of Canaan. And the Noahic oracle of Genesis 9:25-27 is identified by its location there between the two introductions to the table of nations as belonging with that ethnic-national survey. The oracle establishes the destinies of the three Noahic branches and then the development of those lines is traced in Genesis 10:1ff. in such a way that we discern the episodes of curse and blessing prophesied by Noah beginning to take shape in each one. This anticipation of the following (fourth) generations-division by Genesis 9:25-27 near the close of the third division is a characteristic interlocking technique in the structure of the book of Genesis (compare, for example, the relation of Gen 4:25,26 to the second division, Gen 6:1-4 to the third, and Gen 10:21ff. to the fifth).

The fourth generations-division (Gen 10:1-11:9) stands then between the oracular curses and blessings pronounced by Noah and their fulfillment in the redemptive history recounted in the biblical record from Genesis 12 onward. It serves as a prophetic-ethnic glossary for the rest of Scripture, to which the reader can refer and so detect in the course of redemptive events the inexorable fulfilling of the future-shaping word of the Lord through Noah.

It is apparent from the order of the survey of the sons of Noah in Genesis 10 that the interest displayed there in the common history of the nations is subordinated to the paramount biblical purpose of transmitting the history of the Covenant of Grace. That is shown by the reserving of Shem's line for the final position in the arrangement (vv.21-31), the effect of this being to make the chapter lead up to the theme of God's covenant with Shem's descendant Abraham, the theme on which the rest of the Bible is to concentrate. This design of the arrangement is made all the clearer in the fact that Shem's line is taken up again for a separate and distinctive treatment in Genesis 11:10-26, after the intervening Babel episode (11:1-9), which would otherwise break the direct connection with the Abrahamic history. As resumed in Genesis 11:20-26 (itself the fifth generations-division of Genesis) the theme of Shem's descendants does lead directly to Abraham, both in its genealogical contents and in its literary position (cf. 11:26,27).

By dealing first with the nations derived from Japheth and Ham, Genesis 10 makes them the background setting for the central drama of salvation to unfold in the line of Shem-Eber-Abraham. As for the relative order of Japheth and Ham, Japheth's seniority could account for his priority. But perhaps this order was dictated by the desire to proceed from what was chronologically the most distant point to the nearest in terms of the fulfillment of the curse and blessings of the Noahic oracle. Such is, in any case, the order we have. The chapter starts with developments in Japheth's line preparatory to the more remote prospect of his receiving his blessing in the new covenant age. It then moves to Ham's line with the anticipated curse on Canaan in the intermediate, old covenant episode of the Israelite conquest, and so approaches the climactic subject of Shem's line with its promised blessing, soon to be attained in the establishment of the covenant with Abraham.

B. The Sons of Japheth

Significant in the section of "the sons of Japheth" (10:2-5) is the listing of peoples who occupied the area of Asia Minor and southeastern Europe into which the mission of the apostolic ministry of the new covenant advanced when the Lord opened the covenant tent of Shem for the entrance of the Gentiles. And the "coastlands/islands of the nations" mentioned in verse 5 reappear in later prophecy of the outreach of the messianic salvation, especially in the writings of Isaiah, who pictures these distant coasts as waiting for the Lord's deliverance, as being addressed by the Servant of the Lord and having God's glory made known to them (Isa 11:11; 24:15; 42:4; 49:1; 51:5; 60:9; 66:19; cf. Ps 72:10). Read in this light, the centrifugal power seen at work in Genesis 10 dispersing the Japhethites to their distant shores was preparing the situation to which God was going to respond in the new covenant with another centrifugal movement, this one on the part of the church of the Servant, the light of the Gentiles, sent out by great commission and thrust out by persecutions, preaching the Gospel and gathering the dispersed from the ends of the earth to their new heavenly home-focus in Christ.

C. The Sons of Ham

The list of the peoples of Canaan in the "sons of Ham" section (Gen 10:6-20) contains intimations of the eventual fulfillment of Noah's curse on Ham/Canaan, the dispossession of the Canaanites by Israel. For this list (vv.15-19) is distinctly evocative of later lists of the same groups (with some additions or omissions), in which they are described as objects of God's judgment through Israelite conquest (Gen 15:19-21; Exod 3:8,17; 13:5; 23:23; Deut 7:1; 20:17; Josh 3:10; 24:11). The earlier lists in this series (those in Genesis and Exodus) refer to these peoples as elements in the land promised to Abraham. Already implicit in that promise is the inevitable dislodgment of the previous occupants to make room for God's elect nation. This judgment on the Canaanites becomes more explicit in the last list in Exodus (23:23) and is the dominant note in all the subsequent lists in Deuteronomy and Joshua.

Further, certain non-Canaanite groups are mentioned in the Hamitic section which proved to be antagonists of Israel and incurred divine wrath and curse for this hostility to the covenant people. Egypt (Mizraim, v.6) for its oppression of Israel suffered all the affliction and humiliation that attended Israel's victorious exodus (cf. Ps 78:51). Babylonia and Assyria (vv.10,11), authors of Israel's captivity, later received God's retribution. The Philistines (v.14), after prolonged enmity against Israel, were subjugated. And the cities of the plain (v.19) were to become a classic example of God's devastating overthrow of the ungodly.

Something else emerges from the Hamitic section when we step back from the details to catch the bigger picture. Two great world centers appear: Babel and Jerusalem, the rival focus-cities afterwards highlighted in Genesis 11 and 12ff. respectively. Babel in the land of Shinar is the center of attention in the first part of this section (vv.6-14). And the second part (vv. 15-19) delineates the promised land of Canaan, with a hint of Jerusalem in its midst. As observed above, the list of Canaanite peoples in verses 15-19 foreshadows the target-lists of the Conquest, but at the same time it prophetically defines the extent and boundaries of the land destined to become the promised land of the Abrahamic Covenant, for the blessing of Shem's people Israel was to be the corollary of the curse of Canaan. In verse 19, the terminology is explicitly that of tracing boundaries. The northern boundary of Canaan is drawn to Hamath on the northeast edge (cf. Num 13:21; 34:1-8). Then the border of the land on the west is followed from the northern starting point to the southwestern limit, and thence across to the southeastern corner. Viewed in the total perspective of Genesis 10 this area lies at the center of the world-map, where there is an overlapping presence of representatives of all three of the Noahic lines. And among the peoples within the bounds of this central land the Jebusites are prominently listed (v.16). They were the inhabitants of Jerusalem before its conquest by David. Indeed, Jebus was an earlier name of that city (Judg 19:10; 1 Chron 11:4). There at Jebus-Jerusalem the Lord was to establish his typological focus-city, the redemptive restoration of Eden's cosmic mountain, over against Babel and its antichrist aspirations to be the center of the earth. So it is then that in this central, Hamitic section of Genesis 10 two rival cosmic cities stand forth conspicuously, the representative symbols of the great enmity that is the subject of biblical historiography.

D. The Sons of Shem

1. Shem and the Sons of Eber

In an introduction to the heading formula, "the sons of Shem," which stands at the beginning of the section on the third Noahic line (10:22; cf. vv.2,6), Shem is identified as "the father of all the sons of Eber" (v.21). This anticipates the division that was to occur among the Eberites (i.e., Hebrews), a division of a more fundamentally important kind, from the biblical perspective, than those ethnic, national, geographic, and linguistic differences among men noted in the Genesis 10 context. A divine choice was to be made between Eber's two sons, Peleg and Joktan (v.25), making Peleg the elect line which was to lead to Abraham and Israel and Messiah. So significant is this bifurcation of the descendants of Eber and in particular the establishment of the community of redemptive election that the two Eberite lines thus distinguished from each other are not traced within the same genealogical list. The Genesis 10 list continues with only the Eberites of the divergent line of Joktan (vv.26ff.). Treatment of the covenant line of Shem-Eber through Peleg is reserved for its own separate genealogy in Genesis 11:10-26 (cf. esp. vv.16ff.).

The introduction at Genesis 10:21 identifying Shem as father of all the Eberites prepares then not only for the immediately following account of Shem's line, but for his special covenantal genealogy in 11:10-26. The first of these passages (10:22-31) partakes of the character of Genesis 10 as a whole, which is to depict the spreading out of the major lines of mankind and so to display the world-wide network of peoples and configuration of nations. The genealogy of Shem in 11:10-26 does the opposite, narrowing the focus from the universal to the particular elect line. The sequence from Genesis 10:1-11:9, an account of the non-elect branch and world at large, to Genesis 11:10-26, a record of the covenant family, exemplifies the regular pattern for the disposition of the divergent and principal lines throughout the book of Genesis.

2. Peleg

The great division resulting from the covenantal election, which is so heavily underscored by the literary structure with its double genealogy of Shem and the anticipatory notice of Genesis 10:21, is probably what is in view in the statement about Peleg in Genesis 10:25 at the forking of the genealogical way: "The name of the one was Peleg; for in his days was the earth divided (*niplegah*)." Favoring this interpretation is the immediate setting. The statement is embedded in the text just after the declaration that Eber had two sons, with the name of Peleg before it and the name of Joktan after it, so that it divides the two. Related to the verb *plg*, "divide," is the noun *peluggah*, used for family subdivisions (2 Chron 35:5; cf. 1 Chron 1:19). On the use of "earth" for earth's population compare Genesis 11:1.

Otherwise interpreted, Genesis 10:25c refers to the Babel episode. If the verb *plg* had been used in Genesis 11:1-9, the case would be stronger, though *plg* is possibly used in Psalm 55:9(10) in allusion to that event. On this view, it would seem necessary to assume a personal involvement of Peleg's family at least, if not of Peleg himself, in the Babel event. Was he then a king? The expression "in his days" is normally used for the reign of kings or the tenure of prophets. Also, the descendants of Shem populated the Mesopotamian area and one theory regarding the name Arpachshad, the branch of Shem from which Eber came, identifies the last part of it with the name of the Chaldeans. Yet another interpretation of the explanation of Peleg's name is that it refers to the dividing of the land by irrigation canals (a meaning of the noun *peleg*). Genesis 10:25c would then be an aetiological comment attributing to Peleg's days the development of this kind of cultivation. At the same time it would note a dividing of the Eberites into a more sedentary branch (Peleg) and a more nomadic group (Joktan).

On the interpretation preferred above, Genesis 10:25 resumes the series of nomen-omen wordplays of Noah's oracle, a device that heightens the prophetic cast of these intimations of the future course of God's redemptive program. Indeed, Genesis 10:25 resumes the very theme of Noah's covenant blessing on Shem (9:26), marking the narrowing down of the elect channel of Shem-Eber (cf. 10:21) to Peleg, from whom Abraham would descend. This narrowing process continues to be a basic theme in the patriarchal narratives, where a prominent place is given to the similar division that occurred among the offspring of Abraham and then between the twin sons of Isaac. In these instances too, as in the case of Joktan in Genesis 10:25ff., the non-elect lines (of Ishmael, the sons of Keturah, and Esau) moved away from the elect community (of Isaac and Jacob) and merged back into the divergent lines traced in Genesis 10 (cf., e.g., Gen 25:1-6, 10:26-30, and 10:17, particularly Havilah, Sheba, and Dedan). Peleg's name, as explained in Genesis 10:25, celebrated a step in that elective process leading to God's choice of Jacob as the lot of his inheritance. This is the theological motif that Moses, in later retrospect (Deut 32:8,9), singled out as the paramount point of the historical developments of Genesis 10. (We shall return to examine this Deuteronomic passage more closely at the end of this chapter.)

3. The Hebrews

Shem was the father of all the Hebrews (10:21) and Noah's covenant blessing on Shem (9:26) was to be fulfilled in Shem's descendant Abraham. At an appropriate point early in the account of God's covenant dealings with him, Abraham is identified as a Hebrew (Gen 14:13). Clearly, the point is to call attention to Abraham's relationship through Eber to Shem and so to tie the Abrahamic history to the preceding redemptive history and particularly to identify it as the fulfillment of Noah's doxological blessing on Shem. In our analysis of Genesis 9:26 we noted that, soon after identifying Abraham as a Hebrew, the narrative relates how Melchizedek applied that oracular word of Noah to Abraham in a pronouncement that was itself another doxology-benediction (Gen 14:19,20). While the identification of Abraham as a Hebrew is certainly a statement about his ethnic lineage, in the Genesis context this Eber-Shem connection of Abraham is intended to signify the election of his family to become the covenant community that bore the name of God, the destiny Noah drew from the name Shem/Name. To be "the Hebrew" meant that Abraham's family was to become the nation of God's heritage, the holy theocratic kingdom separated from the common kingdoms of the divergent lines of Genesis 10. It meant they were appointed to receive the promised kingdom domain by acting as the agents of the Lord to subjugate the Canaanites. It meant that the Abrahamic Hebrews were to execute Noah's curse on Ham/Canaan. The Genesis 14 context was therefore an appropriate place to note that Abraham was a Hebrew, for in it Abraham is found engaged as a military commander inflicting a defeat on the forces representative of the world-powers as he acts to protect the interests of the covenant community in the land of Canaan.

The accomplishment of salvation, it appears, is not simply a matter of the winning of hearts. It has been from Genesis 3:14,15 onward a warfare against the devil and all his evil hosts on earth and in heaven. It is, therefore, a matter of engaging in judicial ordeals and winning battles. Salvation history features the destroying of the ungodly world in the flood and Pharaoh's army in the sea. At the heart of it is Joshua's conquering of

Canaan and Jesus' slaying of the Satan-Serpent. Only as the sequel to the execution of the redemptive judgment-curse do the saints enter upon the inheritance of Jerusalem, or New Jerusalem. And to be the instruments of God in such judgments is what it was going to mean for the Abrahamites to be Hebrews, the people of blessed Shem in the land of accursed Canaan. That too is the ministry that must at last be performed by all who are the spiritual seed of Abraham, living in a world that knows not God and to which the Lord Jesus will return in flaming fire rendering vengeance to them that obey not the gospel (2 Thess 1:7-10).

An antipathy to this consuming holiness inseparable from genuinely biblical religion accounts in no small measure for certain current sociological reconstructions of Israelite history which replace the prima facie representations of the Old Testament concerning the relation of the Israelite Hebrews to Canaan with something quite the opposite. What the Scriptures present as a movement of Israelite conquest from without is made out to be basically a Canaanite peasants' revolt from within against the oppressive hierarchical organization of the city-states. To the extent such approaches may recognize that the emergent nation Israel included, as one component, some Yahweh-worshippers from outside, that does not essentially alter their interpretation of the movement as primarily a socio-economic enterprise with egalitarian ideals. Indeed, insofar as the covenantal faith of Yahweh figures in these reconstructions, it gets submerged in or is reduced outright to this ideology of political liberation. Substitution of the temporal causes of common grace social-political concerns for the absolutely distinctive purpose and program of eternal salvation is theological confusion at a most fundamental level. Redemptive election's ultimate alignment of saved versus lost cuts across the lines of distinction between peasants and kings with perfect indifference to all such socio-economic partisanship. God's saving grace is no respecter of persons, rich or poor. Neither is his holy judgment. To identify the redemptive kingdom of the God of the Hebrews with the common causes of the city of man is a profaning of the holy, a prostitution of the gospel, a diabolical repudiation of the atonement accomplished by Jesus Christ.

Identifying the biblical Hebrews requires taking note of certain extrabiblical data that have figured significantly in studies of the origin of Israel and of Yahweh worship, including the reconstructions criticized above. As attested in the Amarna letters, one group active in Canaan when the Israelites were solidifying their hold on the territory was the Habiru (or

'Apiru), whose presence is documented all over the Near East for many centuries prior to the Conquest. Their role in Canaan was that of mercenary soldiers, probably dispatched from Syrian centers. These Habiru are, however, often interpreted as a socially disadvantaged class and as such they have been fitted into the peasants' revolt hypothesis of the origin of Israel, being equated with the Hebrews of the biblical narratives. But it is certainly mistaken to identify the Habiru of the Amarna letters with the Abrahamic Hebrews led by Joshua, whatever the possibilities might be of a more general identification of the Habiru as Hebrews in the broader sense of descendants of the Eber of Genesis 10. (One interesting fact of possible relevance is that a king Ebrum ruled at Ebla in Syria at c.2300 B.C.)

For their part, the radical reconstructionists discount the historical value of the ethnic connections outlined in Genesis 10. Proceeding from their conjectured Hebrew-Habiru equation they conclude that the twelve-tribe organization of Israelite Hebrews was not an essentially genealogical structure but a conglomerate of ethnically diverse peoples who shared a common socio-economic grievance and confederated to achieve certain political goals, traditions of the Yahweh cult being in some fashion involved in their political pact. If, however, one is prepared to accept the obvious intent of the data in Genesis 9-14, the Hebrew identity of Abraham and his descendants marks them ethnically and covenantally; ethnically as descended from Eber, and covenantally as the people of God's redemptive election. Abraham's Hebrew descent signalizes the destiny of his seed to be a royal priesthood, to conquer Canaan and establish there not an egalitarian commune in the name of humanity but the holy kingdom of God. The reconstructionists are disconcerted by the fact that their supposed egalitarian, antimonarchical activists so soon reverted to a monarchical government for themselves. As a matter of fact, the rise of the Davidic monarchy was altogether appropriate in the nation which was actually designed of God from the outset to be a prototypal symbol of the eternal kingdom and absolute sovereignty of the royal Christ.

E. Covenant Community: From Shem to Abraham

Genesis 11:10-26 has the same basic pattern as Genesis 5, a formal indication that it is resuming the theme of the covenant community, whose genealogy it in fact carries forward from Shem, son of Noah, where Genesis 5 concluded, to Abraham, son of Terah. God's faithfulness in preserving the covenant community through the prediluvian world was in evidence again after the Flood. In spite of mankind's bent to apostasy betrayed at Babel, a community of faith was being perpetuated in the earth and the history of the oracular promise of the covenant was proceeding unfailingly from Shem, recipient of the blessing-promise, to Abraham, who would be the grantee of the promised covenant. And beyond the preservation of the covenant succession in the line of Shem there was the larger goal of the Gentile restoration projected in the blessing of Japheth; the proximate particularism which we see taking effect in Genesis 11:10-26 was designed as a means to the ultimate universalism of the new covenant.

As in the case of the prediluvian line of Seth (Genesis 5), the covenant was not identified with the line of Shem exclusively or inclusively in the period covered by Genesis 11:20-26. Illustrative instances of this are, on the one hand, the piety shared with Shem by Japheth in the first generation of this period and, on other hand, the idolatry attributed to the Semitic kin of Abraham near its close. But it was among Shem's descendants that the covenant religion prospered most, continuing there in unbroken succession to Abraham's messianic line.

Covenant polity and mission in the era of Genesis 11:10-26 were also much the same as in the era from Seth to Noah. Once again the genealogical form of the record of covenant history in Genesis 11 advertises the constant familial structure of the covenant community. The families of God's people in this era too functioned in both the common and holy spheres. Shem's double genealogy dramatizes this dual status. In the genealogy of Genesis 10:21-31 the Semites are part of the common mass of Noahic humanity, dispersing and forming the kingdoms of this world. (Note also the reference to Noah's role in the development of viticulture [Gen 9:20], comparable to observations in Gen 4 concerning Cain's line.) But Shem's line in Genesis 11:10-26 is distinguished as the covenant family, heirs of the kingdom of God.

In their identity as holy covenant community they were a cultic assembly centered in the altar, which is specifically attested in the family of Noah at the beginning of this period and in the family of Abraham at its close. What was observed previously in the analysis of the Sethite community about the confessional witness entailed in the establishment and maintenance of the altar is again relevant here. And finally, covenantal mission in this era continued to involve the reception and communication of prophetic revelation.

To the covenant people the terms of the world-ordering covenant of common grace were made known (Gen 8:20ff.) and to them was revealed the future outworking of the sanctions of the Covenant of Grace in blessing and curse (Gen 9:25-27). There is also the possibly prophetic naming of Peleg (Gen 10:25). Further, such knowledge of the deliberations and activity of the divine council as is exhibited in the Genesis 11:1-9 record of the judgment on Babel is elsewhere an authenticating mark of the biblical prophets. That account should then be regarded as a tradition originally disclosed to and transmitted through the channel of the covenant community in its privileged role as bearers of the divine oracles. A similar disclosure later made to Abraham involved the revelation of God's presence in the Angel of the Lord, and conceivably that mode of theophanic revelation was a feature of the prophetic experience of God's people in the generations before Abraham.

F. A Mosaic Postscript

In the prophetic lawsuit song of Deuteronomy 32, Moses appeals to "the days of old" (v.7) as he establishes the claims of Yahweh on Israel's covenant allegiance. His reference is specifically to the origins of the nations recorded in Genesis 10: "When the Most High gave the nations their inheritances, when he divided the sons of man (*'adam*)" (v.8a). The verb *prd* used in Genesis 10:5,32 for the dividing of the nations (cf. also Gen 13:9) is found again in Deuteronomy 32:8a, and its object, "the sons of man," harks back to Genesis 11:5. This reference to God's general ordering of the nations serves as a foil for the declaration of his act of redemptive election appointing Israel as his own kingdom inheritance (Deut 32:8b,9) and so placing them under covenantal obligation to him. From this reminder of the Lord's ancient claims on Israel the lawsuit song moves on to a prophetic indictment and judgment of the Israel which would break covenant and undergo the curse of exile, and the song closes with the assurance of a final victory of redemptive judgment.

As we examine Deuteronomy 32:8,9 for its assessment of the theological significance of the historical era covered by the fourth and fifth generations-divisions of Genesis, we encounter particular difficulty in verse 8b. According to the Masoretic Hebrew text it reads: "He assigned the territories of the peoples according to the number (*lemispar*) of the sons of Israel." Since *lemispar* means "one each" or "one apiece" (see, e.g., Num 15:12; Josh 4:5,8; Judg 21:23; 1 Kgs 18:31) and seventy names are listed in the catalogue of nations in Genesis 10, attempts have been made to construe Israel as a seventy-sectioned group, as by appeal to the seventy members of Jacob's household who entered Egypt (Gen 46:27; Deut 10:22).

A satisfactory meaning is not readily yielded by the Masoretic text and most exegetes favor an alternative text (supported by LXX and a Qumran Deuteronomy fragment) which reads "sons of El (God)" instead of "sons of Israel." Some who prefer this text regard "the sons of El" as an allusion to the heavenly council of angels (as specifically read in LXX) and in order to explain the "one apiece" (*lemispar*) correspondence to the seventy nations have recourse to the seventy sons of the god El in Canaanite myth. However, a more general interpretation (and free from the mythological objection) is that God assigned over each nation a "son of El," these being understood as the heavenly "princes" of specific nations, like Persia and Greece, mentioned in Daniel 10:13,20,21 and 12:1. It would then evidently be this relationship viewed from the reverse perspective of the peoples' idolatrous worship of such gods that is referred to in Deuteronomy itself, in 4:19,20 and 29:26(25), passages linked to Deuteronomy 32:8,9 by their common use of key terminology. So understood, Deuteronomy 32:8,9 would assert the national election of Israel as God's own covenantal proprietorship (32:9; cf. Deut 4:20), with the concomitant claim to Israel's worship, and the abandonment of the other nations to the service of creature gods, heavenly princes though they were (32:8; cf. Deut. 4:19; Rom 1:21-25).

If the "sons of El" reading is adopted in Deuteronomy 32:8b, another interpretation may be suggested which takes its cue from "the sons of God (or the gods)" in Genesis 6:2, the human rulers of the prediluvian nations. It is possible that in the song of Deuteronomy 32 Moses casts his eye back over the entire history of the nations, inclusive of the prediluvian world, not just the stage introduced by Genesis 10, for he speaks not of the sons of Noah but of the sons of man (*'adam*; cf. Gen 4:1; 5:1). And in any case, we have seen that the spirit and ideology of the Genesis 6 rulers were revived in the nationalistic developments of Genesis 10 and 11. What Deuteronomy 32:8,9 says then is that for each of the national territories which God established there was a human ruler, "a son of Elohim," as a king might be called either in the sense that he was an agent of the divine justice or that he espoused the divine kingship ideology. But in distinction from these common kingdoms, Israel had God himself as its King: "Truly [or but] the portion of Yahweh is his people; Jacob is his allotted heritage [or the hill of his patrimony]," (Deut 32:9). When in his sovereign government of the peoples of the earth the Lord was organizing the authority structures of the common nations, he had already elected the Israelite descendants of Shem to theocratic status as his own holy kingdom – and had prophesied of this through the oracle of Noah (Gen 9:26).

Depending on how we understand "the sons of El," the contrast drawn here between Israel and the other nations is in terms either of the idolatrous or demon-dominated nature of those nations, or simply in terms of their common, nonholy character. Whatever one's conclusion on the difficult final phrase in Deuteronomy 32:8b, Moses is here recalling "the days of old" as a time when the ancestral line of Israel was being singled out in the midst of the diaspora of the nations for its special vocation as the Lord's holy covenant community.

Chapter Three

THE KINGDOM PROMISED IN THE ABRAHAMIC COVENANT

Redemptive history enters a distinctive new stage with the Abrahamic Covenant but without interrupting the underlying continuity and coherence of the Covenant of Grace. Retained and furthered in the Abrahamic Covenant were the same purpose and way of salvation and the same kingdom goals that characterize the historical administration of redemptive covenant from its inauguration in the revelation recorded in Genesis 3 to the consummation of the new covenant. God's covenantal transactions with Abraham stand in solid continuity with the pre-Abrahamic past and the messianic future. Whatever novelty is initiated under the terms of the Abrahamic Covenant is completely subordinated to the seamless unity of the one continuing Covenant of Grace and its one constant goal of the glory-kingdom.

In Abraham the chosen genealogical line of Shem arrives at that particular Hebrew with whom the ancient prophetic blessing pronounced by Noah on Shem begins to have its focal fulfillment (cf. Gen 14:13,19,20). The ranks of the remnant people were not at once reduced to the Abrahamic community. Fruits of God's redemptive working through pre-Abrahamic covenantal arrangements were still to be found outside the sphere of the Abrahamic Covenant. There was for a while an overlapping of the particular new Abrahamic arrangement with the previous broader covenantal order, associated especially though not exclusively with the line of Shem. That broader expression of covenant life was, however, on the wane, soon enough to disappear from the earth. To the Abrahamic administration of God's saving grace belonged the future of the redemptive realization of the kingdom of God.

The historical function of the Abrahamic Covenant as bridge between the past and future of the one unified Covenant of Grace is mirrored in the position which the account of it occupies in the literary structure of the book of Genesis. Standing in the climactic third division (Gen 11:27-25:11) of the second triad of generations-sections, that account is the capstone of the narratives of genealogical developments and prophetic declarations in the postdiluvian history (Gen 9ff.). It is at the same time the foundation-stone for the remainder of the book of Genesis, and thus for the rest of the

Bible. The remaining two pairs of generations-sections in Genesis elaborate the record of the establishment of the Abrahamic Covenant, relating its confirmation to Isaac and Jacob, and this entire account of covenant-making through the patriarchal era serves as a prelude to the history of salvation recounted in the whole subsequent revelation of the Old and New Testaments.

As simultaneously capstone and foundation stone, the Abrahamic Covenant may be contrasted with the Noahic Covenant. The latter, though similarly occupying a climactic literary position as the third of the first triad of generations-sections, was the terminal episode in the history of the world that then was. But the Abrahamic Covenant, while marking a point of arrival with respect to the developments in Genesis 9-11, possessed germinal significance for all subsequent unfolding of redemptive covenant in the world that now is. Within it were the promises that were pregnant with the whole future of God's covenantal kingdom, both its old covenant and new covenant stages. If the Abrahamic Covenant was the anticipated ripening of the fruit of the tree of covenant revelation in the line of Shem after the Flood, it was fruit that also had within it the seeds of the entire covenantal harvest to come. Agreeably, Paul, from his vantage point as apostle to the Gentiles, roots the new covenant, the final administration of redemptive history, in the Abrahamic Covenant, interpreting God's promise that all the nations would be blessed in Abraham as a preaching of the gospel to him beforehand (Gal 3:8).

In speaking here of the Abrahamic Covenant we have in view the whole complex of God's covenantal transactions with Abraham, Isaac, and Jacob. Within this comprehensive whole can be distinguished separate individual occasions of covenant ratification and confirmation (cf., e.g., Gen 15:9ff.; 17:23ff.; 28:18ff.) and repeated disclosures of the promised blessings of the covenant (cf., e.g., Gen 12:1ff.; 13:14ff.; 15:1ff.). But all of these episodes together constitute one particular administration of God's redemptive rule. Together they produced a single covenant community coherently ordered with respect to its obligations and promises, its historical mission and eschatological inheritance.

I. COVENANT OF PROMISE

Exemplified by the Abrahamic Covenant was the characteristic nature of divine covenants, for it was a commitment transaction with divine sanctioning and it functioned as an instrument of kingdom administration. Under the present heading of Covenant of Promise the commitment aspect of the Abrahamic Covenant will be prominent, especially the divine promissory commitment.

A. Divine Promise and Oath

1. Promise as Gospel-Grace

From its opening salvo of divine promises in Genesis 12 the Abrahamic Covenant confronts us with a way to ultimate human blessedness that stands in stark contrast to the method which the Babelites of Genesis 11 used to achieve their lofty ambitions. What was sought in Shinar by autonomous human effort – the restoration of cosmic-cultic focus and the great name – was bestowed on Abraham as a promissory grant. Babel was man-built, from the accursed ground up towards the heavens. The city promised to Abraham is God-built and descends from the holy heaven to man as the supernatural gift of God's grace (Heb 11:10,16; Rev 21:2,10).

Divine promise in the context of redemptive covenant connotes the principle of grace, the opposite of works. Thus, when Paul in his analysis of the Abrahamic and Mosaic covenants in Galatians 3 identifies the former as promise (v.17; cf. Eph 2:12), he sets it over against the principle of works ("law," v.18) operative in the latter, and says it is received by faith in Jesus Christ (v.22). God's promise arrangement with Abraham is made synonymous with the gospel of grace.

In Romans 4, drawing the same contrast between the works principle of the law and the gospel principle found in the promise to Abraham, Paul emphasizes the faith of Abraham by which the promise was appropriated, a feature which betokens the grace character of God's promise covenant with the patriarch. "It is of faith that it may be according to grace" (v.16). Inheritance of the promise was not through the works principle of the law (v.13), for that is contrary to the promise-grace-faith-forgiveness principle (vv.14,15; cf. vv.4-8). The promise of the kingdom was rather through the righteousness of faith (v.13; cf. v.3). If justification and kingdom inheritance are by works, the glory goes to oneself as a matter of merit and due, "but not to God" – or, as otherwise understood, "yet not against God" (v.2; cf. v.4). But in God's covenant with Abraham justification was by faith's "Amen" to God's promises (v.3; cf. Gen 15:6, on which see my "Abram's Amen," *WTJ* 31,1 (1968), 1-11). It was by believing on him who justifies the ungodly (v.5). In this promise-faith situation the glory goes to God, being a matter of his sovereign grace (vv.4,20).

By its identification with the gospel of Jesus Christ the Abrahamic Covenant is seen to be a promissory anticipation of the new covenant. It is a subadministration of the overarching Covenant of Grace, which as a whole is mediated by the Son as the one who faithfully fulfills the eternal intratrinitarian covenant, the foundation of all redemptive covenant. God's saving grace in and through Christ Jesus is thus the underlying explanation of the redemptive blessings provided through the covenant of promise to Abraham in both its old and new covenant stages of fulfillment. (We shall, however, be observing that the suretyship of Christ does not relate to the typological level of blessings under the old covenant in the way it does to the ultimate soteric realities in view in all administrations of the Covenant of Grace.)

2. Ratification Oath

Initially expressed in the form of simple promise, God's covenantal commitments to Abraham were afterwards formally heightened into oaths. Most striking of these is the episode recorded in Genesis 15, where the specifically covenantal label *berith* is first applied to the promise arrangement with Abraham. The reality denoted by *berith* had been brought into being by the covenantal call and promises of Genesis 12ff. Those promises already contained the essential substance, which subsequent disclosures merely recapitulated and elaborated. But the Genesis 15 event was the formal ratification of the covenant by oath ceremony. (This development from promise, in Gen 12, to oath, in Gen 15, is reflected in Abraham's review of the matter in Gen 24:7 in terms of God speaking to him and swearing to him, the speaking and the swearing being understood as references respectively to Gen 12:7 and 15:18).

Having reassured Abraham that he would yet become father of a line of heirs who would inherit what was promised to him (Gen 15:4,5), the Lord renewed the promise of the land (v.7). Then, in response to Abraham's desire for further corroboration, he sealed that promise with an oath (vv.9ff.). That is the meaning of the ritual of the passage through the midst of the slain and divided animals. Such rituals involving the severing of animals were common in the ratification of covenant commitments (cf. Jer 34:8ff.,18f.). They acted out the judgment-curse which the party taking the oath invoked on himself, should he violate it.

Additional features of the Genesis 15 episode suggest its oath character. An oven and torch were seen passing between the pieces (v.17) and these are mentioned in Mesopotamian documents as implements distinguishing particular kinds of oath ceremonies. There was also the manner of God's personal appearance on this occasion. His presence was manifested in the two ascending columns, one a cloud of smoke rising from the oven and the other the soaring tongue of flame from the torch. This form of theophany will be recognized as an anticipation of the double-columned cloud-and-fire revelation of the Glory-Spirit at the exodus. As we have observed above, these two pillars represented the legs of God, standing in oath stance as divine witness at the Sinai covenant-making. At the ratification of the Abrahamic Covenant they were beheld walking the way of the oath-passage.

Graphically symbolized by the slain and halved animals, soon to be consumed by the birds of prey (Gen 15:11; cf. Jer 34:20), was the curse of dereliction and destruction. To pass through the way between the rows of severed carcasses was to walk through the valley of the shadow of death. The frightful horror of this death-curse was overwhelmingly communicated to Abraham in his experience of the abyss of sleep and the terrors of unnatural darkness (cf. Job 10:21; Ps 55:4,5[5,6]). Such was the malediction that the Lord conditionally invoked upon himself.

Further light is thrown back on the significance of the Lord's walking that oath-passage by a later event which also involved a passage formed by an act of division conceived of as a slaying. That event is the exodus, the occasion of the reappearance of the theophany of the dual pillars of cloud and fire. The Scriptures represent the waters of the Egyptian sea as the Leviathan-Adversary, who was slain in the Lord's dividing of the sea and given as food to be devoured (Ps 74:13,14; cf. Isa 51:9,10; Ps 89:10). By means of this dragon imagery the demonic dimension of Egypt's hostility to God's people is intimated. Also, Israel's redemption is thereby portrayed as a re-creation event. For in ancient mythology the slaying of the dragon Sea by the hero-god is part of the "creation" episode. Thus, Marduk's conquest of Tiamat concludes with the dividing of her vast carcass into two parts, which are then used to frame the world as the waters above and below. Obviously, the identification of the dragon with the waters and the episode of the dividing in two of the vanquished monster's carcass facilitated the use of this mythological event as a figure for the exodus victory of Yahweh over the sea, as celebrated in Exodus 15.

Seen against this conceptual and symbolical background, the curse enacted in the Lord's oath-passage through the divided carcasses in Genesis 15 was one of suffering the terrors of death's destruction and undergoing the fate of the doomed Adversary. God had promised to curse the enemy who cursed Abraham (Gen 12:3; cf. Exod 23:23). No respecter of persons in his administration of justice, he would not spare himself if he, by breaking covenant, showed himself hostile to Abraham. Judge of heaven and earth, God of the oath, he would put himself under the judgment curse he had pronounced upon the satanic Serpent (Gen 3:14).

The terrible self-malediction was conditional: *if* God failed to fulfill his promise. Yet, in the final analysis, it was not merely hypothetical, not merely a contrary-to-fact protasis. Of course, he who keeps covenant forever would not break his covenant with Abraham. However, according to the revelation of the gospel of grace, the glory of the re-creation victory over the dragon involves necessarily the bruising of the heel of the champion-seed of the woman (Gen 3:15). The glory of the redemptive attainment of the kingdom inheritance comes only through the suffering of the seed of Abraham. Only through the promised individual seed who would, as suffering Servant of the Lord, be mediator of salvation to all the nations are the blessings that were covenanted by oath to Abraham secured. And that suffering Savior is the Lord of Glory. So it transpires that though the Lord would not undergo the curse of the Genesis 15 oath-ritual as a covenant-breaker, it was nevertheless only by suffering this curse that he could keep the covenant. Hence, in taking that oath he was pledging that in order to accomplish the promised redemptive re-creation of heaven and earth — and nothing less than that was envisaged in the Abrahamic Covenant — he would undertake the accursed role attributed in the familiar ancient myths to the dragon-power whom the creator-deity slew and cleft asunder.

An indication of the ultimate outworking of God's self-maledictory oath in Messiah's sacrificial death-curse was given in the nature of the animals selected for the Genesis 15 ritual. Bypassed were creatures like the donkey and young dog that are mentioned in ancient texts concerned with covenant ratification practices elsewhere. Chosen instead were the heifer, goat, and ram, the main animals designated for sacrifice at God's altar, along with the dove and pigeon, which according to Levitical regulations were suitable for private offerings. Indeed, all the circumstances of the ceremony in which these sacrificial creatures figured dramatically presaged the sacrificial sufferings to be endured by the Son of God – the darkness, the sword's violence, the broken flesh, accursed death, abandonment. God's oath-passage was a commitment to the death-passage of Jesus in the gloom of Golgotha. It was a covenant to walk the way of the Cross.

Similar to the Genesis 15 ritual was a Hittite ceremony prescribed for an army after defeat in battle. A way was prepared by arranging in rows the halved bodies of a man and three young animals (goat, dog, and pig). In front of the way was set a door, with a fire lit on either side of the entrance. After going through the midst the troops reached the bank of a river and were sprinkled with water. Here then was a cognate way-of-death ritual, with sacrificial significance, beginning with passage through an entrance way, and culminating in an, apparently, restorative sprinkling.

As we contemplate Genesis 15 and this parallel Hittite death-passage ceremony, the cultic procedure envisaged in Hebrews 10:19f. also comes to mind. Indeed, it proves to be a mutually illuminating relationship that emerges when the way through the veil in Hebrews 10:19f. is brought into connection with the prophetic way of the Cross in Genesis 15. Hebrews 10:19 speaks of a way of access, an entrance-way (*eisodos*), which leads into the holy place (the holy of holies). It is provided by (and so virtually consists in) the atoning blood of Jesus (cf. Heb 9:8,12f.). Verse 20, elaborating on this, repeats the same three elements. It refers to the new and living way (*hodos*) of access, which leads through the veil (and thus again into the presence of God's Glory) and consists in the flesh of Jesus, specifically the torn flesh, for it corresponds to the blood in verse 19. Our suggestion will be that the direct identification of the figure of the way with the flesh in verse 20 becomes readily understandable if there is an allusion here to Genesis 15.

We may get at this through the intermediate link of Jesus' own use of the concept of the way in the Gospel of John. Jesus identified himself as the way, the destination of the way being, as in Hebrews 10, the Father in the heavenly temple (John 14:4,6). From the context it is clear that Jesus is the way particularly by virtue of his walking the way of the Cross, the way of his broken body and his blood shed to ratify the covenant. Because he who is the way is also the resurrection and life (John 11:25) that way to the Glory-Presence in the holy of holies, though the way of the death of the Cross, is a "living way" (Heb 10:20). Also found in the Gospel of John is another self-identification of Jesus as the door (10:7,9), an image closely related to the way and like the latter interpreted in terms of Jesus' sacrificial death (10:11,15,17,18). Correspondingly, in Hebrews 10 the way is a way through an entrance, a doorway. (Here we also recall the door set before the way in the Hittite soldiers' ritual. Incidentally, in both the Hittite ritual and the Hebrews 10 imagery, passage through the entrance-way is accompanied by an act of purificatory sprinkling [cf. Heb 10:22]).

Now, the Genesis 15 death-passage is, as we have seen, prophetically a way of the Cross. Like the way in the Gospel of John and Hebrews 10, this oath-ritual involves the broken flesh and shed blood of an act of covenant ratification. And in this Genesis 15 ritual the flesh quite literally constituted the way, for the animal carcasses were not merely broken but ordered in rows that created a pathway between. That, we suggest, is the background image that explains the direct identification of the flesh as the way in Hebrews 10:20. The "flesh" referred to there is the divided flesh that forms the sides of the way. It is the rent flesh of Christ that accounts for the rending of the veil (Matt 27:51; Mark 15:38; Luke 23:45), the tearing apart of the entrance barrier which results in the creation of a way of access to God's Presence. And thus the flesh is tantamount to the way. Even on the alternative exegesis which regards the flesh as the veil, the image would be specifically that of the rent veil (which is in effect the opened way). Hence it would be Christ's flesh as torn (Heb 9:12) that was identified as this divided veil, or way.

The concept of the way in the words of Jesus and in Hebrews 10:19f. can be traced back beyond Genesis 15 to Genesis 3. Driven out of the sanctuary of God because of his breaking of the covenant, man found himself everywhere barred from access back into that holy garden by the fiery sword of the cherubim agents of the Glory-Spirit, wielded all around (Gen 3:24). This was the barrier that was later represented by the veil before the holy of holies in Israel's sanctuary, made of flame colored material with cherubim figures wrought into it (Exod 26:31ff.; cf. my *Images of the Spirit*, p.44) and having the way of approach to it and through it to the Glory-Presence guarded by the altar sword of sacrifice. For outcast Adam and Eve entrance into the holy Presence in Eden was only by way of the judgment sword of the Glory-Spirit and his *parousia* hosts. Only by a death-passage could access be gained to the tree of life. It was this "way of the tree of life" of Genesis 3:24 that was the original of the way of the Cross travelled by "the way, the truth, and the life."

Relating Genesis 3:24 to Genesis 15, the striking fact is highlighted that it was his own judgment of the flaming sword that the Glory-Spirit was summoning against himself in traversing the oath-passage to ratify the Abrahamic Covenant.

3. Confirmatory Oaths

There is a recurrence of the sacrificial cutting symbolism of the Genesis 15 oath ritual on the occasion of a later divine oath to Abraham. Once again and more directly the scene conveys the idea that the divine commitment is to the way of the Cross. Abraham had complied with God's directions to prepare the altar on the mount of Moriah and to proceed with the slaying and offering there of Isaac, his only and beloved son (Gen 22:1ff.). Intervening as Abraham laid hold of the sacrificial knife, the Lord had provided the ram as a substitute offering in Isaac's place. Thereupon, the Lord swore by himself that he would surely perform the full complement of covenant promises, culminating in the gospel promise of the blessing of the nations through Abraham's seed (Gen 22:15-18). Interpreted in its setting, this oath was a commitment by God not to spare his own Son but to deliver him up as our sacrificial substitute (Rom 8:32).

Genesis 22 clarifies and supplements the message of the Genesis 15 oath concerning the divine passage through the sacrificial way of the rent flesh. In itself, as dramatized in the slaughtered beasts whose parted flesh produced the oath-passage of the Genesis 15 ritual, that way was one of death. But God's ratification oath to Abraham (as illuminated by the Gen 22 oath) was in effect a commitment that the messianic Son would pass through that way, and as undergone by the Son, to whom the Father appointed to have life in himself (John 5:26), the way of death is transformed into the way to the Father and thus becomes the way to eternal life. Such it is for all who hear his word and, like Abraham (Gen 15:6), believe on the Father who sent him (John 5:24; 6:40,47), even for those who identify with the Son in his passage through that way, partaking by faith of his flesh (which is the way), given for the life of the world (John 6:51,54).

An instance of the fulfillment of this promise of God's redemptive presence with his people in their undergoing of the judgment is found on the typological level at the exodus. Israel must negotiate a way through the sea. They were faced with a passage through Leviathan, the death power. How fearsome a power of death he was would be demonstrated when the

Egyptian forces, venturing this passage, were overwhelmed and their carcasses were washed up on the shore as a feast for the vultures (Exod 14:30). But this death-passage was transformed for God's people into a path of life. What had been an impassable barrier became an open entrance, a way of access to the promised kingdom. For the Lord their God led them through as a flock by the hand of Moses and Aaron (Ps 77:16-20[17-21]). The Glory-Spirit of the Genesis 15 death-passage, the Creator-Spirit who of old had divided and bounded the mighty waters in preparation for earth's original paradise, was present with Israel on its way to the paradise of Canaan (Exod 13:21,22). In their behalf he encountered the sea, that devouring dragon of death, and swallowed him in victory. He slew Leviathan and divided his flesh, so turning death's flooding depths into a way of resurrection and salvation, a processional way of triumph to the mountain of God.

Taken together the oaths of Genesis 15 and 22 were God's commitment to bring deliverance to his people in their ruinous liability as covenant-breakers under the curse of his sword of judgment. Hope was afforded in the sworn promise that the Lord himself would shoulder the burden of their liabilities and undergo this judgment for them. He would traverse the death-passage, changing it for them into the way of life.

Referring particularly to the Genesis 22 episode, Hebrews 6:13ff. explains that a divine oath was added to the promises of the Abrahamic Covenant as a second immutable commitment of the Lord, given to strengthen the faith-assurance of the heirs of the covenant. Surely such was the purpose of the original ratification oath of Genesis 15, as well as of the Genesis 22 oath which confirmed it. Once the covenant was formally intensified from promise to oath, the force of the oath continued to adhere to it in subsequent renewals. Psalm 105:8-10 joins the successive renewals of the Abrahamic promises to Isaac and Jacob into an extended, unified transaction of establishing a single oath-covenant. The renewal to Isaac (Gen 26:3,4) is said to have been sworn by God to him (Ps 105:9), though it is recorded in the form of simple promise (the purpose of fulfilling the oath to Abraham being, however, expressly stated therein). The renewals to Jacob (Gen 28:13-15; 35:11,12), though not accompanied by oath ritual or designated as oath by an introductory formula, do begin with God's self-designation by name (28:13; 35:11) and this gives them an oath character (see Ezek 20:5; cf. Exod 6:2,6,8).

B. Divine Promise and Divine Sovereignty

Since all God's covenants from the beginning are administrations of his kingship, they are all exercises of his royal sovereignty. Considerable emphasis falls on the divine sovereignty in the revelation of God's grace in the promises of the Abrahamic Covenant. There is the sovereignty of divine purpose expressed in election to the covenant and its promised blessings and the sovereignty of divine power displayed in the supernaturalism of the performance of the word of promise.

1. Sovereign Election

In the earliest prophetic disclosure of the redemptive program in Genesis 3:15 it was announced that there would be a divinely determined division within fallen mankind. A people of God and his Christ would be separated from a people of the Serpent. As the Genesis narrative proceeds we discover that this individual election to salvation is characterized by a constant historical continuity through the succession of generations. Actualization of the election is manifested in the appearance and preservation of a covenant community, whose history is chronicled in a genealogical form (Gen 5). The individual election constitutes the proper continuing core of the covenant but is not coextensive with its genealogical parameters.

The sovereign partitioning that is ever at work dividing mankind as a whole was dramatically externalized in the separation of the ark-community from the rest of the world for deliverance from the flood-judgment. And within the covenant household of Noah the fact that covenant is a broader circle than the election was in evidence. Then in the postdiluvian era this pattern of covenant and election continued. Selection of the branch of the covenant people that would lead to Israel, and through Israel to Messiah, became a most significant aspect of the election process in this period between Noah and Abraham (Gen 9:26; 10:21; 11:14ff.).

The several aspects of election observed in pre-Abrahamic times are found again in the revelation of election in the period of the patriarchs Abraham, Isaac, and Jacob.

Individual election to salvation was part, at least, of what was signified in the call of Abraham and in the appointment of Isaac and Jacob as his patriarchal successors. Indeed, the divine preference for Jacob over Esau made known in the prebirth disclosure is interpreted by Paul in Romans 9 as a double predestination, as an individual election of the one and an individual reprobation of the other.

In this Romans 9 context the apostle is dealing with the problem that would arise in the mind of some as to how God's identity as keeper of his covenant promises could be maintained in the face of the failure of the Israelite community as a whole to enter into the blessings of the new covenant. A two-level structure of the meaning and realization of the promises of the Abrahamic Covenant is presupposed in Paul's answer to that problem. First, there was the level of the typological kingdom of Israel under Moses in the old covenant. In terms of this temporary level of fulfillment all the Israelites were the promised seed, numerous as the sand of the seashore, and their occupation of Canaan was a fulfillment of the land promise (cf. 1 Kgs 4:20,21). But the promises also possessed a second, abiding level of meaning, which in its spiritual aspects found realization even in the patriarchal period, as well as in the old covenant era (here, along with the typological level fulfillment), and which under the new covenant comes to fulfillment in every respect in the antitypical, eternal kingdom of righteousness and peace in the Spirit.

Viewing the promises at this permanent and true (i.e., not merely symbolic) level of meaning, Paul argues that not all the natural descendants of Abraham constituting the Israelite people were the intended seed of promise (Rom 9:6-8). Abraham's promised seed in this sense, according to Paul, is to be identified as Christ and those who are in Christ by faith (Gal 3:16,29), including believers from among the Gentiles (Rom 9:24-26; Gal 3:29). And this believing seed of Abraham, he observes, was ever only a remnant within Israel, a remnant according to the election of grace (Rom 11:5), an individual election within the national election (Rom 11:2,28). Only this spiritual seed of Abraham was intended as the promised seed at the level of Christ's kingdom in the Spirit. Therefore, God's promise had not failed in the falling away in unbelief of the others, the promise not having had reference to them in the first place. As for the seed actually promised to Abraham, the true children of God (Rom 9:8), the elect heirs of the righteousness which is by faith in Jesus Christ (Rom 9:30f.; 11:7), the promise had been unfailingly fulfilled. They had been present in unbroken continuity throughout Israel's history, an elect remnant from within the total covenant community, sovereignly produced by the Creator-Potter. Illustrative evidence of this is cited from the patriarchal period (Rom 9:7-

13), the days of Elijah, Isaiah, and Hosea (Rom 9:25ff.; 11:2-4), and Paul's own day (Rom 11:5).

Now this being the context and rationale of the appeal made in Romans 9:7-13 to God's choice of Isaac and Jacob as over against Ishmael and Esau, it follows as an ineluctable conclusion that the apostle saw in this selection of Isaac and Jacob from within the broader covenant family instances of individual election to the eternal righteousness and kingdom of God in Christ. By the same token, the reverse side of this act of election, the rejection of Ishmael and Esau, must be seen as signifying ultimate reprobation. In the case of Ishmael there is further evidence of such an assessment on Paul's part in Galatians 4:29. In the case of Esau, the Romans 9 context itself cites the prophetic declaration of the subservience of Esau to Jacob (v.11; cf. Gen 25:23). That divine utterance resumed the imagery of the curse on Ham-Canaan in Noah's oracle (Gen 9:25-27), which in turn resumed the curse formula of Genesis 3:14 directed against Satan, and thus it appears that the absolute sanction of eternal reprobation is involved in this entire series.

Theological interests are at work in Romans 9-11 beyond the identification of the election in Christ as a remnant within the total covenant community of Israel, particularly an interest in the sovereign nature of the divine grace and power that provide the righteousness of God and bring to pass the promised blessings of the covenant. The histories of Isaac and Jacob appealed to by Paul as instances of individual election within the broader covenant were doubly apt because they also exemplified this further truth concerning God's sovereign majesty. Isaac's case illustrated the involvement of the divine power in the production of the seed of promise (Rom 9:7b-9); and Jacob's case, the fact that the blessing was gained not by works but according to the sovereign purpose of God's grace (Rom 9:10-12; cf. 11:5). We shall return to these themes below but first must take note of another dimension of the patriarchal election besides the appointment to salvation.

A peculiarity of the election of the three patriarchs who stand at the head of the history of the Abrahamic Covenant is that their personal election to eternal blessings coincided with the selection of their genealogical line as the one that would issue in Israel and Messiah. At this historical juncture, genealogical divisions of major import for the redemptive program were occurring, comparable to the earlier division when Peleg was chosen over

Joktan as the line leading to Abraham (Gen 10:25). As a result, the individual election of the patriarchs, in itself a less perceptible fact, came to more observable expression in the corporate history of their descendants. In that typological national history their individual election was written large and was publicly demonstrated.

Thus the individual election of Jacob and reprobation of Esau came into clear historical visibility, on the one hand, in the national election of the people Israel to constitute the holy theocracy in Canaan under the old covenant and, on the other hand, in the inveterate enmity displayed by the Edomite nation descending from Esau against this typological kingdom of God. Because Israel's national election evidenced the reality of Jacob's individual election, Paul, in Romans 9:13, could cite Malachi 1:2b,3a as confirmatory of the individual election of Jacob, even though in that passage Malachi points to the history of the Israelite and Edomite nations (vv.3b,4) in explanation of the Lord's love for Jacob and his hatred of Esau.

This love-hate idiom used by Malachi expresses emphatic preference for one person or thing over another. It can be applied to a situation where the nonpreferred party is not hated in the psychological sense (Gen 29:30-33; cf. Matt 6:24; Luke 16:13 and Matt 10:37; Luke 14:26). From this we should not, of course, conclude that in this idiom the meaning of hate, in and of itself, is to love to a lesser degree and then make that determinative of one's exegesis of Romans 9:13. What is entailed in the act of preference thus denoted depends on the particular context. In a letter written by a Canaanite vassal to his covenant overlord, the Egyptian pharaoh, we find a complaint that the suzerain is doing the reverse of what his treaty commitments call for, namely, to love his vassal and to hate the enemy, who is not in treaty relationship with him. Here, love and hate are polar opposites, signifying respectively to protect and to oppose. It is this treaty usage of love-hate that is reflected in Malachi 1:2b,3a and Romans 9:13. And in the case of the election-love of Jacob and reprobation-hate of Esau, God's hatred of Esau does involve ultimately that holy revulsion that is directed against accursed Satan, his demonic hosts, and his human seed.

The prominent theme of the election of the patriarchs highlights the sovereignty of God's purposes of grace made known in the promises of the Abrahamic Covenant. In the pre-birth announcement of God's choice of Jacob over his elder twin brother the principle of the sovereignty of redemptive grace according to the divine purpose alone is most unmistakably manifested (cf. Rom 9:11,12). This sovereignty of grace was the solid guarantee of the proferred blessings of the covenant of promise. Informed as it was by the election determined beforehand in heaven, the covenant with Abraham was clearly an outworking of that foundational intratrinitarian covenant of eternity, according to which Christ becomes surety for the elect given him by the Father. Here is absolute sovereignty assuring the fulfillment of the covenant promises, at each stage in accordance with the stipulated terms.

With respect to the antitypical level of fulfillment, realization of the eternal kingdom was a simple matter of pure sovereign grace and would be infallibly accomplished. At the typological level, however, it was more complicated. According to God's promise rightly understood, the old covenant kingdom was only provisional. The sovereignty of God's promise assured the development of the Abraham-Isaac-Jacob line into the people Israel who should experience the national election to become the holy kingdom in the promised land and so continue until Christ should come of them as to the flesh. But there was no guarantee of an unbroken continuance of this privileged national status within the premessianic period nor of a harmonious transition to the messianic, antitypical phase of the kingdom. For in the old covenant, which articulated the national election, it was stipulated that tenure in the enjoyment of the theocratic kingdom was predicated on national fidelity to the Lord. In this restricted sense and sphere a principle of works was introduced under the law economy. Unlike the individual election, which was purely a matter of God's grace in Christ, the surety, the national election could, therefore, be lost. Or, coming at the matter from the opposite direction, the very fact that God finally repudiated the elect nation by desolating judgment compels us to recognize that a principle of works had been injected into the typological phase of fulfillment under the old covenant.

Sovereign individual election defines the intention of the covenant promises at their ultimate meaning level – that is Paul's defense of God's covenant-keeping in the face of Israel's loss of national election. "It is not as though God's word had failed. For not all who are descended from Israel are Israel" (Rom 9:6, NIV). While the sovereignty of divine purpose manifested in election guaranteed the fulfillment of the promises, the election limited the intended beneficiaries of the promises at the antitypical, messianic level. Not all who were of covenant status were children of the promise, chosen according to the purpose of grace. The eternal promise commitment to Abraham coincided not with the bounds of the community established by the Abrahamic Covenant but with the bounds of the Father's commitment to the Son as second Adam in the prior covenant in heaven, the commitment to give him the elect people for whom he should become surety. This equation of the promises to Christ with those to Abraham finds expression in Paul's statement that the promises were spoken to Abraham and to his seed, Christ (Gal 3:16). Promise, in its true and final meaning, coincides with election and election is a narrower circle within the broader circle of the covenant as historically administered. Covenant of promise is covenant of grace and the identification of promise with election signalizes the sovereignty of that grace.

2. Supernatural Execution

Confidence in the fulfillment of the promises of the covenant was further buttressed by the sovereignty of the power possessed by the Promiser. A major theme in the patriarchal narratives is the supernatural overcoming of obstacles that stood in the way of the realization of the promises, particularly the obstacles hindering the appearance of the promised seed in the line leading to Christ.

Isaac's birth is the supreme example of this motif, though it appears again in the case of Jacob, who is born only after Rebekah has experienced a time of barrenness (Gen 25:21). The narratives covering Abraham's life are in fact dominated by the theme of the prolonged delay in the acquiring of the crucial first son of promise, the necessary beginning if there was to be a messianic line of descendants at all and thus a possibility of the fulfillment of the promises of the covenant as a whole.

Even before the covenantal call of Abraham is described, the barrenness of Sarah is mentioned (Gen 11:30), preparing the reader for the series of natural, human difficulties that were long to frustrate Abraham's hope of the promised son, until at last that hope could be realized only by the Lord's supernatural intervention. Sarah's barrenness continued past childbearing age (Gen 17 and 18; Rom 4:19; Heb 11:11). Abraham's policy of concealing his wife's true identity in royal court situations threatened his loss of her altogether (Gen 12:11ff; 20:2ff). Alternative avenues by which Lot or Eliezer or Ishmael would serve instead of a son by Sarah proved unacceptable (Gen 13, 15, and 16). Some hundred years old, Abraham himself was for purposes of procreation as good as dead (Rom 4:19; Heb 11:12). Every human strategy had been defeated and human resources of strength were utterly exhausted. Only then was the promise fulfilled, the child given, the son born to the barren and dead, the Lord visiting Sarah as he had said and doing unto her as he had spoken (Gen 21:1). It took sheer supernaturalism (cf. Gen 18:14). And thereby the truth was indelibly registered that the God of promise is sovereign in power to accomplish what is impossible according to nature in order to fulfill the redemptive hope of his covenant (cf. Matt 19:26; Mark 10:27; Luke 18:27). Here is the basis for Zion's faith and assurance (cf. Isa 51:2; 54:1).

Beyond the account of Isaac's birth, God's sovereignty of power in performing his covenant of promise continues as a central theme in Genesis 22, now mirrored in the faith response of Abraham to the dilemma posed by the prospect of Isaac's death. To sacrifice Isaac as the Lord commanded would seem to extinguish the promised messianic line which had been identified with Isaac as the seed of promise. But had not God given Isaac to Abraham and Sarah as a life out of their deadness in the first place? Accordingly, on Moriah Abraham's faith laid hold on God as the omnipotent One, sovereign in power in this new crisis of covenant-keeping, the One able to do the impossible as this proved necessary to his purpose of grace, able even to raise up a slain Isaac from the altar to father the next son of promise (Heb 11:19).

In Galatians 4 Paul identified the principle operative in the birth of Isaac as "promise" (v.23) and "Spirit" (v.29), in contrast to the "flesh" principle (v.29) that produced Ishmael. And he correlates this contrast with that between the grace of the gospel of freedom in Christ and the works principle that brings into bondage (vv.21ff.). In its historical-covenantal context, the divine supernaturalism so dramatically accented in the Abrahamic narratives is, therefore, expressive of the character of the covenant as one of promise. It is a manifestation of the sovereignty of God's saving grace.

Within the Abrahamic narratives the divine designation El Shaddai makes its first appearance (Gen 17:1; cf. 28:3; 35:11; 43:14; 48:3; 49:25). Its special association with revelation in the patriarchal era is specifically noted by the Lord when directing Moses in his mission of fulfilling the covenant with the patriarchs (Exod 6:3). This El Shaddai name would be a quite specific index of the central significance of the theme of God's sovereign omnipotence in the record of the patriarchal age if the LXX translators were on the right track in rendering it "the almighty (or sufficient) One."

Among current contending etymologies of Shaddai one relates it to a term for mountain; another, to a term for field. If Shaddai is understood as the One of the mountain, the reference would be to God as the One whose presence crowned the mountain of God in Eden, the Glory-Spirit who was omnipotently active in the creation of the world and had appeared to Abraham at the covenant ratification (Gen 15). In the Exodus 6 context, the point would be that this El Shaddai would appear again in the mission of Moses to effect the typological redemptive re-creation. Henceforth, however, his Yahweh name was to be his predominant covenantal designation. Its significance, the Present One, would remind the people that the Presence on the heavenly mountain was omnipotently present with them as their covenantal provider and physician, defender and deliverer.

C. Sovereign Grace and Human Obligation

The promised kingdom blessings would unfailingly be realized to the full extent of the divine commitment. That was guaranteed by the sovereignty of the divine power working according to God's sovereign purpose of grace. At the same time a conditionality of human responsibility necessarily entered into the stipulated terms of the covenant of promise. This conditionality did not negate the guarantee of kingdom fulfillment nor did the obligations enjoined contradict the pure gospel principle of grace that governed the bestowal of the eternal redemptive blessings. Imposition of such requirements in the Abrahamic Covenant is directly expressed in various divine commands, obedience to which is explicitly related to the reception of the promised blessings. Further, though the covenant was based on the suzerain's oath-commitment of sovereign grace, oaths and vows were also taken by the patriarchs and these too reflect the existence of the vassal-obligations.

1. Stipulated Demands

Abraham's call, the initial revelation of the covenant, confronted him as a demand (Gen 12:1), an imperative to which the promises were attached (Gen 12:2,3). It was only as Abraham responded in obedience to the command of God's call that he could enter into the hope offered in the promises. This is not to say that the promised heavenly inheritance was to be secured by the works principle, that is, on the ground of obedience. It does mean that the divine promises of the covenant never existed apart from human obligations.

God's call to Abraham may be likened to Jesus' call to discipleship, the familiar summons to "follow me" (Matt 8:22; 9:9; 19:21; Mark 2:14; Luke 5:27; John 1:43; etc.). Abraham was to set out on a journey following after the Lord who would lead the way to the land he would show his servant. For the disciples of Jesus, following him was associated with his identity as the way, as the One who through his death and resurrection leads his followers to the Father and everlasting life (John 13:36-14:6). Similarly, in the journey Abraham undertook when called out of Ur of the Chaldees, he must follow the Lord in the way of the death-passage that leads to resurrection, as he later learned from the episodes of Genesis 15 and 22.

Succinct as it was, God's opening summons to Abraham to follow him was a declaration of the requirements of covenant life in all the breadth and depth of their demands. Covenantal discipleship under the authority of the Lord Jesus is a denial of self and a following after him on the way of the cross (cf. Matt 10:38; 16:24; Mark 8:34; 10:21; Luke 9:23). It means turning from all idols to serve the Lord (John 12:26; 1 Thess 1:9), leaving home and family for the Lord's sake (Mark 10:28f.; Luke 18:28f.; cf. Luke 5:11; 9:59; 14:26). This was quite literally what God's call required of Abraham: "Leave your country, your people and your father's household" (Gen 12:1, NIV). And judging from Joshua's description of that household (Josh 24:2f.; cf. Gen 29ff., esp. 35:2-4) God's call was a demand that Abraham separate himself from idolatry in order to commit himself in covenantal service to Yahweh. Once we see that the calling of the disciples by the Lord Jesus at the outset of the new covenant was a resumption of his covenantal calling of Abraham of old, we can appreciate more fully the broad scope and significance of the command with which the revelation of the Abrahamic Covenant began. What Genesis 12:1 amounts to is the fundamental and comprehensive law to love the Lord God perfectly.

Obligations are explicitly imposed again in the instituting of the covenant sign of circumcision in Genesis 17. Immediately after the preamble-like self-identification of the Lord as El Shaddai and before any statement of the promises, Abraham's responsibilities are stipulated, once more in concise summary fashion: "Walk before me and be perfect" (v.1b). This terminology matches that used in ancient covenants of grant for the basic obligation to display integrity in allegiance and fidelity in service, the kind of conduct that would meet with the royal approval and reward. Genesis 17:1b is then a general, comprehensive formulation of the law of the covenant of promise. Also included in the Genesis 17 context is the specific standing requirement of the observance of circumcision as a sign of the covenant (vv.9-14).

Further, the presence of human obligation as a component of the covenant of promise is reflected in the attention given in the Genesis narratives to the theme of Abraham's obedience. Hebrews 11:8 observes that it was by faith that Abraham went forth at his call to follow the Lord on the way to the unknown inheritance, but it also styles this manifestation of trust an act of obedience. James appeals to the characterization of Abraham as the "friend" of God (Jas 2:23; cf. 2 Chr 20:7; Isa 41:8) in illustration of his thesis that obedience attests to the validity of confessed faith. Above we have noted that "friend" (or "lover") is treaty terminology for the faithful vassal, so that applied to Abraham it described him as one who obeyed God's commandments. Particularly in view was Abraham's compliance with the ultimate special requirement that he offer up Isaac (Gen 22:2).

Genesis 22:16 and 26:5 are relevant here as statements affirming a causal relationship between Abraham's obedience and fulfillment of the promises. We shall be returning to these texts under a related heading below, but the surprising terminology of Genesis 26:5 should be noticed at this point: "Abraham obeyed my voice and kept my charge, my commandments, my statutes, and my laws." That the characteristic phraseology used for the covenant stipulations in the Mosaic law could be thus applied to the life of Abraham shows that obligations were as natural and integral an element of the Abrahamic Covenant as they were in the Sinaitic and Deuteronomic covenants.

Perhaps the most eloquent testimony to this, however, is the Lord's declaration in Genesis 18:19 that righteousness and justice were the fruits he sought in entering into special covenantal relationship with Abraham. Indeed, this reproduction of his own ethical perfection (note the contextual stress on God's justice, v.25) was inseparable from the realization of the covenant promises (v.19b). Was not this perfecting of the *imago Dei* the very goal of the covenant?

2. Vows of Consecration
Solemn declarations of commitment to the Lord made by the patriarchs were another evidence of the dimension of human obligation in the Abrahamic Covenant. Such oaths of allegiance were appropriate to the fundamental Lord-servant structure of the arrangement. Though a

covenant of promise, governed by a principle of divine grace guaranteed by a remarkable divine ratification oath, this covenant was nonetheless an administration of the kingdom rule of God and could not but place the holy demands of the King of heaven upon his subjects. In the patriarchs' asseverations of loyalty they personally submitted to the suzerain-vassal relationship, pledging themselves in commitment of faith to the covenantal service of the Lord of grace.

It was apparently in connection with the solemnities conducted by Melchizedek, priest of El Elyon (Gen 14:18-20), that Abraham swore the oath to Yahweh, El Elyon, which he afterwards mentioned to the king of Sodom (Gen 14:22). More specifically, that oath would have accompanied Abraham's giving of the tithe of the victory spoils to Melchizedek (Gen 14:16,20; cf. Heb 7:1-4). It articulated the meaning of the tithe as a tribute acknowledging the lordship of Yahweh, El Elyon, and pledged devotion to him as Suzerain-Protector. Since the prerogative of determining the disposition of a vassal's battle spoils belonged to his suzerain, Abraham did not permit the king of Sodom to assume that role (Gen 14:21-24). For Abraham to accept the king's offer to act as benefactor (cf. Luke 22:25) would have been a contradiction of his oath of allegiance to the Lord God.

Covenantal vow is again related to tributary tithe in Jacob's pledge in Genesis 28:22. This came in response to Yahweh's confirmation of Jacob's position in the succession of covenant patriarchs and the promise to be his Protector-Provider (vv.13-15). Jacob vowed that as the Lord thus performed the role of covenant God to him (vv.20,21) he would assume the obligations of serving the Lord in the confessional erection of a cultic center and the tributary rendering of tithe (v.22). In the eventual fulfilling of this vow, Jacob, like Abraham in obedience to his call, must undertake a journey, following in the way of discipleship as the Lord directed him, out of the idolatrous context of Laban's household, back to the promised land, to Bethel and the service of the living God (cf. Gen 31:13; 35:1ff.).

3. Circumcision Oath

Vow of consecration becomes itself a stipulated obligation of the Abrahamic Covenant in the appointing of the ordinance of circumcision [On this subject see further my *By Oath Consigned* (1968), of which the present discussion is a résumé involving some revision.]

The first two verses of the account of the institution of circumcision in Genesis 17 present the scene (a theophany) and the Lord's opening words, which contain a summary of the remainder of this revelation. The Lord begins with his self-identification, the customary preamble in such covenantal promulgations, and a demand stating the covenant servant's fundamental duty of sincere allegiance (v.1). Then, in verse 2, the two subjects are mentioned that will alternate as theme of the four following sections that comprise the rest of Genesis 17. One of these is the promises of the covenant, the multiplication of Abraham's posterity being specifically cited as the most relevant promise at this point (v.2b). The other subject is the circumcision requirement about to be imposed. Though not designated by name here in verse 2a, circumcision is what is referred to when God speaks of a *berith* which he is going to give (*nathan*).

Genesis 17:3-21, containing the remainder of God's speech, is divided into three parts marked by a speech formula at verses 3, 9, and 15, with the particular theme of each section indicated as they are introduced in turn by "as for me" (v.3), "as for you" (v.9), and "as for Sarai, your wife" (v.15). Verses 3-8 review the covenant as already revealed and ratified, with some further specification of the promises. By way of confirmation the Lord assigns Abram the new name of Abraham (v.5) and declares that the divine commitments of this covenant of promise will be fulfilled (v.7). The second section, verses 9-14, deals with the appointment of circumcision, which is identified as a sign of God's covenant. Then, the two themes of the promise and circumcision alternating, verses 15-21 return to the promises with a more particular disclosure concerning the birth of Isaac as the seed of promise. Finally, after the close of the divine discourse, the theme of circumcision is resumed in Genesis 17:22-27. Here it is related that the circumcision ordinance was performed by Abraham and his household, as God had commanded.

In this passage *berith* is used in two ways. In vv. 4,7,19 (cf. 14) it refers to the covenant of promise, the Abrahamic Covenant, as a whole. But the *berith* in vv. 10 and 13 is explicitly identified as circumcision. This should not mislead us into regarding circumcision as a separate covenant in itself alongside the Abrahamic Covenant. For the full-orbed designation of circumcision found in v. 11 is actually *'oth berith*, "sign of the covenant." Clearly then circumcision is to be subsumed as a subordinate part under the previously established Abrahamic Covenant, in the course of whose administration it was promulgated. It was a confirmatory sign of that covenant, and as a prominent part of the berith it could be designated *berith*, *pars pro toto* (vv. 10,13).

Instructive for the interpretation of what is said about circumcision in Genesis 17 are the parallel data found in the case of the Sabbath ordinance. Like circumcision, the Sabbath is designated covenant (*berith*) and everlasting covenant (Exod 31:16; Isa 56:4,6; cf. Gen 17:13), a covenant to be observed (Exod 31:14; cf. Gen 17:10). And the Sabbath is, of course, not a separate covenant standing over against the old covenant ratified at Sinai. Rather it is a seal of that covenant, a sign of the covenant relationship, as is shown by the fact that the Sabbath, like circumcision, is designated an *'oth* (Exod 31:13,17; Ezk 20:12). It is as a confirmatory sign representative of the old covenant that the Sabbath, like circumcision, is at times called simply *berith*. Comparable too is Jesus' identification of the cup of the communion supper as "the new covenant in my blood" (Luke 22:20; 1 Cor 11:25), though that supper is but one element, one sacramental ordinance, of the new covenant.

Genesis 17:2a is then not the announcement of the making of a separate new covenant but simply of the confirming of the existing Abrahamic Covenant by a sign. Indeed, the verb *nathan* found in verse 2a is not used elsewhere for making or ratifying covenants but, precisely as here, for the appointing of covenantal signs of confirmation. Thus, the appointment of the rainbow as a sign (*'oth*, Gen 9:12ff.) of the common grace covenant is denoted by *nathan* (Gen 9:12,13). So also is the assignment of the sabbath as a sign of the Mosaic Covenant (Ezek 20:12; cf. Exod 16:29). (Also to be considered in this connection is the statement that the servant of the Lord is given as a covenant of the people [Isa 42:6; 49:8].)

What then is the symbolic meaning of circumcision? As a covenantal knife or cutting rite, circumcision is quite obviously to be understood, like the dismembering ritual in Genesis 15 − it portrays the curse inflicted by the sword of God's judgment. This becomes explicit in Genesis 17:14. For when it says there that the one who breaks the covenant by failure to observe the circumcision obligation will be cut off, there is an unmistakable interpretive allusion to the act of circumcision. Accordingly, circumcision symbolized excision from the covenant. It threatened too the cutting off of descendants. So one concludes from the contextual concern with the blessing of descendants (v.2ff) and the fact that circumcision was an operation on the organ of generation. Moreover, loss of posterity was a familiar item in the ancient curse repertoire.

Covenantal cutting rites accompanied oaths of commitment, their function being to depict impressively the judgment that would be inflicted by the oath deity on the one who violated his commitment. In the case of circumcision the oath was a response to the Lord's comprehensive demand for covenantal devotion and service (Gen 17:1b,2a). It was an avowal of Yahweh as covenant Lord, a commitment in loyalty to him. Agreeably, Jeremiah commands Israel to "circumcise yourselves to the Lord" (Jer 4:4). In Leviticus 19:23-25 the consecratory import of circumcision is illustrated in a figurative application of the idea to fruit trees. Only in their fourth year did their fruit become "holy;" for the first three years it was "uncircumcised." Thus, the circumcision of the tree would consist in its becoming consecrated to the Lord in the fourth year. Another illustrative example is Abraham's offering up of Isaac (Gen 22). Abraham had circumcised the infant Isaac (Gen 21:4) but in this further cutting ritual at Moriah he was performing the ultimate circumcision, cutting off Isaac altogether. And this circumcision took the form of a "burnt-offering" (v.2), a ritual that symbolizes consecration.

Though circumcision was, like the death passage of Genesis 15, an oath ritual symbolizing divine judgment, it differed from the latter in that it did not function as a covenant ratification rite, not even on the initial occasion described in Genesis 17:23-27. Significantly, Genesis 17:22 notes the withdrawal of the theophanic presence prior to that performance of the circumcision rite. And, of course, circumcision was not limited to that first occasion but was to be observed as a recurring ordinance in the successive generations of the ongoing administration of the covenant. It was not then an inaugural ceremony for the covenant order as such; it rather functioned as a sign marking the incorporation of individuals into the community. Its connection with the point of entrance into the covenant becomes especially clear in the prescription that it was to be performed on the child of eight days.

A sign of judgment might seem a strange entrance rite for the covenant of promise. But the divine judgment must not be construed in a one-sidedly negative way. Within the covenant of promise God's act of judgment takes on unexpected new meaning. It becomes the organ of redemptive grace. Of similarly two-sided meaning was the symbolism of the Genesis 15 oath ritual.   On the one hand, the theophanic oath passage signified, hypothetically, the judgment curse that the Lord would suffer as a covenant-breaker. But in its historical-theological context it also pointed to the redemptive sacrifice of the Son of God in fulfillment of the covenant promise. It was prophetic of that judgment curse of Golgotha that was the salvation of God's people, a death of the One that brought justification and life to the many. Circumcision is in fact employed in the Scripture as an image for that redemptive judgment undergone by Christ. Paul referred to the crucifixion as "the circumcision of Christ" (Col 2:11), seeing it as antitype to the circumcision-sacrifice of Isaac (Gen 22), a "putting off" not merely of a token part but of the whole body of his flesh through death (cf. Col 1:22), a veritable perfecting of circumcision. [See *By Oath Consigned*, pp. 45-47, 71.]

What was signified by circumcision was, therefore, the generic concept of the divine judgment in its twofold potential.   It conveyed the threat of being cut off from God and life for the one who, disclaiming the grace of the covenant and thus breaking it, would undergo in himself the judgment due to Adam's fallen race. But circumcision also presented the promise of the Cross, inviting the circumcised to identify by faith with Christ, to undergo the judgment of God in him, and so find in his circumcision-judgment the way to the Father, to justification and life. Because Paul perceived this gospel option as one specific aspect of the generic judgment significance of circumcision he could interpret it as a seal of the righteousness of faith which Abraham had, yet being uncircumcised (Rom 4:11).

Moreover, it is not enough simply to recognize that this positive redemptive meaning was one specific possibility present in the generic significance of circumcision as a symbol of divine judgment. For circumcision was after all an ordinance of the covenant of promise – of the gospel. And just as the central aim of the Covenant of Grace is the salvation of the elect in Christ, so that same redemptive objective is the proper purpose in view in circumcision.

Both the Old and New Testament expound the theology of circumcision in its proper redemptive meaning. True circumcision, Scripture insists, is a matter of heart-consecration to the covenant Lord (Deut 10:16; 30:6; Jer 4:4; 6:10; 9:25,26; Rom 2:29; 4:11; Phil 3:3).   Circumcision, properly experienced, means identification with Christ in his crucifixion-circumcision as a satisfaction of divine justice and it thus means safe passage through the death-judgment to the resurrection unto justification (Col 2:11ff.; Rom 4:11). To be circumcised in Christ involves further a dying to sin, a putting off of the old man not only in the forensic sense but subjectively in the spiritual transformation of sanctification (Col 2:11ff,; 3:5ff.). In such spiritual, soteric realities does the meaning of circumcision consist, according to the analogy of Scripture. Those who, due particularly to a misguided desire to separate circumcision from baptism, desacralize circumcision, reducing its significance to some sort of Jewish nationalism or territorialism stripped of typological redemptive-covenantal meaning, produce a fiction. The significance of the Abrahamic ordinance of circumcision as consistently interpreted in the Bible is through and through religious, spiritual, covenantal, and indeed Christocentric.

In sum, circumcision was a vow of consecration marking entrance into God's covenant. By this oath-sign one was consigned to a status of discipleship under God's sovereign lordship in expectation of his judgment in accordance with the stipulated terms of his covenant. Reception of circumcision was not an infallible index of faith or election. It was not in a given instance a guarantee of eternal salvation. Circumcision threatened the covenant-breaker with ultimate excision. Nevertheless, its proper purpose was found in its significance as an invitation of grace to undergo God's judgment in the Redeemer-Substitute and so experience the death-passage as the way of life.

Matching circumcision in all major respects is the new covenant ordinance of baptism. In the present context only a brief review can be given of some of the evidence with respect to (1) baptism's meaning as symbolic act, (2) its theological import, and (3) its consecratory function. (For a more extensive treatment see my *By Oath Consigned.*)

(1) Baptism symbolizes the divine judgment ordeal and, indeed, the curse of death. The outstanding water ordeals of the Old Testament are identified in the New Testament as baptisms. (On the Noahic Deluge ordeal, see 1 Pet 3:20-22; and for the Red Sea ordeal, 1 Cor 10:1,2.) John the Forerunner describes Messiah's impending judgment of the covenant community as a baptism and he interpreted his own ministry of water baptism as symbolic of that (Matt 3:11,12). Also, Jesus referred to his death on the cross as a baptism (Luke 12:50).

(2) The New Testament exposition of Chrisitan baptism as a participation with Christ in the judgment ordeal of his death, burial, and resurrection (Rom 6:3ff.; Col 2:11ff.) further evidences the basic, generic symbolism of baptism as a judgment ordeal of death, but at the same time it points to the specific kind of baptismal death properly in view in this rite, namely, death with Christ. According to its proper redemptive purpose baptism speaks of justification, reception of the Spirit with all the attending soteriological benefits; it is an invitation to undergo the baptism and death ordeal in Christ unto resurrection and everlasting life.

(3) In the great commission the coordination of baptizing the nations and enlisting them under the command of Christ, sovereign Lord of heaven and earth (Matt 28:18-20) brings out the function of baptism as an oath sign of consecration, a sign of separation from the profane world and incorporation into the holy covenant community.

The implications of the passages just cited and others for determining the proper recipients of the consecration signs of circumcision and baptism will be developed later, in our discussion of the polity of the covenant community.

4. Compatibility of Promise and Obligation

A certain kind of conditionality attached to the covenant of promise, one consistent with the principle and surety of divine grace. There could not but be demands placed on God's human partner in kingdom-covenant, creational or redemptive. God's holiness is insistent in its expression. Reflection of the ethical glory of God must always be required of all, men or angels, who dwell in fellowship with him. Such divine demand for godliness is therefore found in covenants of works and grace alike. The precise kind of conditionality carried by the imposed obligations differs, however, in these two types of covenant.

In distinguishing the two varieties of conditionality the key question is that of the function of the response of obedience. If the obedience functions as the meritorious ground of reception or retention of the kingdom blessings, the conditionality is that of the works principle, the opposite of the principle of grace. Obedience functions that way in the eternal covenant of the Father and Son, in the Covenant of the Creator with Adam, and in the Mosaic Covenant at the level of the typological kingdom (see further below). But what about the Abrahamic Covenant – how did the response of obedience function there? Our concern at this point, be it noted, is with the broad question of the relation of human obedience to the securing of the kingdom blessings at the antitypical level in Christ. The special question of the relationship of Abraham's obedience to the realization of the typical kingdom is reserved for discussion below.

Under the Abrahamic Covenant human obedience was indispensable. If the fundamental demand for cultic loyalty in authentic commitment to the Lord was not complied with, the covenant blessings were forfeited. Esau is a case in point; for lack of the appropriate covenantal response there was no place for him (Heb 12:16,17). In Romans 9 Paul establishes the basis of this conditionality of human response in the reality of human responsibility. Though sovereign divine predestination lies behind a failure like Esau's, as it does behind all else, God finds fault (Rom 9:19ff., cf. 9:10ff.). The disobedience is attributable to human responsibility. And the avoidance of the fault, or, positively, the fulfillment of the fundamental demand of the covenant, for which man was held responsible, was indispensable to attaining the blessings.

Such indispensability of obedience did not, however, amount to the works principle. For in the Abrahamic Covenant, human obedience, though indispensable, did not function as the meritorious ground of blessing. That ground of the promised blessings was rather the obedience of Christ, in fulfillment of his eternal covenant with the Father. And man's appropriation of salvation's blessing was by faith. Paul took as his text for this point Genesis 15:6, the record of Abraham's faith-Amen to the covenantal promises and the Lord's answering declaration that Abraham was righteous (cf. my "Abram's Amen," *WTJ* 31,1[1968],1-11). This showed that Abraham was not justified by works (Rom 4:3). If justified on the ground of his own works, Abraham would be able to glory in himself (v.2). He would have earned his reward (v.4). But Abraham had in fact found justification through faith in the promising God, by believing in him who justifies the ungodly (vv.3,5). And because he was justified and became heir of the world through faith, it was a matter of grace not works (vv.13,16).

Now, the obedience indispensable to reception of the ultimate blessings of the Abrahamic Covenant is the inevitable accompaniment of the faith through which the righteousness of God is appropriated. For it is included as a fruit of the same divine work of spiritual renewal from which springs faith. They are twin gifts of God's saving grace, twin fruits of the Spirit. And because of this inevitable connection of obedience with faith, obedience functions with respect to the acquisition of the promises as a criterion of the validity of confessed faith. It is a confirmatory witness of the presence of the genuine faith which appropriates the promised gift of grace. Absence of obedience would betray absence of faith. This was James' view of the necessity of obedience (Jas 2:14ff.). Similarly, Paul, refuting the perverse idea that antinomianism follows from his doctrine of grace (Rom 6:15ff.), teaches that the believer's obedience attests to his being truly the servant of righteousness and of God (vv.16-19,22), whose grace provides the free gift of life in Jesus Christ (v.23).

Though it involves a kind of conditionality and has a certain kind of necessity, obedience thus originating and thus functioning is agreeable with the principle and guarantee of grace. Functioning as it does as a confirmation of saving faith it is supportive of the grace-promise-faith principle of salvation. And originating as it does from the renewing grace of God it did not nullify the guaranteed fulfillment of the kingdom promises, the grace that produces it being sovereign grace which infallibly accomplishes its purpose.

More than that, it is not merely that there is compatibility here, but rather that attainment of the covenant blessings is unthinkable apart from this obedient devotion to covenant law. For such obedience is itself one of the promised blessings. Indeed, the acme of the redemptive blessings provided in Christ is the restoration of man, the image of God, to conformity to the glory of such godliness (Rom 8:29,30; Eph 2:10).

5. The Works Principle and the Typal Kingdom

How Abraham's obedience related to the securing of the kingdom blessings in their old covenant form is a special question within the broad topic of the role of human works under redemptive covenant. Several times previously we have had occasion to note that the old (Mosaic) covenant order, though in continuity with the Abrahamic covenant of promise and even an initial fulfillment of its kingdom promises, was nevertheless itself governed by a principle of works. Earlier in this chapter (cf. I,A,1) when we were identifying the Abrahamic Covenant as one of grace and promise, we observed how Paul in Galatians 3:10ff. and Romans 10:4ff. contrasted the works principle which he saw operating in the Mosaic law order with the promise-grace-faith principle of the gospel. It was the apostle's perception of this opposition of the governing principles of the two covenants that obliged him to face the question whether the Abrahamic promise had been annulled by the subsequent Mosaic Covenant (Gal 3:15-17). Stated the other way around, the very fact that Paul raises this question is compelling evidence that he saw a principle operating in the law that was antithetical to promise-faith.

That Paul did indeed assess the Mosaic order in such terms is further supported by his citation of Leviticus 18:5 as an expression of the do-and-live principle of inheritance. In Galatians 3 he points to that verse as evidence from within the Mosaic Covenant itself that "the law" was "not of faith" (v.12; cf. v.18). Similarly in Romans 10:5 he uses that Mosaic formulation as a description of "the righteousness which is of the law," asserting this to be antithetical to "the righteousness which is of faith" (v.6). Romans 9:32, compared with Galatians 3:12, also seems to make the same point. Also, Romans 5:13,14 demands this view of the law.

It was only because Paul thus recognized the presence of this works principle in the law that he could identify the old covenant as an administration of bondage, condemnation, and death in contrast to the new covenant, which he characterized as one of freedom, righteousness, and life (Gal 4:24-26; 2 Cor 3:6-9). This same interpretation of the old covenant emerges in Paul's address in the synagogue at Antioch Pisidia, when, proclaiming justification through Jesus, he says that justification was not provided by the law of Moses (Acts 13:39).

At the same time, Paul affirmed that the Mosaic Covenant did not annul the promise arrangement given earlier to Abraham (Gal 3:17). The explanation for this is that the old covenant order was composed of two strata and the works principle enunciated in Leviticus 18:5, and elsewhere in the law, applied only to one of these, a secondary stratum. There was a foundational stratum having to do with the personal attainment of the eternal kingdom of salvation and this underlying stratum, continuous with all preceding and succeeding administrations of the Lord's Covenant of Grace with the church, was informed by the principle of grace (cf., e.g., Rom 4:16). Because the Abrahamic covenant of promise found continuity in the Mosaic order at this underlying level, it was not abrogated by the latter. The works principle in the Mosaic order was confined to the typological sphere of the provisional earthly kingdom which was superimposed as a secondary overlay on the foundational stratum.

Leviticus 18:5, in stating that the man who performed the covenant stipulations would live in them, declared that individual Israelites must observe the requirements of the law to enjoy the blessings of the typological kingdom community. Even individuals who were elect in terms of eternal salvation would be cut off from that temporal, typological realm as the penalty for various serious infractions of the law. Likewise, the Israelite people corporately could maintain their continuing tenure as the theocratic kingdom in the promised land only as they maintained the appropriate measure of national fidelity to their heavenly King. Failure to do so would result in the loss of the typological kingdom and their very identity as God's people in that corporate, typological sense. If they broke the covenant, they would suffer exile and the loss of their national, typological election. Such was, of course, the actual outcome. Israel became *Lo-Ammi*. The fact of this loss of the national election given to Israel in the Mosaic Covenant compels all who confess the sovereignty of God's saving grace to recognize the presence of a works principle in that covenant. Clearly, the sovereign grace of Christ's suretyship does not relate to the typological realm with its national election and blessings under the old covenant in the way it does to the individual election to the ultimate realities of salvation, which are in view in all administrations of the Covenant of Grace. At the level of the secondary, typological stratum of the Mosaic order, continuance in the election to kingdom blessings was not guaranteed by sovereign grace on the basis of Christ's meritorious accomplishments. It was rather something to be merited by the Israelites' works of obedience to the law.

Paul was resuming Jeremiah's classic analysis of the covenants when he contrasted the new covenant to the old (the old viewed in the restricted but distinctive terms of its typological dimension). In contrast to the new covenant which could not be broken, founded as it was on God's sovereign, forgiving grace in Christ, the old covenant, according to Jeremiah, was breakable (Jer 31:32). Individual members of the new covenant community might prove false and be broken off as branches from a tree while the covenant tree remained intact, pruned and flourishing. But the old covenant's typological kingdom order as such could be and was terminated. The axe of God's judgment was ultimately laid unto the roots of the tree and the tree itself was felled. Jeremiah's identification of the old covenant as breakable was the equivalent of an assertion that it lacked the guarantee afforded by the grace principle and was instead based on the principle of works.

What we have found then is that once the typological kingdom was inaugurated under the Mosaic Covenant, Israel's retention of it was governed by a principle of works applied on a national scale. The standard of judgment in this national probation was one of typological legibility, that is, the message must remain reasonably readable that enjoyment of the felicity of God's holy kingdom goes hand in hand with righteousness. Without holiness we do not see God. But if the ground of Israel's tenure in Canaan was their covenant obedience, their election to receive the typological kingdom in the first place was emphatically not based on any merit of theirs (cf. Deut 9:5,6). Their original reception of this kingdom, as well as their restoration to it after the loss of their national election in Babylonian exile, is repeatedly attributed to God's remembrance of his promissory commitments of grace to Abraham, Isaac, and Jacob (Exod 2:24; 3:6ff.; 6:2ff.; 32:13; Deut 9:27; 10:15; Lev 26:42), pointing to the coming Messiah and the new covenant.

When, however, we trace the matter back to the record of God's covenant revelation to the patriarchs we encounter statements that connect the promissory grant of the kingdom to the faithful service rendered to the Lord by Abraham.

This idea of reward for fidelity is introduced in the Lord's opening assurance to Abraham in the Genesis 15 episode of covenant ratification. Just before this is the account of Abraham's military expedition against the kings from the east (Gen 14:1ff.). In this action Abraham had opposed a foreign suzerain who had invaded the land to which Abraham had laid claim in the name of his Lord and at his direction, as recorded in the immediately preceding narrative (Gen 13:14-18). The invader had also shown himself hostile to people under the care of the Lord's covenant vassal (Gen 14:12-14). Abraham's vigorous response comported with a customary treaty requirement that the vassal take prompt military action to guard the interests of his suzerain, if threatened. Moreover, in the aftermath of the battle, Abraham had stoutly acknowledged himself the oath-bound vassal of Yahweh, rendering his tribute and firmly resisting the temptation to compromise his exclusive allegiance to Yahweh by allowing the king of Sodom to assume the role of his benefactor-suzerain (Gen 14:17ff.). Coming on the heels of this episode, the Lord's word to Abraham (Gen 15:1) has the character of a royal grant to an officer of the king for faithful military service. God identifies himself by the military figure of a shield (cf. Deut 33:29; Ps 18:2), otherwise read as suzerain, and promises: "Your reward will be very great" (also read: "who will reward you very greatly"). The term *sakar*, "reward," is used for the compensation due to those who have conducted a military campaign. In Ezekiel 29:19 it refers to the spoil of Egypt which the Lord gives Nebuchadnezzar as wages for his army (cf. Isa 40:10; 62:11). The imagery of Genesis 15:1 is that of the Great King honoring Abraham's notable exhibition of compliance with covenant duty by the reward of a special grant that would more than make up for whatever enrichment he had foregone at the hands of the king of Sodom for the sake of faithfulness to Yahweh, his Lord. The broader record of the Lord's dealings with Abraham includes numerous key expressions paralleled in the ancient royal grants to loyal servants: such a servant is one who obeys, keeps the charge, serves perfectly, walks before his lord.

Another display of outstanding covenantal obedience by Abraham, the most remarkable of all, was the occasion for a second divine disclosure presenting the blessings of the Abrahamic Covenant as a divine grant for the servant's work of obedience. At the conclusion of the sacrificial episode on Moriah, the Angel of the Lord, the very one who was at last to be the only Son and substitutionary ram of sacrifice, called out of heaven to Abraham: "By myself have I sworn, saith the Lord, because thou hast done this thing and hast not withheld thine only son that in blessing I will bless thee ... because thou hast obeyed my voice" (Gen 22:16-18). Viewing this episode from the perspective of justification by faith in Christ, James expounded Abraham's act of obedience as the work that demonstrated the vital reality of his faith (Jas 2:21ff). But this event is to be seen from the redemptive-historical perspective as well as that of the personal, subjective experience of salvation. It had a special, decisive significance for the subsequent course of covenant history. This is suggested by the double affirmation, at the beginning and close of the oracle, that the promised program of the Abrahamic Covenant would proceed to unfold because Abraham had done this.

That Abraham's obedience had special historic significance as the basis for God's future favorable action towards his descendants is confirmed by the Lord's later repetition of the substance of this oracle, now to Isaac (Gen 26:2ff). Having restated his commitment to fulfill the covenant promises to Isaac and his line, the Lord concluded: "because Abraham obeyed my voice and kept my charge, my commandments, my statutes, and my laws" (Gen 26:5, cf. v. 24). Here the significance of Abraham's works cannot be limited to their role in validation of his own faith. His faithful performance of his covenantal duty is here clearly declared to sustain a causal relationship to the blessing of Isaac and Israel. It had a meritorious character that procured a reward enjoyed by others.

The term 'eqeb, "because," used in Genesis 26:5 (and already in the original revelation to Abraham in Gen 22:18) signifies recompense, reward (cf. Ps 19:11; Prov 22:4; Isa 5:23). This strengthens the case for understanding this as a matter of meritorious works. Moreover, Genesis 26:5 describes Abraham's obedience in language surprising in the Genesis context, the divine demand being denoted by a series of legislative categories such as are later applied to the laws of Moses. A particularly interesting combination of such terms together with 'eqeb, "in recompense for," is found in Deuteronomy 7:12 (cf. 8:20). Quite possibly then, Genesis 26:5 employs the terminology of covenant stipulations from the Sinaitic Covenant, where it describes an arrangement governed by the meritorious works principle, to reenforce the point that Abraham's obedience was also to be understood as having such a meritorious character and that as such it was the ground of the reward enjoyed by his descendants.

Because of Abraham's obedience redemptive history would take the shape of an Abrahamite kingdom of God from which salvation's blessings would rise up and flow out to the nations. God was pleased to constitute Abraham's exemplary works as the meritorious ground for granting to Israel after the flesh the distinctive role of being formed as the typological kingdom, the matrix from which Christ should come. Within this typological structure Abraham emerges as an appointed sign of his promised messianic seed, the Servant of the Lord, whose fulfillment of his covenantal mission was the meritorious ground of the inheritance of the antitypical, eschatological kingdom by the true, elect Israel of all nations. Certainly, Abraham's works did not have that status. They were, however, accorded by God an analogous kind of value with respect to the typological stage represented by the old covenant. Though not the ground of the inheritance of heaven, Abraham's obedience was the ground for Israel's inheritance of Canaan. Salvation would not come because of Abraham's obedience, but because of Abraham's obedience salvation would come of the Abrahamites, the Jews (John 4:22). (See the more general discussion of this aspect of redemptive typology in our earlier comments on Noah as a messianic type.)

On both occasions in Abraham's life where the works-reward motif appears there were symbolic actions prophetic of the sacrificial act of obedience of the Messiah, the meritorious work that secures the ultimate salvation-kingdom for God's people of all times. In Genesis 15 it was the oath-passage of the Lord through the way of death. In Genesis 22 it was the provision of the ram as the sacrificial substitute for Isaac. Placing the disclosure concerning the meritorious role of Abraham's obedience in the context of these powerful pointers to Christ and his obedience, which was the meritorious ground of the antitypical blessings of the covenant, was a safeguard against misconstruing the significance of Abraham's work as extending to the antitypical level. It was limited to the prototypal sphere.

It was only a typological pointer but the obedience of Abraham that God assessed as meritorious on these two occasions was richly symbolic of Messiah's mission. In Genesis 15 the reward was announced in response to a kingly service of deliverance from the Lord's enemies. In Genesis 22 the reward was for a priestly ministry of sacrifice. Together these acts of obedience exhibited the negative and positive aspects of the consecration function of God's servant, guardianship of the sanctuary and tributary offering.

The obedient Abraham, the faithful covenant servant, was a type of the Servant of the Lord in his obedience, by which he became the surety of the new covenant. Like the messianic Servant, the one whose meritorious service secured God's blessings for the many who were his "seed" (Isa 52:15; 53:10-12), so Abraham was one, and the reward of his obedience was the blessings of the typal kingdom for the many who were his seed (cf. Isa 51:2). Yet the antitype was before the type. "Before Abraham was, I am" (John 8:58). The messianic seed of Abraham was before father Abraham. Abraham was among the many who were the "seed" of the One who was his seed, the many who were blessed in that messianic One.

II. PROMISES OF THE COVENANT

Covenant as commitment with divine sanctioning has been our theme thus far in this chapter. Now we turn to the kingdom administration aspect of the matter as we analyze the specific content of the promise sanctions of God's covenant with Abraham. In the introduction to this chapter we remarked upon the continuity of the kingdom program defined in the

Abrahamic promises with the kingdom of God as administered in the earlier covenants. Awareness that the kingdom promised to Abraham is none other than the cosmic kingdom envisaged from the beginning affords basic orientation for an analysis of the several promises in their synchronic and diachronic interrelationships. The continuity of the Abrahamic Covenant with the subsequent administrations of the kingdom is betokened by the promissory form itself. In this section special attention will be given to the relationship between the two stages in the fulfillment of God's kingdom promises to Abraham.

A. Résumé of Roots

Revelation of the promises in the period of Abraham, Isaac, and Jacob (Gen 12:2,3; 13:14-17; 15:4,5,13-16,18-21; 17:2-8; 18:10,14; 22:15-18; 26:3,4; 27:27-29; 28:13-15; 35:9-12; cf. 46:3,4; 48:3,4) continues the series of oracular pronouncements concerning the kingdom recorded in the pre-Abrahamic narratives. Formally, the previous prophetic disclosures were covenant sanction utterances, specifically curses, with correlative blessings attached. The promises given Abraham also belonged, of course, to the category of covenant sanctions but with the blessing sanctions now primary and the curses subordinate. At times the promissory form (e.g., Gen 12:2,3) yields to the mode of the blessing formula (e.g., Gen 14:19; 49:28).

As to substance these promises represent an organic development of the kingdom program as previously disclosed. They resume the redemptive kingdom prophecies of Genesis 3:15 and 9:25-27, which were in turn a resumption of the fundamental kingdom hope of the creational covenant. New details emerge concerning the particular course of its historical unfolding but the kingdom envisaged at the goal of the process is the same consummated creational kingdom symbolically portrayed from the beginning by the Sabbath and tree of life in the garden of God.

The kingdom in Eden was Immanuel's land, the holy place of the Glory-Spirit presence, a theocratic paradise-protectorate where a holy nation of priests lived in covenanted communion with the Lord their Creator. In the Glory-Presence on the mountain of God the Edenic kingdom had a focus, a vertical axis uniting earth with heaven and so with the celestial center, the throne-site of God in the midst of the divine council-court. And mandated in the stipulated program of the kingdom was a fullness to be achieved through a correlated process of multiplying the kingdom people and appropriating the kingdom land. The earth was to be filled and in the appointed hour the eternal Sabbath would dawn and the hitherto earth-bound sanctuary city would be transfigured into Metapolis. There the heavens are opened and the Glory-focus coalesces with the kingdom's cosmic fullness. There God dwells with his people and they see his face and reign forever and ever. Continuation of this original kingdom goal as the ultimate hope of the Covenant of Grace is manifested in the reappearance of various features of the sanctuary kingdom of Eden in redemptive prophecy, notably so in the book of Revelation.

Only gradually, however, did the contours of the eternal city come into view again. Understandably, the earliest redemptive oracles were preoccupied with the situation imposed by the Fall, with the history of conflict with Satan and the victory of salvation to be won by the Messiah. The vision of the ultimate restoration-consummation of the creation-kingdom began to be more definitely modeled in the revelation of the Abrahamic Covenant. But also taken up and carried forward there was the theme of the salvation-history leading to the New Jerusalem. Resumed from Genesis 3:15 and 9:25-27 were the essential promise of restoration of covenant with the Lord for a people identified with his name (cf. the seed of the woman corporately and the line of Shem); their warfare against Satan and an accursed people (cf. the seed of the serpent and Canaan); the climactic triumph of the messianic champion (cf. the seed of the woman as individual); and the universal extension of the covenant blessings (cf. the line of Japheth). All these features, it will be found, have their clear continuing counterparts in the promissory blessings of the Abrahamic Covenant.

The two-stage pattern of the unfolding of the kingdom, which is such a major feature of the historical-eschatological projections in the Abrahamic Covenant, is also resumed there from earlier revelation, having already been intimated in Noah's oracle (Gen 9:25-27). In Shem's blessing (Gen 9:26), pointing to the old covenant and Israel's dispossessing of the Canaanites, we perceive the peculiar ethnocentric phase distinctive of the program of kingdom realization contemplated in the Abrahamic promises, the preliminary phase that would prove transitional to an ultimate coming of the kingdom. And in Noah's prophecy of Japheth's entrance into the covenant tent of Shem there is already discernible the prospect of that ultimate universal stage, the new covenant prospect which is resumed in the gospel promise given to Abraham that all nations would be blessed in his seed.

B. Blessed and Blessing

In their simplest terms the promises of the covenant were that Abraham would be blessed and he would be a blessing. The one involved the other. It was by receiving the blessing that he would become a blessing. The secret of this connection is that the blessing was, in a word, Christ.

According to the parallelism of the several promises in their original formulation in Genesis 12:2f., to be blessed is synonymous with becoming great. The first four promises are set out in an A.B.A.B arrangement. The A-sections promise greatness, greatness of nation (v.2a) and of name (v.2c); the B-sections speak of blessing, of being the object of blessing (v.2b) and of being oneself the blessing (v.2d).

God's blessing empowers his creature to occupy successfully its proper place in the kingdom order. His blessing of the birds and fish in creation's fifth day was equated with his fiat-command that they be fruitful and fill their respective domains of sky and sea (Gen 1:22). And the Creator's blessing of the royal man and woman was linked to his mandate that they multiply and subdue the earth (Gen 1:28). So God's promised blessing of Abraham (Gen 12:2b) would enable him to attain his assigned place of great nationhood in God's kingdom order (v.2a).

The blessing episodes just cited from the creation story, particularly God's blessing of the man and woman, not only illustrate the concept of blessing as a divine empowering but serve to identify the kingdom blessing promised in the Abrahamic Covenant as the redemptive version of the kingdom fullness mandated at the creation. Like the kingdom mandate given to Adam and Eve, so the kingdom promise to the Abrahamites would involve multiplying and filling the contemplated domain. That is, the promised kingdom included the two components of people and territory. Hence, in subsequent elaboration of the promises the kingdom promise is unfolded in terms of the promises of seed and land.

In Genesis 12:2d the promised blessing is imperative in form. This could be viewed as a creational fiat: "Be a blessing." As such it would be a manifestation of the sovereign divine initiative at work here by which the covenant promises would be omnipotently accomplished. Redemptive covenant is a process of re-creation. Or, in this kind of construction the imperative may express the result of the preceding action (cf. Gen 20:7), yielding the translation here: "so that you shall be a blessing." But either way, it is as the one who receives the great name (v.2c) that Abraham becomes a blessing (v.2d).

The literary relationship of the promises of the great nation and great name, constituting as they do the two A-sections in the A.B.A.B structure of verse 2, reflects the fact that the great name is a concomitant of the great nation. This is so because that nation is God's own holy kingdom and thus is the bearer of his great name. Echoed here is Noah's oracular blessing on Shem's line, appointing them as the people to be peculiarly identified with the name of the Lord until the advent out of Shem's lineage of the One who would be the ultimate revelation of God's name. The Babelites sought greatness of name by magnifying the name of man. On Abraham would be bestowed the truly great name of God, particularly as he became the great nation of whom came Christ.

Genesis 12:3 develops the climactic prospect of verse 2d that Abraham's line was to be the source and channel of redemption's blessings. Noah's blessing on Japheth is resumed and surpassed in the promise that in Abraham all the families of the earth would be blessed (v.3c). It would be as receiver of the Christ-blessing that Abraham would become a mediator of blessing. This is not yet explicit in Genesis 12 but subsequent revelation specified that it would be through his seed – through the corporate seed as matrix of the messianic seed and thus more precisely through that individual messianic seed – that Abraham would become a blessing to the world (Gen 18:18; 22:18; 26:4; 28:14; cf. Acts 3:25; Gal 3:16).

It had been intimated already in Genesis 3:15 that the messianic seed's achievement of victory and blessing for the rest of the woman's seed would be by the way of suffering. This does not come to expression in the several passages where the promises are given to Abraham or passed along to Isaac and Jacob. There is a suggestion of it in Jacob's blessing on Judah (Gen 49:11). During the patriarchal period it is most clearly conveyed in the episodes that were typological of the way of the Cross (Gen 15 and 22). Isaiah's insight into this is revealed in his weaving together the themes of the chosen seed and the suffering Servant.

Through Abraham's messianic seed salvation would be mediated beyond the ethnic line of Abraham to the nations (Gen 12:3c). Yet this universal mediator would be a divider of mankind. Not everybody in all the families of the earth would find blessing in him. He would send not peace but a sword on the earth, cleaving apart households (Matt 10:34-37). Those who confessed him before men he would confess before his Father in heaven, but those who denied him before men he would deny before the Father (Matt 10:32,33). Such was Jesus' exposition of God's word to Abraham: "I will bless them that bless thee and him that curseth thee I will curse" (Gen 12:3a,b). We are again reminded that the messianic hope was first given in the context of the enmity of the two seeds (Gen 3:15) and that the covenant blessing on Shem was correlative to the curse on Ham-Canaan (Gen 9:25). In the promise of universal blessing there was a preaching of the gospel beforehand to Abraham (Gal 3:18). That gospel, however, proves to be both savor from life unto life and savor from death unto death (2 Cor 2:16), not only on the mission field of the Gentiles but in the covenant community of Israel (Isa 10:22; Luke 2:34; Rom 9:27-29; 11:28).

We have reflected upon the blessing-curse promise of Genesis 12:3a,b as it relates to the theme of the mediation of blessing through Abraham (v.2d). That dual sanction formula may also be viewed from the perspective of Abraham's reception of the great kingdom (v.2a,b), the theocratic kingdom invested with God's great name (v.2c). Characteristic of covenantal arrangements between the ancient suzerain and his vassal was the commitment that each would be friend to the other's friends, and foe to his foes. That God would bless or curse others in matching response to their blessing or cursing Abraham was an indication that the great Abrahamic nation would be a covenantal protectorate of the heavenly Suzerain. This is part of the pattern of correspondences between the kingdom promised to Abraham and the kingdom of God in Eden, the original theocratic protectorate.

As the revelation of the promised kingdom continues on from Genesis 12 to Genesis 13,15,17,22,26 and 28 and as the promise comes to fulfillment at its two historico-eschatological levels, the distinctive features of the creation kingdom mentioned above (in the résumé of the roots of the Abrahamic promises) emerge more and more into view. It becomes clear that the kingdom promised to Abraham, like that in Eden's garden of God, is a paradise domain flowing with milk and honey, a new heaven and earth with river and trees of life (cf. Isa 51:3), having as its glory the Shekinah Presence of the Lord enthroned among his angels at the focal cosmic axis of Zion (old and new) – all in all, the fitting embodiment of the special covenantal relationship between God and the sanctified human community. And like the kingdom fullness mandated in the creational covenant, the fullness of this kingdom comes through the multiplying of Abraham's seed and their filling-subduing the allotted land (cf. Gen 35:11). The promised great nation blessing (Gen 12:2a) was nothing more nor less than the creation kingdom redemptively restored and consummated.

C. Promised Kingdom on Two Levels

References to the two-level nature of the promises have been unavoidable in various connections in our analysis of the Abrahamic Covenant up to this point but now it is time to focus on this more particularly. In doing so we will sum up the promises under the concept of kingdom, tracing the two-level structure with respect to the kingdom components of king, people, and land.

As the kingdom promises come to fulfillment in two successive stages, each is identified as a divine remembrance of Abraham or of the covenant made with him. In our treatment of God's ark-covenant with Noah we noted that the verb to remember takes on a specialized sense in such contexts, signifying not just recollection but a faithfulness to prior commitment evidenced in performance of what was promised. God's remembering of his covenant with Abraham, Isaac, and Jacob is mentioned at the beginning of the first stage of kingdom fulfillment immediately before the account of the call of Moses to be the agent of that fulfillment (Exod 2:24) and again as the prelude to God's oath to proceed forthwith to deliver the Israelites from bondage and bring them to their promised land (Exod 6:5; cf. also Exod 32:13; Lev 26:42,45). Then at the dawning of the second stage of the kingdom, which was to be brought in through Jesus, mediator of the new covenant, this new development is identified by Zacharias, father of John the Forerunner, as the Lord's remembrance of his holy covenant, the oath sworn to Abraham (Luke 1:72,73; cf. also Luke 1:54,55).

1. The Promised King

At first the promise of kingship came in a general form, as an enhancement of the promise of numerous descendants. If Abraham was to be a father of a great nation and even a multitude of nations, then naturally he would number kings among his descendants (Gen 17:6). So also, if Sarah was to be a mother of nations, "kings of peoples" would come of her (Gen 17:16). When establishing vassal rulers in their kingship, ancient suzerains might assign them dynastic names (cf., e.g., 2 Kgs 23:34; 24:17). Likewise, the Lord gave to Abram and Sarai the new names of Abraham and Sarah when presenting to them a promissory grant of royalty (Gen 17:5,15). Similarly, when renewing to Jacob this promise of royal descendants, God confirmed the change of his name to Israel (Gen 35:10,11; cf. 32:28).

Later, the kingship promise became more specific in Jacob's testamentary blessings on his twelve sons, a forecast of their tribal histories down into the eschatological era (Gen 49:1-28). Judah's blessing was to attain leonine royalty, to become the ruling tribe in the midst of the tribes of Israel (vv.8,9). Once established in Judah the sceptre would continue forever, the royal dynasty culminating in the latter days in the coming One, Shiloh, Lord of all peoples (v.10). As was true in the original messianic prophecy of Genesis 3:15 and as is characteristic of all messianic prophecy in the law, the prophets and the Psalms, so in Judah's blessing redemptive suffering conjoins royal glory in the reign of Shiloh, the prince of peace. His reign is one of paradisaic abundance of milk and wine (v.12). He will engage in a triumphant, vesture-incarnadining trampling of the winepress of God's wrath (v.11b; cf. Isa 63:3; Rev 19:13,15). Yet, it is in trampling the head of the serpent-foe that the champion seed of the woman suffers the heel-wound. And so, it is suggested, the "blood of grapes" with which Shiloh's garment is "washed" is also his own, the blood of the Lamb in which the multitude out of all the nations, saved from the great tribulation, wash their robes and make them white (Rev 7:14). Symbolic too of the sacrificial role he must perform is the animal he comes riding on. For the foal, the donkey's colt (v.11a), is mentioned in an ancient treaty account as the animal that was slain in order to ratify the covenant (cf. Zech 9:9,11).

Two levels of kingship were present in this prophetic blessing. Judah assumed the royal supremacy in Israel in the appointment of David as king. He, with his successors under the old covenant, were level one. Then David's dynasty reached a distinctive second level of kingship in the coming of Jesus Christ, Shiloh, the universal Lord, and his inauguration of the new covenant in his blood. In the kingship of Christ, Judah's sceptre became eternal as well as universal.

When the king promise attained its first level fulfillment, it was embodied in a separate covenant of its own. God gave to his faithful servant David a covenantal guarantee that his dynasty would endure forever and that his descendants would build God's house (2 Sam 7:5ff.). In accounting for all the elements in this covenant it is necessary again to distinguish two levels of fulfillment. Only in the reign of Christ did David's dynasty attain everlasting permanence, but only in terms of dynastic representatives at a premessianic level was the threat of chastisement for the committing of iniquity applicable (v.14). Hence too the promise that a Davidic king would build God's house is rightly seen to have twofold fulfillment, first in Solomon's construction of the Jerusalem temple and later in Christ's building of the church-temple of these last days.

At his advent the messianic king was heralded as the fulfillment of the royal promise sworn to Abraham and covenanted anew to David. Matthew's Gospel opens by introducing Jesus as the long-awaited king: "The book of the generation of Jesus Christ, the son of David, the son of Abraham" (Matt 1:1). Resuming the basic structural formula of the Book of Genesis, Matthew connects Jesus with Abraham through the one link of royal David, so identifying him as the promised king, the ultimate hope of the Abrahamic Covenant. Matthew continues this theme of Jesus' royal identity in the expanded dynastic genealogy that follows (1:2-16) and in the birth narratives. The latter speak of the one who is "born king of the Jews" (2:2), who arises out of Judah as a "governor" and "shepherd" of Israel (2:6). Luke's birth narratives also identify Jesus as the one who is given "the throne of his father David," a kingdom without end (1:32,33), in fulfillment of God's covenant with Abraham (1:69-73).

Here was the greater son whom David saw from afar and called "my Lord" (Ps 110:1; Matt 22:43-45). Ancient dynasts had presumptuously named themselves "sons of the gods," divine kings (Gen 6:1-4), but the great name of God-king belonged in truth to the One who, at the second level of promise fulfillment, was the royal seed of Abraham and son of David. He receives the name which belongs to none but him, "King of kings and Lord of lords" (Rev 19:12,16).

2. The Promised Kingdom-People

We have found that in the course of biblical revelation two distinct levels of fulfillment, one provisional and prototypal, the other messianic and eternal, are clearly distinguishable in the king promise given to Abraham. What is true of the promise of the king must inevitably also be true of the promise of the kingdom, both kingdom-people and kingdom-land.

As carried forward in the revelation of the Abrahamic Covenant the concept of the seed of the woman (Gen 3:15), now in the form of the seed of Abraham, continues to have both individual and corporate significance. There is the individual messianic seed of Abraham, the one through whom the blessings of the covenant were to be mediated to the nations (Acts 3:25,26), the one who was the final fulfillment of the kingship promised to Abraham's descendants. There is also the corporate seed, and the promised seed in this corporate sense is interpreted by the Scriptures as being realized on two levels.

God's blessing on Abraham was such that he would multiply to become a great nation (Gen 12:2). The promise of a kingdom people implicit in that original statement of the promises subsequently became explicit. This people would be as numerous as the dust of the earth, the stars of the sky, the sand by the sea (Gen 13:16; 15:5; 22:17; 26:4; 28:3). Abraham and Sarah would become father and mother of a multitude of nations (Gen 17:4,16).

Development of the twelve sons of Jacob into the twelve-tribe nation of Israel of course constituted a fulfillment of the promise of the kingdom people at one level. Alluding to the promise imagery of Genesis 22:17 (cf. 32:12), 1 Kings 4:20 says that in the days of Solomon's reign "Judah and Israel were many, as the sand which is by the sea in multitude" (cf. 2 Sam 17:11; 1 Chr 27:23f.; 2 Chr 1:9).

Equally obvious is the Bible's identification of a realization of the promise of the Abrahamic seed at another level. As we have seen, when Paul, in Romans 9-11, defends God's covenantal faithfulness in the face of Israel's fall, he bases his case on the identification of the promised seed as the individual election, a remnant-fullness of Jews and Gentiles, spiritual children of Abraham, all like him justified by faith (Rom 9:7,8; cf. Rom 4:16; Gal 3:7). The apostle finds within the Lord's revelation of the promises to Abraham explicit warrant for distinguishing this spiritual seed of Abraham from the physical offspring (Rom 9:7-13; cf. Gen 17:18-21; 21:12,13). What is remarkable is how he bypasses the more literal first level significance of Abraham's seed and takes for granted the second, spiritual level of meaning as *the* meaning of the promise.

Confirming the distinction made in the promise of the seed between literal and spiritual Israelites and pointing particularly to the second, spiritual level of meaning was the inclusion of the nations of the Gentiles among

Abraham's promised seed (Gen 17:4,6,16; Rom 4:11,12,16,17). Manifestly the Gentile seed were not Abraham's physical posterity. Moreover, the promise of the many nations as seed is equivalent to the gospel-promise that Abraham through his messianic seed would mediate blessing to all nations. That is, the promise of the seed is thereby lifted into the messianic, or new covenant, level where Gentile and Jewish believers are gathered together in the united assembly of the heavenly altar. Possibly it is in prospect of this reality that the terminology employed in the promise concerning the many nations is at times that of an assembly (*qahal*) of nations (Gen 28:3; 35:11; 48:4), *qahal* being a standard term for the tribes of Israel as the gathered covenant congregation. Further, in this gospel mystery of the union of the promised kingdom people in the Spirit, the corporate seed (Jewish and Gentile believers) and the individual messianic seed become one, Christ the head and all in him the body (Gal 3:16,29).

The promise of the kingdom people is unlike the promise of the king and the kingdom land in that its two levels of meaning cannot be simply equated with two successive eschatological stages (i.e., old and new covenants). For the second, spiritual level of the promised seed is already in process of realization under the old covenant, being the spiritual election within the national election of Israel.

3. The Promised Kingdom-Land

Step by step what was included in the promised kingdom land at the first level of meaning was more precisely defined. It was a land to be designated later as Abraham followed the Lord (Gen 12:1); the land of Canaan (Gen 12:7); Canaan extending in all four directions (Gen 13:14-17); the area bounded on the northeast by the river Euphrates and on the southwest by the river of Egypt (Gen 15:18) and comprising the territories of a series of specified peoples (Gen 15:19-21). Subsequent reaffirmations of the promise to the patriarchs after Genesis 15 do not further define these boundaries (cf. Gen 17:8; 22:17; 24:7; 26:3,4; 28:13,14; 35:12; 48:4; 49:1ff.; 50:24). That the territory eventually occupied by Israel fully corresponded with the geographical bounds defined in the promise is explicitly recorded in Joshua 21:43-45 and 1 Kings 4:20,21 (cf. Num 34:2ff.; 1 Chr 18:3; Ezek 47:13-20).

From the earliest intimations given at the call of Abraham it began to be apparent that this promised land was laid hold of by the Lord as peculiarly his own, as a holy land removed from the general common grace apportionment of the earth to mankind and set apart for a special covenantal grant to a people of redemptive election. It was a land claimed by the Lord and at his disposal to bestow on Abraham in a manner overriding his ordinary common grace disposition of earthly affairs.

As revelation of the promise progressed it became increasingly evident that appropriation of this royal land grant would be by force. Abraham's arrival in the land was confrontational. The land was not unclaimed terrain but occupied by the Canaanites, in whose midst Abraham erected the altar-claim of his God (Gen 12:6,7). Description of the land in terms of its occupants emphasized the necessity of acquiring it by a process of dispossessing these present owners (Gen 15:19-21; cf. 26:3,4). Most explicit was the prophetic announcement that Abraham's descendants would return from a foreign sojourn to take actual possession of the divine grant at the time when the iniquity of the Amorites would be full (Gen 15:16). Clearly, God's delivering the land to the Abrahamites would be an act of judgment on the Canaanites. It would be through holy war, contravening common grace political processes, that the land promise would be fulfilled.

To possess Canaan, Israel must conquer Canaan in fulfillment of Noah's curse on Ham-Canaan. In this warfare they had God's promise that they would possess the gate of their enemies (Gen 22:17). Established by act of divine judgment as a great nation in God's special domain, the Abrahamites would be the Lord's own protectorate. Also distinguishing this Abrahamic promise of the land from ordinary common grace allotments of territory to other peoples (cf. Deut 32:8; Amos 9:7) is its "everlasting" character (Gen 13:15; 17:8; 48:4). In this feature of permanence the second level of the promise of a kingdom land comes into view. To this we shall return.

There was continuity between the kingdom-land promised to Abraham and the covenant kingdom as it was originally envisaged in the creational covenant and subsequently carried forward in the blessing sanctions of the redemptive covenants. This continuity is already evidenced in the formulation of the promises to the patriarchs and becomes still more pronounced in the record of the fulfillment at the first level under the old covenant. When the time of the promised occupation was at hand the land was described as a new garden of Eden, "flowing with milk and honey" (Exod 3:8,17; 13:5; Deut 6:3; Josh 5:6; etc.). Most illuminating for the connection of this promised land with the garden of God in Eden was the establishing of God's theophanic Presence and dwelling in the midst of it.

Particularly the enthronement of the Glory on the temple mount of Zion declared the essential identity of this old covenant kingdom arrangement with the creational order. Here was the cosmic axis of heaven and earth restored as the focus of a renewed holy, theocratic paradise-protectorate. In the patriarchal era the episode of Jacob's dream at Bethel (Gen 28) was a notable anticipation of the promised land as site of the reestablished kingdom-focus. That episode is presented as a redemptive counterpart to the pseudo-focus enterprise at Babel. And in the teaching of Jesus it is interpreted in terms of the Lord's own identity as the new and true link between heaven and earth (John 1:51)

Fulfillment of the land promise at the old covenant level (cf. 1 Kgs 8:65; 1 Chr 13:5; 18:1-12; 2 Chr 9:26) represented a redemptive renewal of the creation kingdom not merely at its original created stage but at the final eschatological stage contemplated in the God's original covenant with Adam. For, as observed above, Israel's procuring of Canaan is portrayed as arrival at a sabbath-rest (Deut 3:20; 12:9; 1 Kgs 8:56) and Sabbath was the Consummation-goal of the creational covenant. The sabbatical experience of Israel in Canaan was, for one thing, a resting from their enemies. It was a sequel to the "final" judgment of the evil Amorites, just as the gaining of the eternal sabbath-realm will follow upon Christ's final defeat and dispossession of all the enemies of his people.

Israel's attainment of creation's sabbatical goal at a first level of fulfillment coincided with their filling the conquered land of Canaan to its full extent according to the allotments to the twelve tribes. And filling the earth was of course another ultimate objective of the kingdom program of the original covenant in Eden, the reaching of which would coincide with the dawning of the Sabbath upon eternal Metapolis.

By virtue then of both the filling of the land of Canaan and its characterization as a sabbath-land, this first level, Canaanite fulfillment of the land promise is seen to be an anticipatory portrayal of the consummated kingdom-land, the Metapolis kingdom-city of the new heavens and earth which the Creator covenanted to man from the beginning. Canaan represented this in a figure; it was only a limited land, not the cosmic goal of the creation kingdom. Also, as Hebrews 4 teaches, Canaan was not the true Sabbath experience. Even believers under the new covenant still await that. The Canaanite, first level fulfillment of the land promise served the pedagogical purpose of pointing beyond itself to the second level fulfillment, intimated by the "everlasting" nature of the promised possession.

Biblical teaching concerning a cataclysmic overhauling to be undergone by the earth and the emergence of a new heaven and earth at the Consummation presents a problem to any interpretation of the promise of an everlasting land inheritance understood in its specifically Palestinian delineation. The particular configuration of Canaanite territory specified to Abraham will not exist forever. Even apart from the assumption of radical cosmic restructuring at the final judgment, one would have to recognize that the current continental configurations of the earth reflected in the Abrahamic land promise would be altered beyond recognition in future ages by the natural geologic dynamics of the planet.

Moreover, and more decisively, in the New Testament there are clear indications of a positive kind of the shift to the second level of meaning of the land promise. Indeed, with surprising abruptness the New Testament disregards the first level meaning and simply takes for granted that the second level, cosmic fulfillment is the true intention of the promise. In keeping with Old Testament prophecies that Messiah, the royal seed of Abraham, would receive and reign over a universal kingdom (e.g., Pss 2:8; 72:8; Zech 9:10), Paul identifies Abraham's promised inheritance as the world (*kosmos*, Rom 4:13). What is more, the New Testament attributes to Abraham himself as a subjective expectation an eschatological hope based on a second level understanding of the land promise. According to Hebrews 11:10,16 the object of Abraham's faith-longing was not any earthly turf of this evil world-age but a better, heavenly country, the city of the new age, the creation of God.

The promised land at the second level of fulfillment is no less a solidly physical reality than it was at the first level. There is no question here of a docetic kind of spiritualizing away of the geophysical dimension of the kingdom. As we have observed, New Jerusalem, the second level fulfillment of the land promise, is the redemptive version of Metapolis and is, therefore, as much a physico-spatial reality as that consummation world proferred in the original covenant with Adam. Guaranteeing the continuing geophysical nature of the promised inheritance at the second level is the biblical teaching of the resurrection of the body. For those bodies of the risen saints there must be an appropriate cosmic environment. During the present phase of the new covenant the seed of promise on earth are, like

Abraham in his day, still awaiting their inheritance of the heavenly city. They are still a pilgrim people, a church in the wilderness (cf. Rev 12:6), not yet arrived at their Sabbath-land (Heb 4:1,11). But at the advent of the consummated Sabbath-order, the resurrection of their bodies and the expanded, exalted second level realization of their geophysical inheritance will occur together.

Additional New Testament corroboration of the second level meaning of the land promise will come before us as we consider the question of the relationship of the first and second levels of the promise to each other.

D. Typal and Antitypal Kingdom

1. Covenantal and Dispensational Hermeneutics

Dispensationalism is evolving and notice will be taken below of current developments, but it is the earlier, widely popularized form of the Dispensational system that is in view here in the first part of our hermeneutical analysis.

The issue between covenantal and dispensational hermeneutics is not one of spiritualizing versus nonspiritualizing interpretations of the second level kingdom. For, contrary to a common allegation, the covenantal system as well as the dispensational allows for the geophysical dimension of that kingdom. The basic question at issue is rather how to construe the relation of the two levels of the promised kingdom of the Abrahamic Covenant to one another. This amounts to the question of the relationship of the old covenant with Israel to the new covenant with the church, particularly as that comes into focus in the typological connection which the Scripture posits between them.

The fundamental fallacy of the dispensational scheme is its failure to do justice to the Bible's identification of the new covenant (or second level) realization of the kingdom promise as standing in continuity with the old covenant (or first level) realization as antitypical fulfillment to typal promise. While the first level kingdom under the old covenant was itself a fulfillment of the Abrahamic promises, it had the character of prophetic promise when viewed in relation to the second level fulfillment under the new covenant. The latter is *the* fulfillment and the former was prototypal. The Abrahamic promises were in effect restated and elaborated as they were embodied in their symbolic old covenant fulfillment. This typological expression of the promises in the kingdom of Israel developed the picture presented in the verbal promises made to the patriarchs into a dramatically concrete visual model by which the ultimate reality of the promised kingdom could be conceptualized and apprehended until the time of true fulfillment came in the messianic age.

Covenantal hermeneutics properly perceives the prototypal, provisional, passing nature of the first level kingdom and the antitypal, perfective, permanent nature of the second level kingdom. Dispensationalists, failing to see that the first level kingdom becomes obsolete and gets replaced by the antitype in the messianic age, continue the obsolete order on indefinitely into the new age. They assign it a place parallel to the second level kingdom, perhaps even permanently so, while relegating the second level fulfillment to a parenthetical rather than perfective status. In so doing, Dispensationalism radically misconstrues the typological structure of the old and new covenants, reducing typology to mere analogy and obscuring the historical promise-fulfillment relationship of these two covenants.

Dispensationalism's virtual rejection of the typological identity of the first level kingdom finds expression in their literalistic misinterpretation of prophecies that depict the second level kingdom in the typological idiom of the first level model. Hence the difference between the dispensational and covenantal hermeneutics is sometimes described as one of literal versus figurative exegesis. But the terms literal and figurative obscure the precise nature of the difference between these two approaches. The terms literal and figurative suggest the issue is of a more general literary sort, whereas it is primarily of an historical nature. Specifically, it concerns contrary analyses of the relationship of two successive covenantal orders in redemptive history, one approach being nontypological and the other typological.

2. Typological Unity and Succession
Under this heading we shall present some of the more salient biblical support for the covenantal view of the typological continuity between the old and new covenant kingdoms, the continuity characterized by a unified movement from promise-symbol to fulfillment-reality.

In the case of the promise of the king it will be readily seen that the relationship between the two levels of fulfillment was not that of two analogous tracks, coexisting and running parallel to each other in the course of the messianic age. For the relation between the Davidic dynasty under the old covenant and Jesus Christ in the new covenant is clearly one of succession, of movement from the earlier to the later. It is indeed a genealogical succession, Jesus being the scion of David's line, the successor who replaced his ancestral predecessors on the throne. There are not two parallel lines of development of the theocratic kingship but one linear, dynastic succession.

Moreover, as this single dynastic line moves from the first to the second level of realization the succession is not a simple matter of continuity but of climactic fulfillment. There is continuity but with an epochal development marked by the difference between David and Jesus, the successor of David who is David's Lord. The difference is that between a promissory typological symbol and the antitypical reality. In Christ the dynasty finds its permanent representative and embodiment. In him the promised everlasting duration of this kingship (cf. 2 Sam 7:13,16) is attained. What had gone before was, by the same token, obviously something temporary and provisional, which performed its historical purpose and made way for the divine King. There is only the one throne of David and since Jesus has now assumed his place as dynastic heir of David on that throne and occupies it forever (Luke 1:32) there is simply no place for the idea of a restoration of the literal David to that throne over God's people. If Dispensationalists do not wish to suggest the replacement of Jesus by David on that throne (in effect, an antichrist usurpation), they have no alternative in interpreting prophecies of the eschatological reign of "David" (Jer 30:9; Ezek 34:23,24; 37:24,25; Hos 3:5) but to abandon their literalistic (non-typological) hermeneutics and acknowledge the genuinely typological nature of the old covenant order as reflected in the typological idiom of such messianic prophecies.

As it is with the king promise, so it inevitably will be with the kingdom promise. Once again the relationship obtaining between the old and new covenant fulfillments is something quite different from and much more than the mere parallelistic analogy allowed by Dispensationalism. What we find in the Scriptures is that there is a unity of the kingdom-people of the old and new covenants and an identity with respect to their promised kingdom inheritance portion. This is consistent with and corroborates the typological, promise-fulfillment continuity proposed in covenant theology, but it is contrary to the discontinuity introduced by the dispensationalist reconstruction with its two parallel programs of two distinct groups of people coexisting apart from each other in two different messianic orders.

Under the figure of the olive tree in Romans 11 Paul depicts the redemptive covenant institution in its ongoing administration from Abraham through the old covenant and into the new. According to the apostle's representation here, it is in the same tree whose lower portion includes the old covenant community (as well as the patriarchal) that the people of the new covenant participate. The picture is one of organic unity between old covenant Israel and new covenant church. Similarly, Paul elsewhere assures the Gentile Christians that, though formerly excluded as foreigners from citizenship in Israel, they are now fellow-citizens. For Christ has destroyed the dividing barrier and out of the two is creating one new man (Eph 2:11-19).

Besides the institutional continuity of the old and new covenant communities, the olive tree imagery of Romans 11 evidences the unity of the promised seed of Abraham at the second level of election in Christ (discussed above under the heading of Sovereign Election). For though not all the individuals who are in this covenant tree are that promised seed (as we see from the fact that branches of the tree can be broken off), the elect remnant are the constant core of the covenant tree. Such is the burden of Paul's argument in Romans 9-11. Thus, unity of the elect people, extending through old covenant times and on into the Christian church, is also of the organic character illustrated by that one living tree in which all the elect are found. The fullness of elect Israel and the fullness of the elect Gentiles together constitute one spiritual family of father Abraham, the true Israel of God.

Inseparable from the unity of old and new covenant believers as fellow citizens (Eph 2:19) is their identity as fellow heirs (Eph 3:6). As one kingdom-people they participate together in one kingdom-inheritance, in one promised land. Christ's redemptive accomplishment brings to the Gentiles the promised blessing of Abraham (Gal 3:14). With reference to God's oath to Abraham guaranteeing reception of the promised land (Gen 15, esp. vv.8 and 18ff.), Hebrews 6:18 says God gave that oath so that we new covenant believers might be reassured of our eschatological hope.

In Hebrews 11 and 12 the common kingdom inheritance of Jewish and Gentile believers is identified as Zion, city of God. Abraham looked for this city of promise (11:10) but did not receive it (11:13). Neither did any of the other just people of God, prediluvian (11:4ff.) or postdiluvian (11:8ff.), all the way down to the coming of Christ: "These all...received not the promise" (11:39; cf. v.13). For God had ordained that they should attain the perfection of the true eschatological inheritance of the heavenly city only in association with his new covenant people (11:40). Even those who under the old covenant experienced the first level fulfillment are here flatly declared not to have received the promise – so far is it from being the case that the first level realization of the land promise continues alongside the second level as a permanent parallel to it. The statement made in Hebrews 11:39 regards the second level realization as the single real fulfillment, so relegating the first level kingdom land to the status of nothing more than shadowy prototype.

According to Hebrews 12:22,23 the believers of premessianic times have, in the new covenant age, at last been made perfect (cf. 11:40) in that they are now, in Christ, in the true heavenly city. This passage also indicates that the Christian believers are united with them in common eschatological community and kingdom inheritance as fellow-citizens of the city of the living God. That kingdom-inheritance of the church of Christ is identified as "mount Zion." What is thus designated is clearly not the first level mountain and city but "the heavenly Jerusalem." This use of first level imagery for the second level reality demonstrates again that the relationship between the two levels of kingdom realization is one of typological unity, with a continuity of old succeeded by new. Of like import is the utilization of the imagery of the first level kingdom-city in the picturing of the glorified church, the bride of the Lamb, in its eternal inheritance as the new Jerusalem in Revelation 21:2 and 10. Of special interest for the typological unity of the old and new covenant kingdoms is the fact that combined in the architecture of the eternal city are the twelve gates bearing the names of the twelve tribes of Israel and twelve foundations having on them the names of the twelve apostles of the Lamb (Rev 21:12-14).

Not analogy then but typology describes the relationship between the two levels of fulfillment of the kingdom-inheritance. They do not stand in parallel to one another but in a linear succession proceeding from the provisional and transient to the perfective and permanent stage of the kingdom. Kingdom level one is identified with the old covenant and level two with the new covenant, and the new covenant is continuous with the old in a successive manner that involves its replacing of the old. Such, according to the author of Hebrews, is the significance of the designation "new" applied to the covenant mediated by Jesus. Commenting on Jeremiah 31:31-34, he says that in referring to the future covenant as new the prophet identified the Mosaic covenant as old in the sense of that which becomes obsolete and vanishes away (Heb 8:13). In the context he has been arguing the superiority of the priesthood of Christ over the Levitical priesthood, observing that the priestly order of the old covenant was but a shadow of the heavenly reality and had been abrogated and superseded by Christ's historical exercising of his heavenly priesthood (Heb 7:18). And in Hebrews 8:6ff. this relationship of the abrogated Levitical priesthood to the current priesthood of Christ is integrated with the relationship of the old to the new and better covenant. Continuity there is between the two levels of fulfillment, the continuity of the substance and its shadow. It is a continuity in which the old gets annulled and removed, its place being taken by the new, the real and permanent fulfillment of the prophetic promise contained in the old.

The new covenant is not a renewal of an older covenant in the sense of confirming the continuing validity of the old. If we speak of the new covenant as a renewal of the old it must be to express their continuity as two administrations of the Covenant of Grace or, more specifically, the continuity of the new covenant with the underlying, foundational stratum of the old covenant, the substratum of gospel-grace as the way to the ultimate heavenly hope in Christ. But with respect to the old covenant as a typological realization of the promised kingdom realm, the new covenant does not confirm the continuing validity of the old but rather announces its obsolescence and end.

Necessarily so. For, as the Jeremiah 31:31-34 prophecy indicated, the old covenant in its typological kingdom aspect was not a permanent order of the grace-guarantee kind but a probationary arrangement informed by the works principle, hence breakable. And having been broken, it was perforce terminated. Thereby, as Paul observes, all, Jew as well as Gentile, were shut up together under the sentence of having failed to attain the kingdom on the ground of obedience to the law and thus all alike were put in the position of being wholly dependent on the mercy of God's grace revealed in the gospel (Rom 11:32).

3. Dispensationalism at Odds with the Gospel

In the past, Dispensationalism has recognized the presence of the works principle in the old covenant, even making that the identifying hallmark of its dispensation of law. In doing so, it did not comprehend the full complexity of the situation. For it did not perceive that the works principle was confined to the typological kingdom stratum of the Mosaic economy and that there was simultaneously in that economy an underlying stratum that was concerned with the eternal salvation of individuals and their inheritance of the everlasting second level kingdom, a stratum governed by the principle of grace. Law (works) was also seen by Dispensationalism as the operative principle in the millennial kingdom dispensation. That was the logical consequence of Dispensationalism's bracketing out the gospel of grace by its concept of the church dispensation of grace as a parenthesis between the two kingdom dispensations of the law and the millennium. As a result, Dispensationalism ended up teaching that there were two different and contrary ways by which fallen men secured God's eschatological blessings. In particular, according to the logic of the dispensational scheme, Israel's possession of the promised kingdom throughout the millennium dispensation would be on the ground of their meritorious compliance with the demands of the law, apart from the suretyship of Christ, that is, apart from the gospel of grace. For all their being fallen sons of Adam, the millennial Jews, it would seem, would be able to satisfy fully and constantly God's probationary demands in that dispensation of law.

Thereby this earlier form of Dispensationalism contradicts the claim of Jesus Christ to be the one way, the only name given under heaven whereby man must be saved. In effect, it takes its stand with Judaism over against Christianity's witness to Jesus as the Christ. Within nominal Christianity it finds itself in the strange theological company of the extreme ecumenists who, advocating a plurality of valid covenantal traditions, accept Judaism, in spite of its failure to confess Christ, as nevertheless, along with the church, a legitimate development of God's covenant with Abraham.

Dispensationalism's beclouding of the exclusive claim and demand of the gospel is also exposed in its failure to challenge the non-Christian Zionist cause when the latter appeals to the promises of the Abrahamic Covenant to validate its claimed right to the (first level) kingdom territory, apart from faith in Christ. In this Zionist claim we see again the defiance of fallen Adam, caught in his covenant-breaking and banished from the "homeland" with its tree of life, but still perversely bent on seizing the forfeited fruit

(Gen 3:22). It is the spectacle again of the unbelieving nation to whom the spies brought back the discouraging report about the situation in Canaan, condemned to wander in the wilderness outside the promised homeland because of their rebellious unbelief but willfully striving to occupy the kingdom in defiance of God's judgment decree (Num 14:4ff.). What Zionist ideology projects is a grotesque parody of the kingdom of God – a land without the temple, an earthly fullness without a heavenly focus. From the beginning it was not so. And if it be that a temple building is included in the plans of these modern architects of the kingdom, while they yet spurn the claims of Jesus, the promised seed of Abraham, the Christ of God, what is this but another Babel-tower, another titanic attempt to erect the cosmic focus by autonomous human effort, another repudiation of the grace of God and his redemptive provision of the true holy temple-city from heaven? Such a pseudo-temple the man of sin might occupy but the Son of Man, himself the true temple, would ultimately destroy it. Any response from the Christian community, dispensational or other, that does not challenge the Zionists' appeal to God's covenant with Abraham to justify the present Israeli occupation of Palestine represents a tragic failure to confront them with fallen man's absolute lack, in himself, of claim on God's covenanted kingdom and with the sinner's desperate need to find restoration to God's favor through Jesus Christ. To show sympathy to the Zionist in his defiant claim is to hide from him the gospel of God's love and to encourage him on his unbelieving way to perdition apart from Christ, the sinner's only hope.

4. Evolving Dispensationalism

As Dispensationalism undergoes revision some of its major former tenets are being shucked off. For one thing, the revisionists would now acknowledge that the eschatological blessings of the salvation-kingdom are secured not by works but by God's grace in Christ. However, in avoiding the error of propounding two ways of salvation they find themselves confronted with a dilemma. For while they want to affirm that it is only in Christ that the Jew can receive the kingdom blessings, they still cling to the notion that there is a separate millennial kingdom for Jewish believers. But the Scriptures disallow this by insisting that if a Jew is in Christ he is no more a Jew, just as a Gentile is no more a Gentile in Christ. For in Christ there is neither Jew nor Gentile (Gal 3:28,29; Col 3:11; cf. Eph 2:12-14). In the only place where salvation's blessings exist – in Christ, the distinction between Jew and Gentile does not exist.

Identification with Christ by faith automatically and absolutely erases the distinction between Jew and Gentile with respect to the securing of peace with God and the joyous glory of the eschatological inheritance. To suggest that certain Jews who are in Christ will have their own peculiar Jewish experience of the kingdom assumes a continuance of the distinction that Christ abolished. It is to build up again the barrier wall that Christ has broken down. It is to cleave the one new man in Christ apart. All who are in Christ share the same eschatological kingdom destiny. Indeed, as we have seen, it is the teaching of Scripture (for example, Hebrews 11 and 12) that not only do all believers since Christ's coming participate in the one heavenly Zion, but so do all previous believers back to Abraham and even back to the beginnings of redemptive history. Scripture simply will not tolerate this dispensationalist notion of a separate salvation-kingdom for Jewish Christians in a future millennium. There is no place for such a salvation-kingdom outside of Christ and there is no place for it in Christ.

Another difficulty for this dispensationalist tenet of a millennial salvation-kingdom designed for Jewish believers is the biblical teaching that all who are in Christ receive all the fullness of the eternal inheritance. All who have the Spirit of Christ are "heirs of God and joint heirs with Christ" (Rom 8:17). Having delivered up his Son for us God will "with him freely give us all things" (Rom 8:32). Paul assures believers: "All things are yours...the world...things present...things to come; all are yours" (1 Cor 3:21,22). This means, on the one hand, that the inheritance of the Jewish believers is the whole world, not just Palestine, and, on the other, that there is no special reserve, Palestinian or any other, set aside for Jewish believers in preference to Gentile believers since all the world belongs to the Gentile believer too. All believers receive all the kingdom alike. All in Christ without ethnic or any other distinction attain to that kingdom fullness that was mandated to the first Adam and is accomplished by the second Adam. God has put all things under Christ's feet, and the church, his body, is "the fullness of him that fills all in all" (Eph 1:22,23; cf. Ps 8:6; Heb 2:8,9). It is the hope and privilege of every believer to be "filled unto all the fullness of God" (Eph 3:19; cf. 4:13; Col 2:10).

Also, the revised Dispensationalism that purges itself of the teaching of two ways of salvation does so at the cost of abandoning the correct perception of earlier Dispensationalism that a works principle was operating in the Mosaic kingdom. Since these revisionists, no more than the older Dispensationalists, discern the two distinct strata (viz. the typological kingdom overlay and the underlying stratum of eternal salvation) coexisting in the old covenant, they do not perceive the true solution of identifying the works principle with the former while maintaining the continuity of the one way of salvation at the other, foundational level. All they can do is join certain of their covenantal critics in denying that there was a works principle in the old covenant.

Moreover, this form of Dispensationalism, like every other, so misconstrues as virtually to deny the type-antitype relationship of the old and new covenants.

Another change being made in Dispensationalism by its progressive wing involves toning down the sharp discontinuity between the old and new covenants which came to expression in the parenthesis concept of earlier Dispensationalism. The progressives do not accept the relegation of the church to a parenthesis between supposedly earlier and later phases of the first level, Jewish kingdom. They recognize in a general way that the typological, first level realization of the promises was provisional and has been replaced by the antitypical realities of the messianic order. Inconsistently, however, they adopt the dispensationalist hermeneutic in their interpretation of the land promise. While regarding participation in the other promises as the common experience of all, Jew or Gentile, in the church of the new covenant, they detach the land promise from the others, attributing to it a continuing first level, Palestinian application on into the second level stage of kingdom eschatology in the messianic age. And they reserve participation in this specialized form of territorial blessing for Jewish Christians in particular.

This progressive Dispensationalism is condemned by the inconsistency of its hermeneutics. The people and the land aspects of the kingdom are in fact correlative and not to be wrenched apart. Together they represent the twin cultural task of filling the earth with people and subduing the kingdom realm as that creational program gets taken up into redemptive history. Land and people promises must therefore be kept together within each level, whether in the typological embodiment of the cultural program in the old covenant kingdom or in its new covenant version. A hybrid combination of old covenant land and new covenant people violates the conceptual unity of these two cultural components of the kingdom, while at the same time ignoring the discreteness of the typical and antitypical kingdoms. In addition to the hermeneutical inconsistency of this form of

Dispensationalism there is also the problem that it too contradicts the Bible's insistence that in Christ the distinction between Jew and Gentile ceases with respect to kingdom inheritance.

Incidentially, not all are liable to this criticism who interpret Romans 9-11 as anticipating a distinctive, future, covenantal development involving the physical seed of Abraham. In particular, there are those who, though they (mistakenly) understand the grafting back of Jews into the covenant tree as pointing to the conversion of a future generation of Jews comprehensively, nevertheless perceive that nothing in Romans 9-11 would justify the notion that these reingrafted Jewish believers would be assigned a distinctive territorial inheritance, temporarily or permanently. Indeed, they recognize that the imagery of Gentiles and Jews being ingrafted, or reingrafted, together into the one and same tree plainly suggests that all who find their place there at the new covenant stage of the tree share one and the same kingdom experience.

5. Antitype Kingdom and the Millennium

Inevitably discussion of the kingdom promises of the Abrahamic Covenant leads to a consideration of the millennium. We may get at this connection by returning to our critical examination of the evolution of Dispensationalism. One feature of Dispensationalism that persists amid the changes taking place is the expectation of a fulfillment of the kingdom promise in a millennial kingdom, a premillennial kingdom ethnically and geographically delimited, a premillennial kingdom of Jews in Palestine.

Also inseparable from Dispensationalism has been the distinctive view it has spawned of a *parousia*-climaxed prelude to the millennium, a seven-year transition from the church age to the supposed millennial resumption of the old covenant kingdom order. The outline of this eschatological scheme is based on a highly idiosyncratic misinterpretation of the seventy weeks prophecy of Daniel 9:24-27. This very successfully marketed end-time fiction is integral to dispensational premillennialism. To espouse this peculiar eschatology is to be a Dispensationalist. To drop this eschatological hallmark would be not simply a revision of Dispensationalism but a mutating of it into another species. It would mark the evolution of dispensational premillennialism into classic (non-dispensational) premillennialism.

Classic premillennialism is a big improvement over Dispensationalism but its view of the fulfillment of the kingdom promise of the Abrahamic Covenant is still defective. This same verdict applies, indeed, to every form of millennial eschatology that finds in the millennium a fulfillment of the kingdom promise. Postmillennialism (properly so-called) also commits this error. More precisely the mistake made by both premillennialism and postmillennialism is to posit a coming of the promised kingdom of power and glory foretold by the prophets before the Consummation. Both these millennial views recognize that the ultimate coming of the kingdom in heavenly glory transpires at the Consummation but they also suppose there is a preliminary realization of the antitypal theocratic kingdom in the millennium and thus before the Consummation (which of course comes after the millennium on any view of the sequence of the millennium and the *parousia*).

One problem with such millennial views is that biblical prophecy clearly indicates that until the Final Judgment/Consummation event the evil powers will be present, opposing and persecuting the community of faith on earth. Not until the Final Judgment, not until after the total elimination of the satanic forces forever, will the saints of the Most High receive the kingdom of glory and its cosmic, everlasting dominion (cf., e.g., Dan 2 and 7). Only amillennialism is true to this vision of the postconsummation inauguration of the glory-kingdom. Only amillennialism recognizes that the millennium is for the church militant a martyr age – an age of martyr-witness in fulfillment of the great commission, an age of martyr-suffering with Christ and not yet the hour of glorification with Christ.

Another problem with the preconsummation views, both premillennial and postmillennial, is that they muddle the type-antitype structure of redemptive history. According to the Scriptures there is a clear-cut distinction between the typal and antitypal levels of fulfillment of the kingdom domain promised in the Abrahamic Covenant. The typal kingdom is a bounded terrestrial territory set within a temporary world order regulated by the terms of the Covenant of Common Grace. The antitypal fulfillment is a supernal and eternal realm, a heavenly New Jerusalem, a Sabbath-Consummation reality whose presence terminates the common grace order, brings to an end the world that now is and introduces the world to come. The classic premillennialists and the postmillennialists do well in recognizing, over against Dispensationalists, that the kingdom promises must be translated from the old covenant typal idiom into the antitypal reality when moving into the age of new covenant fulfillment. But they garble the translation. Their millennial kingdom blurs the sharp distinction between type and antitype. It cannot be identified with either. Unlike the type it extends beyond Palestine to the whole world. Unlike the antitype it is earthly not heavenly and it is of limited duration not everlasting, its dominion being interrupted by a concluding Gog/antichrist/Har Magedon crisis in which the kingdom people are beset on a global scale and their world witness suppressed. Such a mongrel millennial kingdom finds no place in amillennialism. Amillennialism's postconsummational eschatology alone presents a truly biblical account of the antitypical, messianic fulfillment of God's kingdom promise in the Abrahamic Covenant.

6. Design of the Typal Kingdom

A variety of purposes can be discovered to explain the insertion of the old covenant order and its typal kingdom into the course of redemptive history. Of central importance was the creation of the proper historical setting for the advent of the Son of God and his earthly mission (cf. Rom 9:5). In accordance with the terms of his covenant of works with the Father he was to come as the second Adam in order to undergo a representative probation and by his obedient and triumphant accomplishment thereof to establish the legal ground for God's covenanted bestowal of the eternal kingdom of salvation on his people. It was therefore expedient, if not necessary, that Christ appear within a covenant order which, like the covenant with the first Adam, was governed by the works principle (cf. Gal 4:4). The typal kingdom of the old covenant was precisely that. Within the limitations of the fallen world and with modifications peculiar to the redemptive process, the old theocratic kingdom was a reproduction of the original covenantal order. Israel as the theocratic nation was mankind stationed once again in a paradise-sanctuary, under probation in a covenant of works. In the context of that situation, the Incarnation event was legible; apart from it the meaning of the appearing and ministry of the Son of Man would hardly have been perspicuous. Because of the congruence between Jesus' particular historical identity as the true Israel, born under the law, and his universally relevant role as the second Adam, the significance of his mission as the accomplishing of a probationary assignment in a works covenant in behalf of the elect of all ages was lucidly expressed and readily readable.

Much more than the works-probation aspect of Jesus' task was included in the revelatory design of the typal kingdom. It prepared a public context in world history in which the meaning of Jesus' mission as a whole might be communicated effectively. For example, an exposition of the priest-king role of Jesus was afforded by the institutional integration of the Israelite temple cultus and the Davidic monarchy within the theocratic kingdom.

Besides preparing an appropriate context for the messianic mission, a broadly pedagogical purpose was served by the typal kingdom in that it furnished spiritual instruction for the faithful in ages both before and after the advent of Christ (1 Cor 10:11). Thus, in addition to calling attention to the probationary aspect of Jesus' mission, the works principle that governed the Israelite kingdom acted as the schoolmaster for Israel, convicting of sin and total inability to satisfy the Lord's righteous demands and thereby driving the sinner to the grace of God offered in the underlying gospel promises of the Abrahamic Covenant. (Recognition of this preparatory contribution of the law does not depend on acceptance of the suggested understanding of the *paidagogos* of Gal 3:24,25.)

At this point we may parenthetically note another need met by the kingdomizing of the covenant order. The condemnatory effect of the law just mentioned was intensified by the extensive and detailed elaboration of God's requirements for the community. And the kingdom organization provided by the typal stage in the fulfillment of the Abrahamic kingdom promises was a prerequisite for the formulation of such a comprehensive corpus of legislation. Appropriately, these laws assumed the specific form of covenant stipulations such as were found in the kind of treaty document that was imposed as a kingdom-constitution on a vassal people (cf. my *Structure of Biblical Authority*, pp.76ff.).

Other lessons about the nature of God's eternal kingdom were taught through the history of the typal kingdom. Those who gave thought to it might learn that the heavenly kingdom is to be established by a final holy-war judgment of the world; that the eternal kingdom is a temple domain cleansed of all evil, a realm where piety and prosperity are perfectly wedded, where God's personal Presence is the crowning glory and the beholding of God's Face the ultimate beatitude – and many such things. In short, this typal model of heaven was a master historical parable of the kingdom, dramatically presented by the Lord of history.

Hand-in-hand with the pedagogical function of the typal kingdom went its purpose of contributing to the preservation of the covenant community on earth. Postdiluvian history down to the patriarchal age exhibited the same trend towards the diminution of the ranks of the people of God as had the prediluvian era. A measure of insulation from the corrosive impact of the corruptions of the Gentile world was secured for Israel by its establishment as a separate nation. This end was furthered by constant reminders, as in the system of things clean and unclean, of their holy distinctiveness as God's people.

A more positive countermeasure taken by the Lord against the erosion of the covenant community was his augmenting of the means of grace through which the Spirit worked to propagate the seed of the woman in a world infested by the seed of the devil. And it was in part with a view to this expansion and concentration of revelation as re-creative instrument of the Spirit that the Lord arranged in the Abrahamic Covenant for the typal kingdom stage and the ethnocentralizing of the covenant community that accompanied its kingdomization. The rich parabolic teaching of the symbolic typal kingdom itself would serve to support and strengthen the faith of the remnant. But also in view was the appearance of the Scriptures as the preeminent means of grace unto the preservation of a people for God's name (cf. Rom 3:2). And the linguistically unified and historically continuous community provided by the typal kingdom facilitated and was even necessary for the production of the Scriptures, Scriptures of the organically coherent kind that God gave his covenant people (cf. my *Structure of Biblical Authority*, pp.77f.).

Thus perceived, the ethnic particularism that characterized the typal kingdom was not so much a constriction of the covenant community as it was a strategy to prevent its further perilous decrease. The grand design of this divine arrangement was the preservation of the covenant community to bridge the centuries yet remaining to the fullness of time and, as we have observed above, the preparation of this community as the suitable historical setting for the earthy mission of the Messiah. As a preparation for the mission of the Savior of the world, the ethnocentric typal kingdom of the old order was, in the wisdom of the divine design, a provisional particularistic means to an ultimate universalistic end.

A fundamental perspective that has emerged in our study of the promises of the Abrahamic Covenant is that the fulfillment of these promises in Christ represents the attainment of the eschatological goal set before mankind at the creation. In this messianic accomplishment, overcoming the effects of the Fall, the kingdom focus is restored and its fullness is achieved.

And since the Abrahamic Covenant, as can be seen from its ultimate outcome, was a redemptive resumption of the original universal kingdom program, its inclusion of a particularistic Jewish kingdom in its package of promises ought not to be treated as the launching on a second parallel track of a novel kingdom program. That particularistic kingdom is clearly to be understood as a provisional stage on a single kingdom track, a subordinate stage leading to the new covenant stage and the ultimate universal goal of God's kingdom. Second level fulfillment of the promised kingdom, fulfillment perfect and cosmic, involving "all the fullness of God," leaves no room for the perpetuation of a partial and imperfect first level fulfillment alongside it. Necessarily it replaces the first level fulfillment, which is then seen to have been a typological interim provision, a prophetic sign serving before the fullness of time to point to the kingdom fullness that was to come in Christ under the new covenant.

Chapter Four

PRE-KINGDOM ABRAHAMIC COMMUNITY

Not until the mission of Moses recorded in Exodus through Deuteronomy does the fulfillment of the kingdom promises of the Abrahamic Covenant at their first level get underway. Patriarchal history narrated in Genesis 12-50 antedates any appearance of the promised redemptive kingdom, typal or antitypal. In that sense, the book of Genesis is kingdom prologue. However, though the kingdom as a realm was not yet on the scene, but abeyant, there was already present in the days of the patriarchs an anticipation of the kingdom as a spiritual reign of God in the lives of his people.

In this chapter we shall analyze the era of the patriarchs from this eschatological perspective, developing the point that it was characterized not by kingdom power but by pilgrim politics and polity, not by kingdom glory but by a more veiled divine presence and by an inner transfiguration of God's people. As children of Abraham under the new covenant we observe with particular interest the similarities between the patriarchal age and our own with respect to this pattern of realized and unrealized eschatology, a pattern that distinguishes these two ages from the Israelite kingdom epoch which they bracket.

I. PILGRIM POLITICS AND POLITY

A. Pre-Kingdom Politics

Realization of the twofold kingdom promise of posterity and territory was to be long delayed. As to the promised descendants, progress was impeded by the barrenness of the patriarchs' wives and by other obstacles. Though these hindrances were overcome and Abraham's family developed into a twelve-tribe people during the centuries covered by Genesis 12-50, growth of this community to the promised proportions of great nationhood still lay in the future at the point reached at the close of the Genesis narrative.

Acquisition of the promised land went even slower. Early in the account there is the episode of Abraham's walk about his territorial grant, undertaken at the Lord's behest (Gen 13:17). This was evidently a symbolic legal procedure by which one staked out a land claim (cf. Josh 18:4; 24:3). Customarily it would be a public act in the company of the civil authorities, solemnly sealing the official transference of the title to the property. But in the case of Abraham the circumambulation was performed as a private statement of eschatological faith before the eyes of the Lord, the ultimate sovereign of the territory and bestower of the grant. As far as immediate ownership was concerned, the patriarch was at the end of his walk still only a resident alien in this land.

Subsequently some small pieces of land were obtained by purchase. From Ephron the Hittite Abraham secured the field of Machpelah with its burial cave (Gen 23) and Jacob bought a plot of ground at Shechem from the sons of Hamor (Gen 33:19). These properties served as an earnest of the inheritance to which the hope of the patriarchal community could attach itself. For example, in the return of the body of Jacob for burial in the cave of Machpelah (Gen 50:12,13) faith testified to its expectation of the exodus of all Israel and their eventual occupation of the land in its fullness. But fulfillment was not yet. Indeed at the end of the book of Genesis it seems more remote than ever. Far from having obtained the total territory of the promise, or even an expanded hold therein, the twelve-tribe family actually found itself at that late date living in a foreign land outside the borders of Canaan. This was in accordance with the Lord's prophetic disclosure to Abraham that his more immediate posterity would be "sojourners in a land not theirs," suffering affliction there and only after the lapse of four centuries experiencing an exodus-deliverance and a victorious homecoming (Gen 15:13-16). Meanwhile, before the descent into Egypt, the patriarchal community had to be content with sojourner status in the land of Canaan, dwelling in the land of promise as in a land not their own. They beheld the kingdom from afar and confessed that for the present they were strangers and pilgrims on the earth (Heb 11:9,13; Gen 23:4; 47:9). At the appointed time God would visit his people with redemptive judgment, delivering them from bondage and bringing them in triumph to possess the mountain of God's inheritance. Then the covenant nation would become a theocratic kingdom. However, until the hour came for the Lord's vindicatory judgments on the Amorites (Gen 15:13,14), the covenant people must wait in hope and journey in faith. Theirs was a time for the cultivation of common grace relationships, a time for toleration and cooperation with the occupants of the land.

In relation to the civil rulers in Canaan the patriarchal age was characterized by pilgrim politics. That the covenant community was not yet a theocratic kingdom but a pilgrim family following customary common grace procedures can be plainly seen in the various economic and political dealings of the patriarchs. Of special significance are their covenants and contracts with the Canaanites.

Later, when the Mosaic day of the Lord dawned dark with judgment over the land of Canaan and the command was issued to the theocratic army to storm the land, appropriating it for Yahweh, the Israelites would be forbidden to enter into alliances with the peoples of the land. The inhabitants of Canaan were to be smitten, driven out, utterly destroyed, not shown mercy or received into covenantal relationship (Exod 23:32; 34:12,15; Deut 7:2). Such was the mandate of the intrusion ethic of holy war which obtained when the covenant community, by the Lord's ordaining, became a theocratic institution. But the earlier, patriarchal community, with no apparent hint of divine disapproval, did enter into covenants with their Canaanite neighbors. This tells us two things. One is that the divine institutional norms which govern the functioning of a theocracy are not meant for general application apart from that institutional framework. The second is that the covenant institution in the patriarchal age was nontheocratic.

The particular substance of the covenants made by the patriarchs with the Canaanites further accents this difference between the patriarchal and theocratic periods. Some of these covenants were in settlement of disputes over access rights to wells (Gen 21:22ff.; 26:26ff.). The underlying assumption of the negotiations was that the patriarchs had the status of resident aliens in the land and the arrangements that were concluded defined their rights and obligations as those of merely tolerated sojourners (Gen 21:23,34; 26:3). Tolerated pilgrims, not triumphant possessors – such is the life of the nontheocratic community of faith, waiting while the kingdom is withheld.

One covenant made by Abraham with local Amorites cemented a military confederation (Gen 14:13,24). It is mentioned in connection with an event in which he engaged in a successful skirmish against an alliance of eastern powers. But though he enjoyed a military triumph in the land, the promised kingdom had not yet come. Indeed, the whole episode exhibits the common grace character of the patriarch's relation to the occupants of

Canaan and points up the delay of the hour of the Shem-Abraham dispossession of Ham-Canaan. For Abraham did not contend against the nations of Canaan. Rather, he and the Canaanites were joined in covenant of mutual defense against a common enemy from outside the land of promise, an enemy that included Semite contingents. As a closing touch the narrative cites Abraham's special concern that his Amorite confederates in arms receive their just portions from the joint enterprise. Very different this from the politics of the Mosaic age of theocratic kingdom.

Besides the testimony of the covenants is that of the contracts or business agreements. The very transactions that brought Abraham and Jacob into ownership of at least some fragments of the promised land reminded them that the time had not yet arrived to take possession of the kingdom by holy war. For they were obliged to make these acquisitions by the ordinary process of purchase. There was no aggressive assertion of title deriving from claim to a special divine grant that contravened and overruled the existing rights of proprietorship obtaining by virtue of common grace provisions.

Subordination of the patriarchal pilgrims to the temporal political powers is illustrated by Abraham's purchase of the field of Machpelah. If later Hittite real estate laws embody long-standing Near Eastern legal traditions, the process of negotiations described in Genesis 23 would seem to reflect that legal background. If so, what Abraham tried to avoid, but unsuccessfully, was the socage obligations attendant upon the purchase of an entire unit of property. The effect of his having to buy the whole field instead of just the cave on the edge of it was that Abraham became responsible for the customary fees and services to the civil authorities. And in the performance of these obligations he would be making a specific public acknowledgement that the land God had promised him was at present rightfully under Canaanite jurisdiction and control. Expressed in terms of the New Testament age, Abraham was made more acutely aware by the purchase of the field that he was duty-bound to render unto Caesar that which was Caesar's.

An act of aggression in defiance of common grace politics and economics, a plundering of the Canaanites, is reported in the account of the experience of Jacob's family at Shechem (Gen 34:14ff.). But Jacob's denunciation of this treacherous violence on the part of his sons (Gen 34:30; 49:5-7) underscores the contrast in eschatological situation and ethic between that time and the later age of Israelite conquest, when action formally similar to the reprobated deed of Simeon and Levi was the divine order of the day.

Delayed until the set time (Gen 15:13,14), a day of divine judgment was in store for Canaan when the Lord would terminate the authority of the Canaanite Caesars and confiscate their domains so that the meek folk of the covenant might inherit the land. That would be a day for holy war and intrusion ethics, for seizing Canaan in God's name and establishing his theocratic kingdom there. But the time for theocratic politics is in the Father's hands and it is not for pilgrims to try to change his times. It is not for them, impatient with the unrealized eschatology of their day, to attempt to force the birth of the theocratic kingdom prematurely. Perseverance in faith and patience in tribulation – such graces become the sojourning servants of the Lord in an age of pilgrim politics.

Along with patient, passive endurance, pursuit of the policy of pilgrim politics meant for the patriarchal covenant community a more active and positive role in their world as well. While there were instances enough where the presence of this community of God's people (partly because of failings of its members) was the occasion of strife for other peoples, there were also times when their presence proved to be a blessing to others, bringing them some temporal earthly benefits. Abraham's successful foray against the invading kings resulted in a restoration of captives and plundered goods to neighboring Canaanite cities (Gen 14). Regard for Lot's personal interests in the midst of the Lord's destruction of the cities of the plain led to the sparing of Zoar (Gen 19:21). Laban acknowledged that his flocks had prospered thanks to the presence of Jacob (Gen 30:27). And outstanding as an example of the patriarchal family as agents of common grace blessings to the world of their day was the history of Joseph in Egypt. Wherever Joseph was taken prosperity attended him (Gen 39:3-5,23) and climacticly the nation of the pharaoh, and other affected countries too, were preserved through the famine by virtue of the wise administrative measures of Joseph (Gen 41:41ff.). This blessing role is epitomized in the episode of Jacob blessing pharaoh (Gen 47:7,10). The total contrast between this meeting of Jacob with pharaoh and the confrontation of Moses with the pharaoh in his day, the day of the coming of God's kingdom in judgment, illustrates graphically the pre-kingdom nature of the age of patriarchal pilgrims.

B. Family Polity

Organizationally the covenant community in the patriarchal period was not unlike what it had been through the times before and since the Flood. For the basic picture of patriarchal covenant polity, therefore, it would be useful to consult again the analysis of the earlier periods given above. (See especially Part I, Section B, Chapter Two, II B and C and Part II, Chapter Two, III E.) By reason of the peculiar relationship in which the Abrahamites stood to the future of redemptive history, certain of the institutional forms and functions that were shared with the pre-Abrahamic community took on a special significance. An example would be the particular geographic location of their altars. We shall concentrate here on these distinctive aspects of the Genesis 12-50 period. Special emphasis will be laid on the not-yet-theocratic nature of the patriarchal covenant institution.

It has been observed that covenants of grant such as God gave to Abraham were closely related in concept and terminology to legal formulations pertaining to family inheritance. There was thus congruity between the legal form in which God's promises were bestowed and the family nature of the recipients. Indeed, the covenant of grant to Abraham adopted this family structure of the Abrahamites as its own governmental form. In the patriarchal age, covenant polity was family polity.

1. Family and Covenant Congregation

From the beginning the institution of the family was consistently respected in determining the constituency of the covenant family. (See further on this topic my *By Oath Consigned*, pp.84ff.) The continuation of this administrative principle under the Abrahamic Covenant becomes most prominent and explicit in the regulations governing the covenant sign of circumcision. (See above on the symbolic meaning of this sign.) As a sign performed on an organ of generation, circumcision alluded to the descendants of the one who was circumcised. Thus, in symbolizing the curse on the covenant-breaker, circumcision included a reference to the cutting off of one's descendants and so of one's name and future place in the covenant community. However, insofar as circumcision was a sign of consecration, it signified that the issue of the circumcised member was consecrated to the Lord of the covenant and thereby set aside from profane to holy status, that is, to membership in the covenant institution. Agreeably, God promised to establish the covenant with Abraham's descendants after him (Gen 17:7). In the stipulation that the infant sons of the Abrahamites be circumcised on their eighth day (Gen 17:12) the administrative principle is most clearly expressed that the parental authority of the confessors of the covenant faith defines the bounds of the covenant community. Those under that parental authority are to be consigned to the Lord by the appointed sign of incorporation into the covenant congregation. By divine appointment it is the duty of the one who enters God's covenant to exercise his parental authority by bringing those under that authority along with himself under the covenantal jurisdiction of the Lord God.

Included in the circumcision provision along with Abraham's descendants were his household servants (Gen 17:12,13). Not only parental authority but a broader household authority was, therefore, determinative of the bounds of the covenant congregation at that time. This administrative policy of God's covenant puts one in mind of the ancient suzerain-vassal covenants, for these were made with the vassal king precisely in his status as a king and therefore specifically included his family and the whole domain under his royal authority in the stipulated obligations and sanctions of the treaty, along with himself as swearer of the covenant oath.

When ordering the polity of the new covenant church the Lord continued, as ever, to honor the family institution and its authority structure. This is clearly taught by Paul in connection with his treatment of the covenant in Romans 11:16ff. under the image of the olive tree that represents the old and new covenants in their organic institutional continuity. Directing attention to the holy root of this tree, which would be Abraham, the apostle declares that if the root is holy the rest of the tree deriving from that root is holy. This holiness is not that inward spiritual holiness which is the fruit of the sanctifying work of the Spirit in the elect, for it is shared by those (branches) whose nonelection is betrayed by their eventually being broken off from the olive tree. Hence the olive tree as such does not represent the election but the covenant, and the holiness attributed to the tree, root and branches, is the formal status-holiness of membership in the covenant institution. The affirmation that the holy root imparts holiness to the tree growing up from it is to be understood, therefore, as a figurative expression of the administrative principle that parental authority determines inclusively the bounds of the covenant constituency. This principle, illustrated in the first instance by the relation of Abraham (the root) to his descendants, has repeated application in each generation, beyond the ability of the olive tree metaphor to convey. Each successive part of the tree, as it were, becomes a new holy root imparting holiness to its own branching extensions. The apostle is thus teaching as an ongoing principle of covenant polity that if the parent is a member of the holy covenant, so is the child.

Since the new covenant church is depicted in the Romans 11 imagery as an organic continuation of the old covenant community (vv.17ff.), the root-branches principle of covenantal holiness must continue to apply to at least those Jewish branches of Abraham not cut off but continuing on as the remnant of Israel in the church of the new covenant. But surely there would not be a different policy on covenantal incorporation for Gentiles than for Jews within the church, where the partition wall between the two has disappeared. The holy parent/holy child principle must, therefore, apply to ingrafted Gentile branches as well as to Jews. Confirming all this is Paul's treatment of precisely this same issue in 1 Corinthians 7. There the apostle teaches that even if only one parent is a believer (a holy root-branch) and the other profane, the holy prevails over the profane in the marriage relationship and the child of that sanctified union is holy (v.14). Also, by applying the covenantal blessing of the fifth commandment to the children of Christian parents (Eph 6:1-3; cf. Col 3:20; Exod 20:12) Paul indicates that they are not merely under the call to enter the covenant but are *in* the holy covenant, consigned under its terms of blessing or curse.

Statements in the New Testament concerning household baptisms provide another indication that the children of believers are still, under the new covenant, to be regarded as holy members of the covenant community (Acts 16:15,33f.; 1 Cor 1:16; cf. Acts 10:2,47f.; 11:14; 18:8; 2 Tim 1:16; 4:19; John 4:53). In the rite of baptism we have the ritual sign of the new covenant that demonstrably matches the previous covenant sign of circumcision in all major respects (as indicated above). Baptism corresponds to circumcision in its symbolic depiction of the divine judgment of death, in its proper theological import of identification with Christ in his death leading to resurrection-justification, and in its function as consecration sign of incorporation into the holy covenant community (cf. *By Oath Consigned*, pp.63ff.). Accordingly, the fact that references to households recur in connection with baptism is indicative that membership in the covenant community (the church), of which baptism is the sign, continues under the new covenant as under the old to be based not solely on individual confession of faith but on the principle of parental-household authority as well. (Cf. *By Oath Consigned*, pp.96f. See pp.94ff. for a discussion of the question of the continuation of the broader household approach inclusive of "servants.") In particular, the household baptism data corroborate the conclusion that children under the parental authority of covenant members belong to the church and, therefore, should receive baptism, the sign of that holy status.

These principles of covenant administration are often slighted when the question of the grounds of infant baptism is under discussion. Traditionally, paedobaptist answers have tended to slip into an ecclesiology more compatible with the Baptist position. If due account is taken of these polity principles, the church as an institution of this present world will not be defined simply in terms of election (or believers). Paul included the new covenant as well as preceding times when making the point (in Romans 9-11) that covenant and election do not coincide. As an instance of the different compass of covenant and election in the patriarchal age he cited the case of Esau, recipient of the covenantal sign of circumcision, yet reprobate (9:12,13). And for old covenant times the apostle observed that they are not all Israel who are of Israel (9:6; cf. v.27). Then, recognizing that the same situation obtained in the new covenant church, he warned Gentiles grafted into the holy tree of the covenant institution that they too, like the Israelites, could be broken off (11:21). This means that when we are defining the present covenant community, the church as it exists in this world, we must do so in terms that will accommodate the reality of holy covenantal status that is not necessarily accompanied by inward holiness.

This also means that when we are establishing the ground for baptizing our children into the church our appeal should not be to the "promise," for the promised seed is the election and the covenantal constituency is not delimited by election, nor do we know whether or not our children are elect. In fact, in the case of Esau, it was with awareness, resulting from divine foreannouncement, that he was not the seed of promise (Gen 25:23) that his parents nevertheless circumcised him, in accordance with the Lord's requirement. Speculative considerations about the election or regeneration of our children are irrelevant to their being baptized. It is not a matter of the promise but of the parental authority principle. By virtue of the Lord's directive children under the authority of confessing parents are to be accorded their proper status as members of the holy covenant and are to receive the appointed sign of incorporation into the consecrated community. In presenting them for baptism we do not regard them as holy "in Christ" (which is the equivalent of election) but as covenantally holy.

By baptismal oath they are consigned under the covenantal jurisdiction of the Lord and at the same time they are invited to participate by faith-identification with the Savior in his death-baptism and thereby to enter into the fullness of the blessings covenanted unto father Abraham.

2. Family and Covenant Government

a. Father Abraham: In pre-Abrahamic times the redemptive community as a whole was the composite of all the covenant family units distributed over the earth. Though found to some extent elsewhere, there was a concentration of these families in the lines of Seth and Shem in the prediluvian and postdiluvian eras respectively. In fact, in the earlier era the total covenant community on earth was reduced eventually to the one Sethite family of Noah. A similar tendency set in again after the Flood. This trend was certainly in process by patriarchal times, yet, as the examples of Melchizedek and Job illustrate, the Covenant of Grace, broadly viewed, was still represented here and there by family units other than Abraham's. By the Mosaic age, whatever such exceptions there might have been were rapidly vanishing, leaving the Abrahamites, now the twelve tribes of Israel, as the remnant of the redemptive covenant, the sole surviving covenant family.

Another kind of ethnocentric development in covenant administration took place with Abraham, one that was not simply a restricting of the covenant line to a single ethnic line as a result of attrition in the covenant ranks elsewhere. This one rather followed from the circumstance that a special covenant was established with an individual partriarch making his family *the* covenant family in this particular covenantal arrangement. This had also happened in the case of Noah. In addition to the fact that his family was left as the sole and total surviving remnant of the Covenant of Grace, Noah was the recipient of a special covenant, the ark-kingdom covenant, in which the covenant community was identified specifically and exclusively with his family. The peculiar covenant that God made with Abraham's family had a distinctive purpose and program within the unity of redemptive history. Because this special covenantal order involved the entire future course and consummation of the redemptive kingdom, the effect of identifying it with Abraham and his descendants was that the whole future structure of redemptive covenant took on, in one sense or other, the contours of that Abrahamic family.

Both the Noahic and Abrahamic instances of ethnic particularism in covenant history began with a pre-kingdom stage of waiting, followed in due course by an advent of the kingdom. The Flood-covenant was inaugurated by the divine oath-promise presenting to Noah and his family the grant of the kingdom in the ark. They must, however, first pass through the pre-kingdom stage of the allotted one hundred twenty years (Gen 6:3) during which the evil of those who dwelt on the earth was ripening for wrath. Then, at the judgment, the form of the covenant community was changed and the Noahic family became the kingdom of God in the ark. Similarly, the Abrahamic family, after receiving the kingdom grant in the covenant promises, had to wait through the appointed four hundred years of a pre-kingdom age (Gen 15:13,16) until the iniquity of the Amorites was full. Then with the exodus mission of Moses the covenant family community of the Abrahamites became the covenant kingdom of Israel.

Thus, from the Abrahamic Covenant onwards the institutional form assumed by the redemptive covenant proceeds from the patriarchal pre-kingdom household to the (typological) kingdom-family of the twelve tribes of Israel. It is a major concern of the latter part of the book of Genesis to trace the origins of this kingdom-family back to the twelve great grandsons of Abraham in the chosen line. Then, in terms of the spiritual family of Abraham in the new covenant, the familial polity of the covenant community takes the form in turn of the ecclesiastical household of faith and, finally, the heavenly kingdom-family in the Spirit.

Within this family pattern of covenant formation Abraham had the status of father of all the covenant people. This holds true at the second level of the seed-promise only in and through that special individual seed of Abraham, Christ Jesus, the father by the Spirit of all the rest of Abraham's (spiritual) seed – and of Abraham himself. In this development from type to antitype Abraham is a prefiguration of his messianic son. As paternal source and patriarch of the covenant family (cf. Isa 51:1,2) Abraham was a prototype of the second Adam, the patriarchal father of that new mankind in which the Edenic ideal of the kingdom-family, originally set before Adam, is realized. Out of the deadness of Abraham's century-old body God made the multitudinous covenant family to spring (Heb 11:12), and in this way father Abraham prefigured the Servant of the Lord, who out of the travail of his death as an offering for sin saw his numerous seed come into being (Isa 53:10-12). Reflecting this typological status of the patriarch is the concept of being gathered into Abraham's bosom (Luke 16:22,23), if understood on the analogy of John 1:18 as a figurative equivalent of being welcomed into the embrace of the heavenly Father-Lord (as is favored by the frequent use of *kolpos*, "bosom," in sepulchral epitaphs).

b. Patriarchal Authority: Though the Abrahamic Covenant marked a turning point of epochal dimensions in covenant history, covenant polity continued in the patriarchal era along lines fundamentally similar to what is found in the previous period. As we have seen, the prospect of the external political kingdom was in abeyance in this era of alien residency in Canaan. The covenant family was not yet kingdomized. Their identity as a redemptive covenant community rather consisted in their functioning as a cultic congregation. They simultaneously functioned as a common grace family but their holy covenantal status lay in their worshipping-witnessing role in relation to the holy altar of the Lord. The Abrahamic covenant family was an altar family, a priestly community, a spiritual temple.

The polity of the Abrahamic altar-congregation was familial in that its authority structure coincided with that of the family. There was no specialized priesthood in charge, no separate order of cultic officers. The general authority of the family patriarch extended to the area of the family's covenantal identity as a cultic assembly.

An episode from the life of Jacob illustrates at once the household bounds of the covenantal cultic community and its patriarchal authority structure. On his return to Canaan, Jacob was directed by God to Bethel to build an altar and reaffirm the covenant, fulfilling the vow he had made there long before (Gen 28:20ff.; 35:1). No longer just an individual, as when he made that vow, but head of a great household now, Jacob united them all with himself in his culticly affirmed covenant commitment. Addressing his family as one with authority to exercise covenant discipline over them, he called on them to perform the paramount obligation of covenant worship. Of the entire household he required that they render sole devotion to the Lord God, purging themselves of all the material tokens of idolatry brought from Paddan-aram (Gen 35:1-4). Another expression of the headship of the family patriarchs in the covenant cultus was their pronouncing of the benediction of God in their declarative communication of the covenant blessing to their household (Gen 27:27ff.; 48:14ff.; 49:1-28).

Patriarchal authority over the cultic family had a prophetic dimension. Indeed, in the first appearance in the Bible of the term *nabi`*, the common designation for the Israelite prophets, it is Abraham who is explicitly so identified by the Lord (Gen 20:7). Though with particular reference to the Genesis 20:7 episode, Psalm 105:15 extends the designation of prophet to the other patriarchs. In their exercise of prophetic rule over the covenant community the patriarchs were resuming the tradition of the prediluvian prophet figures Enoch and Noah and anticipating the prophetic office in the kingdom of Israel.

The main privileges and functions that characterize the prophets later raised up in accordance with the provisions of the old covenant (cf. Deut 18:15-19) are for the most part found to be present in the roles performed by the patriarchs in the pre-Mosaic period. Referring to the patriarchs, Psalm 105:15 parallels the term "prophets" with "anointed ones," so describing them by a term that evokes the image of the later prophets as preeminently the covenant officers commissioned by anointing of God's Spirit (cf. the prophetic designation, "man of the Spirit," Hos 9:7). Vouchsafed to the patriarchs was the distinctive prophetic privilege of being confidants of the Lord, admitted into his council presence to be apprised of his secret purposes (cf. Gen 18:17; Num 12:6-8; Jer 23:16-22). Reception of special disclosures of the word of the Lord is a recurring feature of the patriarchs' experience. To each of them the Lord is said to have appeared and to have spoken. Various modes of divine revelation are mentioned: theophany, vision, dream.

Inspired prophetic utterance is attributed to the patriarchs. Their blessings on the heirs of the covenant (Gen 27:27-29; 49:1-27), while functioning legally as testamentary disposition and cultically as priestly pronouncement, constituted a prophetic forecast of the future outworking of the covenant curses and blessings in redemptive history. Such concern with the covenant sanctions is the constant and pervasive theme of biblical prophecy. Illustrative of the continuity of patriarchal and Israelite prophecy is the close relationship between Jacob's testamentary blessings on his sons (Gen 49:1-27) and the final covenantal blessings bestowed on the tribes of Israel by Moses, the paradigm prophet of the old covenant (Deut 33). Jacob's prophetic blessings are also notable for the long range of their vision, reaching down into "the latter days" (Gen 49:1) to the messianic lion of the tribe of Judah, whose sceptre should be universal and eternal (Gen 49:8-12).

Intercession was another function of the Israelite prophet (cf., e.g., Ps 99:6f.; Jer 15:1; 27:18; 1 Kgs 13:6) and this role too is attributed to the patriarchs. Thus, it is precisely in his capacity as a "prophet" that Abraham is to pray for king Abimelech (Gen 20:7; cf. 18:22-32).

Within the patriarchal order, as in the Mosaic economy, the covenantal office of prophet carried prerogatives and functions of the priestly and royal offices. We have observed that the prophet-patriarchs ruled over their family community and they performed priestly acts like officiating at the altar, offering intercession, and pronouncing blessings. However, the prophetic office in the patriarchal era is distinguished from that in the Mosaic age of the twelve-tribe kingdom by its amalgamation with the position of the patriarch, and by the consequent genealogical succession of the office. This fusion of the office of the prophet with the status of patriarch in the covenant polity of the Genesis 12-50 era is another index of its pre-kingdom nature.

II. PRE-PAROUSIA PRESENCE

A. Pre-Kingdom Cultus

The theocratic kingdom instituted in the Mosaic age was a redemptive renewal of the paradise-sanctuary of Eden and a prototypal preview of the eternal theocratic sanctuary of the Consummation. As a reconstituting of the Edenic cultus it involved a reappearance of the Glory-Presence in association with the mountain of God as cultic focus for a kingdom fullness. Previously, in the patriarchal period, theophany and cultus were of a pre-Glory character, which evidenced the pre-kingdom nature of that age.

1. Angel Theophany

Theophany adjusts its form to the eschatological hour. Advent of the King as the Glory-Presence *is* the coming of the kingdom of glory in power. So it is at both levels of the kingdom promised in the Abrahamic Covenant. When that kingdom was inaugurated at the old covenant, typical level, theophany assumed the form of the fiery cloud of the Glory-Spirit, who led the afflicted sojourners out of Egypt into their inheritance and brought final judgment on the Amorites. Again at the antitypical, messianic level the *parousia* of the Son of Man on the clouds of heaven in the Glory of the Father with all the holy angels introduces the fiery world judgment that brings in the order of the consummated kingdom-temple in the Spirit. The day of final judgment and the descent of the kingdom-temple is marked by the revelation of the Glory-Spirit, who is the temple.

In the days of the patriarchs, when the Lord was still withholding his revelation in Glory until a later eschatological moment, his appearances on earth were in the form of the Angel of the Lord. That is how Jacob described, by way of general review, the divine presence which he and Abraham and Isaac before him had experienced (Gen 48:15,16). In the light of such a summation we should probably assume that during this period not only divine appearances specifically identified as the Angel (Gen 16:7ff.; 18:1ff.; 21:17; 22:11,15; 24:7,40; 31:11) but those too without specification of the form of manifestation were instances of Angel of the Lord theophany.

In Jacob's testimony to the constancy of the Angel's shepherding care during his pilgrimage (cf. Gen 47:9) there is an indication that the Angel is a self-manifestation of God. For in this passage the Angel who has redeemed Jacob from all evils is placed in apposition to the God who has tended him all his life, the God before whom Abraham and Isaac had walked. What is disclosed elsewhere concerning the Angel confirms his identity as a manifestation of the Son of God. "The Angel's possession of the divine nature is expressly affirmed in God's declaration that his 'name' was 'in' the Angel (Exod 23:21). In the biblical contexts referring to the Angel from Genesis on there is an oscillation between him and God and there is no satisfactory accounting for this alternation in all the variety of circumstances in the relevant passages apart from the recognition that the Angel was a form of God's self-manifestation (cf. Gen 16:7-14; 21:17; 22:11-16; 31:11-13; 48:15,16). The place where the Angel appeared was by virtue of his presence holy ground, a divine sanctuary to be guarded against profanation, hence mandating the removal of profaned shoes (cf. Exod 3:5; Josh 5:15). His was the exclusively divine prerogative to forgive sin (cf. Exod 23:21). Malachi, calling him 'the Angel of the covenant,' equates his coming with the coming of the Lord (Mal 3:1)." [*Images of the Spirit*, pp.70,71.]

There is, of course, a close bond between the Angel of the Lord and the Glory-Spirit congruent with the mysterious union in the Godhead of the second and third persons of the Trinity, to which these two forms of theophany were particularly related. "The oscillation we have mentioned in the texts is at times specifically between the Angel and God's theophanic revelation in the Glory-cloud. Thus, in Exodus 14:19 the statement that the Angel of God moved from before to the rear of the Israelite hosts is paralleled by the statement that the pillar of cloud did so. For reflections on the exodus event making the same identification, see Numbers 20:16 and Isaiah 63:9." [*Images of the Spirit*, p.71.]

For our present purpose of distinguishing the form of theophany in the patriarchal era from that in the Mosaic age of kingdom inauguration it is important to observe that the Angel of the Lord might appear either in union with the Glory theophany or apart from it. Comparable is the incarnate manifestation of the Son of God, first in a stage of humiliation but then in exaltation in the bright majesty of the Glory-Spirit at the consummation of the kingdom.

It is on the distinction between these two modes of the Angel's appearance that the negotiations between Moses and the Lord in Exodus 32 and 33 turned. The Lord declared that he intended to send the Angel apart from the Glory before Israel in their advance on Canaan, but Moses prevailed in his plea that the Glory-cloud should also be present in their midst. (See further *Images of the Spirit*, pp.71-75.) During the pre-kingdom age of the patriarchs the mode of theophany was the Angel apart from the awesome splendor of the Glory-Spirit. So subdued a manifestation of the divine presence was this appearance of the Angel of the Lord, at times accompanied by other similarly ordinary appearing angel figures, that the patriarchs could entertain angels unawares (Heb 13:2; Gen 18:1ff.; 19:1ff.; Judg 13:3ff.; cf. Luke 24:15ff.). It was precisely the concern of Moses in his intercession for Israel that they not be led forward by the Angel apart from the Glory-cloud. Moses did not want the eschatological clock turned back. His plea was in effect that the day of judgment and kingdom possession having been ushered in by the exodus-redemption and covenant-making, there should be no reversion to the pre-kingdom, patriarchal state of affairs.

The *parousia*-sign of kingdom advent was not a feature of the patriarchal age. Only partial foretastes of the future manifestation of the Glory-Spirit were afforded in this earlier period. For example, it was in a theophanic form anticipating the pillars of cloud and fire that the Lord traversed the death-passage in the covenant oath ceremony of Genesis 15. There were also occasions when the angels of the Glory-council appeared in association with the Angel of the Lord. Thus, agents of the heavenly court were in attendance upon the Lord when, in his judgment mission against the cities of the plain (Gen 18:20ff.; cf. Gen 11:6ff.), he visited at the tent of Abraham (Gen 18:1ff.). Two such experiences are recorded of Jacob. One of these was his vision of God in his dream at Bethel (Gen 28:11ff.). He was also met by the angels of God at Mahanaim (Gen 32:1,2) in conjunction with his night encounter with the Angel of the Lord (Gen 32:24ff.; cf. Hos 12:4). These divine disclosures differed from the continuing public Glory-theophany of the kingdom age in their occasional, private, and, in part, visionary character. In sum, the radiant light of glory remained veiled in theophanic disclosures of the Angel and other representatives of the Glory-council to Abraham, Isaac, and Jacob and this absence of the Shekinah-Presence in glory identifies their time as a pre-kingdom stage in the history of redemption.

2. Prophetic Altars

Theophany and altar are closely related. Developments in the history of theophany are accompanied by corresponding modifications in the role and meaning of the altar in the covenant community. It is in the context of their pre-Glory setting that the significance of the patriarchal altars must be understood. Glory-*Parousia* brings triumphant judgment by the King of heaven and the consequent establishment of his kingdom of glory, with his temple-house, the seat of his sovereignty, as the focus in the midst of the kingdom fullness. We may better perceive how the pre-Glory, patriarchal altars stood in relation to the covenanted kingdom focus and fullness by comparing them with the later (Glory stage) altars.

a. Altar and Kingdom Focus: With the appearance of the continuing Glory-cloud theophany in the days of Moses, the continuing central altar was instituted in Israel. Allowance was still made for other special altars (cf., e.g., Deut 27:2-8) but a central altar was now introduced for the regular or official theocratic cultus (cf., e.g., Deut 12:5ff.). Further, with the kingdomization of the covenant community and particularly the renewal (on the typological level) of the Edenic theocracy in the promised land of Canaan, there was a typological restoration of the mountain of God as the sanctuary focus of the kingdom. Being situated at this holy mountain in the royal tabernacle court of the Glory-Presence, the central altar participated in the significance of the theophanic mountain. The altar became part of the typological expression of the promised restoration of the cultic focus of the kingdom of God.

Sinai was the mountain of God where the Glory-altar was first erected. But the typological symbol of the mountain-focus underwent historical extension. It moved from Sinai to Zion, the holy mountain where the central altar eventually came to rest. Sinai-Zion together constituted the complex symbol of focus-mountain with which the identity of the altar of the Glory-sanctuary was correlated. Reflective of the Sinai-Zion fusion is the way the Sinai and Zion events, both of which had the pattern of divine conquest crowned by the erection of the divine dwelling, are merged in the victory celebration song of Exodus 15 (especially vv.13-18).

It was the presence on Sinai and Zion of the heavenly Spirit-temple, the tent of assembly in the highest, the archetypal Glory-temple of which the Sinaitic tabernacle and Zion's temple were replicas, that made those earthly mountains holy mountains of God. This Glory-Spirit temple, the mountain-house of God in its archtetypal reality, accompanied Israel en route from Sinai to Zion. It was the continuing, unifying reality throughout the transition from the ectypal tabernacle of Mount Sinai to the ectypal temple of Mount Zion.

Foreshadowed by the two-stage Sinai-Zion typology was a corresponding pattern in the revelation of the Glory and the establishing of the kingdom in the messianic age. The initial but impermanent stint of Sinai as the location of the Glory-Presence has its counterpart in the occasional manifestations of the heavenly Glory associated with the first advent of Christ and his Pentecostal erection of the church as the house of God in the wilderness of this world-age. The more permanent enthronement of the Glory-Spirit on Zion in the Sabbath-Paradise land of Canaan anticipated the reappearance of the Glory from its present heavenly withdrawal from visibility in the awaited *parousia* unveiling of the Lord Jesus and the descent of New Jerusalem, heavenly Zion, as the abiding sabbatical temple of the Glory-Spirit, the consummated kingdom-house of God.

Back in patriarchal times no peak in the promised land of Canaan served as cultic focus of the kingdom of God. To be sure, according to the mythological world-view of the Canaanites, Zaphon, a mountain in northern Canaan, was the residence of Baal, an earthly counterpart to the cosmic court of the gods. But the day was coming when the Lord God of heaven and earth would enter into judgment with the Canaanites for this idolatrous myth and counter the claims of their Olympus, their rival Har Magedon, by establishing Zion (type and antitype) as the true Har

Magedon, the true mountain-city of assembly of the Great King (Ps 48:2,3). Before Sinai-Zion, however, there was not yet either Glory-Spirit theophany or restoration of God's mountain city. Apart from such a theocratic kingdom setting, the patriarchal altars did not yet carry the connotations of cosmic mountain-focus of the kingdom and holy site of the Glory-Presence that would later arise through the association of the altar with Zion.

At the same time the patriarchal altars are set forth in the narratives from Genesis 12 on as the beginning of God's response to the apostate Babel attempt to reestablish the cosmic mountain focus apart from the redemptive grace of God (cf. Gen 11). That effort of the city of man had resulted in yet worse dispersion and loss of coherence. Over against that humanistic failure God promised in the Abrahamic Covenant to produce a true restoration of the kingdom. Although the completion of this divine response to Babel at the typological level would be found in Mount Sinai-Zion of the Israelite kingdom, the fulfilling of the promise already began to take place in the Genesis 12-50 history. The patriarchal altars were a preliminary step pointing towards Jerusalem, the type of the eternal New Jerusalem, the true Mount Zaphon. No patriarchal altar had the status of holy mountain focus of the kingdom; they were, however, all located within the promised kingdom-boundaries and so were a sign that within this set-apart territory God would fulfill his promise to Abraham. Here in Canaan he would re-create his holy paradise-kingdom with his Glory-Presence enthroned on the mountain-focus in the midst, at the place which he would choose.

One patriarchal altar was actually erected on what would become the temple mountain. In 2 Chronicles 3:1 the site of Solomon's temple is identified as the Mount Moriah to which the Lord directed Abraham for the sacrifice of Isaac (Gen 22:2). The Abrahamic altar on Moriah was a veiled anticipation of the site's later identity as Zion, but like other patriarchal altars it was not yet a kingdom focus, not yet adorned by the Glory-Presence.

In this connection the possibility may be mentioned that such altars as Abraham's on Moriah, places of burnt-offerings (cf. Gen 22:2), were in their form symbolic of the cosmic mountain of God. At least, that would be the case if we generalized from Israel's central altar of burnt-offering and regarded as relevant to that altar Ezekiel's identification of his visionary altar of burnt-offering as *har`el* (Ezek 43:15), understanding that as "mountain of God."

The altar that Jacob erected at the place he called Bethel carried Zion-like symbolic connotations of focus-mountain by reason of the visionary experience he had there earlier (Gen 28:10-21; 35:7). That dream episode was designed as a counterpart to Babel. The angel-traversed stair-ascent set down on the earth, its top ("head") in the heavens, was God's true provision answering to the debacle of Babel's staircase tower which assayed in vain to lift its head into the heavens. The stair-structure of Jacob's dream represented the cosmic axis, the holy mountain-focus, the Presence-place of the Lord of glory, attended by angelic hosts. Jacob so identified the site, "house of God" and "gate of heaven" (28:17), memorializing the visionary appearance with a form reflective of it, a pillar monument rising up from the place sanctified by the Lord's standing there. It is the visionary basis of the association of the Glory-Presence with the site of Jacob's Bethel altar that distinguishes this altar in terms of focus-mountain identity from the temple altar on Zion, where there was the more objectively manifested and abiding presence of the divine Glory. Though not the destined site of God's house, Jacob's Bethel vision and altar spoke prophetically to the fact that Canaan was the land that God was separating out of the profane world for his own holy dwelling and within which he would appoint the mountain of God.

b. **Altar and Kingdom Fullness:** Altars erected before Abraham (and those set up by the godly who continued on into patriarchal times but outside the Abrahamic Covenant) served as testimonies to the Lord as Creator-Owner of all the earth. They were prophecies too that his lordly proprietorship would assert itself in eschatological judgment, removing the rebellious and allotting the world to his people. When Abraham and the patriarchs of his line, living within the land promised in covenantal grant to their descendants, built and maintained altars there in Canaan, they were professing their faith that this particular land lay under the special claim of Yahweh, one day to be bestowed as an inheritance on his covenant children. Only indirectly did their altars witness to their Lord's claim upon the world as a whole and present a prophetic warning of that final judicial intervention when he would lay hold on his universal domain, sanctifying it through the expulsion of the ungodly whose presence he had tolerated in forbearance, taking possession of it all for his redeemed people. Only indirectly through typological symbol did these patriarchal altars point to that universal kingdom of God and its antitypical realization, their more immediate reference being to the kingdom in Canaan, the envisaged first level of fulfillment of the covenant promise to Abraham.

The significance of these patriarchal altars as land claims for Yahweh emerges in the record of the first altar built by Abraham in the land. Led by God into Canaan (Gen 12:1; Josh 24:3), Abraham arrived at Shechem in the center of the land. There the Lord appeared to him and identified this as the land he would give to Abraham's descendants (Gen 12:7). Implicit in the Lord's promise was the declaration of his own sovereign ownership of this land. It was his to give. And in this disclosure was revealed the intention to establish Canaan at the appointed time as a provisional, typological theocratic kingdom. This assertion of his ownership and his purpose to appropriate Canaan as his own special kingdom in the midst of the nations on earth was made in the face of an existing Canaanite presence and proprietorship. As Genesis 12:6b advises us: "the Canaanite was then in the land." For Abraham, this circumstance, seemingly adverse to the promises, was part of the testing of his faith. He must trust the Lord to bestow the land grant in spite of its present occupation by the Canaanites. His building of the altar (v.7b) in response to God's promise (v.7a) was an expression of such faith. And it was Abraham's confessional witness to Yahweh's lordship over Canaan and his special claim upon it. Let the builders of the city of man in Canaan be reminded that their jurisdiction there was a subordinate, temporary common grace arrangement, and that Yahweh, Abraham's God, the Creator of all, reserved the right to assert his ultimate claim.

In their particular reference to the land of Canaan rather than the world in general the patriarchal altars were like the later, Israelite altars in that land, but with a difference. The latter functioned as virtual victory pillars, declarations of Yahweh's present royal occupation of the conquered territory. In the Mosaic legislation, as noted previously, for the Lord to appoint an altar-tent site was to put his name there (Deut 12:5,21; 14:24; cf. 12:11; 14:23; 16:2,6,11; 26:2), which, in extra-biblical legal-political usage, signifies to make a claim of ownership and, in a military context, to erect a victory monument in subjugated territory. The patriarchal altars, however, functioned more like a *kudurru*-stone that marked out a land claim, that claim being in the case of the altars a prophetic statement of hope for the future. Thus, Abraham's first passage through the land, punctuated by the erection of the altars at Shechem and Bethel (Gen 12:1-10), was a prospective registration of claim in the name of Yahweh. Like the circumambulation of the land recorded in Genesis 13:14-17, the procedure that validated acquisition of a piece of property, so the tour of Canaan described in Genesis 12:1-10 was from boundary to boundary, from Abraham's entrance on the northeast to his exit into Egypt in the southwest. The origin of the Shechem and Bethel altars within this historical context is suggestive of their *kudurru*-like significance.

Looking back on that original passage of Abraham through Canaan, peaceful as it was, we see the emerging shape of the future campaign of conquest by which the Israelite army of the Lord took possession of the promised land. Abraham's establishing of altar tent-sites at Shechem and Bethel (Gen 12:7,8; 13:3,4) divided the land into northern, central, and southern sections. Joshua's campaigns at the time of the Israelite conquest of Canaan are distinguishable according to the pattern of these three areas of the land, with key events transpiring at the two altar sites (cf. Josh 7:2; 8:9,30ff.) located, as they both were, on an east-west crossroad on the main north-south route over the central mountains.

In Joshua 8:9 the geographical details concerning the ambush between Bethel and Ai seem to be a conscious echo of the description of the location in Genesis 12:8. More significantly, the altar building episode at Mt. Ebal near Shechem (Josh 8:30ff.) was itself another land-claiming ceremony, the victorious counterpart answering to Abraham's prophetic altar-sign of faith. The occasion was the concluding second act in the renewal of the covenant that had been begun under Moses in Moab before Israel crossed the Jordan. The Deuteronomic treaty, the documentary embodiment of the first act in the ratificatory process, had called for this second, sealing ceremony to take place after Israel's penetration of the land under the direction of Moses' appointed successor (Deut 27:2ff.). Standing at Shechem, that central location within the land where God had originally identified Canaan as the promised land and Abraham had erected an altar, Israel, now led by Joshua, proceeded to carry out the Deuteronomic instructions. The altar they built there was a treaty pillar proclaiming Yahweh as Lord of this land by sovereign right. It was a victory stele celebrating the Lord's vindication of his claim to Canaan by his triumph over the gods of Canaan in the judicial ordeal of the passage through the Jordan (Josh 3 and 4) and in the subsequent supernaturally abetted victories of his people (Josh 6-8).

What we have noted about intimations of the future in the case of Abraham's altars we observe again in the life of Jacob. The pattern of events that culminated in the building of altars at Shechem (Gen 33:20) and Bethel (Gen 35:7) by Israel the individual foreshadowed the history of the homecoming triumph of Israel the nation. For these altars followed upon Jacob's re-entry into the land from the west, after an exodus-like flight from Laban, in the process of which he despoiled his erstwhile oppressor (Gen 31), and after preliminary successes in the Transjordan area (Gen 32:1-33:17). By pointing prophetically ahead to Israel's occupation of Canaan the patriarchal altars gave due warning to the native occupants that latent in the priestly service of these altars by the patriarchal cultic congregation was a priestly mission of sanctifying that land to Yahweh, a mission that must ultimately find expression in a holy war directed against the Canaanites and their defiling idolatries. Sounded by these altars was the ancient Noahic curse-threat against Ham-Canaan.

But in keeping with the "not-yet" eschatological nature of the times the message of the patriarchal altars was not yet a declaration of holy war judgment but still only a prophetic warning. They represented the complaint stage in God's lawsuit against the Canaanites. More positively stated, they were a summons to repentant turning from the worship of idols and a call to reconciliation with the God of Abraham, Isaac, and Jacob, the Creator of heaven and earth. They were a missionary-evangelistic witness. Apparently neither this witness of the patriarchal altars nor the total impact of the godly presence of the patriarchs and the manifest favor of God in their affairs was notably fruitful in the conversion of those outside the covenant community. Nevertheless, in their function of summoning to covenantal commitment to the Lord of redemptive promise, these altars afforded an intimation of a coming day when the reconciling call of the altar of Calvary would be heard in all the earth, when the gospel of Christ would go forth in the power of the Spirit to the Gentiles and the promise would be fulfilled that in Abraham's seed all the nations would be blessed with the salvation of God. While the patriarchal altars renewed the curse-threat of God's oracle against Canaan, they also heralded anew Noah's prophetic blessing on Japheth, promising entrance into the covenantal inheritance of Shem-Abraham.

B. Re-creating Spirit-Presence

If the Spirit as Glory-theophany was withheld in the patriarchal age, the Spirit was nevertheless present within, present in the hearts of God's people as re-creating divine power-paradigm. This inner working of the Spirit, replicating the divine likeness, is discernible in the biblical record beneath the surface description of the outward course of the lives of the patriarchal family. The emphasis in the Genesis 12-50 history of the Spirit's work of renewal is on the restoration of the ethical dimension of the glory-image in man. This is what one would expect in this pre-kingdom age, in contrast to the Mosaic age when the emphasis in the treatment of Israel's re-creation in the divine image shifts to the dimensions of the physical and especially the judicial glory. Genesis 18:19 should be noted again here with its specific divine declaration that righteousness and justice, the ethical glory of the heavenly King, were the objectives of Abraham's covenantal vocation.

The Genesis account develops the theme of inward transformation in the spiritual life both of the individual partriarchs and of the community of Jacob's family as a covenantal body.

This subjective religious aspect of the redemptive experience is pursued with sustained interest in the narratives about Abraham. The record details Abraham's steadfast persistence in Spirit-wrought faith through a lifelong succession of intense testings of his confidence in God and the covenant promises. Noteworthy in the life of Isaac is his remarkable exhibition of submissive obedience to the revealed will of the Lord at the altar on Moriah. But it is in the treatment of Jacob's life pilgrimage that we find the most pronounced emphasis on spiritual conversion and sanctification as a paramount purpose of God's covenantal engagement with his people. Epitomized in the change of names from Jacob to Israel is the story of the patriarch's spiritual transformation.   The earlier Jacob is the young supplanter who grasped at the blessing by deceptive stratagems, and as an immediate consequence of these efforts found himself a frustrated exile, far from family and homeland. Highlighted in the narrative is the critical midway turning point in Jacob's spiritual journey (Gen 28:10ff.). The circumcised son of the covenant experienced conversion in an arresting "Damascus road" encounter with the Lord of hosts at Bethel. In this eye-opening vision, Jacob was set in a new direction, henceforth to seek the kingdom through reliance not on self but on Yahweh, gracious God of the covenant promises, to whom he made his covenantal vow. The later Israel is the wrestler with the Angel, vanquished by God, reduced to helplessness in himself, but triumphant through his importunate plea to the grace of the God of the redemptive judgment ordeal (Gen 32; cf. Hos 12:3,4). And in the spiritual maturity of his old age, seasoned now in the patience of faith, the patriarch Jacob assumed under the hand of the Spirit the stature of a prophetic figure, invoking God's benediction on pharaoh and family, announcing the future course of God's kingdom among the twelve tribes of Israel.

Further examples of spiritual transformation are afforded by the individual lives of Jacob's sons, especially Judah and Joseph, but the final generations-division of Genesis (37:2-50:26) adds another dimension to the picture. Distinctive in this part of the story is the corporate aspect of the Spirit's work. He is depicted as refashioning the covenant family of Jacob as a total community.

Episodes narrated at the beginning of this section of Genesis expose Jacob's family as a house divided. Tensions among the rival mothers spilled over into the relationships of their sons. Paternal favoritism and special tokens of Joseph's destined supremacy sparked smoldering jealousies among the brothers. Malicious resentment festered to the extreme of a readiness to murder the favorite and the actual selling of him into bondage, a deed deceitfully concealed in cruel disregard of their father's broken heart (Gen 37). Widening the rifts in the unity of the covenant family was Judah's move into Philistine territory, leading to his marriage to a Canaanite woman, with its shameful repercussions (Gen 38).

In later episodes (Gen 42-45) the earlier unbrotherly strife and disunity give way to repeated demonstrations of qualities and conduct more becoming to the covenant community of the godly. Cooperative joint endeavor is undertaken by the brothers for the common good of all the household of faith. They display compassionate concern to spare their aged father further grief and they show tender solicitude for Benjamin, Joseph's replacement in old Jacob's affections. There is willingness to accept personal sacrifice for the sake of the family. Estrangement between Joseph and his brothers yields to reconciliation. Supreme among these expressions of the Spirit-changed hearts of these sons of the covenant is the plea of Judah that he might be substituted for Benjamin as a bondman in Egypt (Gen 44:33), a plea that makes one think of the love shown by Judah's royal descendant Shiloh, who would offer himself as the substitute for his transgressing people. The Spirit, re-creatively present, had remolded the family divided into a covenant community of faith, united in brotherly love and filial devotion to the covenant patriarch.

In this history of Jacob's family there is a premessianic anticipation of the mission of the Spirit of Pentecost, who takes those in times past alienated but now reconciled with the heavenly Father through Jesus Christ and fashions them into the sanctified community of the new covenant. Once again in this forming of the church there were divisions at the human level that had to be overcome. The Spirit must bond together in faith and love as the family of the Lord Jesus peoples separated by geographic, political, social, and cultural barriers with their attendant tensions and antagonisms. He must take Jews and Gentiles, between whom the old covenant itself had raised a partition, and join them into one body in the Spirit, one new man in Christ Jesus. By tracing the formation of the church-family of the new covenant to the working of the Spirit in the hearts of Christ's people the New Testament revelation casts the light of theological explanation back on Genesis 37-50, uncovering the inner process behind the transformation of the family of Jacob related there. It is as thus illuminated by the New Testament revelation that the Genesis record of individual and corporate spiritual renewal in Jacob's family can be read as an account of the acts of the Spirit in the patriarchal age.

More particularly, in the light of the New Testament's exposition of the Spirit's church-creating mission, his similar mission back in the patriarchal age can be seen as one of re-creating the covenant community in the image-likeness of the Glory-Spirit. For the New Testament depicts the church, the new covenant creation of the Spirit, as a replica of the Glory-temple. Indeed, the church is portrayed as incorporated into the Glory-temple and thus as not only a likeness but an extension of it. Hebrews 12:22-24 advises the Christian community of its participation in the heavenly assembly of the Glory-Spirit. The book of Revelation unveils the transforming work of the Spirit as he brings the church from its creation as candle-like image of the Glory-light of Christ (Rev 1) to the perfecting of this Glory-image in the church at its ultimate merging with the heavenly Glory-community in the eternal temple-city (Rev 21). The church will at last be angel-assembled into the clouds of Christ's *parousia*, his presence in the Glory of the Father with all the holy angels of the Glory-council. Another intimation of the intertwining of the church and the heavenly council before the Consummation is the evidence of the involvement of angels in the earthly gatherings of the saints (1 Cor 11:10; cf. 1 Cor 13:1). Moreover, the new covenant community is identified with the holy court of the heavenly assembly by its very designation as *ekklesia*. In its secular application this term is used for political bodies assembled for deliberative purposes. But most significant is the equivalence of *ekklesia* with *qahal*, which in the Old Testament is preeminently the assembly at Sinai-Zion, the gathering of the covenant people at the site of the presence of the Glory-Spirit, the King of Glory enthroned in the midst of his angelic retinue (cf. Acts 7:38; Heb 12:18-25). Reflective of the character of the *ekklesia* as likeness-extension of the heavenly council are the governmental-judicial functions attributed to it (cf., e.g., Matt 16:18,19; 18:15-20). Indeed, the total role of the church as an assembly for the adoration of God, the celebration of the sabbatical enthronement of the Creator-Redeemer, and the service of the Lord reveals it to be a replication of the Glory-Spirit assembly in the heavenly Zion.

By virtue of its anticipations of the new covenant acts of the Spirit re-creating the covenant people in the image of God, the patriarchal age is seen to have been an age not without its realized eschatology. It was a pre-kingdom age for it was not yet time for the Glory-Spirit-Parousia and the inheritance of the kingdom realm. But the kingdom was already present in the reign of God through his re-creating Spirit within.

INDEX OF BIBLICAL REFERENCES